My Mother Was a Computer

My Mother Was a Computer

DIGITAL SUBJECTS AND LITERARY TEXTS

N. Katherine Hayles

The University of Chicago Press   CHICAGO AND LONDON

N. KATHERINE HAYLES is the Hillis Professor of Literature at the University of California, Los Angeles. She is the author of four books, most recently *How We Became Posthuman: Virtual Bodies in Cybernetics, Literature, and Informatics.*

The University of Chicago Press, Chicago 60637
The University of Chicago Press, Ltd., London
© 2005 by The University of Chicago
All rights reserved. Published 2005
Printed in the United States of America

14 13 12 11 10 09 08 07 06 05   1 2 3 4 5

ISBN: 0-226-32147-9 (cloth)
ISBN: 0-226-32148-7 (paper)

Library of Congress Cataloging-in-Publication Data

Hayles, N. Katherine.
    My mother was a computer : digital subjects and literary texts /
N. Katherine Hayles.
        p. cm.
    Includes bibliographical references and index.
    ISBN 0-226-32147-9 (cloth : alk. paper) — ISBN 0-226-32148-7 (pbk. : alk. paper)
    1. Computational intelligence.   2. Human-computer interaction.
    3. Computers in literature.   4. Virtual reality.   5. American literature—
    20th century—History and criticism.   I. Title
    Q342.H39 2005
    006.3—dc22

                                                2005006276

To my mother, who was not a computer

Contents

Acknowledgments

In the four or five years this book has been swirling around in my thoughts, it has benefited from the insights of many friends and colleagues who have been generous enough to converse with me and to read all or part of the manuscript. I began this project, and to some extent finished it, feeling intensely ambivalent about the Regime of Computation, and so I found this input from others an invaluable way of testing and refining my ideas. Among those who read and commented on drafts or offered valuable insights in conversation are Jay Bolter, Nathan Brown, Dino Buzzetti, John Cayley, Bruce Clarke, Mats Dahlström, Johanna Drucker, Michael Dyer, Dene Grigar, Mark Hansen, Linda Henderson, Jerzy Jarzebski, John Johnston, Michael Kandel, Matthew Kirschenbaum, Kate Marshall, Jerome McGann, Brian McHale, Anne Mellor, Adelaide Morris, Mark Poster, Jessica Pressman, Rita Raley, Mark Rose, Stephanie Strickland, Peter Swirski, Thom Swiss, Joseph Tabbi, John Unsworth, Carol Wald, and Noah Wardrip-Fruin. Greg Egan, Shelley Jackson, Karl Sims, and Neal Stephenson received drafts graciously and provided material help. Alan Liu, a reader for the University of Chicago Press, made many valuable suggestions for revision in a report that was exceptionally helpful. David Toole's astute copyediting made many improvements in the manuscript. Other colleagues too numerous to name provided thoughtful and useful comments along the way, and to all of them I owe a debt of gratitude.

My work was greatly facilitated by a Senior Fellowship from the National Endowment for the Humanities; a President's Research Fellowship from the University of California; a fellowship from the Zentrum für Literaturforschung in Berlin, Germany; several Senate Research Grants from the University of California, Los Angeles; a Rockefeller Foundation Fellowship for

Residence at Bellagio; and research funds provided by the John Charles Hillis Endowed Chair. I am grateful for this generous support. Alan Thomas at the University of Chicago Press awaited the manuscript with patience and gave unfailing support throughout the process. Carol Wald, Nathan Brown, and Michael Fadden provided valuable research assistance and generous intellectual exchanges. Thomas Wortham and Lynn Batten helped more than I can say with their superb administrative skills and their generous accommodation of teaching requests so as to allow concentrated research time.

I owe a special debt of gratitude to my good friend Marjorie Luesebrink, whose suggestions, support, readings, and comments thread through this book and make it better than it otherwise would have been. My husband Nicholas Gessler provided so many ideas, comments, suggestions, references, and information that I scarcely know where to start acknowledging his contributions, except to say that the book would not have been the same without him.

In somewhat different form, chapters of this book have appeared as essays, and I am grateful for permission to reprint the following: Chapter 3 appeared as "Escape and Constraint: Three Fictions Dream of Moving from Energy to Information," in *From Energy to Information*, edited by Linda Henderson and Bruce Clarke (Stanford: Stanford University Press, 2002), 235–54; © 2002 by the Board of Trustees of the Leland Stanford Jr. University, used by permission of the publisher. Chapter 4 appeared as "Translating Media: Why We Should Rethink Textuality," *Yale Journal of Criticism* 6, no. 3 (2003): 263–90; used by permission of The Johns Hopkins University Press. Chapter 5 was published as "Performative Code and Figurative Language: Neal Stephenson's *Cryptonomicon*," in *The Holodeck in the Garden: Science and Technology in Contemporary American Fiction*, edited by Peter Freese and Charles B. Harris (New York: Dalkey Archive Press, 2004), 2–27; used by permission of the publisher. Chapter 6 appeared in significantly different form as "The Invention of Copyright and the Birth of Monsters: Flickering Connectivities in Shelley Jackson's *Patchwork Girl*," *Postmodern Culture* 10, no. 2 (January 2000), http://www.iath.virginia.edu/pmc. Chapter 8 appeared as "Simulated Narratives: What Virtual Creatures Can Teach Us," *Critical Inquiry* 26, no. 1 (Autumn 1999): 1–26. Most of this material was also presented at various conferences and invited lectures, and I am grateful to all those who offered valuable comments that helped me rethink and refine my arguments.

Finally, my greatest debt is to my family, and especially my mother, without whom none of this would have been possible. To them I give my deepest thanks and affection.

Prologue
Computing Kin

On the Title

In Neal Stephenson's *Cryptonomicon*, the fictional mathematical genius Lawrence Pritchard Waterhouse is showing off his new mechanical invention to his supervisor, Lieutenant Colonel Earl Comstock. Comstock inquires:

"If you had to give a name to the whole apparatus, what would you call it?"

"Hmmm," Waterhouse says. "Well, its basic job is to perform mathematical calculations—like a computer."

Comstock snorts, "A computer is a human being." (600)

The dialogue reflects the historical fact that in the 1930s and 1940s, people who were employed to do calculations—and it was predominantly women who performed this clerical labor—were called "computers." Anne Balsamo references this terminology when she begins one of the chapters in her book *Technologies of the Gendered Body* with the line I have appropriated for my title: "My mother was a computer."[1] Balsamo's mother actually did work as a computer, and she uses this bit of family history to launch a meditation on the gender implications of information technologies. For my purposes, the different interpretations of the sentence from World War II to the end of the twentieth century mark a shift from a society in which the intelligence required for calculations was primarily associated with humans to the increasing delegation of these labors to computational machines. The sentence stands, therefore, as a synecdoche for the panoply of issues raised by the relation of Homo sapiens to Robo sapiens, humans to intelligent machines.[2]

The semantic shock the sentence is likely to give us today is rooted not only in the shift from human to machine labor, but also in the feeling that a kinship category essential to human society has been violated. In this sense, the sentence alludes to what Hans Moravec, among others, has called our "postbiological" future: the expectation that the corporeal embodiment that has always functioned to define the limits of the human will in the future become optional, as humans find ways to upload their consciousness into computers and leave their bodies behind.[3] In *How We Became Posthuman*, I argued strongly against this vision of the posthuman, ending the book with a call to contest for versions of the posthuman that would acknowledge the importance of embodiment and be conducive to enhancing human and nonhuman life on the planet.

In the half decade since the publication of that book, computational technologies have penetrated even further into the infrastructure of developed countries. Pervasive computing, mobile communication devices, satellite networks, and Internet traffic have spread dramatically; and, correspondingly, economic, manufacturing, transportation, and communication technologies have been tightly integrated into globally mediated networks. As a result, the interplay between the liberal humanist subject and the posthuman that I used to launch my analysis in *How We Became Posthuman* has already begun to fade into the history of the twentieth century. In the twenty-first century, the debates are likely to center not so much on the tension between the liberal humanist tradition and the posthuman but on different versions of the posthuman as they continue to evolve in conjunction with intelligent machines.

In juxtaposing the posthuman with the liberal humanist tradition, I argued that despite many important differences, some versions of the posthuman continued to reinscribe the disembodiment that was a prominent feature of the liberal tradition, insofar as it associated self with mind and saw the body as a mere container for the mind's operations. As new and more sophisticated versions of the posthuman have evolved, this stark contrast between embodiment and disembodiment has fractured into more complex and varied formations. As a result, a binary view that juxtaposes disembodied information with an embodied human lifeworld is no longer sufficient to account for these complexities. Although I have not abandoned my commitment to the importance of embodiment, it seems to me that contemporary conditions call increasingly for understandings that go beyond a binary view to more nuanced analyses. From my perspective, this development requires repositioning materiality as distinct from physicality and re-envisioning the material basis for hybrid texts and subjectivities. The thinking I did for my book *Writing Machines* has been crucial in allowing me to work out the arguments advanced here. *Writing Machines*, *How We Became Posthuman*, and this book form a trilogy that arcs from the mid-twentieth century to the present, a trajectory that moves from a binary opposition between embodiment and information through an engagement with the materiality of literary texts to a broadening and deepening of these ideas into computation and textuality.

Materiality, as I defined it in *Writing Machines*, is an emergent property created through dynamic interactions between physical characteristics and signifying strategies. Materiality thus marks a junction between physical reality and human intention. Following Bruno Latour's call for a turn from "matters of fact" to "matters of concern," I like to think of materiality as the constructions of matter that matter for human meaning.[4] This view of materiality goes hand in hand with what I call the Computational Universe, that is, the claim that the universe is generated through computational processes running on a vast computational mechanism underlying all of physical reality. For scientists making the strong claim for computation as ontology, computation is the means by which reality is continually produced and reproduced on atomic, molecular, and macro levels. In *A New Kind of Science*, Stephen Wolfram extends the claim to include biological systems and, indeed, complex behaviors of every kind, including social and cultural systems.[5] In this context, "My mother was a computer" can be understood as alluding to the displacement of Mother Nature by the Universal Computer. Just as Mother Nature was seen in past centuries as the source of both human behavior and physical reality, so now the Universal Computer is envisioned as the Motherboard of us all.

The appearance of the Computational Universe at a moment in human history when computers have achieved unparalleled scope and importance is obviously not coincidental. We might draw an analogy with eighteenth-century commentators who, impressed by the reductive power of Newton's laws of motion and the increasing sophistication of time-keeping mechanisms, proclaimed that the universe was a clockwork.[6] As Marjorie Hope Nicolson pointed out in the 1940s, the clockwork metaphor worked powerfully to express the orderliness and predictability of a universe that moved with beautiful precision.[7] At the same time, it occluded other aspects of reality that subsequently found expression in such diverse developments as Romantic poetry, quantum mechanics, and complexity theory. Similarly, the Computational Universe enables deeper insight and new intuitions into certain aspects of reality; we may safely assume that it also obscures other aspects of reality, including constructions of subjectivity that have traditionally found expression in the humanities and social sciences. The friction between traditional views of subjectivity and a computational perspective is one focus of this inquiry, but other foci are new configurations that put traditional and computational perspectives into synergistic cooperation with one another.

In the course of this book, I offer my own commentary on the Computational Universe, including a critical interrogation of current research claims. My primary interest, however, is not in separating the Computational Universe as the means by which reality is generated from its function as a metaphor for understanding natural and cultural processes. Rather, I am interested in the complex dynamics through which the Computational Universe works *simultaneously* as means and metaphor in technical and artistic practices, producing and also produced by recursive loops that entangle with one another and with the diverse meanings of computation as technology, ontology, and cultural icon. This dynamic interplay of recursive, multiple causalities becomes, I argue, the fertile ground for re-envisioning and remaking a wide variety of cultural artifacts, including computer simulations and literary texts.

In addition to its associations with the Computational Universe and Mother Nature, the title also alludes to Friedrich Kittler's influential argument that reading functions as "hallucinating a meaning between letters and lines."[8] In *Discourse Networks*, Kittler notes that with the introduction of phonics in the nineteenth century, children were taught to read by sounding out words, first articulating them out loud and then subvocalizing them.[9] These practices gave "voice" to print texts, particularly novels—and the voice most people heard was the same voice that taught them to read, namely, the mother's, which in turn was identified with Mother Nature and a sympathetic resonance between the natural world and human meaning. In the contemporary period, reading as "hallucination" has been displaced in part by the instant messaging, chat rooms, video games, e-mail, and Web surfing that play such a large role in young people's experiences. To an extent, then, the mother's voice that haunted reading has been supplanted by another set of stimuli: the visual, audio, kinesthetic, and haptic cues emanating from the computer. If the mother's voice was the link connecting subjectivity with writing, humans with natural environments, then the computer's beeps, clicks, and tones are the links connecting contemporary subjectivities to electronic environments, humans to the Computational Universe. One strand of my analysis interrogates the effects of these pervasive interactions on the construction of subjectivity and contemporary reading practices, charting the resulting shifts by locating both print and electronic texts in relation to computational practices.

Turning to the title's kinship implications, we can also understand "My mother was a computer" as the answer an artificial-life simulation might give if asked who its parent was. Researchers in the field frequently evoke human kinship terminology to describe computer simulations; it is common, for example, to say that the computer (or more precisely, the program) "gives birth" to evolving artificial biota. Such usage promiscuously mingles anthropomorphic projection with descriptive intent. In this sense "My mother was a computer" articulates a certain kind of anthropomorphic projection that creates (mis)understandings of the computer's functioning. Mystifying the computer's actual operation, anthropomorphic projection creates a cultural Imaginary in which digital subjects are understood as autonomous creatures imbued with human-like motives, goals, and strategies. This projection also has a reverse undertow, for it brings into question the extent to which human beings can be understood as computer programs. The "digital subjects" of the subtitle alludes to this dialectical positioning of humans and artificial creatures in relation to each other. Read as a phrase delineating an area of inquiry, "digital subjects" punningly connects the subject of digitality, especially the Computational Universe, with these hybrid subjectivities.

Why literary texts, the other half of the subtitle? I am indebted to Alan Liu, a reader for the University of Chicago Press, for challenging me on this issue. In the first draft, I took the inclusion of literature to be more or less self-evident. I am, after all, a literary critic (among other things). On further reflection, however, I understand the question both as an indication of literature's increasingly marginal position in mainstream culture, where it competes and cooperates with such cultural phenomena as blockbuster movies and best-selling computer games, and as an invitation to rethink the role of literature in creating the contemporary cultural Imaginary.

To elucidate my decision to include literary texts, I begin from a fundamental question. What resources do we have to understand the world around us? As Nicholas Gessler, among others, has pointed out, these resources can be grouped into three broad categories: mathematical equations, simulation modeling, and discursive explanations.[10] Of mathematical equations, I have little to say, other than to note the point that Harold Morowitz, Stephen Wolfram, and others make about the limited usefulness of mathematics in describing complex behaviors. Because complex systems exhibit nonlinear behaviors that typically cannot be described by equations having explicit solutions, the kind of mathematics that gave us classical mechanics and other triumphs of modern science has little traction in the case of complex systems, which leaves us with simulations and discursive explanations.

There are, of course, many different forms of discursive explanations, including such preeminent nonliterary forms as history, philosophy, and cultural anthropology. Among these discourses, literature is distinct for creating, as Marie-Laure Ryan puts it, "possible worlds."[11] Kittler's proposition that reading novels is like a hallucination highlights one of literature's main fascinations: its ability to create vividly imagined worlds in which readers can "hallucinate" scenes, actions, and characters so fully that they seem to leap off the page and inhabit the same psychic space as the readers themselves. In this respect, literature functions more like simulations than do other discursive forms, because like computer simulations such as Karl Sims's "Evolved Virtual Creatures" (discussed in chapter 8), literary texts create imaginary worlds populated by creatures that we can (mis)take for beings like ourselves.

There are also important differences between simulations and literary texts. Whereas computation is essential for simulations that model complex phenomena, literature's stock-in-trade is narrative, especially in the contemporary period when novels have become the preeminent literary form. Narrative is much older than simulation modeling in artificial media—almost as old, many anthropologists believe, as the human species itself. Narrative, with its evocation of the human lifeworld, speaks to subjectivities that remain rooted in human perceptual systems, human languages, and human cultures. Simulations, by contrast, are essentially numerical calculations. Although they can be rendered in visual forms that evoke the perceptible world that humans see (as is the case for Karl Sims's simulations), these appearances are generated through algorithms that operate first and foremost with numerical quantities. Because computers are much better equipped than human minds to carry out the staggeringly tedious calculations involved in creating simulations, simulations are closely associated with artificial intelligence and with postbiological subjectivities. The dynamic tensions between simulation and narrative thus involve a dialectic between the human lifeworld and the (relatively) inhuman world of massive numerical calculations.

The traffic between language and code that this similarity/opposition sets up is one of the principal ways in which digital subjects and literary texts are interrogated and articulated together in this book. The two other modalities highlighted here are the interpenetration of print and electronic text, and the dialectic between analog and digital representations. Together, these three dynamics can be parsed as making (language and code), storing (print and electronic text), and transmitting (analog and digital). Making, storing, and transmitting can be thought of as modalities related to information; they also help to constitute the bodies of subjects and texts. Another way in which literary texts and digital subjects are articulated together is by analyzing the effects of these modalities on their bodies. As an embodied art form, literature registers the impact of information in its materiality, in the ways in which its physical characteristics are mobilized as resources to create meaning.

This entanglement of the bodies of texts and digital subjects is one manifestation of what I call "intermediation," that is, complex transactions between bodies and texts as well as between different forms of media. Because making, storing, and transmitting imply technological functions, this mode of categorization insures that the different versions of the posthuman will be understood, in Kittlerian fashion, as effects of media. At the same time, in my analysis of literary texts and especially in my focus on subjectivity, I also insist that media effects, to have meaning and significance, must be located within an embodied human world. In refusing an either/or choice between media effects and a human lifeworld, I again invoke the necessity, as I did in my repositioning of materiality, to think in terms of multiple causalities, complex dynamics, and emergent possibilities. As both computer simulations and literary texts recognize, autonomous agents interacting recursively with one another and their environments can never be reduced to linear dynamics or simple causalities. The final and most important significance of *My Mother Was a Computer: Digital Subjects and Literary Texts*, as a title and as a book, is to insist on the irreducible complexity of contemporary posthuman configurations as they continue to evolve in digital subjects and literary texts, computer programs and human mindbodies.

Method and Scope
I turn now to the book's methodology and organization. Three main parts explore the distinct but related processes of making (through language and code), storing (as print and electronic text), and transmitting (through analog and digital encoding). As noted earlier, making, storing, and transmitting imply technological functions that are intimately co-involved. Their division here into separate parts helps to clarify their specific functionalities but should not obscure the fact that they constantly engage one another in dynamic and multiple recursive interactions.

Within each part, different chapters emphasize theory, technology, and thematics. In discussions of electronic literature and computer simulations, the emphasis on technology ensures that the analysis takes place not only at the level of the screen but also at the level at which screenic effects are achieved. The emphasis on thematics allows me to integrate into the discussion close readings of different kinds of texts, ranging from print novels and electronic literature to computer simulations used in scientific research. Both the technological and thematic analyses have theoretical implications, which the chapters emphasizing theory explore explicitly in ways that the other chapters test, confirm, modify, and extend. Theory, technology, and thematics are, of course, in constant interaction with one another, so all the chapters have some of each, although usually one strand is predominant. The order in which I take up these three strands of inquiry varies from part to part. For example, the chapter devoted predominately to theory comes second in part 1, first in part 2, and last in part 3, whereas the chapter devoted to technology comes first in part 1, last in part 2, and second in part 3. In this regard, the organization of the book is flexible.

Part 1, "Making: Language and Code," focuses on the signifying processes of language and code. To set the stage, chapter 1 develops the concept of intermediation and relates it to the technologies driving the Regime of Computation. As a result of these developments, code assumes new importance as the lingua franca of nature. This raises the issue of how code can be related to theoretical frameworks for the legacy systems of speech and writing, the topic of chapter 2. From a systematic comparison of Saussure's semiotics, Derrida's grammatology, and programming languages, implications emerge that reveal the inadequacy of traditional ideas of signification for understanding the operations of code. In instances where code becomes important—as is the case for virtually all forms of textuality in the digital age—the dynamics at work bring into question such long-held verities as the arbitrariness of the sign, while simultaneously highlighting processes given relatively little attention in Saussurean semiotics and Derridean grammatology, such as the act of "making discrete." The result is a significant shift in the plate tectonics of signification, with a consequent rethinking of the processes through which texts emerge. The point is not simply to jettison the worldviews of speech and writing—even if by some miraculous fiat this were possible—but rather to understand the processes of intermediation by which they are in active interplay with the worldview of code. This endeavor necessarily assumes an understanding of the differences and similarities between these three worldviews, so in this sense chapter 2 lays the groundwork for the chapters that follow.

Chapter 3 shows how bodies are interpolated differently as the technology transforms from the passive code of the telegraph to the active code of sophisticated cybernetic devices and computer programming, moving through Henry James's "In the Cage" (1898) to Philip K. Dick's *The Three Stigmata of Palmer Eldritch* (1966) and James J. Tiptree's "The Girl Who Was Plugged In" (1973). The protagonists of these narratives share a common desire to escape from the constraints of life within a capitalistic regime, yearning to partake of an informational realm where goods flow freely and life escapes from being a zero-sum game. As the technology becomes more sophisticated, this dream is not fulfilled; instead, embodied subjects are interpolated ever more tightly into a circuit controlled by capitalistic dynamics. As bodies enter more completely into the circuit, subjects cease to be *circumscribed* by these dynamics and are *constructed* through them, a process enacted in Tiptree's story with disconcerting literalness. The complex dynamic created when language meets code proves to be crucial in all three narratives, highlighting the processes of intermediation that cycle through these fictions.

Part 2, "Storing: Print and Etext," emphasizes the interactions of print and electronic literature as production systems. Chapter 4 is theoretically oriented and argues that received ideas of the foundational concepts of work, text, and document should be reconceptualized to take materiality more fully into account. As I indicated above, materiality on this view cannot simply be collapsed into physicality but is an emergent property generated by interactions between a work's signifying strategies and the physical characteristics it mobilizes as resources for its operations. This chapter argues that taking materiality seriously requires different models of subjectivity than those usually assumed in textual editing, as well as changed concepts of how embodied texts relate to one another. Here the cycles of intermediation are illustrated through the complex dynamics by which novels, films, Web sites, and other media forms interact with one another. Rather than holding up as an ideal a unitary convergent work to which variants can be subordinated (for example, by considering a novel as the "real" work and a film based on the novel as a more or less faithful enactment of the original), this chapter argues that we should conceptualize texts as clustered in assemblages whose dynamics emerge from all the texts participating in the cluster, without privileging one text as more "original" than any other. To articulate this approach further, I compare and analyze the contrasting ideas of Jorge Borges, Warren Weaver, and Walter Benjamin toward linguistic translation.

Chapter 5 asks in what ways a text's existence as an electronic document matters, if its final output form is a print novel. Do the intervening stages, when the document consisted not of durable marks on paper but of flickering voltages in a digital computer, leave their mark on the visible surface of the print book? Although the question might be easily answered in the affirmative for print books that use computer technology to create innovative typography and other visual effects difficult to achieve without a computer, more challenging are the far more numerous instances of books that are entirely conventional in appearance, such as Neal Stephenson's *Cryptonomicon*. In the admittedly somewhat idiosyncratic case of *Cryptonomicon*, written by a print author who is also a computer programmer, digital processes are deeply implicated in the text's construction and expressed through a subterranean narrative propelled by dialectical interactions between mutating terms. At issue in this subterranean narrative are tensions between figurative language and performative code, between hackers who yearn to make information free and capitalistic moguls who want to convert it into a market commodity. In the convoluted configurations the text assumes, it both mimics and obscures its relation to a digital computer, at once celebrating its form as a print book and suggesting that hidden within it is a powerful command core based on code. Intermediation here is figured as an engine driving narrative reconfigurations, deriving its motive force from complex feedback loops between language and code, print novels and computer programs.

Exploring the relation between fragmented subjects, multiple distributed authorship, and digital textuality, chapter 6 builds on the argument of chapter 2 that code goes farther in the direction of "making discrete" than speech and writing. Locating this electronic work in the context of Mark Rose's analysis of copyright battles in the eighteenth century, this chapter uses his conclusions, specifically the links he establishes between the literary work as intellectual property and the liberal humanist subject, as the backdrop against which Shelley Jackson's *Patchwork Girl* (1995) can be seen as a contestation of the ideology implicit in the print novel as a literary form. Pushing toward new forms of subjectivity even as it enacts different kinds of textual configurations, *Patchwork Girl* both reinscribes the print novel and uses this reinscription to invent a form suitable for digital media. For the principal narrator, subjectivity cannot be separated from the digital technology that produces the work, leading to speculation about what it might mean to be a digital rather than analog subject. Intermediation here manifests itself in a complex entanglement of print and electronic text, continuous and discrete consciousness, language and code.

Part 3, "Transmitting: Analog and Digital," takes up the distinction between the analog and digital, specifically with reference to its implications for subjectivity. Chapter 7 focuses on the intermediation between analog consciousness and digital program within a single creature; chapter 8 explores the dynamics between digital creatures living in computers and humans interacting with them; and chapter 9 takes up the highly speculative "postbiological" future when humans make digital computerized Copies of themselves that live in computers. As the ramifications broaden, at issue are the feedback loops not only between computation and human consciousness but also between human consciousness and the nature of reality, envisioned as the result of computational processes. In a recursive loop appropriate to intermediation, the epilogue cycles back to reconsider in a new light the issues raised in the first chapter, rethinking computation and embodiment not as opposed visions of a posthuman future but as intermediating modalities, both of which are crucial to the human world in the present.

As all of these chapters illustrate, making, storing, and transmitting are not so much distinct arenas of interaction as they are different analytical slices through the multidimensional dynamics of intermediation. The implications for rethinking digital subjects and literary texts are extensive and include: understanding how the worldview of code is positioned in relation to the worldviews of speech and writing; forging new ways to think about the foundational terms "work," "text," and "document"; recognizing the different ways in which print and electronic texts mobilize the processes that produce them; and exploring how computer simulations may be related to human subjectivity and consciousness. The intermediating processes that I partially and incompletely describe are operating in the contemporary moment to challenge received ideas about language, subjectivity, literary objects, and textuality, including both print and electronic forms. If nothing else, I hope this book will convince you that literary and cultural critics steeped in the print tradition cannot simply continue with business as usual. Needed are new theoretical frameworks for understanding the relation of language and code; new strategies for making, reading, and interpreting texts; new modes of thinking about the material instantiation of texts in different media; and new ways to put together scientific research with cultural and literary theory. Rethinking digital subjects and literary texts as intermediation will not be accomplished in a single moment or by any one person. It is necessarily a collective and ongoing enterprise, to which I hope this book contributes.

1 MAKING
Language and Code

1 Intermediation
Textuality and the Regime of Computation

Language and Code

Unnoticed by most, new languages are springing into existence, proliferating across the globe, mutating into new forms, and fading into obsolescence. Invented by humans, these languages are intended for the intelligent machines called computers. Programming languages and the code in which they are written complicate the linguistic situation as it has been theorized for "natural" language, for code and language operate in significantly different ways. [1] Among the differences are the multiple addressees of code (which include intelligent machines as well as humans), the development of code by relatively small groups of technical specialists, and the tight integration of code into commercial product cycles and, consequently, into capitalist economics. Although virtually everyone would agree that language has been decisive in determining the specificity of human cultures and, indeed, of the human species, the range, extent, and importance of code remain controversial. Many people would argue that natural languages are much more broadly based than programming languages, a stance that relegates code to the relatively small niche of artificial languages intended for intelligent machines. Recently, however, strong claims have been made for digital algorithms as the language of nature itself. If, as Stephen Wolfram, Edward Fredkin, and Harold Morowitz maintain, the universe is fundamentally computational, code is elevated to the lingua franca not only of computers but of all physical reality.

Given these complexities, it has become an urgent task to understand in nuanced and theoretically sophisticated ways interactions between code and language. The scholarship on human languages is, of course, immense, and a smaller but still enormous quantity of research exists on programming languages. To date, however, criticism exploring feedback loops that connect the two kinds of language has been minimal.[2] At issue are the semiotically and materially distinct ways in which code and language operate, as well as the different contexts in which they emerge and develop. The task of understanding these differences is impeded by the diversity of the expert communities attending to them, comprising humanists and linguists on the one hand and computer programmers and software engineers on the other. Despite the general lack of communication between these communities, programming code and language interact continually in millions of encounters every day. The trading zones in which these negotiations occur are global in scope, penetrating deep into nearly every aspect of environments that rely on computers to carry out everyday tasks. Language alone is no longer the distinctive characteristic of technologically developed societies; rather, it is language plus code.

This project aspires to contribute to our understanding of these complexities by creating a theoretical framework in which language and code (in both its narrow and broader senses) can be systematically thought together. In addition, it explores through a series of case studies implications of the interactions of language and code for creative, technological, and artistic practice. The case studies focus on a range of issues, including the relation of print to electronic textuality, the constitution of subjectivity through bits as well as words, and the (mis)understandings through which humans interact with analog patterns functioning as metaphors for digital processes.

In the next chapter, I consider the three principal discourse systems of *speech*, *writing*, and *digital computer code*. To focus my discussion, I choose as representative of speech the semiotic theories of Ferdinand de Saussure,[3] and of writing, the early texts of Jacques Derrida, especially *Of Grammatology*, *Positions*, *Writing and Difference*, and *Margins of Philosophy*, works where he discusses the language system as theorized by Saussure and contrasts it with his theory of grammatology. My remarks on code are drawn from a number of sources; particularly important is the work of Stephen Wolfram, Edward Fredkin, Harold Morowitz, Ellen Ullman, Matthew Fuller, Matthew Kirschenbaum, and Bruce Eckel.[4] Further, I claim that theories about speech, writing, and code as represented by these sources are fraught with presuppositions, premises, and implications, in effect constituting what, for lack of a better term, I call "worldviews." The worldviews of speech, writing, and code are inextricably entwined with the technological conditions enveloping the theorists that developed these ideas, the philosophical, linguistic, and scientific traditions in which they claimed lineage, and the purposes toward which they wanted their work to contribute. From the comparison of these worldviews emerges a series of tensions and problematics that will form the basis for the arenas of interaction—*making, storing,* and *transmitting*—central to contemporary creative practices in scientific simulations, digital arts, electronic literature, and print literature.

The Regime of Computation

To facilitate the comparison of speech, writing, and code, I want to explore the larger context in which code as performative practice is located. For this inquiry, let us backtrack for a moment to consider the relation of computation (and hence of code, the language in which computation is carried out) to preexisting models for understanding truth statements, especially classical metaphysics. Perhaps no philosopher in the last century has been more successful than Jacques Derrida in exposing the impossible yearning at the heart of metaphysics for the "transcendental signified," the manifestation of Being so potent it needs no signifier to verify its authenticity. Yet Derrida repeatedly remarks that we cannot simply leave metaphysics behind.[5] He frequently asserts that metaphysics is so woven into the structure of Western philosophy, science, and social structures that it continually imposes itself on language and, indeed, on thought itself, creeping back in at the very moment it seems to have been exorcised. In this sense, classical metaphysics plays the role of the hegemonic influence that makes Derrida's resistant writing necessary and meaningful as a cultural practice. Derrida's discourse, as he himself remarks, is "entirely taken up with the reading of [others'] texts" and in this sense can be considered parasitic.[6] In his early writings, this preoccupation focuses specifically on texts that reinscribe the metaphysical yearning for presence that he devotes himself to deconstructing. To paraphrase a notorious remark, if metaphysics did not exist, Derrida would have been forced to invent it.

The worldview of computation also offers new answers to metaphysical questions, although in a very different way than Derridean grammatology. "Computation" in the sense it is used here connotes far more than the digital computer, which is only one of many platforms on which computational operations can run. Computation can take place in a variety of milieu and with almost any kind of material substrate. Leonard M. Adelman has pioneered the use of solutions of DNA as computational platforms for solving certain topological problems; Daniel Hillis recounts that as a child he made a computer out of Tinkertoys; John von Neumann, brooding over the birth of the digital computer, envisioned computation taking place with giant iron I beams adjacent to a factory that could assemble them into patterns representing binary code.[7]

If computation is not limited to digital manipulations, binary code, or silicon, what is it? Alan Turing gave a formalist definition of computation in his famous 1936 article describing an abstract computer known as the Turing machine, the most general version of which is called the Universal Turing machine. The Universal Turing machine, as its name implies, can perform any computation that any computer can do, including computing the algorithm that constitutes itself.[8] The computational regime continues in the tradition of Turing's work by considering computation to be a process that starts with a parsimonious set of elements and a relatively small set of logical operations. Instantiated into some kind of platform, these components can be structured so as to build up increasing levels of complexity, eventually arriving at complexity so deep, multilayered, and extensive as to simulate the most complex phenomena on earth, from turbulent flow and multiagent social systems to reasoning processes one might legitimately call thinking.

The wide-reaching claims made for the Regime of Computation are displayed in Stephen Wolfram's *A New Kind of Science*. The ambition of this book is breathtaking, especially considering the modesty with which scientists have traditionally put forth their claims. The book makes a fascinating contribution to the Regime of Computation, demonstrating through Wolfram's twenty years of research into cellular automata that simple rules can indeed generate complexity through computational means. Cellular automata have been around for decades. John von Neumann experimented with them, learning from Stanislaw Ulam how they could be reduced to a grid of two-dimensional cells;[9] Konrad Zuse in the 1950s suggested that they could form the basis for the physical universe;[10] in the 1990s researchers at the Santa Fe Institute, particularly Christopher Langton and his colleagues, explored the conditions under which cellular automata create, modify, and transmit information;[11] and John Conway showed that they could give the impression of living systems in his famous *Game of Life*.[12]

The basic idea is disarmingly simple, illustrated through this typical configuration.[13] Imagine a square grid, with each square representing a cell that can be either "on" or "off"; further suppose that we represent these states by black or white. An initial state is defined for each cell, as well as a set of rules telling each cell how to update its state. For example, a cell might have a rule specifying that it is "on" if two or more of its four neighbors are "on"; otherwise it is "off." Each cell in parallel then canvases the state of its neighbors and updates its state accordingly, while all of the other cells do the same. This update results in a new state for the system, which transforms in yet another iteration during which all the cells again canvas their neighbors and update their states accordingly. With contemporary computing power, it is possible to run through hundreds or thousands of iterations in a relatively short time. Through extensive research into various categories of cellular automata with simple rules, Wolfram shows that these conceptually simple systems are nevertheless capable of emergent behaviors in which astonishingly complex patterns appear. In particular, he discovered that the one-dimensional cellular automata described by Rule 110 yielded a Universal Turing machine, previously thought possible only in complex cellular automata of high dimensions.[14] That it should prove possible to create a Universal Turing machine in a system this simple is indeed a remarkable discovery.

Wolfram is not slow to draw sweeping implications from his work. He summarizes them in the Principle of Computational Equivalence, explored at length in chapter 12 of *A New Kind of Science*. In one of its formulations, the principle states, "Whenever one sees behavior that is not obviously simple—in essentially any system—it can be thought of as corresponding to a computation of equivalent sophistication" (5). The principle, as I read it, has three interlocking claims. The first is that all complex behavior can be simulated computationally, up to and including human thought and action (at least in principle). The second claim is that complex systems are "computationally irreducible" (6). Although the computations may be generated through simple rules (as are the cellular automata Wolfram discusses), there is no way to shorten the labor of computing the system's behavior (for example, by reducing it to mathematical equations). Simulating the behavior of these complex systems requires roughly the same amount of computation as the system itself puts forth to generate its actions, which implies a redistribution of intellectual labor. In a classical system susceptible to explicit solution, the equations may be difficult to solve but, once solved, serve to explain a wide variety of disparate behavior. For the cellular automata Wolfram discusses, the rules are extremely simple, but the labor of computing the behavior is intensive, requiring hundreds (or thousands or more) of iterations. The third claim, often not stated explicitly, is implied by the sweeping consequences Wolfram envisions for his research. This is the strong claim that computation does not merely *simulate* the behavior of complex systems; computation is envisioned as the process that actually *generates* behavior in everything from biological organisms to human social systems.

Wolfram's slide from regarding his simulations as models to thinking of them as computations that actually generate reality can be tracked at several places in his massive text. For example, he comments that "countless times I have been asked how models based on simple programs can possibly be correct, since even though they may successfully reproduce the behavior of some system, one can plainly see that the system itself does not, for example, actually consist of discrete cells that, say, follow the rules of a cellular automaton" (366). He answers this objection by claiming that "there is no reason that the model should actually operate like the system itself" (366). Elsewhere, however, he equivocates:

My approach in investigating issues like the Second Law is in effect to use simple programs as metaphors for physical systems. But can such programs in fact be more than that? And for example is it conceivable that at some level physical systems actually operate directly according to the rules of a simple program? . . . At first the laws might seem much too complicated to correspond to any simple program. But one of the crucial discoveries of this book is that even programs with very simple underlying rules can yield great complexity. . . . And so it could be with fundamental physics. Underneath the laws of physics as we know them today it could be that there lies a very simple program from which all the known laws—and ultimately all the complexity we see in the universe—emerges. (434)

In this passage and in similar ones, Wolfram introduces a crucial ambiguity into his claims for the Computational Universe. At issue is whether computation should be understood as a metaphor pervasive in our culture and therefore indicative of a certain "climate of opinion" (in Raymond Williams's phrase) at the turn of the millennium, or whether it has ontological status as the mechanism generating the complexities of physical reality. Rather than attempting to argue one side or the other of this controversial issue, I explore the implications of what it means to be situated at a cultural moment when the question remains undecidable—a moment, that is, when computation as means and as metaphor are inextricably entwined as a generative cultural dynamic. As we shall see, this entanglement has extensive implications for the positioning of humans in relation to intelligent machines and the broader landscape of the Computational Universe.

What does it mean to say that the Computational Universe functions simultaneously as metaphor and means? One way to understand their entanglement is through feedback loops that connect culturally potent metaphors with social constructions of reality, resulting in formulations that imaginatively invest computation with world-making power, even if it does not properly possess this power in itself. In *The Second Self* and *Life on the Screen*, Sherry Turkle shows compellingly that such feedback loops can dramatically influence how people perceive themselves and others. This influence extends even to the interactions of young children with intelligent toys. One of my favorite examples comes when one of her respondents, a shy and socially inept young man, comments, "Reality is not my best window."

A second kind of feedback loop emerges when belief in the Computational Universe is linked with an imagined future through which anticipation cycles to affect the present. A striking example of the Regime of Computation's ability to have real effects in the world, whatever its status in relation to the underlying physics, is the initiative to reorganize the U.S. military to pursue "network-centric warfare." Presupposing the ontology of code, military strategists argue that information has become a key military asset and that the U.S. military must be reorganized to take full advantage of it. They aim to abandon a centralized command/control structure in favor of a highly mobile and flexible force, a transformation that involves moving from platform-based strategies (based on tanks, airplanes, ships, etc.) to "network-centric" structures in which units are seen not as independent actors but as "part of a continuously adapting ecosystem."[15] Vice Admiral Arthur K. Cebrowski of the U.S. Navy and his collaborator, John J. Garstak, writing for the *Naval Institute Proceedings Magazine*, proclaim, "We are in the midst of a revolution in military affairs (RMA) unlike any seen since the Napoleonic Age." They quote Chief of Naval Operations Admiral Jay Johnston to the effect that network-centric warfare marks a "fundamental shift" in military thinking (1).

A principal advantage of network-centric warfare is the presumed ability to create "lock-out" effects through superior flexibility and speed. (The textbook example of lock-out occurred when video producers made the decision to produce for VHS equipment instead of Beta, thus converting a slight numerical advantage in the marketplace into interrelated equipment-content-consumption networks that decisively locked out Beta, despite the fact that in some ways it was technically superior to VHS). Cebrowski argues that lock-out can happen even faster in warfare and be even more decisive. Creating lock-out in military terms means acting fast and flexibly enough so that the opponent's very ability to plan strategically is disrupted. Cebrowski argues that such action demands a high-performance information grid combined with interoperable sensor and engagement grids. Moreover, it also requires the ability to achieve "self-synchronization" in which the commander's intentions, instead of filtering from the top slowly down the chain of command, are activated through the bottom-up organization of flexible units called "swarms," which can continually reorganize and restructure themselves (the nomenclature is no doubt indebted to the artificial-life software called "Swarm," designed to create self-organization and emergent behaviors).

Anticipating a future in which code (a synecdoche for information) has become so fundamental that it may be regarded as ontological, these transformations take the computational vision and feed it back into the present to reorganize resources, institutional structures, and military capabilities. Even if code is not originally ontological, it becomes so through these recursive feedback loops. In *Wetwares*, Richard Doyle makes a similar observation about the belief that we will someday be able to upload our consciousness into computers and thereby effectively achieve immortality. Doyle comments, "'Uploading,' the desire to be wetware, makes possible a new technology of the self, one fractured by the exteriority of the future. . . . Uploading seems to install discursive, material, and social mechanism for the anticipation of an *externalized* self, a techno-social mutation that is perhaps best characterized as a new capacity to be affected by, addicted to, the future" (133).

We will return to the entanglement of means and metaphor in chapter 9 through an analysis of Greg Egan's "subjective cosmology" trilogy: *Quarantine, Permutation City*, and *Distress*. An enormously inventive writer, Egan is arguably the most admired and influential novelist associated with the Regime of Computation. In the trilogy, feedback cycles between human cognition and the Computational Universe function to construct the nature of both reality and human beings. The novels will be contrasted with Slavoj Žižek's analysis of the symptom, which presupposes that such phantasmatic imaginations function as symptoms pointing toward repressed trauma and underlying psychopathologies. Thus in the final chapter we return to the issues raised here through a sharp contrast between a view that sees the Computational Universe as metaphoric and symptomatic, and one that sees the Computational Universe as physically real and deeply bound up with human thought. Through the encounter staged in chapter 9 between Egan and Žižek, the book cycles back to the beginning, although from the changed perspective articulated in the epilogue.

I am, however, getting ahead of my story. The third way in which the Computational Universe functions indeterminably as means and metaphor is through its current status as a provocative hypothesis that has neither won wide consensus nor been definitively disproved. Although many physicists remain skeptical of Wolfram's claims and of the Computational Universe generally, the idea of the Computational Universe has also attracted considerable attention and speculation. To understand the controversy in more detail, let us return to explore the different levels at which the Computational Universe has been postulated to run. To this end, it will be useful to summarize where we are at this point by indicating how the Regime of Computation positions itself in relation to classical metaphysics.

The regime reduces ontological requirements to a bare minimum. Rather than an initial premise (such as God, an originary Logos, or the axioms of

Euclidean geometry) out of which multiple entailments spin, computation requires only an elementary distinction between something and nothing (one and zero) and a small set of logical operations.[16] The emphasis falls not on working out the logical entailments of the initial premises but on unpredictable surprises created by the simulation as it is computed. The consequences of a simulation are not logically entailed by the starting point, which is why there is no shortcut to the computational work of running the simulation, and why the behaviors of complex systems cannot be compressed into more economical expression such as mathematical equations. Consequently, the Regime of Computation provides no foundations for truth and requires none, other than the minimalist ontological assumptions necessary to set the system running. Far from presuming the "transcendental signified" that Derrida identifies as intrinsic to classical metaphysics, computation privileges the emergence of complexity from simple elements and rules. Underscoring the point, Wolfram comments that "throughout most of history it has been taken almost for granted that such complexity—being so vastly greater than in the works of humans—could only be the work of a supernatural being" (3). Now complexity is understood as emerging from the computational processes that constitute the universe, and that changes everything. "The crucial idea that has allowed me to build a unified framework," Wolfram summarizes, ". . . is that just as the rules for any system can be viewed as corresponding to a program, so also its behavior can be viewed as a computation" (5).

Thinking along similar lines, Edward Fredkin has proposed a worldview that he calls "digital philosophy," a term that, like Wolfram's remarks, implicitly positions itself as providing answers to metaphysical questions. Fredkin argues that the discrete nature of elementary particles indicates that the universe is discrete rather than continuous, digital rather than analog. Electrons, protons, and neutrons always have charges represented by a small integer (–1, +1, 0); atomic nuclei are composed of neutrons and protons that are always (relatively) small integers; other qualities like spin and charm are either integers or halves of integers. These observations are consistent with Fredkin's major thesis: that the universe is digital all the way down and, moreover, can be understood as software running on an unfathomable universal digital computer. "Digital Philosophy carries atomism to an extreme in that we assume that everything is based on some very simple discrete process, with space, time, and state all being discrete."[17] Moreover, the discreteness he takes as axiomatic implies that information is conserved, a radically different view than, for example, Ilya Prigogine's view of thermodynamic dissipative systems.[18] "Digital Philosophy supports the beliefs that at different levels information is often best thought of as digital, and processes can often be best understood as digital processes. Thus anything in the world of Digital Philosophy that is changing or moving does so in a manner similar to how things are made to change or move in the memory of a computer."[19]

Acknowledging that quantum mechanics in some sense "works," Fredkin argues that the theory is ugly because it is largely ad hoc, concluding that we should prefer digital mechanics because it yields a more intuitively plausible and beautiful picture, one so simple and coherent it can be grasped by schoolchildren. His theory implies that quantum mechanics may describe what happens at the quantum level but fails to penetrate into the essential mechanisms generating the behavior. These mechanisms, in his view, are discrete and computational. The proof that digital mechanics underlies quantum mechanics will be demonstrated, Fredkin believes, when his research team is able to show that quantum mechanics *emerges* from the underlying digital mechanics base (a goal so far not achieved, although some progress toward it has been made). He remarks, "As one really understands the ideas of DM [digital mechanics], the currently accepted models of time, space, and process begin to seem mystical. From a Digital perspective, contemporary models of fundamental physics are a bit like looking at an animated cartoon while assuming that it's reality: that the images are moving continuously. So far, everyone we have interviewed who buys into Digital Philosophy has come to the conclusion that ordinary physics is a subject full of magic."[20]

Although Fredkin's claims are not as sweeping as Wolfram's, he too remains confident that a computational approach will explain living as well as nonliving systems. "Most biologists do not think about the processes of life in the same ways as would a Digital Philosopher," he remarks. "Yet some kind of information processing in living things begins with the informational process of sperm and egg combining and continues with differentiation as a kind of computation based on inherited information, and finally, as is obvious for all creatures that move, behavior involves information processing at a more familiar level."[21] Yet most of his examples are drawn from particle physics and quantum mechanics, realms that operate at a much lower level of complexity than living organisms.

Ray Kurzweil's criticism of Wolfram is telling in this regard; as Kurzweil points out, the cellular automata that Wolfram explores evolve complex patterns at what might be called the first level of complexity, but these complex patterns never self-organize to create further levels of emergence and complexity.[22] They do not, for example, self-organize to create bacteria or even viruses, never mind more complex organisms such as a duck or a human.

Even if Wolfram and Fredkin are correct in their claims that at the particle level the universe is a computer, this claim does not preclude higher levels of complexity emerging from different mechanisms, including analog processes (which can, of course, also be represented as computation, that is, analog computation rather than digital). Kurzweil further criticizes Wolfram for downplaying the role of evolution as a mechanism favoring the emergence of complexity; Kurzweil suggests that emergence at higher levels of complexity may well require the selective pressures and fitness criteria essential to evolutionary explanations.[23]

At best, then, the claims of Fredkin and Wolfram are incomplete, especially with regard to the emergence of higher-order from lower-order complexity. This is where the views of Harold Morowitz and like-minded researchers become important, for they offer a way to think about emergence as a process that not only operates at a single level of complexity but also continues up a dynamical hierarchy of linked systems to produce complexities out of complexities. In *The Emergence of Everything: How the World Became Complex* (a glitzy title for a good book), Morowitz reviews twenty-eight stages in the history of the cosmos to show that they can be characterized as emergent processes, each of which builds on the complexities that emerged from the preceding level.

"Emergence" carries special weight in this discourse. The term refers to properties that do not inhere in the individual components of a system; rather, these properties come about from interactions between components. Emergent properties thus appear at the global level of the system itself rather than at the local level of a system's components. Moreover, emergences typically cannot be predicted because the complex feedback loops that develop between components are not susceptible to explicit solution. As with Wolfram's simulations, the only way to determine the behavior of such a system is to run the simulation and see what emerges.

The new idea Morowitz adds is the insight that the emergences of a first-order complex system become properties that a second-order system can use to create a new dynamics from which further emergences will come. To the second-order system can be added a third-order system, a fourth-order system, and so on, with each level creating new emergences made possible by the emergences of the previous system. Multileveled complex systems synthesized in this way are called "dynamical hierarchies" (sometimes, significantly, "dynamic ontology"),[24] and the complexities they generate are potentially unlimited in scope and depth. Building on these ideas, Morowitz groups his twenty-eight events into four main stages: the emergence of the cosmos; the emergence of life; the emergence of mind; and the emergence of mind contemplating mind, or reflexivity. Presently, he believes, we are on the threshold of this last stage, whose development will be the catalyst for further evolution of the human into the posthuman in the centuries and millennia ahead. He finds the noosphere, the distributed global intelligence postulated by Pierre Teilhard de Chardin as the next stage in the evolution of intelligent life, suggestive of what might lie ahead for this fourth period.[25]

Whatever the future, the implications of this view for the present are clear, and it is here that the links between the "emergence of everything" and the Computational Universe become explicit. When the scope expands to the universe, simulations that could compute such behaviors become impossibly large, or in the terminology of the field, "transcomputable." To understand what "transcomputable" means, suppose that all the computing power on the planet was harnessed together and programmed to compute a given simulation. If the simulation qualified as "transcomputable," even this powerful array would not make more than a dent in the problem the simulation represented. For transcomputable situations, researchers must use pruning algorithms and selection rules to identify from an extremely large possibility space the conditions most likely to apply. The application of successive constraints, then, is crucial. What emerges has the force of an explanation but differs significantly from typical explanations in the physical sciences because it is not causal in nature and frequently is retrodictive rather than predictive.

These modes of explanation are necessary because complex systems cannot be described by mathematical equations that would allow precise prediction through linear causality. Like Wolfram and Fredkin, Morowitz emphasizes that the kinds of systems for which equations can be used constitute only a small set of all possible systems. According to Morowitz, although the traditional mathematical approach will continue to be useful, it will be understood increasingly as a specialized tool applicable only in (relatively) few situations. Future progress, he maintains, lies largely in the realm of computation and simulation. In a revealing analogy, Morowitz likens the invention of calculus and its central importance to the rise of modern science to the invention of the digital computer and the crucial role it plays in simulation. What calculus has been to physics and mathematics, the digital computer will be to understanding complex systems, evolution, and emergence.

Although the simulations and complex systems Morowitz discusses are not teleological (a characteristic related to the ontological minimalism of their starting points and to the lack of entailments these starting conditions embody), there is nevertheless directionality at work in their operations. The arrow of emergence points in the direction of increasing complexity, both for the preferred simulations and, presumably, for the evolution of the universe itself (a proposition endorsed by Stuart Kauffman in his work on the evolution of life through autocatalytic networks).[26] In Morowitz's view, humans are the most complex systems yet to emerge, and they now have sufficient complexity to emulate the very processes of emergence that created them and everything else. Far from needing to presume or construct a separation between the observer and the observation—a premise necessary in the classical understanding of science to ensure objectivity—the computational perspective endorsed by Morowitz, Wolfram, and Fredkin has no need of such a stipulation. These researchers can account for the presence of the observer simply by introducing a component into the simulation that performs this function. Indeed, in Morowitz's view the human observer plays an indispensable role in the jump from the third stage (emergence of mind) to the fourth stage (emergence of reflexivity), for our ability to simulate complex processes within computers makes possible the next stage of emergences.[27]

The Regime of Computation, then, provides a narrative that accounts for the evolution of the universe, life, mind, and mind reflecting on mind by connecting these emergences with computational processes that operate both in human-created simulations and in the universe understood as software running on the "Universal Computer" we call reality. This is the larger context in which code acquires special, indeed universal, significance. In the Regime of Computation, code is understood as the discourse system that mirrors what happens in nature and that generates nature itself.

Having looked at the claims, I turn now to a critical examination of them. From my perspective, all of these researchers claim much more than they actually demonstrate. Wolfram's assertion that cellular automata underlie and explain the complexity of living systems, including human culture and social processes, is a giant (and mostly unwarranted) leap from the simple systems he has explored. He shows convincingly only one level of emergence, from individual cells to group behavior. He does not show how this group behavior, however complex, provides the basis for further emergences that would build upon it. In my view, analog processes are undervalued in Fredkin's and Wolfram's accounts and are likely to play a central role as first-level complexities evolve into second-level complexities and further levels beyond that. Moreover, Wolfram often does not tie his cellular automata models to actual mechanisms at work in physical systems, a connection that must be made to validate the kind of ontological claims he advances. In this sense, Fredkin's program is more ambitious, for it tries to show how phenomena described by particle physics can emerge from the group behavior of cellular automata. If this result can be achieved, it would indeed be a striking accomplishment and might well lead to radical rethinking of such foundational concepts as space and time, as he believes. Even in this best-case scenario, however, the leap Fredkin makes to higher-level complexities would remain to be demonstrated.

As for Morowitz, the novel component he adds is the interpretive framework of dynamical hierarchical emergences. Virtually all the phenomena he instances are well-known within their respective fields (cosmology, origins-of-life biology, evolution, psychology, etc.). Although he offers a compelling overall picture, he does not explicate the mechanisms that link one level of emergence to another, other than as a precondition (for example, there must be a planet before life can emerge on that planet). This sort of linear causality is well-known and offers nothing new. What would be new is a detailed understanding of how one dynamical level enchains and emerges from the next lower one through their intersecting dynamics. This he does not show, nor does he explore the specific mechanisms that bring it about.

In fact, no one to date has demonstrated clearly how complex dynamics in simulations can progress more than one level. Accordingly, such a demonstration has become the goal of the community of artificial-life researchers, who are devoting several major conferences to the problem in addition to organizing a special issue of the *Artificial Life Journal* on dynamical hierarchies.[28] History provides many examples of scientific and technological breakthroughs that occurred because researchers became convinced a certain goal was achievable and were willing to devote significant resources to accomplishing it (often aided by substantial government funding), from mapping the human genome to building an atomic bomb. In my view, it is likely that within the next three or four years multilevel dynamical hierarchies will be created in simulations, and I expect that much will be learned from detailed studies of their dynamics. Whether these insights will significantly alter the current picture remains to be seen.

The central problem of achieving emergence through more than one level is bound up tightly with issues of representation. As Nicholas Gessler, among others, has pointed out, one way to think about this process is to imagine a mechanism whereby the patterns that emerged at the first level are represented by a different kind of mechanism, which then uses these representations as primitives to create new emergent patterns, which in turn would undergo further re-representation and be turned into primitives for the third level, and so on.[29] This schema suggests a new interpretation of Wolfram's interaction with his cellular automata.

As noted above, one weakness of Wolfram's argument is his underestimation of the importance of analog processes, and especially of the productive interplay between analog and digital processes. Take DNA replication for example. DNA is often understood to operate as a digital code, in the sense that it is discrete rather than continuous. With the sequencing of the human genome, however, it has become clear that sequence is only part of the story, perhaps even the less important part. Protein folding, an analog process that makes use of continuous transformation in form, is essential to understanding how the genome actually functions. The *combination* of the two processes, the digitality of DNA sequences and the analog process of protein folding, gives the gene its remarkable power of information storage and transmission. Similar cooperations between digital and analog processes occur everywhere in nature and in contemporary technologies. Music CDs, for example, which Jean Baudrillard famously and mistakenly characterized as purely digital, rely on analog processes (such as microphones and other analog equipment) to capture the morphology of sound waves, which then can be represented numerically and transformed into computer code. That the combination of analog and digital should prove far more powerful than either by itself is no mystery, for each has properties that complement the other. As explained more fully in chapter 2, digital representations allow for precise error control, extreme fragmentation and recombination, whereas analog processes have the advantages of the continuum, including the ability to transmit informational patterns between differently embodied entities.

Consider now the moment when Wolfram bends over the output of one of his cellular automata and perceives in it patterns strikingly similarly to the shell of a mollusk. What exactly is happening in this scene? One way to understand it is as a re-representation of the patterns that emerged from the first-level operations of the cellular automata by another kind of analog mechanism we can call Wolfram's consciousness (assume for purposes of this discussion that consciousness is analog, even though in fact it may well be an emergent phenomenon itself produced by the synergistic interaction of analog and digital components). This kind of interaction between digital mechanisms and analog consciousness happens all around us every day, often resulting in emergent reorganizations across many levels of complexity, for example when digital technologies are re-represented in the consciousness of military strategists and used as the basis for reorganizing military units to create and facilitate emergent behaviors.

This larger vision of synergistic cooperation between consciousness and computer, language and code, epitomizes the kind of complex interactions to which this study is devoted. Notwithstanding the problems with the claims of Wolfram, Fredkin, and others, the computational worldview these researchers advocate contains valuable insights that should not get lost in the skeptical scrutiny to which their claims are rightfully subjected. Especially crucial are the entwined concepts of emergent processes and dynamical hierarchies, which represent ways of thinking that are powerful heuristics through which to understand the dynamics of complex systems of many different kinds. Whatever their limitations, these researchers fully understand that linear causal explanations are limited in scope and that multicausal complex systems require other modes of modeling and explanation. This seems to me a seminal insight that, despite three decades of work in chaos theory, complex systems, and simulation modeling, remains underappreciated and undertheorized in the physical sciences, and even more so in the social sciences and humanities.

Meanwhile, the pervasiveness and importance of computing in contemporary culture continue to reinforce the idea that computation is a fundamental process. Even if many of the claims associated with the Universal Computer are disproved, it is unlikely that the idea will die out altogether, particularly in communities of researchers concerned with the development of code and the construction of simulations. Already circulating are versions of the Universal Computer based on different mechanisms than cellular automata. Seth Lloyd, among others, has proposed that "the universe is a quantum computer: life, sex, the brain, and human society all arise out of the ability of the universe to process information at the level of atoms, photons, and elementary particles."[30] Significantly, this proposition came in response to "hard-edge" questions posed by popular science writer and literary agent John Brockman, questions that "render visible the deeper meanings of our lives, redefine who and what we are."[31]

Intermediation

For my purposes, I find the Regime of Computation valuable for articulating the context in which code takes shape within the worldview of computation. Speech and writing also have extensive links with their respective worldviews, which, as noted above, for the purposes of this project I identify with Saussurean semiotics and Derridean grammatology, respectively. Like computation, these worldviews imply distinctive ways of constituting communities, dealing with evolutionary changes, accommodating technological interventions, and describing the operations of systems. A thorough understanding of the interactions in which speech, writing, and code participate requires more than knowing the details of the three systems. Also at stake are the diverse conflicts and cooperations between their respective worldviews. As the worldview of code assumes comparable importance to the worldviews of speech and writing, the problematics of interaction between them grow more complex and entangled. These complex and entangled interactions are what I call "intermediation," a term suggested by Nicholas Gessler.[32]

An important aspect of intermediation is the recursivity implicit in the coproduction and coevolution of multiple causalities. Complex feedback loops connect humans and machines, old technologies and new, language and code, analog processes and digital fragmentations. Although these feedback loops evolve over time and thus have a historical trajectory that arcs from one point to another, it is important not to make the mistake of privileging any one point as the primary locus of attention, which can easily result in flattening complex interactions back into linear causal chains. The contemporary indoctrination into linear causality is so strong that it continues to exercise a fatal attraction for much of contemporary thought. It must be continually resisted if we are fully to realize the implications of multicausal and multilayered hierarchical systems, which entail distributed agency, emergent processes, unpredictable coevolutions, and seemingly paradoxical interactions between convergent and divergent processes.

A case in point is the current tendency to regard the computer as the ultimate solvent that is dissolving all other media into itself. Since sound, image, text, and their associated media (such as phonography, cinema, and books) can all be converted into digital code, many commentators, including Lev Manovich and Friedrich Kittler, have claimed that there is now only one medium, the digital computer.[33] Asserting that "one century sufficed to transform the ancient storage monopoly of writing into the omnipotence of integrated circuits," Kittler writes that "all data flows end in a state n of Turing's universal machine: numbers and figures become (in spite of romanticism) the key to all creatures."[34] This claim has the effect of flattening into a single causal line—the convergence of all media into one—social and cultural processes that are in fact much more complex. To take the case of books, clearly it matters that print has now become a particular kind of output for digital text. As I argue in chapter 5 with regard to Neal Stephenson's print novel *Cryptonomicon*, digitization leaves its mark even on print texts that remain entirely conventional in appearance and functionality. Moreover, a stroll through any major bookstore will confirm that print books in general have moved toward the visual and away from straight text, a tendency that bears witness to their interactions with other media.

Nevertheless, it is also true that any book, conventional or not, participates in the rich historical contexts and traditions of print that influence how books are designed, produced, disseminated, and received. The sub-vocalization that Kittler associates in *Discourse Networks* with the advent of phonetics and the ability of readers to hallucinate an imagined world does not disappear simply because blockbuster movies attract millions of viewers, any more than it evaporates because cinema and books are increasingly interpenetrated by digital techniques.[35] If anything, print readers relish all the more the media-specific effects of books precisely because they no longer take them for granted and have many other media experiences with which to compare them.[36] Although Sven Birkerts draws a different lesson from media proliferation in *The Gutenberg Elegies*, his book can be understood as a demonstration of the fact that print no longer exists in isolation from other media (even as it also illustrates the tendency to flatten complex interactions into a single causal chain). Recognizing entangled causalities and multiple feedback loops enables us to understand how media can converge into digitality and *simultaneously* diverge into a robust media ecology in which new media represent and are represented in old media, in a process that Jay Bolter and Richard Grusin have called "remediation."[37]

Grusin and Bolter define remediation, in one formulation, as "the formal logic by which new media technologies refashion prior media forms."[38] They trace feedback loops between the seemingly opposed but nonetheless correlated strategies of "immediacy" (the tendency of media to represent their productions as transparent and naturally accessible) and "hypermediacy" (the tendency of media to draw attention to their modes of representation and the media-specific strategies they use). This coevolution of apparently opposed trends, like the simultaneous coevolution of convergence and divergence in media, is characteristic of complex systems with multiple feedback loops.

Think, for example, of an ecological system in which predator and prey develop opposing strategies because each is involved in a feedback loop with the other. The opposition looms large if we look only at a single interaction between predator and prey (that is, position them in a linear causal relationship). In the more comprehensive context of the complex dynamics formed by their continuing interactions over generations of coevolution, however, the opposition becomes part of a larger picture in which one strategy catalyzes the opposing strategy, which in turn catalyzes a further development of the first one. In a similar way, extensive research on the Prisoner's Dilemma, a famous thought problem in which players must choose between competitive and cooperating strategies, demonstrates that the dynamics of this system change dramatically when the game is iterated, that is, subjected to repeated interactions between players.[39] Coevolution that extends over many cycles, such as that instantiated in iterated Prisoner's Dilemma simulations, is typical of media interactions in contemporary society, including the interactions that help to form (and in-form) the complex dynamics of textualities.

Grusin and Bolter's arguments in *Remediation* demonstrate insightfully that complex feedback occurs between the oppositional strategies of immediacy and hypermediacy. Nevertheless, for my purposes I prefer the term "intermediation." "Remediation" has the disadvantage of locating the starting point for the cycles in a particular locality and medium, whereas "intermediation" is more faithful to the spirit of multiple causality in emphasizing interactions among media. In addition, "remediation" (thanks to the excellent work Grusin and Bolter have done in positioning the term) now has the specific connotation of applying to immediate/hypermediate strategies. Because the dynamics I want to explore go far beyond this particular cycle, I would rather use the lesser known "intermediation" (which, being not as well known, is more open to new interpretations). To make the term more useful for my purposes, I want to expand its denotations to include interactions between systems of representations, particularly language and code, as well as interactions between modes of representation, particularly analog and digital. Perhaps most importantly, "intermediation" also denotes mediating interfaces connecting humans with the intelligent machines that are our collaborators in making, storing, and transmitting informational processes and objects.

In emphasizing intermediation, I have been instructed by studies that adopt different strategies to achieve different ends. I regard this project as complementary to these studies, for I see both these studies and my own project as useful in developing new frameworks with which to understand where we are and where we may be heading, both in literary studies and the broader context of contemporary Anglo-American-European culture. To some extent, this project is also intended as a corrective to the tendency in other studies, useful as they are, to privilege one medium and/or mode of interaction to the exclusion of others and thus to fall again into the trap of linear causality. By keeping the focus on intermediation, I hope to incorporate some of the insights from other studies while clarifying how the recognition of multiple causalities leads to different conclusions.

Media Technologies and Embodied Subjects

To help situate this project, let us consider the contrasting approaches of Friedrich Kittler and Mark B. N. Hansen. Kittler's strategy for escaping from the confines of humanist discourse is to focus on media rather than subjects. In *Discourse Networks*, he argues that subjects speak within discourse systems, and that discourse systems are constituted by the technological apparatuses enabling them to operate. "Media determine our situation," he proclaims in the preface to *Gramophone, Film, Typewriter*, asserting that "technologies that not only by-pass writing but suck in and carry off so-called humanity render their own description impossible" (28), thus making post-print media the sea in which we posthuman fish swim. Although Kittler does not ignore bodies and subjectivities, he positions them as being constituted by the media they use. "In order to optimize writing for machines," he asserts with typical hyperbole "it must no longer be dreamt of as an expression of individuals or as a trace of bodies. The forms, differences, and frequencies of letters have to be reduced to formulas. So-called man becomes physiology on the one hand and information technology on the other."[40] The rhetoric of force ("must no longer," "have to be") performs an epistemic break reminiscent of the early Foucault, with the important difference, as Kittler himself has observed in critiquing Foucault, that his focus is on the media technologies that produce discourse systems ("discourse networks") rather than on discourse systems themselves.[41]

Strenuously resisting Kittler's coercive rhetoric, Hansen, in *New Philosophy for New Media*, performs a violence of his own by attempting to reduce Kittler's argument to a linear causal chain that rests solely on the truth or falsity of Shannon's information theory. "What remains decisive for Kittler," he argues, "are precisely the formal properties of Shannon's model: as the basis for the technical de-differentiation that constitutes the logical culmination of the historical decoupling of information from communication, Shannon's model allows Kittler to postulate an informational posthistory. From the standpoint of the optoelectronic future, the human or so-called Man—as well as the entire range of media effects said to comprise a media ecology—must be revalued as the purely contingent by-product of a preparatory phase in the evolution of information toward truly autonomous circulation" (77). To show that this foundation cannot stand, Hansen instances Donald MacKay's alternative approach to information, which was developed contemporaneously with Shannon's. In contrast to Shannon's separation of information and meaning, MacKay develops a concept of information that places the embodied receiver at the center of his theory.[42] Hansen's recourse to MacKay is somewhat disingenuous, for it ignores the fact that it was the Shannon/Wiener theory, and not Mackay's work, that was important for the development of information theory, for the good reason that MacKay's theory, although more encompassing in correlating information with meaning, could not be reliably quantified with technologies available in the 1950s (and still cannot today). Moreover, Hansen's refutation concerns only one line of reasoning in Kittler's extensive oeuvre, and for this reason is insufficient to discount his approach entirely, as Hansen seems to imply.

In contrast to Kittler, Hansen privileges embodiment as the locus of subjectivity, reading new media through its effects on embodied users and viewers. "Correlated with the advent of digitization, then, the body undergoes a certain empowerment, since it deploys its own constitutive singularity (affection and memory) not to filter a universe of preconstituted images but actually to enframe something (digital information) that is originally formless. Moreover, this 'originary' act of enframing information must be seen as the source of all technical frames (even if these appear to be primary), to the extent that these are designed to make information perceivable by the body, that is, to transform it into the form of an image" (10). It is no accident, I think, that coercive rhetoric similar to Kittler's appears here ("must be seen"), for Hansen wants to unseat Kittler's media focus in order to place the embodied subject at the center of his own "new philosophy for new media."[43]

Notwithstanding their opposed viewpoints, Hansen and Kittler share a mode of argumentation that privileges one locus of the human/machine feedback loop at the expense of the other. For Kittler it is all about media: the technical configurations they impose on representations, and the content of representations that reflect and reinscribe these configurations. For Hansen it is all about embodied subjects: the perceptual and cognitive processing they incorporate as a result of the media they encounter, specifically media images, and the representations within new media that catalyze and foreground these incorporations. From where I stand, it looks like Kittler and Hansen are perched on a seesaw that teeters up and down while they fail to notice that both ends are connected by a fulcrum joining the two in correlated actions.

Certainly media are dependent on embodied subjects, not only for their reception and significance but also because researchers extensively investigate the precise nature of computer/human interfaces to develop and design networked and programmable media that will have certain effects. There would be no media without humans to invent them, and no purpose to them without humans to give them meaning and significance (notwithstanding the futuristic scenarios evoked by Kittler, Moravec, Kurzweil, and others of a postmedia, posthuman age in which media are autonomously created by other media and/or intelligent machines).[44] On the other hand, media clearly determine and help constitute humans' embodied responses, which include not only the historically specific conditioned reactions of a given epoch but also the evolutionarily evolved cognitive and perceptual capabilities that Hansen evokes. Moreover, in certain contexts the body itself becomes a medium at the same time as it is in-formed by other media, a complex dynamic ingeniously enacted by Sha Xin Wei's "Tgarden," in which performers strive to create new gestural languages in association with motion sensors and virtual projections.[45] Surely a fuller account—to which I hope to contribute by focusing on intermediation—would take into consideration both of the vectors that Hansen and Kittler mobilize, acknowledging, on one hand, the role technical configurations play and, on the other, the centrality of embodied subjects to new media productions. The trick, as I see it, is to enlarge the scope of inquiry so that it includes *both* Wolfram and his cellular automata, the embodied human and his perceptions *along with* the computational processes that he creates and that work to coconstitute him and his perceptions. In a strikingly literal sense, Wolfram and his cellular automata coevolve together in a synergistic dynamic that allows emergences to occur across many levels of complexity.

A similar pattern emerges from the contrast between Espen Aarseth's *Cybertext* and Jerome McGann's *Radiant Textuality*. Like the work of Kittler and Hansen, these texts are seminally important studies deserving close attention. Defining "ergodic literature" as literature requiring "nontrivial effort" to "allow the reader to traverse the text" (1), Aarseth makes a point of including print books as well as computer games and electronic interactive fiction. He slyly takes a poke at the literary establishment by remarking that to limit his analysis to computer-driven texts "would be an arbitrary and unhistorical limitation, perhaps comparable to a study of literature that would only acknowledge texts in paper-printed form" (1). Nevertheless, if computer games, electronic hypertexts, and interactive fiction were not on the scene, no one (including Aarseth) would have been likely to find it necessary to define "ergodic literature" as a category of analysis. In this sense, his analysis is motivated primarily by the kind of literature the computer has made popular, especially computer games, now his principal focus of interest. The centrality of computers to his analysis is indicated, among other places, by his defense of the cybertext perspective as necessary because no other existing approach takes into account "the text as a material machine, a device capable of manipulating itself as well as the reader" (24), a description much more relevant to computers than to books. Moreover, he develops several important distinctions—including "scriptons" as strings the reader sees versus "textons" as strings generating the text—that are crucially important for computer texts but infrequently so for codex books and print texts in general. The computer orientation also helps to explain why his analysis is heavily weighted toward functionality. Most of the terms he defines to develop his typology have to do with functions available to the player/user or with functions that elements within a text can perform. Since most print texts differ little from one another in their functionality, this emphasis is an additional indication that Aarseth's perspective is oriented primarily toward computer-generated texts.

There is nothing wrong, of course, with a computer orientation. This orientation is part of what makes *Cybertext* an invaluable contribution to the field of electronic textuality, which continues to be too often seen through a print-centric perspective. More problematic is the fact that Aarseth's functionalist approach tends to flatten multiple causalities into linear causal sequences determined by a work's functionality. This flattening can be seen both in his relative neglect of the political, social, and cultural contexts in which texts are used and in the "textonomy" he develops for his typology (58). Similarly, he also neglects interactions of different modalities within electronic texts. Even though many of his examples include visual displays and animations, he defines a text as "any object with the primary function to relay *verbal* information" (62, emphasis added), leaving out of account visual, graphic, sonic, kinetic, and other nonverbal signifiers. Although he recognizes that materiality should be part of the picture, his analysis pays scant attention to the material specificity of texts. He asserts—astonishingly, given the contemporary legal and political debates over Gnutella and Napster—that in "the transition from long-playing records to compact discs in the music industry," the "analog-to-digital shift of the artifact did not change any substantial aspects of the cultural production or consumption of music" (59). To be fair, it is much easier to see the importance of these issues in 2004 than it would have been in 1997, when *Cybertext* was published, for the intervening seven years have seen remarkable growth in the visuality of electronic media and the accelerating digitization of all media. Nevertheless, there remains an important gap between Aarseth's emphasis on typology as a list of static functionalist components located on a grid of 576 positions, and the kind of dynamic multicausality required to understand complex emergent processes characterized by entangled feedback loops cycling back and forth between different levels.

In contrast to Aarseth's methodology is the approach Jerome McGann takes in *Radiant Textuality*. As I argue at more length in chapter 4, McGann's primary interest lies in using electronic textuality to deepen our understanding of how print literature works. In this the book is successful, as its deserved recognition by the James Russell Lowell Prize indicates. A brilliant reader of print literature, particularly poetry, McGann continues to argue that even modest works in the print tradition are far better, as literature, than the most complex and interesting works of electronic literature.[46] This is a judgment I do not share, and in my view it stems largely from a tendency to apply to electronic literature the same reading strategies one uses for print, while underappreciating or perhaps simply not recognizing the new strategies available to electronic literature: animation, rollovers, screen design, navigation strategies, and so on. Whereas Aarseth faces forward and reads print literature through a matrix developed in the context of computer games, McGann faces backward and reads electronic literature through a matrix developed in the context of print literature. McGann has been a pioneer in arguing for multidimensional models to explain how print texts come into being. However, despite his leadership in creating and implementing the D. G. Rossetti Hypermedia Archive, an important Web site, one looks in vain in *Radiant Textuality* for similar deep insights into the multiple causalities, complex feedback loops, and emergent processes through which electronic texts are made, stored, and disseminated.[47]

Of course, it is much easier to characterize in general terms what should be done than it is to do it, especially when attempting to work against the grain of something as entrenched and powerful as linear causal models. My arguments will stand or fall not on general claims and caveats about seminal texts but on in-depth explorations of the complex dynamics with which I want to engage. Accordingly, I turn now from this chapter focused on technology to a comparison of the theoretical frameworks and worldviews of speech, writing, and code.

2 Speech, Writing, Code
Three Worldviews

The Locus of Complexity

Speech, writing, code: these three major systems for creating signification interact with each other in millions of encounters every day. Each, as it has been theorized, comes with its own worldview, associated technologies, and user feedback loops. In the progression from speech to writing to code, each successor regime reinterprets the system(s) that came before, inscribing prior values into its own dynamics. Now that the information age is well advanced, we urgently need nuanced analyses of the overlaps and discontinuities of code with the legacy systems of speech and writing, so that we can understand how processes of signification change when speech and writing are coded into binary digits. Although speech and writing issuing from programmed media may still be recognizable as spoken utterances and print documents, they do not emerge unchanged by the encounter with code. Nor is the effect of code limited to individual texts. In a broader sense, our understanding of speech and writing in general is deeply influenced by the pervasive use of code (my deliberate situating of them as legacy systems above is intended as a provocation to suggest the perceptual shifts underway). This chapter will show how the worldview of computation sketched in chapter 1 manifests itself in the specific case of the digital computer. It will also indicate ways in which commonly accepted ideas about signification need to be reevaluated in the context of coding technologies. Finally, it will suggest terms for analysis that, although not absent in speech and writing, assume new importance with code and therefore lead to new theoretical emphases and foci of attention.

In drawing comparisons of code with speech and writing, one is faced with an embarrassment of riches. One thinks, for example, of the embodied views of speech explored by practitioners and theorists as diverse as Walter

Ong and Oliver Sacks; of such preeminent theorists of writing as Paul de Man and J. Hillis Miller. Out of many possibilities, I have chosen to focus on Ferdinand de Saussure's view of speech and Jacques Derrida's grammatological view of writing partly because these theorists take systemic approaches to their subjects that make clear the larger conceptual issues. Like them, I want to take a systemic approach by focusing on the conceptual system in which code is embedded, a perspective that immediately concerns programming for digital computers but also includes the metaphysical implications of the Regime of Computation. In addition, both Saussure and Derrida have been extremely influential in shaping contemporary views of speech and writing. By addressing their work in detail, I can by implication address the large number of related projects these two theorists have inspired. An additional advantage is Derrida's engagement with Saussure's theories of the speech system; Derrida's work has an intimate relation with Saussure's, which is richly documented in Derrida's writings, especially his early work. Moreover, one of Derrida's critical points is that writing exceeds speech and cannot simply be conceptualized as speech's written form. Similarly, I will argue that code exceeds both writing and speech, having characteristics that appear in neither of these legacy systems. This project, then, is not meant as a general comparison of code with structuralism and deconstruction but as a more narrowly focused inquiry that takes up specifically Saussure and Derrida.

Before turning to a systematic comparison of code with Saussure's speech system and Derrida's grammatology, I want to establish a general framework for my remarks. Derrida's remarkably supple and complex writing notwithstanding, much of his analysis derives from a characteristic of writing that would likely spring to mind if we were asked to identify the principal way in which writing differs from speech. Writing, unlike speech (before recording technologies), is not confined to the event of its making. It can be stored and transmitted, published in dozens of countries and hundreds of different editions, read immediately after its creation or a thousand years hence. In a sense it is no surprise that Derrida summarizes this difference between writing and speech by fusing "difference" with "defer," for the ability to defer indefinitely our encounter with writing leaps out as perhaps the most salient way in which it differs from speech. Derrida, of course, complicates and extends this commonsense idea by linking it with a powerful critique of the metaphysics of presence—but these complexities have their root in something most people would identify as a constitutive difference between speech and writing.

If we were to ask about the parallel characteristic that leaps to mind to distinguish code from speech and writing, an obvious contender would be the fact that code is addressed both to humans and intelligent machines. A further distinction is implied when we note that computers, although capable of performing diverse and complicated tasks, have at the base level of machine language only two symbols and a small number of logical operations with which to work. As Stephen Wolfram eloquently testifies in relation to his cellular automata, the amazing thing about them is that starting from an extremely simple base they can nevertheless produce complex patterns and behaviors.

This train of thought suggests the following question: Where does the complexity reside that makes code (or computers, or cellular automata) seem adequate to represent a complex world? In his critique of speech and the metaphysics of presence, Derrida makes clear that complexity was vested traditionally in the Logos, the originary point conceptualized as necessarily exceeding the world's complexity, since in this view the world derived from the Logos. For Derrida's grammatology, complexity is conceptually invested in the trace and by implication in the subtle analysis that detects the movement of the trace, which can never be found as a thing-in-itself. For code, complexity inheres neither in the origin nor in the operation of difference as such but in the labor of computation that again and again calculates differences to create complexity as an emergent property of computation. Humans, who have limited access to their own computational machinery (assuming that cognition includes computational elements, a proposition explored in chapter 9), create intelligent machines whose operations can be known in comprehensive detail (at least in theory). In turn, the existence of these machines, as many researchers have noted, suggests that the complexities we perceive and generate likewise emerge from a simple underlying base; these researchers hope that computers might show us, in Brian Cantwell Smith's phrase, "how a structured lump of clay can sit up and think."[1] The advantages of the computational view, for those who espouse it, is that emergence can be studied as a knowable and quantifiable phenomena, freed both from the mysteries of the Logos and the complexities of discursive explanations dense with ambiguities. One might observe, of course, that these characteristics also mark the limitations of a computational perspective.

It is not an accident that my analysis starts by inquiring about the locus of complexity, for the different strategies through which Saussurean linguistics, Derridean grammatology, and the Regime of Computation situate complexity have extensive implications for their respective worldviews. From this starting point I will develop several ways, not all of them obvious, in which code differs from speech and writing. My purpose is not to supplant these legacy systems and especially not to subordinate speech and writing to code (an important point, given Saussure's historic claim that writing must be subordinate to speech, and Derrida's insistence that, on the contrary, speech is subordinate to writing). Rather, for me the "juice" (as Rodney Brooks calls it) comes from the complex dynamics generated when code interacts with speech and writing, interactions that include their mundane daily transactions and also the larger stakes implicit in the conflict and cooperation of their worldviews.

Saussurean Signs and Material Matters

Let us begin, then, where Saussure began, with his assertion that the sign has no "natural" or inevitable relation to that which it refers; "the linguistic sign is arbitrary," he writes in *Course in General Linguistics*.[2] Partly for this reason, he excludes from consideration hieroglyphic and idiomatic writing. As he makes clear in a number of places, he regards speech as the true locus of the language system (*la langue*) and writing as merely derivative of speech. "A language and its written form constitute two separate systems of signs. The sole reason for the existence of the latter is to present the former. The object of study in linguistics is not a combination of the written word and the spoken word. The spoken word alone constitutes that object" (24–25). Objecting to the primacy Saussure accords to speech, Derrida sees in this hierarchy indications that Saussure remains bound to a metaphysics of presence and to the Logos with which speech has traditionally been associated; in an interview with Julia Kristeva, he remarks that "the concept of the sign belongs to metaphysics."[3]

Derrida marshals numerous arguments to insist that writing, far from being derivative as Saussure claims, in fact precedes speech; "the linguistic sign implies an original writing."[4] This counterintuitive idea, to which we will return, depends on his special understanding of writing as grammatology. In addition, he critiques Saussure's notion of the arbitrariness of the sign, asking if the "ultimate function" of this premise is to obscure "the rights of history, production, institutions etc., except in the form of the arbitrary and in the substance of naturalism" (*Of Grammatology*, 33). Of course he recognizes that the arbitrariness of the sign as Saussure posits it refers to the absence of a necessary connection between sign and referent, but his critique implies that Saussure's formulation tends to suppress the recognition that constraints of any kind might encumber the choice of sign. The productive role that constraints play in the Regime of Computation, functioning to eliminate possible choices until only a few remain, is conspicuously absent in Saussure's theory. Instead, meaning emerges and is stabilized by differential relations between signs. Jonathan Culler, writing his influential book on Saussure just as Saussure was becoming well known in the United States, makes explicit this implication: "The fact that the relation between signifier and signified is arbitrary means, then, that since there are no fixed universal concepts or fixed universal signifiers, the signified itself is arbitrary, and so is the signifier. . . . Both signifier and signified are purely relational or differential entities."[5]

Culler's interpretation helps explain why material constraints tend to drop out of Saussure's theory as appropriated by American poststructuralism, with a corresponding emphasis on differential relations and shifting uncertain ties to reference and, indeed, to the material conditions of production altogether (interpretations that have been contested by later commentators seeking to recuperate Saussure for various purposes).[6] Although Derrida's suggestion that Saussure had erased "the rights of history, production, institutions, etc." remains underdeveloped in his writing, the recognition that materiality imposes significant constraints becomes crucially important in code, and arguably in speech and writing as well. Why, for example, are there no words in English (and so far as I know, in any other language) that have one hundred or more syllables? Obviously, we have no such words because they would take too long to pronounce. In contrast to the erasure of materiality in Saussure, material constraints have historically been recognized as crucial in the development of computers, from John von Neumann in the 1950s agonizing over how to dissipate heat produced by vacuum tubes to present-day concerns that the limits of miniaturization are being approached with silicon-based chips. Moreover, material constraints have played a central role in favoring the shift to digital computers over analog.

To understand why digital computers have been favored, consider Transistor to Transistor Logic (TTL) chips, where the binary digit zero is represented by zero volts and the binary digit one by five volts. If a voltage fluctuation creates a signal of .5 volts, it is relatively easy to correct this voltage to zero, since .5 is much closer to zero than to five. Error control is much more complex with analog computers, where voltages vary continuously. For code, then, the assumption that the sign is arbitrary must be qualified by material constraints that limit the ranges within which signs can operate meaningfully and acquire significance. As we shall see, these qualifications are part of a larger picture that tie code more intimately to material conditions than is the case either for Saussure's speech system or Derrida's grammatological view of writing. In the worldview of code, materiality matters.

Culler was not wrong in emphasizing differential relations rather than material constraints, for it is clear that Saussure's view of the sign tended toward dematerialization. "The physical part of the [speech] circuit can be dismissed from consideration straight away," he says (13). Although he later acknowledges that "linguistic signs, although essentially psychological, are not abstractions," he sees their materiality as "realities localized in the brain" and distinguishes this mediated materiality from linguistic structure, where "there is only the sound pattern" (15). He argues that differences in pronunciation should be excluded because they "affect only the material substance of words" (18). Considering the sign to consist of signifier and signified, he insists that the signifier is not the acoustic sound itself but the "sound pattern" or "sound image," that is, an idealized version of the sound, whereas the signified is the concept associated with this image. The advantage of defining an immaterial pattern as the signifier is obvious; through this move, he dispenses with having to deal with variations in pronunciation, dialects, and so on (although he does recognize differences in inflection, a point that Johanna Drucker uses to excavate from his theory a more robust sense of the materiality of the sign).[7]

This is Saussure's way of coping with the noise of the world, whereby idealization plays a role similar to the function performed by discreteness in digital systems. It is worth reflecting on the differences between these two strategies. Rectifying voltage fluctuations could be compared to Saussure's "rectification" of actual sounds into idealized sound images. Importantly, however, rectification with code happens in the electronics rather than in the (idealized) system created by a human theorist. Thus it is a physical operation rather than a mental one, and it happens while the code is running rather than retrospectively in a theoretical model. These differences again illustrate that code is more intrinsically bound to materiality than Saussure's conception of *la langue.*

The disjunctions between Saussure's theory and the materially determined practices of code raise the question of whether it makes sense to use such legacy terms as "signifier" and "signified" with code. Many theorists concerned with electronic textuality are starting from new frameworks that do not rely on these traditional terms. In chapter 1, for example, I introduced Espen Aarseth's "textonomy," which sweeps the board clean and works from fundamental considerations to create a taxonomic scheme for analyzing ergodic literature. Similarly, a group of German researchers at the University of Siegen are working together in a project they call "Medienumbrüche" (Media Upheavals). They "regard the semiotic difference between strings and nets of signifiers as the foundation of a theory of 'net literature' which calls basic concepts such as 'author,' 'work,' and 'reader' into question."[8]

Although valuing these new theoretical frameworks as necessary interventions, I think it is important also to undertake a nuanced analysis of where code does and does not fit with traditional terms, especially for this project with its focus on intermediation. The exchanges, conflicts, and cooperations between the embedded assumptions of speech and writing in relation to code would be likely to slip unnoticed through a framework based solely on networked and programmable media, for the shift over to the new assumptions would tend to obscure the ways in which the older worldviews engage in continuing negotiations and intermediations with the new. For my purposes, then, the comparison is vital. Later I will perform the reverse operation of trying to fit the speech and writing systems into the worldview of code, and here too I expect the discontinuities to be as revealing as the continuities.

In the context of code, then, what would count as signifier and signified? Given the importance of the binary base, I suggest that the signifiers be considered as voltages—a suggestion already implicit in Friedrich Kittler's argument that ultimately everything in a digital computer reduces to changes in voltages.[9] The signifieds are then the interpretations that other layers of code give these voltages. Programming languages operating at higher levels translate this basic mechanic level of signification into commands that more closely resemble natural language. The translation from binary code into high-level languages, and from high-level languages back into binary code, must happen every time commands are compiled or interpreted, for voltages and the bit stream formed from them are all the machine can understand.[10] Thus voltages at the machine level function as signifiers for a higher level that interprets them, and these interpretations in turn become signifiers for a still higher level interfacing with them. Hence the different levels of code consist of interlocking chains of signifiers and signifieds, with signifieds on one level becoming signifiers on another. Because all these operations depend on the ability of the machine to recognize the difference between one and zero, Saussure's premise that differences between signs make signification possible fits well with computer architecture.

Derrida's *Différance* and the Clarity of Code

This continuity between computer architecture and Saussure's understanding of signification becomes a discontinuity, however, when Derrida transforms difference into *différance*, a neologism suggesting that meanings generated by differential relations are endlessly deferred. Speaking metaphorically, we may say that whereas Saussure focuses on two (or more) linguistic signs and infers a relationship connecting them, Derrida focuses on the gap as the important element, thus converting Saussure's presumption of presence into a generative force of absence: "*différance is not*, does not exist, is not a present-being (*on*) in any form. . . . It has neither existence nor essence. It derives from no category of being, whether present or absent."[11] To name this generative force, Derrida coins any number of terms in addition to *différance*: "trace," "arche-writing," "non-originary origin," and so on. Whatever the name, the important point is that the trace has no positive existence in itself and thus cannot be reified or recuperated back into a metaphysics of presence. "*Différance* is not only irreducible to any ontological or theological—ontotheological—reappropriation, but as the very opening of the space in which ontotheology—philosophy—produces its system and its history, it includes ontotheology, inscribing it and exceeding it without return" (*Margins*, 6). Always on the move, the trace resides everywhere and nowhere, functioning as the elusive and fecund force that makes possible all subsequent meaning. In this sense the trace, as the arche-writing that enables signification, precedes speech and also writing in the ordinary sense. The notoriously slippery nature of the trace has authorized the widely accepted idea, reinforced by thousands of deconstructive readings performed by those who followed in Derrida's footsteps, that meaning is always indeterminate and deferred.

Let us now consider how this claim for difference/deferral looks from the point of view of code. In the worldview of code, the generation of meaning happens in ways that scholars trained in the traditional humanities sometimes find difficult to understand and even more difficult to accept. At the level of binary code, the system can tolerate little if any ambiguity. For any physically embodied system, some noise and, therefore, possible ambiguities are always present. In the case of digital computers, noise enters the system (among other places) in the voltage trail-off errors discussed earlier, but these are rectified into unambiguous signals of one and zero before they enter the bit stream.[12] As the system builds up levels of programming languages such as compilers, interpreters, scripting languages, and so forth, they develop functionalities that permit increasingly greater ambiguities in the choices permitted or tolerated. The Microsoft Word spell checker is a good example. Given a letter string not in the program's dictionary, it looks for the closest matches and offers them as possibilities. No matter how sophisticated the program, however, all commands must be parsed as binary code to be intelligible to the machine.

In the context of digital computers, even less tenable than ambiguity is the proposition that a signifier could be meaningful without reference to a signified. In Derrida's view, Saussure's definition of the sign undercuts the metaphysics of presence in one sense and reinforces it in another. He argues that the very idea of a signified as conceptually distinct from the signifier (although for Saussure, indissoluble from it) gives credence to a transcendental signified, and to this extent reinscribes classical metaphysics. The distinction between signifier and signified, Derrida writes, "leaves open the possibility of thinking a *concept signified in and of itself,* a concept simply present for thought, independent of a relationship to language, that is of a relationship to a system of signifiers" (*Positions,* 19). At the same time, the distinction also opens the possibility that any signified, extracted from one context and embedded in another, could slide into the position of the signifier (for example, when one concept entails another). Since the idea of a transcendental signified implies that there is nothing above or beyond this originary point, the dynamic of signified-becoming-signifier threatens to undermine the absolute authority given to the transcendental signified. In this sense, Saussure's theory (as interpreted by Derrida) can be seen as working against the metaphysics of presence in which it otherwise remains complicit. This background helps to explain why, in deconstructive criticism, the focus tends to fall on the signifier rather than the signified. Indeed, I venture to guess that in contemporary critical theory, "signifier" is used thousands of times for every time "signified" appears.

In the worldview of code, it makes no sense to talk about signifiers without signifieds. Every voltage change must have a precise meaning in order to affect the behavior of the machine; without signifieds, code would have no efficacy. Similarly, it makes no sense to talk about floating signifiers (Lacan's adaptation of Derrida's sliding signifier) because every change in voltage must be given an unambiguous interpretation, or the program is likely not to function as intended.[13] Moreover, changes on one level of programming code must be exactly correlated with what is happening at all the other levels. If one tries to run a program designed for an older operating system on a newer one that no longer recognizes the code, the machine simply finds it unreadable, that is, unintelligible. For the machine, obsolete code is no longer a competent utterance.

Because it is a frequent point of confusion, I emphasize that these dynamics happen before (or after) any human interpretation of these messages. Whatever messages on screen may say or imply, they are themselves generated through a machine dynamics that has little tolerance for ambiguity, floating signifiers, or signifiers without corresponding signifieds. Although the computational worldview is similar to grammatology in not presuming the transcendental signified that Derrida detects in Saussure's speech system, it also does not tolerate the slippages Derrida sees as intrinsic to grammatology. Nor does code allow the infinite iterability and citation that Derrida associates with inscriptions, whereby any phrase, sentence, or paragraph can be lifted from one context and embedded in another. "A written sign carries with it a force that breaks with its context, that is, with the collectivity of presences organizing the moment of its inscription. This breaking force [*force de rupture*] is not an accidental predicate but the very structure of the written text."[14] Although Derrida asserts that this iterability is not limited to written language but "is to be found in all language" (*Limited Inc*, 10), this assertion does not hold true literally for code, where the contexts are precisely determined by the level and nature of the code. Code may be rendered unintelligible if transported into a different context—for example, into a different programming language or a different syntactic structure within the same language. Only at the high level of object-oriented languages such as C++ does code recuperate the advantages of citability and iterability (i.e., inheritance and polymorphism, in the discourse of programming language) and in this sense become "grammatological."[15]

Ellen Ullman, a software engineer who has been a pioneer in a field largely dominated by men, has written movingly about the different worldviews of code and natural language as they relate to ambiguity and slippage.[16] Asked in an interview with Scott Rosenberg if code is a language, she replied, "We can use English to invent poetry, to try to express things that are very hard to express. In programming you really can't. Finally, a computer program has only one meaning: what it does. It isn't a text for an academic to read. Its entire meaning is its function."[17] Emphasizing the unforgivingness of code, Ullman underscores its functionality. Code has become an important actor in the contemporary world because it has the power to change the behavior of digital computers, which in turn permeate nearly every kind of advanced technology. Code can set off missiles or regulate air traffic; control medical equipment or generate PET scans; model turbulent flow or help design innovative architecture. All of these tasks are built ultimately on a base of binary code and logic gates that are intolerant to error. Above all else, the digital computer is a logic machine, as Martin Davis shows elegantly in *The Universal Computer*, where he discusses the history of the logic on which the digital computer is based.

In *Close to the Machine*, Ullman illustrates vividly the contrast between the worldviews of code and human language when she discusses a software system she was commissioned to create that would help deliver information to AIDS patients. She recounts working in her San Francisco loft with a small group of programmers she had hired. They worked around the clock to meet the deadline, speaking in rapid-fire phrases about the structure of the program, the work-arounds they could devise, the flow charts that showed how the code would be processed. Junk food abounded, dress was disheveled, courtesy was a waste of precious minutes, and sleep became a distant memory as they subordinated all other concerns to the logic of the machine (1–17). Then, as the independent contractor responsible for the system, she met with the staff whose clients would be using the software. Suddenly the clear logic dissolved into an amorphous mass of half-articulated thoughts, messy needs and desires, fears and hopes of desperately ill people. Even as she tried to deal with the cloud of language in which these concerns were expressed, her mind raced to translate the concerns into a list of logical requirements to which her programmers could respond. Acting as the bridge arcing between the floating signifiers of natural language and the rigidity of machine code, she felt acutely the strain of trying to reconcile these two very different views of the world. "I had reduced the users' objections to a set of five system changes. I would like to use the word 'reduce' like a cook: something boiled down to its essence. But I was aware that the real human essence was already absent from the list I'd prepared. An item like 'How will we know if the clients have TB?'—the fear of sitting in a small, poorly ventilated room with someone who has medication-resistant TB, the normal and complicated biological urgency of that question—became a list of data elements to be added to the screens and database" (13–14).

One of the book's poignant scenes comes when Ullman, emotionally stressed by events in her life, decides to take her computer apart and put it back together, in a kind of somatic therapy that soothed by putting her physically in touch with the parts that functioned in such perfectly logical fashion (65–94). The scene illustrates another way in which the worldview of code differs from Saussure's dematerialized view of speech and Derrida's emphasis on linguistic indeterminacy. Although it is possible to view computer algorithms as logical structures that do not need to be instantiated to have meaning (the received view of many computer science departments), in practice any logical or formal system must run on some kind of platform to acquire meaning, whether a human brain or a digital computer. Without the ability to change the behavior of machines, code would remain a relatively esoteric interest of mathematicians working in areas such as the lambda calculus (where algorithms were used for research purposes in the 1930s, prior to the invention of the digital computer).[18] Code has become arguably as important as natural language because it causes things to happen, which requires that it be executed as commands the machine can run.

Code that runs on a machine is performative in a much stronger sense than that attributed to language. When language is said to be performative, the kinds of actions it "performs" happen in the minds of humans, as when someone says "I declare this legislative session open" or "I pronounce you husband and wife." Granted, these changes in minds can and do result in behavioral effects, but the performative force of language is nonetheless tied to the external changes through complex chains of mediation. By contrast, code running in a digital computer causes changes in machine behavior and, through networked ports and other interfaces, may initiate other changes, all implemented through transmission and execution of code. Although code originates with human writers and readers, once entered into the machine it has as its primary reader the machine itself. Before any screen display accessible to humans can be generated, the machine must first read the code and use its instructions to write messages humans can read. Regardless of what humans think of a piece of code, the machine is the final arbiter of whether the code is intelligible. If the machine cannot read the code or if the program does not work properly, then the code must be changed and corrected before the machine can make things happen. In *Protocol*, Alexander R. Galloway makes this point forcefully when he defines code as executable language. "But how can code be so different from mere writing?" he asks. "The answer to this lies in the unique nature of computer code. . . . Code is a language, but a very special kind of language. *Code is the only language that is executable.*" [19]

This character of code stands in striking contrast to the communities that decide whether an act of speech or a piece of writing constitutes a legible and competent utterance. As Saussure observes, no one person can change the spoken language system. "A language, as a collective phenomenon, takes the form of a totality of imprints in everyone's brain. . . . Thus it is something which is in each individual, but is none the less common to all. At the same time it is out of reach of any deliberate interference by individuals" (*Course*, 19). It takes many individual adopters of a change and a (relatively) long time for changes in the speech system to occur. (To some extent this claim requires modification in light of mass media such as television and newspapers, where a single speaker or small group of speakers can change the system if given enough press coverage. Saussure's point remains valid, however, in the sense that only if the speech acts of such privileged speakers are widely adopted can they actually change the system.) For Derrida, writing differs from Saussure's view of the speech system because inscriptions can endure over centuries or millennia, and thus can be cited, and therefore embedded, in a potentially infinite number of different contexts.

Moreover, Derrida reads the qualities of iterability and citation back into speech, instancing precisely the phenomena (e.g., quotations and speeches performed by actors in a theatrical performance) that Austin excluded from his speech act theory because he viewed them as anomalous.[20] In Derrida's grammatology, the more or less coherent community of speakers that Saussure presumes fractures into historically and geographically diverse contexts of different writing (and speaking) practices, different communities of general or expert readers, and different criteria for what constitutes competence and legibility. As William R. Paulson, among others, has observed, Derrida's complex writing style itself performs this diversity, insofar as it creates a class of "priestly" interpreters who can understand his writing, in contrast to many nonspecialist readers who have found it unintelligible.[21]

Like esoteric theoretical writing, code is intelligible only to a specialized community of experts who understand its complexities and can read and write it with fluency. There is, however, a significant difference between the worldview of code, on one hand, and, on the other, the community of speakers Saussure presumes and the infinitely diverse inscription contexts Derrida invokes. With code, a (relatively) few experts can initiate changes in the system that are often so significant they render previous systems illegible, as when Microsoft creates a new operating system such as Windows XP, which is not backward compatible with Windows 95 and earlier versions. Moreover, in code the breaks are much sharper and more complete than with either speech or writing. Occasionally I meet people who are using hardware and software that have been obsolete for years. Although they can still produce documents using these versions, they are increasingly marooned on an island in time, unable to send readable files or to read files from anyone else. Whereas undergraduates can understand (with some help) the Middle English of Chaucer's *Canterbury Tales* or the Elizabethan English of Shakespeare, thus making a connection over the hundreds of years that separate them from these works, no such bridges can be built between Windows 95 and Windows XP (separated by a mere seven or eight years), without both massive recoding and fluency in the nastily complex code of Windows programming.

Although code may inherit little or no baggage from classical metaphysics, it is permeated throughout with the politics and economics of capitalism, along with the embedded assumptions, resistant practices, and hegemonic reinscriptions associated with them. The open source movement testifies eloquently to the centrality of capitalist dynamics in the marketplace of code, even as it works to create an intellectual commons that operates according to the very different dynamics of a gift economy.[22]

The Hierarchy of Code

As we have seen, code differs from speech and writing in that it exists in clearly differentiated versions that are executable in a process that includes hardware and software and that makes obsolete programs literally unplayable unless an emulator or archival machine is used. Moreover, the historical strata of code do not involve a troublesome metaphysical inheritance but a troublesome deep layer of assembler code that can be understood and reverse engineered only with great difficulty, as demonstrated by attempts to excavate it and correct the problems associated with the Y2K crisis. The ways in which the historical character of code influence its alterations is a subject that requires understanding the difference between change within a given slice of time (synchrony) and change across time (diachrony).

For Saussure, the proper object of study for the semiotics of the speech system is the synchronic orientation. He points out in the introduction to *Course in General Linguistics* that his analysis reorients the field of study from the historicist and philological emphasis it had in previous generations to an understanding that regards the language system as a (more or less) coherent synchronous structure (1–8).[23] For Derrida, the diachronic manifests itself as the (allegedly) inescapable influence of classical metaphysics, whereas the synchronic ceases to have the force it does for Saussure because inscriptions, unlike speech prior to the invention of recording technologies, can be transported into historically disparate contexts, and so exist as rock does: in historically stratified formations that stretch back for thousands of years. Derrida writes, "This citationality, this duplication or duplicity, this iterability of the mark is neither an accident nor an anomaly, it is that (normal/abnormal) without which a mark could not even have a function called 'normal.' What would a mark be that could not be cited? Or one whose origins would not get lost along with way?" (*Limited Inc*, 12).[24]

Along with these differences in conceptualizing the sign and delineating its operations across and through time go related differences in how signs work together to comprise a semiotic system. When Saussure argues that differential relations between signs constitute the engine that drives signification, he identifies two vectors along which these relations operate, working at multiple levels within the speech system. The syntagmatic vector points horizontally, for example, along the syntax of a sentence. By contrast, the paradigmatic vector operates vertically, for example, in the synonyms that might be used in place of a given word in an utterance. Derrida makes little use of these terms in his grammatology, focusing instead on the hierarchical relations between concepts by which a privileged term posits a stigmatized term as the "outside" to its "inside." For Derrida, perhaps the primary instance of this hierarchical relation, in the context of Saussure's theory, is Saussure's attempt to relegate writing to a purely derivative role. Derrida's deconstruction of this hierarchical arrangement is typical of his treatment of hierarchical dichotomies in general, for he shows that the privileged term must in fact contain and depend on what it tries to exclude. "The exteriority of the signifier is the exteriority of writing in general, and I shall try to show . . . that there is no linguistic sign before writing. Without that exteriority, the very idea of the sign falls into decay" (*Of Grammatology*, 14).

Like speech, coding structures make use of what might be called the syntagmatic and paradigmatic, but in inverse relation to how they operate in speech systems. As Lev Manovich observes in *The Language of New Media*, in speech or writing the syntagmatic is what appears on the page (or as patterned sound), whereas the paradigmatic (the alternative choices that could have been made) is virtually rather than actually present (229–33). In digital media using dynamic databases, this relationship is reversed. The paradigmatic alternatives are encoded into the database and in this sense actually exist, whereas the syntagmatic is dynamically generated on the fly as choices are made that determine which items in the database will be used. In this sense, the syntagmatic is virtual rather than actual. This insight opens onto further explorations of how databases and narratives interface together, especially in electronic literature and the more general question of literariness.

In *Reading Voices*, Garrett Stewart argues that literary language is literary in part because of its ability to mobilize "virtual" words—related by sound, sense, or usage to those actually on the page—that surround the printed text with a "blooming buzz" of variants enriching and extending the text's meanings. Although operating according to a different dynamic than envisioned by Saussure, the luminous fog created by these variants resembles the paradigmatic vector that Saussure theorized for the speech system. When electronic literature offers the user hypertextual choices that lead to multiple narrative pathways, the strategy of evoking "virtual" possibilities happens not only on the level of the individual word but at the narrative level where different strands, outcomes, and interpretations mutually resonate with one another. This richness is possible, of course, only because all these possibilities are stored in the computer, available to be rearranged, interpolated, followed or not. Somewhat paradoxically, then, the more data that are stored in computer memory, all of which are ordered according to specified addresses and called by executable commands, the more ambiguities are possible. Flexibility and the resulting mobilization of narrative ambiguities at a high level depend upon rigidity and precision at a low level. The lower the level, the closer the language comes to the reductive simplicity of ones and zeros, and yet it is precisely the ability to build up from this reductive base that enables high-level literariness to be achieved. In this sense, the interplay between the virtual syntagmatic sequences and the actual paradigmatic database resembles the dynamic that Wolfram, Fredkin, and Harold Morowitz envision for computer simulations, with high-level complexity emerging out of the brute simplicity of binary distinctions and a few logical relationships. Literariness, as it is manifested in the panoply of choices characteristic of hypertext literature, here converges with the Regime of Computation in using the "simple rules, complex behavior" characteristic of code to achieve complexity.

Along with the hierarchical nature of code goes a dynamic of concealing and revealing that operates in ways that have no parallels in speech and writing. Because computer languages become more English-like as they move higher in the "tower of languages" (Rita Raley's phrase),[25] concealing the "brute" lower levels carries considerable advantage. Knowing how to conceal code with which one is not immediately concerned is an essential practice in computer programming. One of the advantages of object-oriented languages is bundling code within an object, so that the object becomes a more or less autonomous unit that can be changed without affecting other objects in that domain. At the same time, revealing code when it is appropriate or desired also bestows significant advantage. The "reveal code" command in HTML documents, for example, allows users to see comments, formatting instructions, and other material that may illuminate the construction and intent of the work under study, a point Loss Pequeño Glazier makes effectively in *Dig[iT]al Poet(I)(c)s*. With programs such as Dreamweaver that make layers easy to construct, additional dynamics of concealing and revealing come into play through rollovers and the like, re-creating on the screen dynamics that both depend on and reflect the "tower of languages" essential to code.[26]

These practices of concealing and revealing offer fertile ground for aesthetic and artistic exploration. Layers that reveal themselves according to timed sequences, cursor movements, and other criteria have become an important technique for writers seeking to create richly dense works with multiple pathways for interaction. One such work is Talan Memmott's *Lexia to Perplexia*, a notoriously "nervous" digital production that responds to even minute cursor movements in ways a user typically does not expect and finds difficult to control. Layering in this work is arguably the principal way by which complex screen design, text, animation, and movement interact with one another. Another example is M. D. Coverley's *The Book of Going Forth by Day*, where the visual tropes of revealing and concealing resonate with the multiple personae, patterned after ancient Egyptian beliefs, that cohabit in one body. The layers are instrumental in creating a visual/verbal/sonic narrative in which the deep past and the present, modern skepticism and ancient rituals, hieroglyphs and electronic writing merge and blend with one another.

The "reveal code" dynamic helps to create expectations (conscious and preconscious) in which the layered hierarchical structure of the tower of languages reinforces and is reinforced by the worldview of computation. The more the concealing/revealing dynamic becomes an everyday part of life and a ubiquitous strategy in everything from commercial Web pages to digital artworks, the more plausible it makes the view that the universe generates reality though a similar hierarchical structure of correlated levels ceaselessly and forever processing code. Similarly, the more the worldview of code is accepted, the more "natural" the layered dynamics of revealing and concealing code seem. Since these dynamics do not exist in anything like the same way with speech and writing, the overall effect—no doubt subtle at first but growing in importance as digital cultures and technologies become increasingly pervasive and indispensable—is to validate code as the lingua franca of nature. Speech and writing then appear as evolutionary stepping stones necessary to ratchet up Homo sapiens to the point where humans can understand the computational nature of reality and use its principles to create technologies that simulate the simulations running on the Universal Computer. This, in effect, is the worldview Morowitz envisions when he writes about the fourth stage (after the evolution of the cosmos, life, and mind) as mind reflecting on mind.[27] The more "natural" code comes to seem, the more plausible it is to conceptualize human thought as emerging from a machinic base of computational processes, a proposition explored in chapter 7.

As I argue throughout, however, human cognition, although it may have computational elements, includes analog consciousness that cannot be understood simply or even primarily as digital computation. Speech and writing, in my view, should not be seen as predecessors to code that will wither away but as vital partners on many levels of scale in the evolution of complexity. As I said in chapter 1, not Wolfram *or* his cellular automata alone, but *both* together—hence my emphasis on narrative and subjectivity as these are intermediated with computation. It is not the triumph of the Regime of Computation that can best explain the complexities of the world and, especially, of human cultures but its interactions with the stories we tell and the media technologies instrumental in making, storing, and transmitting.

Making Discrete and the Interpenetration of Code and Language

Let us now shift from interpreting code through the worldviews of speech and writing to the inverse approach of interpreting speech and writing through the worldview of code. An operation scarcely mentioned by Saussure and Derrida but central to code is digitization, which I interpret here as the act of making something discrete rather than continuous, that is, digital rather than analog. The act of making discrete extends through multiple levels of scale, from the physical process of forming bit patterns up through a complex hierarchy in which programs are written to compile other programs. Understanding the practices through which this hierarchy is constructed, as well as the empowerments and limitations the hierarchy entails, is an important step in theorizing code in relation to speech and writing.

Let me make a claim that, in the interest of space, I will assert rather than substantiate: the world as we sense it on a human scale is basically analog. Over millennia, humans have developed biological modifications and technological prostheses to impose digitization on these analog processes, from the physiological evolution needed to produce speech to sophisticated digital computers. From a continuous stream of breath, speech introduces the discreteness of phonemes; writing carries digitization farther by adding artifacts to this physiological process, developing inscription technologies that represent phonemes with alphabetic letters. At every point, analog processes interpenetrate and cooperate with these digitizations. Experienced readers, for example, perceive words not as individual letters but as patterns perceived in a single glance. The synergy between the analog and digital capitalizes on the strengths distinctive to each. As we have seen, digitization allows fine-tuned error control and depth of coding, whereas analog processes tie in with highly evolved human capabilities of pattern processing. In addition, the analog function of morphological resemblance, that is, similarity of form, is the principal and indeed (so far as I know) the only way to convey information from one instantiated entity to a differently instantiated entity.

How do practices of making discrete work in the digital computer? We have already heard about the formation of the bit stream from changing voltages channeled through logic gates, a process that utilizes morphological resemblance. From the bit pattern bytes are formed, usually with each byte composed of eight bits—seven bits to represent the ASCII code, and an empty one that can be assigned special significance. At each of these stages, the technology can embody features that were once useful but have since become obsolete. For example, the ASCII code contains a seven-bit pattern corresponding to a bell ringing on a teletype. Although teletypes are no longer in use, the bit pattern remains because retrofitting the ASCII code to delete it would require far more labor than would be justified by the benefit. To some extent, then, the technology functions like a rock strata, with the lower layers bearing the fossilized marks of technologies now extinct.

In the progression from speech to writing to code, each successor regime introduces features not present in its predecessors. In *Of Grammatology*, Derrida repeatedly refers to the space between words in alphabetic writing to demonstrate his point that writing cannot be adequately understood simply as the transcription of speech patterns (39, passim). Writing, he argues, exceeds speech and thus cannot be encapsulated within this predecessor regime; "writing is at the same time more exterior to speech, not being its 'image' or its 'symbol,' and more interior to speech, which is already in itself a writing" (46). Not coincidentally, spaces play an important role in the digitization of writing by making the separation of one word from another visually clear, thus contributing to the evolution of the codex book as it increasingly realized its potential as a medium distinct from speech. Similarly, code has characteristics that occur neither in speech nor in writing—processes that, by exceeding these legacy systems, mark a disjunction.

To explore these characteristics, let us now jump to a high level in the hierarchy of code and consider object-oriented programming languages, such as the ubiquitous C++. (I leave out of this discussion the newer languages of Java and C#, for which similar arguments could be made). C++ commands are written in ASCII and then converted into machine language, so this high-level programming language, like everything that happens in the computer, builds on a binary base. Nevertheless, C++ instantiates a profound shift of perspective from machine language and also from the procedural languages like FORTRAN and BASIC that preceded it. Whereas procedural languages conceptualize the program as a flow of modularized procedures (often diagrammed with a flowchart) that function as commands to the machine, object-oriented languages are modeled after natural languages and create a syntax using the equivalent of nouns (that is, objects) and verbs (processes in the system design).

A significant advantage to this mode of conceptualization, as Bruce Eckel explains in *Thinking in C++*, is that it allows programmers to conceptualize the solution in the same terms used to describe the problem. In procedural languages, by contrast, the problem would be stated in real-world terms (Eckel's example is "put the grommet in the bin"), whereas the solution would have to be expressed in terms of behaviors the machine could execute ("set the bit in the chip that means that the relay will close"; 43). C++ reduces the conceptual overhead by allowing both the solution and the problem to be expressed in equivalent terms, with the language's structure performing the work of translating between machine behaviors and human perceptions.

The heart of this innovation is allowing the programmer to express her understanding of the problem by defining classes, or abstract data types, that have both characteristics (data elements) and behaviors (functionalities). From a class, a set of objects instantiate the general idea in specific variations—the nouns referred to above. For example, if a class is defined as "shape," then objects in that class might be triangle, circle, square, and so on (37–38). Moreover, an object contains not only data but also functions that operate on the data—that is, it contains constraints that define it as a unit, and it also has encapsulated within it behaviors appropriate to that unit. For example, each object in "shape" might inherit the capability to be moved, to be erased, to be made different sizes, and so on, but each object would give these class characteristics its own interpretation. This method allows maximum flexibility in the initial design and in the inevitable revisions, modifications, and maintenance that large systems demand. The "verbs" then become the processes through which objects can interact with each other and the system design.

New objects can be added to a class without requiring that previous objects be changed, and new classes and metaclasses can also be added. Moreover, new objects can be created through inheritance, using a preexisting object as a base and then adding additional behaviors or characteristics. Since the way the classes are defined in effect describes the problem, the need for documentation external to the program is reduced; to a much greater extent than with procedural languages, the program serves as its own description. Another significant advantage of C++ is its ability to "hide" data and functions within an object, allowing the object to be treated as a unit without concern for these elements. "Abstraction is selective ignorance," Andrew Koenig and Barbara E. Moo write in *Accelerated C++*, a potent aphorism that speaks to the importance in large systems of hiding details until they need to be known.[28] Abstraction (defining classes), encapsulation (hiding details within objects and, on a metalevel, within classes), and inheritance (deriving new objects by building on preexisting objects) are the strategies that give object-oriented programs their superior flexibility and ease of design.

We can now see that object-oriented programs achieve their usefulness principally through the ways they anatomize the problems they are created to solve—that is, the ways in which they cut up the world. Obviously a great deal of skill and intuition goes into the selection of the appropriate classes and objects; the trick is to state the problem so it achieves abstraction in an appropriate way. This often requires multiple revisions to get it right, so ease of revision is crucial.

Some of the strategies C++ uses to achieve its language-like flexibility illustrate how it makes use of properties that do not appear in speech or writing and are specific to coding systems. Procedural languages work by what is called "early binding," a process in which the compiler (the part of the code hierarchy that translates higher-level commands into the machine language) works with the linker to direct a function call (a message calling for a particular function to be run) to the absolute address of the code to be executed. At the time of compiling, early binding thus activates a direct link between the program, compiler, and address, joining these elements before the program is actually run. C++, by contrast, uses "late binding," in which the compiler ensures that the function exists and checks its form for accuracy, but the actual address of the code is not used until the program is run.[29] Late binding is part of what allows the objects to be self-contained with minimum interference with other objects.

The point of this rather technical discussion is simple: there is no parallel to compiling in speech or writing, much less a distinction between compiling and run-time. The closest analogy, perhaps, is the translation of speech sounds or graphic letter forms into synapses in the human brain, but even to suggest this analogy risks confusing the *production* of speech and writing with its *interpretation* by a human user. Like speech and writing, computer behaviors can be interpreted by human users at multiple levels and in diverse ways, but this activity comes after (or before) the computer activity of compiling code and running programs.

Compiling (and interpreting, for which similar arguments can be made) is part of the complex web of processes, events, and interfaces that mediate between humans and machines, and its structure bespeaks the needs of both parties involved in the transaction. The importance of compiling (and interpreting) to digital technologies underscores the fact that new emphases emerge with code that, although not unknown in speech and writing, operate in ways specific to networked and programmable media. At the heart of this difference is the need to mediate between the natural languages native to human intelligence and the binary code native to intelligent machines. As a consequence, code implies a partnership between humans and intelligent machines in which the linguistic practices of each influence and interpenetrate the other.[30]

The evolution of C++ grew from precisely this kind of interpenetration. C++ is consciously modeled after natural language; once it came into wide use, it also affected how natural language is understood. We can see this two-way flow at work in the following observation by Bruce Eckel, in which he constructs the computer as an extension of the human mind. He writes, "The genesis of the computer revolution was in a machine. The genesis of our programming languages thus tends to look like that machine. But the computer is not so much a machine as it is a mind amplification tool and a different kind of expressive medium. As a result, the tools are beginning to look less like machines and more like parts of our minds, and more like other expressive mediums like writing, painting, sculpture, animation or filmmaking. Object-oriented programming is part of this movement toward the computer as an expressive medium" (*Thinking in C++*, 35). As computers are increasingly understood (and modeled after) "expressive mediums" like writing, they begin to acquire the familiar and potent capability of writing not merely to express thought but actively to constitute it. As high-level computer languages move closer to natural languages, the processes of intermediation by which each affects the other accelerate and intensify. Rita Raley has written on the relation between the spread of Global English and the interpenetration of programming languages with English syntax, grammar, and lexicon.[31] In addition, the creative writing practices of "codework," practiced by such artists as MEZ, Talan Memmott, Alan Sondheim, and others, mingle code and English in a pastiche that, by analogy with two natural languages that similarly intermingle, might be called a creole.[32]

The vectors associated with these processes do not all point in the same direction. As explored in chapter 8, (mis)recognizing visualizations of computational simulations as creatures like us both anthropomorphizes the simulations and "computationalizes" the humans. Knowing that binary code underlies complex emergent processes reinforces the view that human consciousness emerges from similar machinic processes, as explored in chapter 7. Anxieties can arise when the operations of the computer are mystified to the extent that users lose sight of (or never know) how the software actually works, thus putting themselves at the mercy of predatory companies like Microsoft, which makes it easy (or inevitable) for users to accept at face value the metaphors the corporation spoon-feeds them, a concern explored in chapter 6. These dynamics make unmistakably clear that computers are no longer merely tools (if they ever were) but are complex systems that increasingly produce the conditions, ideologies, assumptions, and practices that help to constitute what we call reality.

The operations of "making discrete" highlighted by digital computers clearly have ideological implications. Indeed, Wendy Hui Kyong Chun goes so far as to say that *software is ideology*, instancing Althusser's definition of ideology as "the representation of the subject's imaginary relationship to his or her real conditions of existence."[33] As she points out, desktop metaphors such as folders, trash cans, and so on create an imaginary relationship of the user to the actual command core of the machine, that is, to the "real conditions of existence" that in fact determine the parameters within which the user's actions can be understood as legible. As is true for other forms of ideology, the interpolation of the user into the machinic system does not require his or her conscious recognition of how he or she is being disciplined by the machine to become a certain kind of subject. As we know, interpolation is most effective when it is largely unconscious.

This conclusion makes abundantly clear why we cannot afford to ignore code or allow it to remain the exclusive concern of computer programmers and engineers. Strategies can emerge from a deep understanding of code that can be used to resist and subvert hegemonic control by megacorporations;[34] ideological critiques can explore the implications of code for cultural processes, a project already evident in Matthew Fuller's call, seconded by Matthew Kirschenbaum, for critical software studies;[35] readings of seminal literary texts can explore the implications of code for human thought and agency, among other concerns. Code is not the enemy, any more than it is the savior. Rather code is increasingly positioned as language's pervasive partner. Implicit in the juxtaposition is the intermediation of human thought and machine intelligence, with all the dangers, possibilities, liberations, and complexities this implies.

3 The Dream of Information
Escape and Constraint in the Bodies of Three Fictions

The Economy of Information

The worldviews of speech, writing, and code discussed in chapter 2 are not, of course, merely theoretical models. They are enacted through media, and media are in turn deeply embedded in economic and social structures. Intermediating feedback circulates between these sites, connecting technological change with theory, theory with economics, economics with technological change. This chapter explores these intermediating cycles in the effects registered on bodies and subjectivities as they are represented in fictions from the close of the nineteenth century to three-quarters of the way through the twentieth century, roughly the period of time it took to go from the passive code of the telegraph to the executable code of the digital computer. At issue here are not so much the bodies of texts themselves—topics to which we will turn in the next set of chapters—but the bodies *within* texts and their relation to the human lifeworld as it is reconfigured by interpolating humans with machines that, as they become intelligent, increasingly interpenetrate and indeed constitute human bodies.

Throughout this period, the dream of information beckoned as a realm of plenitude and infinite replenishment, in sharp contrast to what might be called the regime of scarcity. The regime of scarcity is based on the fundamental assumption that energy and matter are conserved (i.e., every slice of pie that goes in your mouth is one that I cannot eat, or if I do manage to grab it from you and eat it, I cannot eat it again). This regime has prevailed throughout most of modern history and is a foundational premise for everything from G. M. Foster's "Limited Good" to the first and second law of thermodynamics (the first law states that energy is conserved, and the famous second law, more pessimistic, states that in closed systems every exchange tends to result in the loss of energy for useful purposes).[1]

Consider, for example, such terms as "exchange value" and "surplus value"; they presume that matter and energy are conserved and must be balanced by accounting for their transformations and movements through economic structures.

The dream of information is much more recent and emerges from the radically different economics of information. As Mark Poster and others have observed, information does not operate according to the same constraints that govern matter and energy.[2]

If I have a disk and make a copy for you, we both have the information. Like the fabled magic pot, information promises to proliferate virtually without cost. At the beginning of the new millennium, as information technologies move toward nano-components, optical storage media, and photonic switches, this promise sings its siren song louder than ever. Charles Ostman, senior fellow at Global Futures, a consultant firm that anticipates near-future technological development, predicted recently that once nanotechnology is developed, all shortages will disappear. The "coveting of stuff, territory, physical things will no longer be an issue because there won't be any reason for it—you can make what you need. Wars, conquests, enslavement of peoples, malevolent dictatorships—all the stuff driven by predation—will be obsolete."[3]

As I argued in *How We Became Posthuman*, assumptions that may not be immediately apparent link the conservation laws of thermodynamics with the formation of the liberal subject. If, as Ostman predicts, people could make whatever they desire virtually without cost, private property would cease to be meaningful (a utopian vision Neal Stephenson both accepts and contests in *The Diamond Age*).[4] Along with the demise of private property would go an idea of selfhood based on the notion that in the first instance one owns oneself, a proposition that C. B. Macpherson has called possessive individualism and that he identifies as foundational to liberal philosophy.[5] If these constraints fall away, surely others can follow. Operating in the economy of information, one can dream that social position and economic class will cease to matter, dream even of loosening the constraints of living in a single body located at a single position in space and time.[6] These utopian visions invite resistant readings of the kind articulated by Robert Markley in his critique of the information superhighway.[7] Rightly criticizing the rhetoric of free information, Markley points to the ecological and social costs involved in developing a global information network, from junked computer monitors leaking lethal heavy metals into the groundwater of the developing countries that buy them as scrap, to infrastructure costs that add significantly to governmental and university budgets, to upheavals in the U.S. economy as dot-coms go bust and skilled technical jobs move abroad to India, China, and other countries.

Yet important issues remain obscured if the emphasis falls solely on recuperating the dream of information back into the constraints governing matter and energy. To understand fully the dynamics at work, it is necessary to look at the intermediating feedback cycles connecting the regime of scarcity with the economy of information. How are these dynamics configured? On one side the dream of freely flowing information strains to escape scarcity, restricted physical space, class, gender, embodiment, time, and mortality; on the other side the claims of corporate profit, stratified social structures, physical confinement, gender inequalities, marked and failing bodies reassert their inevitability. Connecting the two are complex feedback loops. Since technologies of communication make the dream possible, one kind of feedback articulates bodies together with prostheses of communication. Another loop initiates the changes that subjectivities undergo as they are reconfigured for an economy of information and then, in continuing intermediating cycles, reconfigured again, as bodies and subjects are pulled back into the constraints of energy and matter. Processes of signification are also involved, for as we saw in chapter 2, the dynamics of signs change as they move from the flat, durable inscriptions of print to the hierarchies of code characteristic of electric and electronic communication technologies. The change from flat marks to hierarchical structures opens the possibility of interventions into the encoding/decoding chains. Because these interventions typically require humans to interact with communication technologies, the changed nature of signification ties back into the prostheses joining humans and machines. Signification, technology, and subjectivity coevolve.

I will use three fictions, stretching across the span of most of the twentieth century, to interrogate these intermediating dynamics. Henry James's "In the Cage," written in 1898, explores intimations of an information regime through telegraphy. As the woman in the telegraph cage sends out messages and uses her active imagination to reconstruct dangerous sexual liaisons from the sparse codes, she also contemplates her own future marriage to Mudge the grocer, a transaction firmly rooted in the constraints of scarcity. Vacillating between the dream of information and the restrictions of matter and energy, the telegraphist attempts to code her interactions in ways that would inscript them into the regime of information. Her struggle is not so much to perform a subjectivity appropriate to information as to reinterpret actions performed under the regime of scarcity so that their significance escapes that regime. In Philip K. Dick's *The Three Stigmata of Palmer Eldritch*, written two-thirds of a century later, the issue is not reinscription but transubstantiation, a dream of translation into an economy of information that fundamentally changes the nature of subjectivity. A corporate battle between the purveyors of two drugs (one merely relocates traditional subjects, and the other radically alters the experience of subjectivity) sets the stage for moving beyond information considered as passive code to information as simulation. Once posited as simulation, information develops the power to infect reality, making *it* appear to be a simulation. In this way *The Three Stigmata of Palmer Eldritch* anticipates the Regime of Computation, in which reality itself is conceptualized as a kind of simulation running on the Universal Computer. The last text is James Tiptree's "The Girl Who Was Plugged In," a fiction whose title resonates with James's girl in the cage. This 1973 story is sufficiently later than Dick's fiction to envision the economy of information not as competing with reality but as interpenetrating and, indeed, indistinguishable from it. In this respect, Tiptree's fiction seems to hearken back to James's story, but with the crucial difference that here subjectivity is split between two bodies. One body exists in a real-life dream in which scarcity drops away; the other body participates in that dream but at the same time endures extreme physical constraints.

The trajectory formed by these three fictions displays a clear pattern. First the dream of information is figured as an escape, but the more powerfully it exerts its presence as a viable place in which to live, the more it appears not as an escape at all but rather as an arena in which the dynamics of domination and control can be played out in new ways. What changes is finally not the regime of scarcity but the subjects within and through whose bodies the informational codes are transmitted.

Code as Reinscription: "In the Cage"

"In the Cage" is structured through a series of oppositions that dramatizes the contrast between the constraints of ordinary life and the freedom of information. Confined in the small space of the telegraph cage where she endures the inquiries of Mr. Buckton and the elbows of the counter clerk, the girl feels that her nervous system, and especially her imagination, extend outward through the telegraph network, until there "were times when all the wires in the country seemed to start from the little hole-and-corner where she plied for a livelihood" (153).[8] The messages she is given by her customers operate according to a similar dual logic. In one guise they are words to be counted, commodities that make money for the company. However, decoded by her imagination, they become tokens of the secret lives of the aristocrats making use of her services; she imagines that these aristocrats constitute an economy in which calculation is transformed into passion, constraint into glorious freedom. "More than ever before it floated to her through the bars of the cage that this at last was the high reality, the bristling truth that she had hitherto only patched up and eked out—[in which] . . . all the conditions for happiness actually met" (146).

The different economy in which her imagination operates, compared to the economy of her mundane life, is illustrated through the diverse effects her imaginings have on the future, compared to those of her betrothed, Mr. Mudge. In the informational economy, imagining the future makes it blossom with possibility. The girl eagerly anticipates the visits of the dashing Captain Everard, whom she intuits is having an adulterous liaison with Lady Bradeen, variously encoded in the telegrams as "Mary," "Cissy," or "Miss Dolman." In this dream, the more the girl imagines, the more there is. In contrast are the anticipations of Mudge, who seems to wear the future out by fingering it over and over in his calculations, as though his imaginative life operates according to laws of conservation that subtract anticipated pleasures from lived pleasures in a strict balancing of quantities.[9]

Operating in an economy of scarcity privileges possession, and possession takes place within a dialectic of presence and absence: one has money or loses it; one possesses an object or gives it away. Information is not a presence or an absence and so does not operate within that dialectic. Rather, information emerges from a dialectic of pattern and randomness, signal and noise.[10] With information, it is not a question of possession but access. In James's story, the contrast is played out in the different strategies adopted by the girl and Mrs. Jordan, the clergyman's widow who aspired to a not undesirable social standing before her husband died. We never know precisely what happened to the father under whose protection the girl aspired to like status; we know only that when it failed, she, her mother, "lost brother," and sister began skidding toward the bottom from "which she alone had rebounded" (141). Mrs. Jordan hopes to regain status by arranging flowers for the wealthy, a service that allows her to enter their homes. This physical proximity to wealth gives her, according to her account, chances much superior to those the girl enjoys. She urges the girl to join her in her enterprise, intimating that this is the way for the girl to find a wealthy husband. Trapped in her cage, the girl has no physical entry into spaces of wealth and privilege, but she does have access to the messages they send. As she hesitates between joining Mrs. Jordan and continuing to send messages, the girl is forced to confront what, exactly, the dream of information can do to help her.

The matter comes to a head in a meeting the girl allows to happen outside the cage between herself and Captain Everard. For weeks she has made a detour on her way home that takes her past his lodgings, and finally she meets him "by chance" outside his door. Strolling together into the park, they sit down on a bench. At stake for the girl in this encounter is the regime into which her actions will be inscribed. If they take place in the regime of scarcity, her initiatives can be read only as the advances of a shop girl to a gentleman; the girl realizes that if such advances were to proceed to a sexual encounter, they would not even be considered significant enough to count as infidelity on the captain's part toward his lover, Lady Bradeen. Moreover, the encounter could easily slide into casual prostitution, as Ralf Norrman shows in a careful reading that traces how the girl's thoughts of blackmail—which she briefly entertains and quickly rejects—slip into a covert evocation of prostitution.[11] Indeed, after this encounter the captain appears to offer the girl money, as if in anticipation of sexual favors. "It was either the frenzy of her imagination or the disorder of his baffled passion that gave her once or twice the vision of his putting down redundant money—sovereigns not concerned with the little payments he was perpetually making—so that she might give him some sign of helping him to slip them over to her" (215). Norrman also argues that the girl's ultimate goal in meeting with Everard is to get him to marry her. This may indeed form part of her intention, but as the meeting progresses, it becomes clear to her that an equally likely—in actuality, far more likely—possibility is that she might become his mistress, in which case she would be ruined, having neither the rank nor financial resources Lady Bradeen has to get away with this kind of scandal. Desperate to avoid this interpretation of their relation, the girl struggles to define the realm in which their interactions take place as something beyond and above the regime of scarcity, an economy in which she is in a position to be extravagantly generous toward the captain rather than the other way around and in which the relation between them will be "not a bit horrid or vulgar" (193).

Significantly, this realm turns out to be the dream of information. The girl has an opportunity to exercise her generosity by recalling for the captain an intercepted telegram that Lady Bradeen had sent to him. Emphasizing the informational nature of the exchange, the telegram, which was intended to be transcribed into Morse code, is itself written in code, a series of numbers correlated with events in the physical world through undisclosed encryption rules. The girl had already intervened in the coding chains when she corrected Lady Bradeen's code for the place-name that corresponded with the pseudonym "Miss Dolman."[12] Whether this "correction" was a mistake that led to the telegram's interception we do not know.[13] However this may be, the arbitrary nature of the code is underscored when the Captain announces that "It's all right if it's wrong," possibly because the number code passed on to him secret information that the mistake exonerated him from knowing (223).

These events, left mysterious by the narrator, have the effect of emphasizing the arbitrariness of codes. It is important to note that this arbitrariness is of a different nature than Saussure's assertion that the relation between the signifier and signified is arbitrary. As discussed in chapter 2, Saussure denied that a "natural" relationship exists between a word and a thing. After Saussure, his conceptual distinction between signifier and signified became the occasion for an increasing emphasis on the signifier, until the signified seemed to recede from view. However, as we have seen, in codes the signified does not disappear. Rather, at every level the relation between signifier and signified is specified precisely by rules governing the transformations of encoding and decoding. Nevertheless, mistakes happen, and a symbol in the object code may be correlated incorrectly with the matching symbol in the target code. These mistakes do not testify to an inevitable undecidability in the relation between signifier and signified, mark and concept, such as a deconstructionist reading would display. Rather, coding errors point instead to the inevitability of noise in the system, a shift bound up with the conceptualization of the sign as a product of a series of transformations between different levels of code.

This shift from the arbitrariness of language to the noise of code signals a change of emphasis from the limitations of language in producing meaning to the limitations of code in transmitting messages accurately. Whereas the arbitrariness of language implies the inability of language to ground itself in originary meaning, the arbitrariness of code leads to multiple sites for intervention in the coding chains and thus to a focus on the fragility of messages as they are encoded, sent through communication channels, and decoded through prosthetic articulations between humans and machines. Whereas deconstruction focuses on economies of supplementarity, coding theory focuses on techniques of supplementation that graft together organic components with communication technologies. Deconstruction implies a shift from the authority of a speaking subject to the instabilities of a writing subject, whereas coding theory implies a transformation from the writing subject to a posthuman collective of encoders/decoders.

Significantly, in James's story the girl is only infrequently depicted as working the sounder; her efforts tend not toward a seamless integration with the machine but in the opposite direction of transforming words from commodities into intuitions. Before the telegrams are translated into code, the girl operates selectively on some of them to encrypt them into other combinations. "Most of the elements swam straight away, lost themselves in the bottomless common, and by so doing kept the page clear. On the clearness, therefore, what she did retain stood sharply out; she nipped and caught it, turned it and interwove it" (156). The girl's selective attention is here represented as a coding operation, a physical rearrangement of marks on the page that erases some of the "elements" and makes others into signifiers resonant with meaning, a hallucinated action she will later enact physically when she takes the telegram from Lady Bradeen, erases one of the words, and puts another in its place. Commenting on the above passage in highly condensed prose that might itself be called telegraphic, Jennifer Wicke points out the importance of the girl's interventions into the coding sequences. "This putative action mystifies the process of the sending out of the telegrams, but also alters it, produces it back so that the nameless intermediary of the process of communication reorchestrates that information, as James calls it, that ceaselessly traverses the cage."[14]

Viewing language as a code rather than as a loose network of floating signifiers also entails different reading techniques. At issue is the difference between a language that cannot unambiguously say what it means, and a message that cannot be encoded and decoded without undergoing transformations as interventions distort the codes and thereby produce noise in the system. Thus in code what is available for readerly inspection is not so much the ambiguity of meaning—we never find out what the numbers in the telegram refer to—but places in the text where interventions in the coding chain occur, as when the girl alters the telegram. A characteristic of code, as distinct from natural language, is the leverage that comes about through multiple coding correlations, as when a single keystroke changes the entire appearance of a text on screen, or when a single mistake in transcribing DNA code leads to drastic physical changes when that gene is expressed in an organism. This characteristic enters James's story through a plot that makes the fate of Captain Everard and Lady Bradeen hang upon a change in the coded telegram. That the climax depends upon a mistake in the coding sequence, not simply on ambiguities in language, indicates that the story, like the yearnings of the protagonist, locates itself within an economy of information.

Yet matters are not quite so simple. At the close of the nineteenth century, the economy of information had not penetrated far enough into the infrastructure of the society to maintain itself as a separate space. Although the story's climax validates the power of information when the girl displays her power by dangling the message the captain so desperately needs to recover just out of his reach, this proves to be a momentary—if satisfying—triumph rather than the establishment of an economy of information as a place where one might live. The end of the story reasserts the power of the regime of scarcity, albeit with some reservations; it arrives when the girl learns from Mrs. Jordan that she is to be married. The encounter escalates into a contest for preeminence based on who knows the most information about the scandalous affair between Lady Bradeen and Captain Everard. Mrs. Jordan knows, as the girl does not, information having to do with presence and absence. She tells the girl that Lord Bradeen discovered that Lady Bradeen had taken an object—"It's even said she stole it!"—and given it to Captain Everard (240). But the girl knows that the object to which Mrs. Jordan refers in her formulation ("something was lost—something was found") was a telegram, or more precisely the message the telegram contained (240). Since her office has destroyed the physical copy of the telegram, it is only through a memory made eidetic by the excitement of her imaginative decodings that she remembers the number sequence and can reproduce it for the captain. What is produced, then, is not a presence or an absence but a pattern where the crucial issue is whether a mistake has been made in the code.

Mrs. Jordan believes it is only because Lady Bradeen is able to rescue the captain by "stealing" the object that he agrees to marry her, whereas the girl has the bittersweet knowledge that it was she, not Lady Bradeen, who produced the message that saved the captain and Lady Bradeen. This information she simultaneously gave away to the captain and kept for herself, an exchange possible only within an economy of information. This doubleness is soon to end, however, for the dream of information cannot sustain its powers, cannot offer a real space in which to live. Her exciting double life, one strand of which was spun in an informational realm replete with mystery and the promise of infinite expansion, is about to collapse into a single lifeline whose unwinding in the regime of scarcity is all too easily foreseen. As the girl and Mrs. Jordan exchange confidences, the girl holds back the information that it was she who saved the captain. But this very hoarding indicates that she has fallen back into a regime of scarcity, for if she gives this news to Mrs. Jordan, she will lose the sense of superiority she savors by knowing something those around her do not. She has become an inhabitant of Mudge's world, where her secrets, like his anticipations, are worn out if they are fingered too often. Resigned to the inevitability of her return to the regime of scarcity, she resolves to postpone her marriage no longer and in fact to hasten it. Nor does this reassertion of scarcity claim her as its only victim. Mrs. Jordan will enter into marriage with a butler because, as she admits in an incautious burst of emotion, "it has led to my not starving!" (236), and the captain will enter into a marriage in which his authority in the household is very much diminished, because it is Lady Bradeen who has the fortune while he has mostly debts.

In opening the informational realm to view, exploring its dynamics and possibilities, and finally allowing it to be folded again into a regime based on conservation, James writes what might be called the prequel to the story of information in the twentieth century. The girl may feel a doubleness in her life, but she never doubts such fundamental facts as where her body is located or what, in an ordinary sense, her identity is. As the economy of information expands in force and scope, and as technologies of communication sink deeper into the infrastructure of society, these anchors in everyday physical reality begin to drift, and finally come unmoored. The passive code of the telegraph opened issues connected with the transmission and intervention of messages, but it did not penetrate nearly as far into the bodies of subjects as would be the case in the next century with the emergence of intelligent machines. As the century progresses, information increasingly determines the constitution of subjects and, as we saw in chapter 1, the construction of reality itself. A writer who not only anticipated this development but wrote about it with incandescent intensity is Philip K. Dick.

Code as Transubstantiation: *The Three Stigmata of Palmer Eldritch*

Published in 1965, *The Three Stigmata of Palmer Eldritch* reflects the emerging awareness in the United States of hallucinogenic drugs. Dick gives this awareness his own twist in making drugs a communication technology. Colonists on Mars ingest Can-D to relieve the unbearable bleakness of their lives on an inhospitable alien planet, where they are housed in underground dwellings so dismal they are appropriately called hovels. Under the influence of the illegal Can-D, the colonists collectively project their consciousness into miniature dolls, Perky Pat and Walt, modeled on Barbie and Ken. While inhabiting the dolls, each person knows the thoughts of others sharing the same doll, highlighting the drug's function as a communication technology. The drug is further linked to communication technologies by satellite broadcasts that push the drug and use encrypted messages to tell the colonists when the next drop will take place. In sharp contrast to the regime of scarcity that the colonists inhabit in mundane reality, the drug creates a space of promise and infinite expansion characteristic of the realm of information. In the Perky Pat world, the women are all buxom and beautiful, the men all drive fast sports cars, and every day is Saturday. Moreover, these common goods are achieved without sacrificing individual identity.

Although the women all enter Perky Pat and the men enter Walt (no transgendering for Dick), each person retains her or his sense of self and individual agency. The dolls' imagined actions in the carefully realistic miniature sets, "minned" precisely to resemble Earth artifacts, are the result of the desires of the majority of people occupying the doll. If two of the women want Pat to go swimming and the third does not, Pat will go swimming, and Walt will follow her into the water only if the majority of men occupying him agree he should. Thus the drug, despite its hallucinogenic properties, preserves intact fundamental aspects of the liberal subject, including agency and a sense of individual identity based on possession, for it is primarily through the display and consumption of commodities that the Perky Pat world is made to seem real.

The narrative viewpoint nevertheless marks a clear boundary between the illusory world of Perky Pat and the reality of the colonists' everyday lives. While the colonists are experiencing themselves as the glamorous Pat and Walt, the narrator describes them as an objective eye would see them, sprawled in the hovel with drool dripping from their mouths from the chewed-up Can-D. When the drug wears off, the colonists, too, see the scene the narrator describes and are snapped back into the reality they never in fact escaped. As in James's story, the dream of information promises an escape it cannot deliver. This firm basis in the reality of scarcity is reinforced by the capitalistic market that links Perky Pat dolls with Can-D. As the colonists scramble to get together enough truffle skins to purchase the legal layouts and the illegal drug (in Dick's satirically rendered economy, truffle skins circulate as currency because they are the only objects that cannot be successfully simulated), it is clear that liberal subjectivity, capitalism, an essential self, and narrative realism are all part of the same cultural configuration—a configuration based in laws of conservation and corresponding systemic inequalities.[15] The high living standard on Earth requires the dismal existence of the Martian colonists, for the draft that forces some people to emigrate to Mars drains off surplus population and provides a continuing strong market for certain products, chief among them Perky Pat and Can-D.[16]

Whereas for James the collapse of the dream of information provided the story's resolution, in Dick the folding of information back into a regime of scarcity functions as prologue rather than conclusion. Can-D has a rival, Chew-Z. Palmer Eldritch—a "mad capitalist," as Darko Suvin has called him (instead of a mad scientist)—has returned from a decade-long trip out of the solar system with a new drug that promises to remedy the deficiencies of Can-D and, more importantly, hand over the ultimate prize of religion. "God promises eternal life," the Chew-Z slogan boasts, "We can deliver it" (160). The promise is based on one of Chew-Z's two major differences from

Can-D. Whereas Can-D preserves conventional time, Chew-Z creates a subjective perception of time that is much longer than the actual time elapsed. Someone under the influence of Chew-Z might experience hours, days, even months of time passing, while in the real world, only a few seconds have gone by. As users soon learn to their dismay, however, time by itself means little; if it passes in a nightmare world, long duration is not a blessing but a curse. What makes the Chew-Z world so unpleasant is a fact that users discover only gradually. Whereas actions in the Can-D world happen as a net result of all the users' agencies, in the Chew-Z world one person alone determines the rules by which the world operates—Palmer Eldritch. Moreover, the stakes are alarmingly raised, for if one dies in the Chew-Z world, one is dead in the real world as well.

Leo Bulero, the corporate mogul who markets the interdependent products Perky Pat and Can-D, would never win an election for sainthood, but his self-interestedness pales in comparison with that of Palmer Eldritch, who ruthlessly intends to use Chew-Z to take over Earth as well as Mars. Dick's work from this period often sets up a contrast between two types of capitalism. The more beneficent kind folds family relationships into the corporation, and the bonds between employer and employee include claims of loyalty and friendship. This is the case with Leo Bulero and Barney Mayerson, Leo's "pre-fash" consultant whose job is to use his precognition to determine which Earth products are about to become hits on the home market so they can be "minned" and made ready for the Martian market. Involved with Barney is a subordinate pre-fash consultant and sometime lover, Roni Fugate, who is gunning for Barney's job. Discussions between this trio naturally focus on the firm's business; equally of concern to them, however, are bonds of allegiance, especially actions that indicate loyalty or betrayal. The profit motive, although not lacking, is tempered by other considerations. In some deep way the stability of the subject in Dick's work is bound up with this kind of capitalism, as if he intuited that the liberal subject, capitalism, and the family are as inextricably entwined as Perky Pat and Can-D.[17]

By contrast, the more rapacious kind of capitalism represented by Palmer Eldritch has left behind any consideration of the subject as capable of loyalty or betrayal. Palmer Eldritch does not intend merely to make a profit. Rather, his goal is to infect everyone in the solar system with himself, as if he were eating them from the inside and displacing their subjectivities with his own. "It's Palmer Eldritch who's everywhere, growing and growing like a mad weed," Leo thinks, having been captured by Eldritch and given Chew-Z involuntarily (196). Palmer Eldritch's inhuman ambitions are signified by the prostheses he sports as a result of multiple accidents and that constitute his three stigmata: a distended jaw line covering huge metal teeth, an artificial forearm and hand, and artificial eyes with horizontal slots instead of irises.

Just as Palmer Eldritch eats people from the inside, so Chew-Z eats reality from the inside. Leo first discovers its powers when he finds himself in the Chew-Z world and, realizing that events in the Chew-Z world happen within a subjective realm, escapes by thinking into being a stairway to his office. Safely back at his desk, he begins to conduct business as usual, only to find that through his secretary's normal appearance the three stigmata of Palmer Eldritch begin to gleam, as though reality has become a mere husk that at any moment might disappear, revealing the Chew-Z world underneath. The narrative viewpoint that revealed the Can-D world as illusory appears powerless to constitute this difference with Chew-Z. Moreover, users of Can-D assumed the drug-induced surfaces were "accidental" while the interiors remained "essential." Extending this convention to the Chew-Z world leads to a disconcerting insinuation, for now reality is the exterior husk and the simulation is the underlying essence that keeps breaking through. Posing as a dream of information that can satisfy the deepest desires of humans, the Chew-Z world reveals itself not as a refuge but as a rapacious dynamic that preys on the autonomy of the liberal subject and, indeed, on the autonomy of the world itself.

This is the nightmare vision that, once articulated, the narrative tries to draw back from by a series of strategies, none of which is entirely successful. The narrative reacts as if the vision is too horrific to bear, but any attempt to mitigate it is unsatisfactory because then the narrative has failed to do justice to the strength of the vision. Consider the following sequence of events. Hoping to exploit Barney's feelings of loyalty, Leo gives him a brain-rotting chemical that Barney is to take and blame its effects on Chew-Z. As part of this plan Barney, now living on Mars, is supposed to communicate with a satellite broadcaster using a code book the broadcaster has given him. When he opens the book he finds it blank, presumably because by that time he is an inhabitant of the Chew-Z world—or rather, has been inhabited by it—and Palmer Eldritch has intervened in his perceptions so he cannot read the code. Here is an instance where intervention in the chain of coded signifiers appears to cause a decisive turn of plot, much as it did in James's story.

The difference between Dick's text and James's epistemological assumptions can be measured by what happens next. Under the influence of Chew-Z, Barney time-travels into the future and learns that his refusal to ingest Leo's brain-rotting chemical was not crucial after all, for as more people take Chew-Z, they realize it is a con and the drug is banished without his help. Instead of following through on a chain of events in which the issue is loyalty or betrayal, the plot twists to throw the emphasis elsewhere. The person who reveals this information to Barney is his future self, who helpfully reassures him that the experiences the present-day Barney is having are hallucinations that will wear off in time. The issue here, then, is whether the narrative can regain ontological stability. The future Barney reinforces this stab at stability by making reality depend on a congruence of subjectivity and time; he argues that he is real because he is in his own time, whereas the present-day Barney is a phantasm because he has traveled out of his time. After he offers this reassuring parsing of events so that they fall neatly into the categories of fantasy and reality, however, Barney's future self begins to display the stigmata of Palmer Eldritch, throwing doubt on which Barney is phantasmatic, which real—if indeed either is real. Moreover, his assurances to Barney that the Chew-Z world will wear off in time are scarcely trustworthy, since they are offered by the perpetrator of the world himself. His cover blown, Palmer Eldritch tells Barney that the best way he can spend the subjective eons before the drug wears off is as an inanimate object. When Barney tries to project his consciousness into a wall plaque, Eldritch intervenes to switch bodies with him. First the code book is the site of intervention, then the body. The first intervention destroys the cipher that allows different levels of signifiers to be correlated; the second breaks the indecipherable complexities that unite mind and body. Unmoored from its basis in embodied physicality, the "self" becomes increasingly destabilized, subverting the narrative's earlier attempts to regain ontological security.

The switch of bodies provides the climax. It threatens to be fatal, for Eldritch at that moment in "real" time is on a defenseless space cargo ship about to be shot to smithereens by Leo Bulero's heavily armed gun ship. This would appear to be the real world, its authenticity guaranteed by the finality of death. Again, the narrative reaches toward the stability of a secure ontology, albeit in a different time and place than before. Just before the fatal shot is fired, however, the effects of the drug wear off and Barney is translated back into his own body in a Martian hovel. Present again in his own time and space, Barney is confident this is reality. He later realizes that the switch back into his "real" body was not complete, however, for he retains some trace of Palmer Eldritch within himself, just as he has left some trace of himself in Eldritch. It appears that subjectivity cannot be transmitted from one body to another without change, for noise in the channel amounts to an irreversible alteration of identity. Thus even when reality is apparently restored, it differs in some degree from what it was before the interventions happened. In this space-opera mixture of the fantastic with the melodramatic, it is not so much the dizzying turns of plot that are remarkable as the dizzying reversals of which world is authentic and which fake, which subject is a simulacrum and which a real person. The net result of the narrative's veering now toward ontological security, now toward destabilization, is to break down the distinctions that enabled the fake and the real to be constituted as separate categories. To an indeterminate extent, the fake and the real have infused into one another. Significantly, the erosion of the real/simulation distinction has been achieved by the absorption into the body of a drug capable of functioning like a communication medium. The technology of communication has literally become indistinguishable from the constitution of the subject in a narrative that blends this anticipation of the Regime of Computation with a devastating deconstruction of the self.

Also subverted is the status of the body as a guarantor of identity, a physical presence inhabited by an essential self within. The status of Palmer Eldritch's body has been peculiar from the beginning. We first see him when he interrogates the captive Leo Bulero. The interrogation is carried out not by Palmer Eldritch in the flesh, however, but by an electronic box encrusted with mechanical appendages that serves as a surrogate for Eldritch's body. A similar strangeness occurs when Palmer Eldritch appears on Mars to talk with Barney Mayerson. When Barney contemplates attacking Eldritch, the body bounces high up into the air as if it were a balloon and is drawn into the spaceship by a tether. These events are explained by the growing (and accurate) suspicions of several characters that an alien has eaten Palmer Eldritch from the inside during his long interstellar journey and taken over his body. Palmer Eldritch's three stigmata are not so much artificial aids to a natural body, then, as they are signifiers that the entire body is a prosthesis manipulated by the alien. The body itself has become a prosthesis of communication, for Palmer's body and its surrogates are brought into play primarily when Palmer wishes to communicate with someone. The implicit threat to the liberal subject when possessive individualism no longer functions as a foundation for subjectivity is here realized through the science fiction trope of the alien. The irony, of course, is that this subversion has been achieved without realizing information's dream of endless plenitude. The liberal subject may be eaten from the inside, but capitalism continues more rapaciously than ever. Indeed, Kim Stanley Robinson has suggested that the alien who takes over Palmer Eldritch's body can be taken as "representing the spirit of capitalism, just as his product Chew-Z could be thought of as the ultimate consumer item." [18]

After the narrative's wild veering between ontological stability and destabilization, a resolution can scarcely be achieved by coming down on one side or the other, for the oscillation suggests that the opposite outcome was equally likely, in which case the resolution would have no more authority than a roulette wheel that stops on red rather than black. Instead, the text offers different strategies for dealing with a world that cannot be unambiguously categorized as either real or fake. In the instant that Barney is translated into the alien's body, he briefly shares Palmer's consciousness. Barney senses that the alien is immensely old, so old that Barney decides he must be what humans have called "God." Authorized by this ultimate signifier, the alien appears to be definitively named, thus stabilizing the regression into ontological uncertainty. However, Anne Hawthorne, a character represented ambiguously as both a pilgrim to Mars bent on converting colonists to her religion and a spy for Leo Bulero, disagrees with Barney's assessment. "The key word happens to be *is*," she asserts. "Don't tell us, Barney, that whatever entered Palmer Eldritch *is* God, because you don't know that much about Him; no one can. But that living entity from intersystem space may, like us, be shaped in His image. A way He selected of showing Himself to us. If the map is not the territory, *the pot is not the potter*. So don't talk ontology, Barney; don't say *is*" (232). Here the oscillation does not disappear but rather is made irrelevant to living one's life. Ontological security is sacrificed, but Anne implies that it is possible to live a perfectly satisfactory life without this security. A key element in her calm acceptance of the alien/Palmer Eldritch is the modesty of her expectations. The crucial gap between "is" and "appears," ontology and experience, inheres in the signifier called Palmer Eldritch, but this signifier is not confined to that body, as the replication of the stigmata within other bodies indicates. In a deep sense, the stigmata are not manifestations of God but of a reality whose ontology cannot be unequivocally stabilized. Even though Anne also takes on the stigmata from time to time, she is not bothered by her inability to bridge the gap between experience and ultimate reality, because her faith paradoxically allows her to give up ontology.

Leo Bulero practices a different strategy, based on continuing contestation and the exercise of personal power. The grander the claim or the more ambitious the project, the more likely it is that the stigmata will reappear. In contrast to Anne's acceptance is Leo's conviction that he can triumph over Palmer Eldritch. Leo believes his thinking is more elevated than the ordinary person's, since he has been taking E-therapy radiation treatments from Dr. Denkmal's evolution clinic. With his supposedly more evolved brain, he hatches the plan to become a Protector of Earth, gathering other humans evolved through E-therapy into a group that will become a watchdog society protecting Earth from Palmer Eldritch. Although he sports the stigmata, he convinces himself that inside is a core of authenticity, a belief that transcends his personal identity and that therefore constitutes "something *in* me that even that thing Palmer Eldritch can't reach and consume because since it's not me it's not mine to lose. I feel it growing. Withstanding the external, nonessential alterations, the arm, the eyes, the teeth—it's not touched by any of these three, the evil, negative trinity of alienation, blurred reality, and despair that Eldritch brought back with him" (244). Leo intends to draw on this core to save himself and the Earth. But when he pokes "with his non-artificial elbow the semi-thing beside him" (his lieutenant Felix Blau, who also displays the stigmata), Felix responds laconically, "Anything you say, Leo," whereupon Leo fails to recognize his own name (245). Even if we accept Leo's claim that his project will be successful—which the text effectively undercuts through Felix's response—at best he can win only the battle, for the war to maintain his human identity has already been lost.

More successful is the modest plan Barney decides upon. During the brief moment Barney shared Eldritch's mind, he realized that the alien intended to spend his days taking over Barney's life on Mars. Far from finding it unbearable, the alien delighted in such small pleasures as perfectly seasoned eggs. Barney reasons that if life on Mars is good enough for the alien, it can be good enough for him as well, and he resolves to enjoy it. Compared to the fatal attractions and illusory promises of the realm of information, the regime of scarcity ends up looking not so bad after all. It is significant that Barney intends to share this life with Anne Hawthorne, the pilgrim who is content to admit she can never grasp ultimate reality.

These modest accommodations notwithstanding, *The Three Stigmata of Palmer Eldritch* represents a more profound subversion of conventional reality than does James's "In the Cage." More is at stake than revealing the emptiness of information's promise as a dream of effortless plenitude. If Can-D points to the sweetness of this illusion, Chew-Z points to the scarier possibility that, instead of a person consuming the drug, the drug will consume the person. With Chew-Z the space of simulation acquires an ominous agency of its own, including the power to usurp reality. Nevertheless, this usurpation is not absolute. Hideous as the stigmata are, they bring a degree of epistemological stability to the narrative, for they function as markers that indicate, more or less reliably, the realm within which the characters are operating. If the stigmata are absent, the character is in conventional reality or in the translated world of Can-D; if present, the character is operating in the Chew-Z world, where Palmer Eldritch makes the rules and infects all subjectivities with his alien identity. The stigmata thus have the effect of marking the space of simulation and constituting it as a distinguishable phenomenon. The next step is a fiction in which these markers are lost and there is no distinction between simulation and reality.

Tiptree's "The Girl Who Plugged In" takes this step. The self becomes a message to be encoded and decoded, but the self the receiver decodes is never exactly the same self the sender encoded. The liberal subject, distributed between a privileged and stigmatized body connected by a noisy channel, is not so much lost as reconstituted as a dream of the machine. The focus thus shifts from how the self expresses its agency to questions of who controls the machine.

Code as (Re)incarnation: "The Girl Who Was Plugged In"

In the near-future world of Tiptree's story, advertising has been banned. The communication conglomerate GTX has responded by airing shows that follow beautiful people around the world, the real purpose being strategic product placement. Beautiful people tend to be unreliable from a commercial viewpoint, however, so GTX has a new idea. They decide to build a beautiful person from scratch, a genetically engineered body without a functioning brain, to be operated remotely by a cybernetically modified human who will control the body as a "waldo." For the operator they use P. Burke, a wretched, deformed woman off the streets who hitherto has looked up to beautiful people as gods. Immured in an underground cavern at the heart of a high-tech research center, P. Burke undergoes numerous operations that extend her nervous and sensory system into wires. After months of practice, she learns to inhabit the beautiful fifteen-year-old girl-body as if it were her own, a body that GTX advertising whizzes name Delphi. P. Burke still needs to tend to her own body as well, so while Delphi "sleeps" (i.e., returns to a vegetative state when her operator has withdrawn), P. Burke falls back into her own loathsome flesh and carries out the routines that enable her to continue living: eating, exercising, excreting.

Like Dick's novel and James's story, Tiptree's fiction constructs a sharp contrast between an informational realm and a "real" world of severe constraints that operates according to the laws of conservation. On the one hand, Delphi lives in a world of seemingly endless possibility, expansive in its glittering displays of wealth and privilege; on the other hand, P. Burke lives a severely controlled Spartan existence in an underground cavern where her every move, including her physiological responses, are closely monitored. Yet there are important differences between Dick's novel and Tiptree's fiction, illustrated by the comparison with Perky Pat. Both the Perky Pat layouts and Delphi's glamorous life exist to market commodities. Whereas the dolls are inanimate and move only in the drug-enhanced imaginations of the participants, Delphi appears to those around her as a normal person, complete with small talk and conspicuous consumption.

Recall that in Dick's story the colonists maintained their sense of individual identities while their minds were projected into the doll. On some level, they knew the difference between the "real" bodies and the doll's physique. For P. Burke, the projection into Delphi's body is so complete that she perceives it as her own. During the time of projection she experiences her identity as Delphi, all the more strongly because Delphi is everything she might have wished to be and so painfully is not. With Perky Pat, the narrative viewpoint constituted a sharp distinction between the dismal locale of the hovel and the privileged world of Perky Pat; but in Tiptree's story the bodies themselves are clearly distinguished: P. Burke's deformed flesh versus Delphi's heavenly features. In Dick's novel, the binary division between the colonists' lives in the hovel and their expansive existences in the Perky Pat world was used to mark one as real, the other as illusory. Even when the Chew-Z world threatens to displace the autonomy of the real world, there is still a clear conceptual division between reality and illusion, the world as it is in itself and the world as it is created by Palmer Eldritch's mind.

By contrast, in Tiptree's story both spaces are real. Indeed, in some respects Delphi lives a more "real" life than P. Burke in her secret niche within the research complex, for Delphi moves in a socially constructed space that, filmed by the media and beamed out to communication networks throughout the world, represents the epitome of the autonomy, freedom, and agency of the liberal subject. The irony lies not in the illusory nature of this world but in the apparent freedom and luxury of Delphi's life as it is broadcast around the globe, in contrast to the constant surveillance and discipline to which both she and P. Burke are in fact subject, an irony especially evident in light of the fact that GTX is dedicated to "freeing the world from garble" (46). The issue, then, is not which world is real, for Delphi's high-flying life and P. Burke's spartan physical existence are both located in real time and space. Rather, the focus in on the connections that make the two bodies into an integrated cybersystem—the kinds of discipline, surveillance, and punishment to which the bodies are subject, and the distribution of agency between these two different sites in the cybersystem.

The joint between bodies is not altogether seamless. There is a gap of a few seconds between the time that P. Burke thinks the command and Delphi's body enacts it, a temporal reflection of the physical space separating them. Delphi's body also does not work in exactly the same way as other human bodies. She sees and hears as well as normal humans, but to conserve bandwidth the engineers left her with little sense of touch, almost no smell, and only enough kinesthesia for the body to work correctly. It is no accident that the senses she needs for broadband communication with the TV networks are left intact, while the intimate senses most deeply bound up with pleasure are diminished, making sex for her mostly a cerebral experience. Moreover, the diurnal pattern of waking and sleeping does not, in her case, signify that her body is refreshing itself. Rather, the pattern reflects and enacts the distribution of agency, consciousness, and subjectivity between the two bodies according to a strict law of conservation: P. Burke's body must "sleep" while the consciousness is inhabiting Delphi, and Delphi's body must "sleep" while the consciousness is back in P. Burke's body. Intervening in both the media-constructed public world of Delphi and the secret research-dominated existence of P. Burke are the corporate structure and politics of GTX. The conglomerate controls the communication channels through which subjectivity-as-message flows and decides how the distribution of subjectivity will be parsed. Thus the time gap does more than signify that agency is distributed; it also indicates that multiple sites are available for intervention by the corporation.[19] GTX no longer finds it necessary to discipline the bodies directly, for Delphi/P. Burke can be controlled more effectively by intervening in the messages that flow between the bodies.[20]

Discipline becomes necessary when Delphi attracts the attention of Paul Isham, son of a top-ranking executive at GTX. In a script familiar from the 1960s, Paul uses the power and access bestowed on him by his family connections to make satirical TV shows critical of capitalism and the dominant ideologies. Delphi interests him not only because of her alluring combination of innocence and sexiness, but also because she is naive enough to object when the products she displays do not live up to their promises. As infatuated with Paul as he is with her, Delphi willingly accompanies him on romantic excursions, tolerated by GTX in a precise calculation that balances the leeway she is allowed against the strength of her ratings. Intending to annoy the corporation, Paul deliberately makes plans he knows will interfere with Delphi's filming schedules. Finally a "ferret-face" twerp at GTX, plotting for advancement, convinces his superiors that he should be allowed to discipline P. Burke/Delphi, which he does by twisting the dials that control the communication flow between the bodies. The result is excruciating pain for them both. Paul, seeing Delphi writhe in pain, comes to the erroneous conclusion that she has had an implant placed in her brain. Furious at this interference with his desires and the defilement of his love object, he plots to "free" Delphi from her imprisonment.

He can do so, he thinks, by using a wire mesh cage he has constructed to cut off the signals sent to Delphi's brain. As if in ironic reversal of James's story, he plots to rescue Delphi from the realm of information by placing her in the cage. He hires a pilot to drive a small plane and whisks Delphi away from her keepers, in a wild dash for freedom that is undercut when GTX tracks the plane's precise location through its computers. When Paul tries to place the cage over his "bird" (as he thinks of Delphi), she resists, knowing that if she is put in the cage she will cease to be the person Paul loves, in fact will cease to be a person at all. Alarmed that his intervention does not free Delphi, Paul directs the plane toward the research center, determined to force the researchers to remove the supposed implant. His mistake is thinking that Delphi is an autonomous subject whose free will has temporarily been disrupted; in reality, Delphi's subjectivity cannot be separated from the integrated cybersystem that also includes P. Burke. The irony is inscribed into Delphi's name, which GTX coined when they discovered that the "P" in P. Burke stood for Philadelphia, home of the Liberty Bell and American individualism.

The climax comes when Paul bursts into the research center and demands to have Delphi "freed." P. Burke, inhabiting Delphi's body, knows that Paul is coming, and as he enters the inner sanctum to which her cubicle is attached, she bursts through the doors, croaking his name in a scarcely intelligible voice. Overwrought, Paul fails to recognize her as a part of the cybersystem that includes Delphi; instead, he sees her as an independent and remarkably hideous creature scarcely recognizable as human because of her surgically altered body and its trailing equipment. His response is to shoot her, whereupon Delphi also collapses, since there is now no one to operate her body.

But there is a twist. After Delphi/P. Burke had fallen in love with Paul, anomalies began occurring that should have been technically impossible. Delphi stirred in her "sleep" and once or twice murmured Paul's name, as if the waldo was somehow breaking into consciousness by itself. Meanwhile P. Burke, knowing a crisis was coming, had been fighting with all her might to leave her own flesh and force herself into Delphi's body.[21] The narrative intimates that in some measure one or both of these attempts may have partially succeeded, for after P. Burke dies, Delphi retains enough consciousness to say plaintively, "I'm Delphi," asserting the right to become the autonomous subject she can never be (78). The implication is that some measure of the possessive individual can survive, if only momentarily. If the corporation can intervene in the channels to discipline the bodies, perhaps the bodies can also intervene to send messages the corporation has not authorized. Such an intervention, however transitory, is by no means trivial, for GTX's "nightmares are about hemorrhages of information, channels screwed up, plans misimplemented, garble creeping in" (46).

As the narrative races toward its conclusion, the narrator reveals that Delphi's name is doubly significant, for the ferret-face twerp rescues his career by ferreting out the next big technical development in the corporation research labs, the ability to time-travel. In classical myth, Delphi is the site of the oracle, the voice that can reveal the future. Throughout, the narrator has been calling her story a tale of the future.[22] As if anticipating Ostman's utopic vision, the narrator's ironic tone mocks the reader for thinking that communication technologies will soon create a realm of information that will bestow endless plenitude on those of us fortunate enough to enter it. Instead, the future itself has become a commodity, one of many sites available for sale through the miracle of communication technology. Like subjectivity, time can now be sent through the wires and so is subject to distribution according to corporate needs. The implication is that both subjectivity and time itself may be transformed, but capitalism continues intact.

Code as Female Subjectivity:
What Can a Girl Sell When She Really Needs To?

Another way to think about the trajectory formed by "In the Cage," *The Three Stigmata of Palmer Eldritch*, and "The Girl Who Was Plugged In" is to trace the restricted ways in which the female characters can engage in commerce. As we have seen, the girl in the cage briefly considers prostitution as an option. "Horrid and vulgar" as causal prostitution is to her, it nevertheless is a transaction firmly based in possessive individualism, for it assumes that she owns her own body and therefore has the right to sell it, albeit in a way legally proscribed by the capitalistic system in which she is enmeshed. As many historians have argued, the social arrangements of Victorian London virtually required prostitution, for the large numbers of "surplus" women would otherwise have starved. Beds, even more than telegraph offices, are notorious sites of the exchange of information. Jennifer Wicke says of James's story that "women come to mediate exchange. Communication flows through them, telegraphically or otherwise enhanced; information traveling along class lines collocates in them; the mechanisms of mass cultural transfer of libidinal, commodity desire are set up with 'woman' as the switch point."[23]

One might generalize this argument by noting that it applies to anyone occupying the subject position of woman. There is historical evidence that at the time James wrote the story he may have been aware of recent scandals involving telegraph boys and prostitution. In Ric Savoy's reading of the story, the allusions to prostitution stand in for the more scandalous prospect of male homosexual prostitution and the fear that the lower-class telegraph boys would testify against their aristocratic clients.[24] The effect of this reading is to position prostitution centrally within the story's dynamics, making it crucial to the outcome, rather than the girl's passing thought. Whatever one makes of this argument, the fact remains that the girl's interpolation into the market economy depends upon her ownership of her body. Correspondingly, the narrative locates complexity in the girl's consciousness rather than in the message or the channel. Placing the locus of complexity, agency, and possession in the (conscious) mind indicates that the liberal subject remains largely intact.

In Dick's novel, implicit bargaining to exchange sex for goods occurs in both the real and virtual worlds. Roni Fugate sleeps with Barney Mayerson and uses this intimacy to gain information that enables her to compete successfully for his job. We see these events through Barney's consciousness, so the narrative positions Roni as a mingled temptation and threat, at times appearing loyal to Barney and genuinely helpful, at other times treacherous and bent on achieving her success at his expense. As we have seen, this oscillation between loyalty and betrayal is characteristic of Dick's representations of a relatively benign capitalism in which familial relationships are folded into a corporation. Still, there remains a significant difference between male and female characters. Whereas the narrative is focalized in the consciousness of male characters and so makes their actions comprehensible if not commendable, we are never taken into Roni's mind, a partitioning of narrative viewpoint that makes her motives obscure and her actions more threatening than they otherwise would be.[25] Like Barney, Leo Bulero finds Roni both attractive and threatening. After he returns from the Chew-Z world, he propositions her, offering to make her his mistress and install her in his estate on a space satellite. When she refuses, Leo takes his revenge by wishing that she was a hundred years old, "forgetting" that for those infected by Chew-Z, thoughts have the power to create reality. As a result of the wish, Roni becomes an animate horror, for she dies before reaching one hundred, and her decayed body reassembles into a nightmare of the living dead. Roni had declined Leo's offer because she did not find his evolved "bubblehead" attractive, so her refusal was not only an exercise of personal agency but also an assertion of her own desires. As punishment, she is interjected into a world where she no longer owns her body, where her body is not even a commodity but a thought-object under the control of a vindictive male. Possessive individualism does not hold because there is no individual.

Another scene foregrounding male/female bargaining for sex is the exchange between Fran and Sam in the Martian hovel when he tries to convince her to have virtual sex with him by entering Perky Pat and Walt. As an inducement, Sam offers Fran a gift of Can-D, which she can choose to accept or not; but once she has entered the Can-D world, her agency in consummating virtual sex is less clear, for they are joined by other colonists who have their own ideas. Nevertheless, as we have seen, the Can-D world complicates rather than eradicates possessive individualism. Once the Can-D world is displaced by Chew-Z, prostitution gives way to a construction of subjectivity in which powerful males do not have to bargain because they can think revenge or pleasure as they choose. It is surely no accident that after Leo Bulero has spent time in the Chew-Z world he resolves to fire Roni Fugate, deciding that her independence is a threat he does not have to put up with. The narrative here generates complexity largely by indeterminate oscillations between real and simulated realms, an ambiguity mirrored by the indeterminate fusion of the subjects' bodies with the stigmata of Palmer Eldritch. The subversion of the autonomous self moves in conjunction with the subversion of an autonomous world.

In Tiptree's story, P. Burke is so totally under the sway of the GTX corporation that they do not need to buy her body. Instead, she gives it to them freely in exchange for being able to project her consciousness into Delphi's beautiful girl-body. After P. Burke dies, the corporation takes this expensive commodity and hooks it up with another operator. If P. Burke does not own the waldo, she does not own her body either, for her multiple operations and prostheses mean that she can live only so long as GTX is willing to maintain her life supports. At the critical moment when Paul is rushing toward the research complex, the ferret-face twerp gives the order to administer a fatal drug dose to P. Burke. P. Burke lives long enough to meet her ironic fate only because the female nurse in charge refuses to carry out the order, continuing to see her as a "she" rather than an "it," the pronoun the narrator uses for the dying Delphi after P. Burke has been killed. The dramatic climax makes clear that P. Burke has ceased to be an individual. Rather, she/it is a component in a cybersystem, which is how the male technician who trained her and who alone mourns her death thinks about her. Any claim to possessive individualism based on ownership of the self has thus been co-opted by a merger between corporate capitalism and communication technologies so potent that it operates in the intimate territory of nerve and muscle as well as global networks. Coincident with this penetration, the narrative locates complexity neither in the sender nor the receiver but in the channel, the focus for such decisive events as discipline, noise, and time-delay (and eventually, we are told, time-manipulation).

Following the trope of prostitution and the locus of complexity through these stories reveals the continuing force of gender hierarchies, which do not disappear as possessive individualism collapses but rather continue to operate differentially for male and female characters. Although both genders are threatened by the collapse of possessive individualism, men continue to exercise more power, autonomy, and individual choice than women. What has changed is not the historical power difference between genders but the distribution of subjectivities in relation to the Regime of Computation. Information goes from being an imagined realm of plenitude in James's story, to a marked realm that interpenetrates reality in Dick's novel, to reality in Tiptree's fiction. The shifting locus of complexity, which is one focus of the analysis I started in chapter 1, here shows that both subjectivity and reality itself are increasingly entangled with communication media. As Timothy Lenoir has suggested, Baudrillard's prediction of a hyperreality that will displace reality has proven too conservative to keep up with the transformative power of information technologies.[26] Tiptree's story suggests that we will not call what emerges from this ongoing transformation "hyperreality" but simply "reality." In this sense, the Regime of Computation, marking a shift from the construction of complexity as it occurs in speech and writing to complexity as an emergent result of computation, is implicit in the trajectory these fictions enact. Despite the differences in historical contexts and authorial voices that give these fictions distinctive visions, they concur in puncturing the dream of an informational realm that can escape the constraints of scarcity. Finally it is not scarcity and market relations that are transformed, but the subjects who are constrained and defined by how they participate in them.

2 STORING

Print and Etext

4   Translating Media

From Print to Electronic Texts

In "The Don Quixote of Pierre Menard," Borges uses his technique of re-viewing nonexistent books to explain Pierre Menard's fantastic project of re-creating *Don Quixote* in the twentieth century.[1] Although Menard's creation reproduces Cervantes' masterpiece word for word, Borges explains that it is an utterly different work, for the changed cultural context makes thoughts that were banal for Cervantes virtually unthinkable for a twentieth-century intellectual. Borges's mock-serious fantasy recalls more mundane operations carried out every day around the globe. Suppose *Don Quixote* is transported not into a new time but a new medium, and that the word sequences on the computer screen are identical to Cervantes' original print edition. Is this electronic version the same work? Subversive as Borges's fiction, the question threatens to expose major fault lines running through our contemporary ideas of textuality.

To explore these complexities, I propose to regard the transformation of a print document into an electronic text as a form of translation—"media translation"—which is inevitably also an act of interpretation. In invoking the trope of translation, I follow the lead of Dene Grigar. As she observes, the adage that something is gained as well as lost in translation applies with special force to print documents that are imported to the Web.[2] The challenge is to specify, rigorously and precisely, what these gains and losses entail and especially what they reveal about presuppositions underlying reading and writing. My claim is that they show that our notions of textuality are shot through with assumptions specific to print, although they have not been generally recognized as such. The advent of electronic textuality presents us with an unparalleled opportunity to reformulate fundamental ideas about texts and, in the process, to see print as well as electronic texts with fresh eyes. For theory, this is the "something gained" that media translation can offer. It is a gift we cannot afford to refuse.

The issues can be illustrated by the William Blake Archive, a magnificent Web site designed by three of our most distinguished Blake scholars and editors.[3] It is no exaggeration to say that the William Blake Archive establishes the gold standard for literary Web sites. The site is informed throughout by an enlightened editorial policy, for the editors state that they take the "work" to be the book considered as a unique physical object. They thus declare implicitly their allegiance to an idea that Jerome McGann, among others, has been championing: the physical characteristics of a text—page size, font, gutters, leading, and so on—are "bibliographic codes," signifying components that should be considered along with linguistic codes.[4] The editors make canny use of the computer's simulation powers to render the screen display as much like the printed book as possible. They provide a calibration applet that lets users set screen resolution so the original page dimensions can be reproduced. They include a graphical help section that uses illustrations of pages to indicate the site's functionalities and capabilities. Clearly an enormous amount of thought, time, and money has gone into the construction of this site.

The editors of the archive are meticulous in insisting that even small differences in materiality potentially affect meaning, so they have gone to a great deal of trouble to compile not only different works but extant copies of the same work. Yet these copies are visually rendered on screen with a technology that differs far more in its materiality from print than the print copies do from one another. The computer accurately simulates print documents precisely because it is completely unlike print in its architecture and functioning. The simulation of visual accuracy, which joins facsimile and other editions in rescuing Blake from text-only versions that suppress the crucial visual dimensions of his work, is nevertheless achieved at the cost of cybernetic difference. Consider, for example, the navigation functionality that allows the user to juxtapose many images on screen to compare different copies and versions of a work. To achieve a comparable (though not identical) effect with print—if it could be done at all—would require access to rare books rooms, a great deal of page turning, and constant shifting of physical artifacts. A moment's thought suffices to show that changing the navigational apparatus of a work changes the work. Translating the words on a scroll into a codex book, for example, radically alters how a reader encounters the work; by changing *how* the work means, such a move alters *what* it means. One of the insights electronic textuality makes inescapably clear is that navigational functionalities are not merely ways to access the work but part of a work's signifying structure. An encyclopedia signifies differently than does a realistic novel in part because its navigational functionalities anticipate and structure different reading patterns (a clash of conventions that Milorad Pavić has great fun exploiting in *Dictionary of the Khazars: A Lexicon Novel*).

In terms of the William Blake Archive, we might reasonably ask: if slight color variations affect meaning, how much more does the reader's navigation of the complex functionalities of this site affect what the texts signify? Of course, the editors recognize that what they are doing is simulating, not reproducing, print texts. One can imagine the countless editorial meetings they must have attended to create the site's sophisticated design and functionalities; surely they know better than anyone the extensive differences between the print and electronic Blake. Nevertheless, they make the rhetorical choice to downplay these differences. For example, there is a section explaining that dynamic data arrays are used to generate the screen displays, but there is little or no theoretical exploration of what it means to read an electronic text produced in this fashion rather than the print original. Great attention is paid to the relation of meaning to linguistic and bibliographic codes and almost none to the relation of meaning to digital codes. Matthew Kirschenbaum's call for a thorough rethinking of the "materiality of first generation objects" in electronic media is very much to the point.[5] Calling for a closer relationship between electronic textuality (focusing on digital work) and textual studies (traditionally focused on print), he lays out a framework for discussing electronic texts in bibliographic terms, including the nomenclature "layer, version, and release"; "object"; "state"; "instance"; and "copy."[6] As his argument makes clear, electronic texts often have complex bibliographic histories that materially affect meaning, to say nothing of differences between print and electronic instantiations of a work. Concentrating only on how the material differences of *print* texts affect meaning, as does the William Blake Archive, is like feeling slight texture differences on an elephant's tail while ignoring the ways in which the tail differs from the rest of the elephant.

What Is a Text?

Tackling the whole elephant requires rethinking the nature of textuality, starting with a basic question: what is a text? In "Forming the Text, Performing the Work," Anna Gunder, in an effort to clarify the relations between electronic and print media, has undertaken a meticulous survey of textual criticism to determine how editors employ the foundational terminology of "work," "text," and "document" in the context of print bibliographic studies. A work is an "abstract artistic entity," the ideal construction toward which textual editors move by collating different editions and copies to arrive at their best guess for what the artistic creation should be (86). It is important to note that the work is ideal not in a Platonic sense, however, for it is understood to be the result of editorial assumptions that are subject to negotiation, challenge, community norms, and cultural presuppositions. (Jerome McGann's attacks on the principle of defining the work through an author's "final intentions" is a case in point.)[7] Next down the scale comes the text. Gunder points out that the "work as such can never be accessed but through some kind of text, that is, through the specific sign system designated to manifest a particular work" (86). Texts, then, are abstract entities from which editors strive to excavate the work. In this respect, she notes, texts of poems are unlike paintings. Whereas no one would claim it makes sense to talk about a painting separate from the substrate in which it is embodied, editors presume that it does make sense to talk about a text as something separate from its physical embodiment in an artifact. Only when we arrive at the lowest level of the textual hierarchy, the document, is the physical artifact seen as merging with the sign system as an abstract representation.

Gunder's analysis is consistent with the terminological practices of Peter Shillingsburg, one of the editors she surveys. In *Scholarly Editing in the Computer Age*, Shillingsburg defines a text as "the actual order of words and punctuation as contained in any one physical form, such as a manuscript, proof or book." To forestall misunderstanding, he clarifies that "a text (the *order* of words and punctuation) has no substantial or material existence, since it is not restricted by time and space. . . . The text is contained and stabilized by the physical form but is not the physical form itself" (46). Driving the nail farther into this terminological coffin, he insists "it is possible for the same text to be stored in a set of alphabetic signs, a set of Braille signs, a set of electronic signals on a computer tape, and a set of magnetic impulses on a tape recorder. Therefore, it is not accurate to say that the text and the signs or storage medium are the same. If the text is stored accurately on a second storage medium, *the text remains the same though the signs for it are different.* Each accurate copy contains the same text; inaccurate or otherwise variant copies contain new texts" (47, emphasis added). Some hundred pages later, he admits that "proponents of the bibliographic orientation have demonstrated beyond argument, I believe, that the appearance of books signifies a range of important meanings to their users" (150); but apparently he does not think this imbrication of physical form with meaning requires a different notion of textuality. To be fair to Shillingsburg, he has since defined "text" as a compound of matter, concept, and action.[8] Nevertheless, there are no doubt many editors and literary scholars—I dare say the majority—who assume much the same definitions of "work," "text," and "document" that he formulates. Moreover, Shillingsburg's more nuanced explanations of "text" and "work" in his recent analysis result in an alarming proliferation of terms, so that "work," "text," and "version" all split into multiple subcategories. This scheme is reminiscent of the Ptolemaic model of the universe as it piled epicycles upon cycles in an effort to keep the earth at the center of the universe. The problem with the Ptolemaic universe was not that it could not account for celestial motion; rather, it was the cost of increasing complexity required for its earth-centric view. Perhaps it is time for a Copernican revolution in our thinking about textuality, a revolution achieved by going back and rethinking fundamental assumptions.

We can begin this reassessment by noticing how Shillingsburg's definitions are perfectly crafted to trivialize differences between print and electronic media and to insulate "text" and even more so "work" from being significantly affected by the specificities of media. To return to his examples, he claims that a Braille version of a novel is the same text as a print version, yet the sensory input of the two forms is entirely different. Moreover, it is clear that one medium—print—provides the baseline for the definitions, even though they are postulated as including other media as well. Thinking of the text as "the *order* of words and punctuations" is as print-centric a definition as I can imagine, for it comes straight out of the printer's shop and the lineation of type as the means of production for the book. We can see how Shillingsburg imports this print-centric notion into electronic media when he refers to "computer tape" in the quotation above, for this construction unconsciously carries over the notion that the text resides at one physical location, even though it is at the same time alleged to be "not restricted by time and space." When a text is generated in an electronic environment, the data files may reside on a server hundreds of miles distant from the user's local computer. Moreover, in cases where text is dynamically assembled on the fly, the text as "the actual order of words and punctuation" does not exist as such in these data files. Indeed, it does not exist as an artifact at all. Rather, it comes into existence as a *process* that includes the data files, the programs that call these files, and the hardware on which the programs run, as well as the optical fibers, connections, switching algorithms, and other devices necessary to route the text from one networked computer to another.

An even more serious objection to Shillingsburg's definition is its implicit assumption that "text" does not include such qualities as color, font size and shape, and page placement, not to mention such electronic-specific effects as animation, mouseovers, instantaneous linking, and so on. In most contemporary electronic literature, screen design, graphics, multiple layers, color, and animation, among other signifying components, are essential to the work's effects. Focusing only on "the actual order of words and punctuation" would be as inadequate as insisting that painting consists only of shapes, ruling out of bounds such things as color, texture, composition, and perspective. The largely unexamined assumption here is that ideas about textuality forged in a print environment can be carried over wholesale to the screen without rethinking how things change with electronic text, as if "text" were an inert, nonreactive substance that can be poured from container to container without affecting its essential nature.

Moreover, the comparison with electronic text reveals by implication how limited this definition of "text" is even for print media. Although Shillingsburg gives a nod to those of the "bibliographic orientation," he does not begin to deal in a serious way with Jerome McGann's brilliant readings of poets ranging from Lord Byron to Wallace Stevens and with his repeated demonstrations that bibliographic effects are crucial in setting up meaning play within the texts. To exclude these effects from the meaning of "text" is to impoverish criticism by cutting it off from resources used to create artistic works. How can one find these effects in a text if "text" has been defined so as to exclude them? Although Shillingsburg's definition of "work" may not be Platonic in an ideal sense, there is nevertheless a Platonic yearning on display in his definitions, for he seeks to protect the "work" from the noisiness of an embodied world—but this very noise may be the froth from which artistic effects emerge.

The desire to suppress unruliness and multiplicity in order to converge on an ideal "work" is deeply embedded in textual criticism. However the criteria facilitating this convergence are defined, textual editors have largely agreed that convergence is the ideal. Hans Zeller, arguing in 1975 for a shift of the editorial perspective from the author's "final intentions" to a broader historical viewpoint, observes that "the editor searches in the transmitted text for the one authentic text, in comparison with which all else will be a textual corruption."[9] Not arriving at a single authoritative text, editors argue, risks plopping the reader into a rat's nest of complexly interrelated variants, thus foisting onto her the Sisyphean labor of sorting through the mess and arriving at a sensible text that most readers would prefer to have handed to them. In this view, readers want a text they can take more or less at face value so that they can get on with the work of interpreting its meaning and explicating its artistic strategies. Here the comparison of editing with translation is especially apt, for the editor, like the translator, makes innumerable decisions that can never be fully covered by an explicit statement of principles. As McGann points out, these decisions inevitably function as interpretations, for they literally construct the text in ways that foreground some interpretive possibilities and suppress others.

When texts are translated into electronic environments, the attempt to define a work as an immaterial verbal construct, already problematic for print, opens a Pandora's box of additional complexities and contradictions, which can be illustrated by debates within the community formulating the Text Encoding Initiative (TEI). The idea of TEI was to arrive at principles for coding print documents into electronic form that would preserve their essential features and, moreover, allow them to appear more or less the same in complex networked environments, regardless of platform, browser, and so on. To this end, the community (or rather, an influential contingent) arrived at the well-known principle of OHCO, the idea that a text can be encoded as an ordered hierarchy of content objects. As Allen Renear points out in his seminal analysis of this process, the importation of print into digital media requires implicit decisions about what a text is. [10] Expanding on this point, Mats Dahlström, following Michael Sperberg-McQueen, observes that the markup of a text is "a theory of this text, and a general markup language is a *general theory* or conception of text." [11]

With respect to the general theory of OHCO, Renear identifies three distinct positions within the text encoding community, which correspond roughly to three historical stages. The first stage held that a text consists of a hierarchical set of content objects such as chapters, sections, subsections, paragraphs, and sentences. This view asserted that the hierarchy is essential to the production of the text and so must occupy center stage in transforming print text into digital code. This belief in hierarchy informed how the community used SGML (Standard Generalized Markup Language) to create protocols and standards that would ensure that the content objects were reproduced in digital media, and moreover reproduced in the same hierarchy as print. [12] Although most of these researchers thought of themselves as practitioners rather than theorists, their decisions, as Renear points out, constituted a de facto theory of textuality that was reinforced by their tacit assumption that the "Platonic reality" of a text really is its existence as an ordered hierarchy of content objects.

The next stage, which Renear identifies as pluralism, was propelled by the realization that many texts consist of not just one hierarchy but several interpenetrating hierarchies; the standard example is a verse drama, which can be parsed as sentences and metrical lines. Epistemologically, this realization led to a view of texts as *systems* of ordered hierarchies, and refinements such as

Document Type Definitions (DTDs) were designed to introduce more flexibility into the system. The third stage, which Renear calls antirealism, draws the conclusion that the text does not preexist encoding as a stable ontological object but is brought into existence through implicit assumptions actualized through encoding procedures. Renear quotes Alois Pichler as exemplifying this approach: "Our aim in transcription is not to represent as accurately as possible the originals, but rather to prepare from the original another text so as to serve as accurately as possible certain interests in the text."[13] Renear, who identifies himself as a pluralist, astutely points out the tautologies and ambiguities in the antirealist position—for example, indeterminacies in identifying which "certain interests in the text" are to be served.

My interest in this controversy points in a different direction, for what strikes me is the extent to which all three positions—Platonist, pluralist, and antirealist—focus almost exclusively on linguistic codes, a focus that allows them to leave the document as a physical artifact out of consideration. I can illustrate the implications of this erasure by returning to the William Blake Archive. The editors of the archive, as we have seen, take into account the book as a physical object. Their encoding practices make clear, however, that they implicitly understand the bibliographic almost exclusively in terms of the visual. Other aspects of the text as physical object, such as the lovely feeling of a leather binding or the musty smell of old paper, are not reproduced in digital codes. To undertake the *complete* bibliographic coding of a book into digital media would be to imagine the digital equivalent of Borges's Library of Babel, for it would have to include an unimaginable number of codes accounting for the staggering multiplicity of ways in which we process books as sensory phenomena. To reduce this impossible endeavor to manageable proportions, editors must identify some features of particular interest, and it makes excellent sense to emphasize the visual aspect of Blake's works. But we lose important insights if we naturalize this process and allow ourselves the illusion that Blake's books—or any books, for that matter—have been faithfully reproduced within digital media. Rather, *choices* have been made about which aspects of the book to encode, and these choices are heavily weighted toward the linguistic rather than the bibliographic. Moreover, the choices have further implications in the correlations they establish between linguistic, bibliographic, and digital codes. Thus in his rigorous analysis of how markup languages such as SGML relate to the Hjelmslevian distinction between content and expression (the physical instantiation of a text), Dino Buzzetti shows that these languages do not solve the problems raised by thinking of the text as an abstract entity; rather, they amplify implicit problems and further complicate the situation.[14] Only if we attend to the interrelations of linguistic, bibliographic, and digital codes can we grasp the full implications of the transformations books undergo when they are translated into a digital medium.

The debates about encoding assume implicitly that there is some textual essence that can be transported from print to digital media. Even the anti-realist position assumes an essence, although now it is an essence created by an editor. All three positions elide from electronic texts the materiality of books and their physical differences. A more accurate perception would focus on the editorial process of choice, which is always contextual and driven by "certain interests," although these reside not exclusively in the text but in the conjunction of text, editorial process, and cultural context. In my view, the ontology card is not worth playing. There is no Platonic reality of texts. There are only physical objects such as books and computers, foci of attention, and codes that entrain attention and organize material operations. Since no print books can be completely encoded into digital media, we should think about correspondences rather than ontologies, entraining processes rather than isolated objects, and codes moving in coordinated fashion across representational media rather than mapping one object onto another.

The issue goes to the heart of what we think a text is, and at the heart of the heart is the belief that "work" and "text" are immaterial constructions independent of the substrates in which they are instantiated. We urgently need to rethink this assumption, for as long as it remains intact, efforts to account for the specificities of print and electronic media will be hamstrung. Without nuanced analyses of the differences and similarities of print and electronic media, we will fail to grasp the fuller significance of the momentous changes underway as the Age of Print draws to a close and print—as robust, versatile, and complex as ever—takes its place in the dynamic media ecology of the twenty-first century. For an appreciation of these changes we will require a more workable sense of materiality than has traditionally accompanied theories of textuality, which invoke it only to dismiss it as something to be left behind through the labor of creating the ideal work.

Physicality, Materiality, and Embodied Textuality

There are, of course, good reasons why editors have sought to separate the idea of the work from its physical instantiation. If the "work" is instantiated in its physical form, then every edition would produce, by definition, another "work," and textual form would never be stable. Whether textual form should be stabilized is a question at the center of Jerome McGann's "experiments in failure," which he discusses in *Radiant Textuality*. As both Mats Dahlström and McGann point out, the two imperatives guiding most textual criticism are, if not contradictory, at least in tension with one another: editors want to converge on the ideal work and at the same time provide readers as much information as possible about textual variants.[15] The Web promises to allow these dual imperatives to be more successfully integrated than ever before, as the William Blake Archive and McGann's work on the D. G. Rossetti Hypermedia Archive demonstrate. At the same time, perhaps ironically, the Web's remarkable flexibility and radically different instantiation of textuality also draw into question whether it is possible or desirable to converge on an ideal "work" at all. Educated by his work with the D. G. Rossetti Hypermedia Archive, McGann argues against convergence as a critical and theoretical principle, attempting to show through cogent readings of poetic works and other strategies that a text is never identical with itself.[16]

Instead he argues for the practice of what he calls "deformation," a mode of reading that seeks to liberate from the text the strategies by which it goes in search of meaning. Following the ideas of Galvano della Volpa, an Italian critic writing in the 1960s, McGann argues that meaning is not the goal of critical explication but a residue left over after critical interrogation is finished. Meaning itself cannot be the goal of critical explication, for "this would run the risk of suggesting that interpretation can be adequate to poiesis. It cannot" (*Radiant Textuality*, 130). Indeed, explication cannot be adequate even to its own understanding of itself, which can be accomplished only through an explication of the explication, which in turn requires another explication to try to get at the residue left over when these two explications are compared, and so on to infinity or to the exhaustion of the critical will. Underlying this argument is an implicit analogy. Just as textual criticism has traditionally tried to converge on an ideal work, so hermeneutical criticism has tried to converge on an ideal meaning. Echoing deconstructive theory more than he acknowledges, McGann asks what would happen if both kinds of enterprise were to abandon the movement toward convergence and were to try instead to liberate the multiplicities of texts through a series of deformations. Thus he is more interested (at least theoretically) in what deformations of Rossetti's images in Photoshop reveal about their composition than in the accomplishments of the William Blake Archive in simulating the color tones and sizes of the paper documents.[17]

This kind of argument opens the way for a disciplined inquiry into the differences in materiality between print and electronic textuality. As editor of the D. G. Rossetti Hypermedia Archive, McGann has had ample—one might almost say, painful—opportunity to appreciate the differences between the print and electronic text. Indeed, it is precisely this gap that leads him to think that John Unsworth's essay "The Importance of Failure" is so important. McGann's project is to convert the failure to make electronic textuality perform as an exact duplicate of print into a strength by using "deformation" as a tool for critical insight. He emphasizes the importance of *doing* and *making*, suggesting that practical experience in electronic textuality is a crucial prerequisite for theorizing about it. In this sense, his work represents an important advance over the rhetoric of the William Blake Archive (though not necessarily over its technical accomplishments), for he sees that electronic textuality can be used as something other than a simulacrum of print. Rather, he understands that it can provide a standpoint from which to rethink the resources of the print medium.

The impact of his experience is readily apparent in his redescriptions of print texts in terms that make them appear fully comparable to electronic texts. He argues, for example, that all texts are marked; he regards paragraph indentations and punctuation as forms of marking equivalent to HTML, the Hypertext Markup Language used to format documents for electronic environments. Moreover, he proposes that all texts are algorithmic, containing within themselves instructions to generate themselves as displays (the display form of the document here being considered distinct from the data and algorithms used to create it). So extensive and detailed are his redescriptions that one wonders if electronic text has any distinctive features of its own. The burden of his argument would suggest that it does not, an implication strengthened by his overly casual dismissal of the cases made by Janet Murray and Espen Aarseth for the specificities of electronic textuality.[18]

When push comes to pixel, it is clear that McGann's primary allegiance is to print rather than electronic textuality. He repeatedly asserts that the resources of the electronic medium pale in comparison to print.[19] Speaking specifically of fiction, he argues in *Radiant Textuality* that "there is no comparison . . . between the complexity and richness of paper-based fictional works, on the one hand, and their digital counterparts—hypermedia fiction—on the other" (130). Although he is too astute a critic to make comparisons directly, by juxtaposing in the next sentence Stuart Moulthrop with Italo Calvino, McGann implies that Moulthrop, a contemporary pioneer in electronic hypertext, is not as good a writer as Calvino, or at any rate does not produce literature of the same quality. Like many arguments McGann mounts to prove the superiority of print, the implied comparison here between print and electronic literature is seriously flawed. It is obviously inappropriate to compare a literary medium that has been in existence for fifteen years with print forms that have developed over half a millennium. A fairer comparison would be print literature produced from 1550 to 1565, when the conventions of print literature were still in their nascent stages, with the electronic literature produced from 1985 to 2000. I believe that anyone familiar with both canons would be forced to agree it is by no means obvious that the print canon demonstrates conclusively the superiority of print as a medium for literary creation and expression. Given five hundred years in which to develop—if we can possibly stretch our imaginations this far—electronic literature may indeed prove itself equal or superior to print.

If, as Mrs. Malaprop observes, comparisons are odorous (i.e., odious), this one is especially so. As McGann acknowledges, it should not be a question of pitting one medium against the other but of understanding the specificities of each. By using electronic textuality to better understand print, McGann opens the way for important insights into its possibilities. Unfortunately, he is not as successful in using print to understand the specificities of electronic textuality. When problems crop up in his arguments, they almost always stem from this source. He asserts, for example, that print text differs from itself, and he uses close readings to argue the point. But his argument confuses what happens in the mind of the reader with the stability of print in a given document. To demonstrate that print is unstable even at the level of a document, he scans a document with an optical character reader and reports that the machine gives different readings on different scans. However, this experiment does not demonstrate that print is not self-identical, but only that the translation between print and electronic text is unstable.

In other arguments, he conflates the instability of a text—for example, variations in different copies of an edition or between different editions—with the instability of a print document, again to argue that print, like electronic text, is fluid and unstable.[20] The stubborn fact remains, however, that once ink is impressed on paper, it remains relatively stable and immovable. The few exceptions that might be invoked—for example, an artist's book created with thermochromic ink that changes color when heated by a hand touch, or print impressed on cutouts that move—should not be allowed to obscure the general observation that the print of a given document is stable for (more or less) long periods of time, in dramatic contrast to the constant refreshing of a computer screen many times each second. Moreover, print does not normally move once impressed onto the paper fiber, again in contrast to the animations, rollover, and other such features that increasingly characterize electronic literature. No print document can be reprogrammed once the ink has been impressed onto the paper, whereas electronic texts routinely can. These differences do not mean, of course, that print is inferior to electronic text, only that it is different. Admitting these differences does not diminish the complexity and flexibility of print books, which have resources different than those of electronic texts; but it does pave the way for understanding the specificities of electronic textuality and, thereby, coming to a fuller appreciation of its resources.

What, then, are these differences, and what are their implications for theories of textuality? Mats Dahlström tackles this question in his exploration of how notions of a scholarly edition might change with electronic textuality.[21] He makes the important point, also noted by Anna Gunder in "Forming the Text, Performing the Work," that with electronic texts there is a conceptual distinction—and often an actualized one—between storage and delivery vehicles, whereas with print the storage and delivery vehicles are one and the same. With electronic texts, the data files may be on one server and the machine creating the display may be in another location entirely, which means that electronic text exists as a distributed phenomenon. The dispersion introduces many possible sources of variation into the production of electronic text that do not exist in the same way with print, for example, when a user's browser displays a text with different colors than those the writer saw on her machine when she was creating it. More fundamental is the fact that the text exists in dispersed fashion even when it is confined to a single machine. There are data files, programs that call and process the files, hardware functionalities that interpret or compile the programs, and so on. It takes all of these together to produce the electronic text. Omit any one of them, and the text literally cannot be produced. For this reason it would be more accurate to call an electronic text a *process* than an object. Certainly it cannot be identified with, say, a diskette or a CD-ROM, for these alone can never produce a text unless they are performed by the appropriate software running on the appropriate hardware.

Let me emphasize that this processing is necessarily prior to whatever cognitive processing the user performs to read and interpret the text. Although print readers perform sophisticated cognitive operations when they read a book, the printed lines exist as such before the book is opened, read, or understood. An electronic text does not have this kind of prior existence. It does not exist anywhere in the computer, or in the networked system, in the form it acquires when displayed on screen. After it is displayed, of course, readerly processing may occur, as with print. But we should not indulge in the logical confusion that results when it is assumed that the creation of the display—a process that happens only when the programs that create the text are activated—entails the same operations as a reader's cognitive processing. In this sense, electronic text is more processual than print; it is performative by its very nature—independent of whatever imaginations and processes the user brings to it, and regardless of variations between editions and copies.

Acknowledging these differences, Mats Dahlström argues that electronic text should be understood as consisting, at bottom, of binary code, the sequences of ones and zeros that underlie all the languages built on top of them. But defining electronic text in this way, a move reminiscent of Friedrich Kittler's argument in "There Is No Software,"[22] inexplicably privileges binary code over all the other things necessary to produce the text as a document a user can read. In insisting further that electronic text is above all a pattern, Dahlström risks reinscribing the dematerialization so prominently on display in Shillingsburg's definition of "text" as a sequence of words and pauses. If the idea of *print* text as a dematerialized entity is already a fiction (however convenient), how much more fictional is the idea of an electronic text as binary code, when how that code is stored, processed, and displayed is utterly dependent on the nature of the hardware and software? Perhaps it is time to think the unthinkable—to posit a notion of "text" that is not dematerialized and that does depend on the substrate in which it is instantiated. Rather than stretch the fiction of dematerialization thinner and thinner, why not explore the possibilities of texts that thrive on the entwining of physicality with informational structure?

This is where I think McGann is trying to go with his argument that texts are never self-identical, an insight he is developing further in his present work on the quantum nature of textuality (i.e., textuality that is unresolvably ambiguous until a reader interacts with it in a specific way). As we have seen, if one accepts the physicality of the text, then the door opens to an array of infinite difference, with no text identical to any others because there are always differences between any two physical objects, however minute. Although McGann does not fully develop the point with regard to electronic textuality, his argument that a text is not physically self-identical (which he applies mostly to print) is mere common sense with electronic texts. Consider, for example, the time it takes images to appear on screen when they are being drawn from a remote server. Certainly the time lag is an important component of the electronic text, for it determines in what order the user will view the material. Indeed, as anyone who has grown impatient with long load times knows, in many instances it determines whether the user will see the image at all. These times are difficult to predict precisely because they depend on the individual computer's processing speed, traffic on the Web, efficiency of data distribution on the hard drive, and other imponderables. This aspect of electronic textuality—along with many others—*cannot be separated from the delivery vehicles that produce it as a process with which the user can interact.* Moreover, for networked texts, these vehicles are never

the same twice, for they exist in momentary configurations as data packets are switched quickly from one node to another, depending on traffic at
the instant of transfer. In this respect and many others, electronic texts are
indeed not self-identical. As processes they exhibit sensitive dependence on
temporal and spatial contexts, to say nothing of their absolute dependence
on specific hardware and software configurations. Rita Raley points to this
aspect of electronic textuality in her emphasis on performance. Seeking to
locate the differences between print and electronic texts, she remarks, "The
operative difference of hypertext can only be revealed in the performing and
tracing of itself, in its own instantiation."[23]

What are the consequences of the idea that textuality is instantiated rather
than dematerialized, dispersed rather than unitary, processual rather than
object-like, flickering rather than durably imprinted? The specter haunting
textual criticism is the nightmare that one cannot then define a "text" at
all, for every manifestation will qualify as a different text. Pervasive with
electronic texts, the problem troubles notions of print texts as well, for as
physical objects they also differ from one another. But this need not be a
catastrophe if we refine and revise our notion of materiality.

Let us begin rethinking materiality by noting that it is impossible to
specify precisely what a book—or any other text—is as a physical object,
for there are an infinite number of ways its physical characteristics can be
described. Speaking of an electronic text, for example, we could focus on the
polymers used to make the plastic case or the palladium used in the power
cord. The physical instantiation of a text will in this sense always be indeterminate. What matters for understanding literature, however, is how the text
creates possibilities for meaning by mobilizing certain aspects of its physicality. These will necessarily be a small subset of all possible characteristics.
For some texts, such as Edwin Schlossberg's artist's book *Wordswordswords*,
the activated physical characteristics may include the paper on which the
words are impressed. For other texts, the paper's contribution may be neg-
ligible.

The following definition provides a way to think about texts as embodied
entities without falling into the chaos of infinite difference: *The materiality of an embodied text is the interaction of its physical characteristics with
its signifying strategies.*[24] Centered in the artifact, this notion of materiality
extends beyond the individual object, for its physical characteristics are the
result of the social, cultural, and technological processes that brought it into
being. As D. F. McKenzie has argued in the context of the editorial theory of
"social texts," social processes too are part of a text's materiality, which leads

to the conclusion that it is impossible to draw a firm distinction between bibliographic and interpretive concerns. In *Bibliography and the Sociology of Texts*, his influential Panizzi lectures, McKenzie comments, "My own view is that no such border exists" (23). Because materiality in this view is bound up with the text's content, it cannot be specified in advance, as if it existed independent of content. Rather, it is an *emergent* property. What constitutes the materiality of a given text will always be a matter of interpretation and critical debate; what some readers see as physical properties brought into play may not appear so to other readers. But this is not the end of the world as textual criticism has known it. Indeed, it is normal procedure for literary scholars to consider a "text" as something negotiated among a community of readers, infinitely interpretable and debatable. McKenzie's definition of "text" includes "verbal, visual, oral and numeric data, in the form of maps, prints, and music, of archives of recorded sound, of films, videos, and *any* computer-stored information" (5). Moreover, he emphasizes that the recognized negotiations that occur with print works should be extended to electronic works.

Work as Assemblage

The specter of never being able to claim that different documents constitute the same text now appears much less threatening. Critical debate will explore whether there are sufficient differences in materiality (which in this definition cannot simply be collapsed into physicality) between two documents to warrant considering them different texts. If strong cases can be made for differences in how the materialities of the two documents are mobilized, then perhaps they should be considered different texts. Common sense is not violated by supposing that a penny broadside bound in a handsome red cover and signed for with due ceremony in the Rare Book Room of the British Museum is a different text than the same broadside snatched from the gutter and quickly scanned in Shakespeare's London. Indeed, it would strain credulity to suppose that the different physical instantiations of these two documents has no effect on how and what they signify (I speak here only of the physical differences, not the inevitable differences also introduced by culture, language, etc., though these too obviously play a role in how materiality will emerge). In this account of embodied textuality, texts would spread out along a spectrum of similarity and difference, and clusters would emerge. Texts that differed only slightly would occupy adjacent points (say, different editions that closely matched each other in physical characteristics), whereas outlying members of the cluster might include texts in different media (Braille rather than print, an electronic version of a print text, a film version of a novel, etc.).[25] These clusters could usefully be considered to constitute a "work," without implying that "work" is a single convergent object. Editors might argue, for example, that a given edition should be privileged because it is positioned at the center of a cluster, or they might discuss an edition in terms of some notion of a weighted average. In a sense, of course, editors already work in this way. What would change is not so much editorial practice as the conceptual framework and vocabulary invoked to explain and justify an edition.

Perhaps the most important consequence to emerge from this new framework would be preventing the text from being thinned out of existence as a physical object. Texts would be routinely discussed in terms of *both* their conceptual content and their physical embodiments. In some instances, a text would remain relatively constant over many documents, assuming that debate led to agreement that the physical differences between the documents were not important as signifying components. In other instances, there could be as many texts as there are documents. Neither document, text, nor work would be considered immaterial; all would be invested with nuanced senses of their materialities, a viewpoint that would further energize and foreground discussions of how physical characteristics, verbal content, and nonverbal signifying strategies work together to produce the object called "text."

These changed senses of work, text, and document make it possible to see phenomena that are now obscured or made invisible by the reigning ideologies. For example, with the advent of the Web, communication pathways are established through which texts cycle in dynamic intermediation with one another, which leads to what might be called Work as Assemblage, a cluster of related texts that quote, comment upon, amplify, and otherwise intermediate one another. One form of such an assemblage is illustrated by L. J. Winson's Dark Lethe, a science-fiction Web site at which collaborators contribute stories loosely related to one another. Another example, suggested by David Silver, is the cluster of texts associated with *Myst*. This cluster includes, in addition to the computer game and its companion game *Riven*, Web sites populated by devotees of the games, as well as the associated print novels that expand upon the narratives in the games and that supply backstories and other plot details missing from the games.[26]

Yet another example is the cluster of texts around *House of Leaves*, Mark Danielewski's brilliant contemporary print novel. *House of Leaves* was published on the Web before being instantiated in print. The print novel itself exists in four different editions, each significantly different from the others. Also in the cluster is a Web site devoted to the novel, on which hundreds of readers make postings exploring details of the print novels. Still other examples include the now common practice of setting up Web sites to go along with the release of new films. Although most of these sites are merely publicity vehicles, a new genre is emerging in which the site is an independent aesthetic production initiating media-specific strategies to transform, subvert, and play with the film's material. The fascinating site for *Requiem for a Dream* includes pseudo-advertisements, graphic mutations of scenes and characters from the film, and reinscriptions of scraps of dialogue recontextualized visually and verbally to interrogate their meanings—an assemblage that constitutes a new art form, according to Jack Post's compelling argument.[27]

Going along with the idea of Work as Assemblage are changed constructions of subjectivity. The notion of the literary work as an ideal immaterial construction has been deeply influenced by a unitary view of the subject, particularly in the decades when editors sought to arrive at the work by determining an author's "final intentions." The work as it was formulated using this principle in turn reinforced a certain view of the author as a literary figure. As the discussion in chapter 6 on the history of copyright will make clear (in a different context), the unitary work and the unified subject mutually reinforced and determined each other. As the rest of critical theory and cultural studies deconstructed the unified subject and exposed the problematic ideological bases on which it rested, editorial criticism underwent similar revisionist movements, particularly in Jerome McGann's arguments for the "social text."[28] Perhaps now it is time to think about what kinds of textuality a dispersed, fragmented, and heterogeneous view of the subject might imply.

An appropriate model may present itself in Gilles Deleuze and Félix Guattari's rhizomatic Body without Organs (BwO), a construction that in its constant deterritorialization and reterritorialization has no unified essence or identifiable center, only planes of consistency and lines of flight along which elements move according to the charged vectors of desire.[29] The rather esoteric vocabulary invoked here is part of Deleuze and Guattari's project to change the emphasis from objects to processes, and from hierarchical structures to rhizomatic ones. The examples given above of the Work as Assemblage (which by analogy can be abbreviated as the WaA) illustrate clusters of texts that take the distinctive form of rhizomatic tendrils branching out from one another in patterns of fractal complexity. WaA in this view is not an aberration but a paradigmatic configuration that writes large the dynamics of intermediation and media specificity at work in all embodied texts. Rather than being bound into the straitjacket of a work possessing an immaterial essence that textual criticism strives to identify and stabilize, the WaA derives its energy from its ability to mutate and transform as it grows and shrinks, converges and disperses according to the desires of the loosely formed collectives that create it. Moving fluidly among and across media, its components take forms distinctive to the media in which they flourish, so the specificities of media are essential to understanding its morphing configurations.

To see such possibilities—to bring the Work as Assemblage into sight at all—requires a fundamentally different view of authorship than that which undergirds the idea of the work as an immaterial verbal construction. The subjectivity implied by the WaA cannot by any stretch of the imagination be considered unified, a point that Deleuze and Guattari make in another context by replacing a coherent subject with the flows of desire associated with the Body without Organs. Similarly, the subjects producing the WaA are multiple in many senses, both because they are collectivities in and among themselves, and also because they include nonhuman as well as human actors, a dynamic I will explore in chapter 6 by considering the monstrously fragmented and dispersed narrator of Shelley Jackson's *Patchwork Girl*. As this work emphasizes, with an electronic text the computer is also a writer, and the software programs it runs to produce the text as process and display also have complex and multiple authorship (not to mention the authoring done by hardware engineers in configuring the logic gates that create the bit stream). A robust account of materiality focusing on the recursive loops between physicality and textuality is essential to understanding the dynamics of the WaA. Once we let go of the assumption that the literary work must be an expression of an immaterial essence—a line of thought dominant in literary criticism at least since the eighteenth century—we see the new forms of textuality that, racing ahead of textual theory, are already cycling through diverse media in exuberant and playful performances that defy the old verities even as they give rise to the new.

The present moment presents us with a rare opportunity to break out of assumptions that have congealed around the technology of print, rendered transparent by centuries of continuing development, refinement, and use. This opportunity is powerfully present in the implicit juxtaposition of print and electronic textuality. The game is to understand both print and electronic textuality more deeply through their similarities and differences. McGann's project of revitalizing our understanding of print by redescribing it in terms usually used for electronic text is a seminal contribution. The very comprehensiveness that makes his redescriptions so valuable, however, also works to obscure differences between the two media. But a nuanced understanding of the differences is as important to the project as a deep appreciation for the similarities.

The primary difference is the fact that an electronic text is generated through multiple layers of code processed by an intelligent machine *before* a human reader decodes the information. McGann argues that print texts are also coded, but this point relies on slippage between the narrow sense of code as it applies to computers and a more general sense of code as Roland Barthes envisions it, including codes of social decorum, fashion, polite conversation, and so on.[30] In the narrow sense in which code operates in computers, code can be defined as a system of correspondences that relate the elements of one symbol set to another symbol set, for example, when Morse code associates dots and dashes with alphabetic letters. Unlike Morse code, however, code within the computer is *active*, for it functions as instructions that initiate changes in the system's behavior.

Working with these instructions, writers develop a nuanced sense of code as a form of writing with its own stylistic elegance and formal possibilities. Increasingly, writers of electronic literature view code as a resource for signifying practices. Reviewing some of this work, Loss Pequeño Glazier, a distinguished writer of electronic poetry as well as a critic, observes that programming *is* writing (a point also made by John Cayley).[31] In *Dig[iT]al Poet(I)(c)s*, Glazier argues that users who want to understand how an electronic text works cannot afford simply to stay at the surface level of the screenic text, any more than a writer can afford to know nothing about how screenic text is generated and displayed. Agreeing with McGann that the defining characteristic of literary language is the impulse to investigate its conditions of possibility, Glazier names literary writing as "writing that, whether or not it serves other ends, has an engagement with its own formal qualities" (54). He sees print and electronic text on a continuum, arguing that "innovative literature" in both media "has explored the conditions that determine . . . the procedure, processes, and crossed paths of meaning-making, meaning-making as constituting the 'meaning'" (32). As Glazier points out, print writers have also explored the materiality of the medium, from the typewriter poems of Ian Hamilton Finlay to the Mimeo movement and concrete poetry. The specificity of electronic media, he implies, lies in its distinctive materiality: "materiality is key to understanding innovative practice" (22).

These useful insights are somewhat offset by Glazier's tendency to elevate his preferred genre—poetry—and his preferred set of literary strategies at the expense of narrative and "non-innovative literature," a back formation that certainly does not do justice to the complexity of other literary strategies. Although he has a remarkable sense of the possibilities for electronic poetry, his remarks on non-innovative literature are flat to the point of unintentional parody. "Non-innovative literature," he writes, "can be said to possess a number of distinguishing textual features. These can include narrative, plot, anecdotal re-telling of human experiences, logical descriptions, chronological sequence of events, a reliance on factual information, a view of language as a transparent (at most, tinted) bearer of meaning, and an attachment to a Modernist aesthetic" (47). The underlying culprit in his view is "the position of the 'I,'" which non-innovative literature constructs by asserting "forms of authority" and creating "a nonpermeable (or semipermeable) filter between the ego and the world" (48). Although Glazier tends to identify these qualities with narrative, which apparently for him is virtually synonymous with bad literature, I suspect that non-innovative literature as he characterizes it is an empty set. Does there exist any important Modernist text for which a convincing critical argument could not be made that it destabilizes language, subjectivity, and consciousness? As Johanna Drucker comments in her review of Glazier's book, "The traditions of innovation from which Glazier draws for support are often broader in their scope and of much more complex development than his taking up them within late twentieth century references would imply."[32]

These caveats notwithstanding, Glazier makes an important point when he says that innovative literature tends to interrogate its materiality, an observation that returns us to our starting place with renewed urgency. If literature and materiality are indeed closely entwined, what happens when a text is translated into a different medium than that in which it was originally created? I began this chapter with a reference to Borges's "The Don Quixote of Pierre Menard," which suggests slyly that the same words in the same order can nevertheless mean something utterly different when transported into a new context. In this sense Pierre Menard's project is analogous to the translation of a literary text into a new medium, for the same words appear in the same order, yet like Menard's "Don Quixote," they may mean something very different than in the original. Indeed, I use the term "media translation" to suggest that recreating a text in another medium is so significant a change that it is analogous to translating from one language to another. Unlike Pierre Menard's project, language translation changes both the words and their order, and in this sense is unlike (most) media translation. Nevertheless, the analogy with language translation can offer useful insights into the problems and possibilities that haunt media translation. I turn now to explore in more depth the resonances evoked by this imperfect and yet provocative analogy.

Intermediating between Language Translation and Media Translation: Implications for Textuality

As we saw in chapter 2, the performative power of networked and programmable media that enables them to simulate print texts so successfully is deeply related to what Rita Raley calls the "tower of programming languages," a point John Cayley explicates when he refers to "machine code, tokenized code, low-level languages, high-level languages, scripting languages, macro languages, markup languages, Operating Systems and their scripting language," and so on, all stacked in different levels.[33] Raley's phrase alludes, of course, to the Tower of Babel, a mythic origin story that was also important to Warren Weaver's seminal memorandum of July 15, 1949, subsequently published as an essay.[34] In "The New Tower," a foreword to the volume in which his essay appeared, Weaver suggested that machine translation should be seen as a "Tower of Anti-Babel," since in his optimistic expectation it promised to allow "men to communicate freely" despite differences in language.[35] In the essay he relates an incident in World War II in which a cryptographer successfully decrypted a message in Turkish, although he did not know that the source text was written in Turkish and did not himself read Turkish. Weaver recounts sending a letter to Norbert Wiener in which he suggested that machine translation should be treated as a problem in cryptography: "It is very tempting to say that a book written in Chinese is simply a book written in English which was coded into the 'Chinese code.' If we have useful methods for solving almost any cryptographic problem, may it not be that with proper interpretation we already have useful methods for translation?" (22).[36] Raley rightly criticizes the hegemonic implication here that all languages are in some sense already English.[37] Additionally, there is a fallacy, as W. J. Hutchins points out in his critique of the memorandum, that stems from Weaver's equation of decryption and translation.[38] Whereas a successful decryption can render a message exactly as it was before it was encrypted, no translation, no matter how successful, ever renders the original exactly the same as it was in the source language. The problem, of course, lies in the fact that languages and cultures are inextricably entwined; words resonate with connotations that drift like fragrances on a breeze, impossible to duplicate in all their subtleties and complexities in another language.[39]

To be fair to Weaver, he acknowledged that literary language constituted a special case. His proposal was aimed at utilitarian texts where only the information is important, such as when a plane would take off or how to install a carburetor. Nevertheless, even this much more modest project had a theory of language undergirding it, and it is here that his project recalls contemporary claims that the computer is the ultimate medium capable of dissolving all other media in itself. Returning to the Tower of Babel metaphor, he asks us to "think, by analogy, of individuals living in a series of tall closed towers, all erected over a common foundation. When they try to communicate with one another, they shout back and forth, each from his own closed tower. It is difficult to make the sound penetrate even the nearest towers, and communication proceeds very poorly indeed. But, when an individual goes down his tower, he finds himself in a great open basement, common to all towers. Here he establishes easy and useful communication with the persons who have also descended from their towers" (23).[40] In context, Weaver believed that the "great open basement" would be a universal substratum common to all languages. His hope finds a different instantiation in the coding of many different kinds of documents—not only words but also sounds, images, films, etc.—in the binary code that operates in the "basement" of the tower of languages.[41] Not a universal grammar, then, but a universal machine that has its own grammar of code.

Today, code and linguistic translation come together in machine translation, which normally consists of a dictionary that matches terms in one language with those in another, plus a context interpreter. Although great strides have been made in machine translation—a highly technical field that has expanded far beyond Weaver's ideas—many instances remain where human translators are necessary. Even here, however, computers have dramatically changed how translations are done. Jules van Lieshout, co-owner of a translation company in the Netherlands, has writes compellingly in "The New Alchemists" about his experiences translating documentation for the automobile industry.[42] He notes that the practices of the software industry are rapidly becoming the accepted business model for companies that, in Nicholas Negroponte's phrase, "manufacture atoms rather than distribut[e] bits." Van Lieshout observes, "You do not buy software, you rent a first draft, [in a] beta society that markets patches rather than engineer[s] innovation. There may be failures, but no product recalls. In . . . a genuine marketing triumph, the buyer has turned into an unpaid beta tester with the software automatically reporting errors to the developer" (1). Taking its cue from the software industry, the manufacturing sector dreams of documentation that flows frictionlessly between media and languages, that is produced at a speed comparable to the short life span of documentation itself, and that is driven by the relentless cycles of innovation and obsolescence characteristic of capitalist practices.

To minimize costs, manufacturers now use software such as Content Management Systems and Workflow Systems, which control and regulate the authoring and production of documentation. When a new version of a document is needed, they use software such as Translation Memory Systems and Machine Translation Systems to identify and extract all the required changes, recycling everything that has not changed directly into the new version from the old. This practice in itself impacts language use, for manufacturers instruct their technical writers not to correct or change anything that is not absolutely necessary (e.g., punctuation errors or stylistic infelicities), because every change, no matter how trivial, will be routed to the human translators, and so cost them money. Thus language is driven to the lowest common denominator even before the translators receive it.

Moreover, what the translators receive are now only snippets, often phrases or parts of phrases and sometimes only single words. Rarely is the full context available to them, making it impossible for them to translate accurately words or phrases that change meaning according to context. Presumably they could look up the context in earlier versions of the documentation, but this would cost time and money that the manufacturers are not willing to pay. "Ensuring that only the new information is translated," van Lieshout writes, "documentation and translation tools help manufacturers meet their cost-efficiency and time-to-market requirements. The underlying idea is: translate once, never look back" (2). As a result, he concludes, "documentation has become a continuous flow of information. Documentation is an ongoing process where the lack of time and money dictate that information be reused as many times as possible for as many different audiences as possible. In the process, the atom of documentation has been reduced to what may be called an Information Entity, Information Unit, or Information Block. . . . It is the documentation equivalent of component carry-over from one model to the next, component interchangeability between models, and nameplates sharing platforms" (2). Here the fragmentation of code that in programmable media translates into high-level flexibility operates, directly and indirectly, to fragment language and reduce its complexities to small pieces. Slightly modifying van Lieshout's nomenclature, we might call these pieces TIB (The Information Block), mirror image of the BIT (Binary Digit). Cramming language into the Procrustean bed of TIB would have disastrous effects, were it not for the fact that documentation is increasingly written to fulfill legal requirements rather than to produce something buyers can use to understand the products they have purchased.

Faced with these relentless practices that aim to produce only instrumental prose (at best), I can almost sympathize with the tack taken by Walter Benjamin in his famous essay, "The Task of the Translator." He begins by ruling out of court the utilitarian considerations that were paramount for Weaver. "What does a literary work 'say'? What does it communicate? It 'tells' very little to those who understand it. Its essential quality is not statement or the imparting of information" (69). He asserts that only bad translations "perform a transmitting function" of relaying information (69). Rather, he proposes that all languages necessarily embody perspectives that are historically and culturally specific; if they were somehow all to contribute their perspectives to make up a totality, this impossible and elusive entity would be language itself, "pure language" (79). The translator, in Benjamin's view, aims to find the echo or reflection of pure language in the source text and highlight it, bringing it from its hidden implicitness into the light by activating within the historical specificity of the target language a comparable resonance. "It is the task of the translator to release in his own language that pure language which is under the spell of another, to liberate the language imprisoned in a work in his re-creation of that work" (80). In this way, translation contributes uniquely to the literary enterprise, Benjamin suggests, by creating an *emergence*, a glimpse of the pure language that could not be seen as clearly without the conjunction of the source and target languages that the translation performs.

Compare this vision, and the metaphors Benjamin mobilizes to express it, with Weaver's metaphor of separate towers connected by a subterranean basement. Whereas Weaver wants to go down to find the common elements—down to universal grammar, code elements, or in contemporary usage, BITS and TIBS—Benjamin consistently uses metaphors suggesting that the appropriate action is to go up, asserting that "the ultimate purpose toward which all single functions tend is sought not in its own sphere but in a higher one" (72). In translation, he insists, "the original rises into a higher and purer linguistic air" (75). Whereas Weaver focuses on fragmentation and the benefits it can bestow, Benjamin envisions fitting together the fragments into larger wholes. "Languages are not strangers to one another, but are, a priori and apart from all historical relationships, interrelated in what they want to express," he writes (72). This interrelation he imagines as the gluing together of a broken vessel, whose fragments "must match one another in the smallest details, although they need not be like one another. In the same way a translation, instead of resembling the meaning of the original, must lovingly and in detail incorporate the original's mode of signification, thus making both the original and the translation recognizable as fragments of a greater language, just as fragments are part of a vessel" (78).

The problem with this idealistic view, as I see it, is its insistent evocation of "pure language," a transcendental mode of signification so "pure" that it "no longer means or expresses anything but is, as expressionless and creative Word, that which is meant in all languages" (80). Whereas Weaver proposes to overcome Babel by going into the basement, Benjamin evokes the Tower of Babel as a subtext and seems to imply that we can return to the "pure language" spoken before languages differentiated or, even better, before the language of "man" separated from the Word of God. It is scarcely surprising, then, that he ends his essay by evoking the "Holy Writ," where "language and revelation are one without any tension" (82). At that ideal point, media would cease to matter, for language would have escaped from historical specificity, cultural perspective, and material instantiation to become the pure and perfect Word, impervious to the operations of reference and signification. So mystical a vision can have its justification only in an intense desire to rescue literature, translation, and language itself from base and instrumental purposes. However understandable the desire, this is not a theory that describes language as it actually works and as it is instantiated and performed in media.

Positioned somewhere between Weaver and Benjamin is Jorge Luis Borges. Here we may refer profitably to the brilliant work Efrain Kristal has done on Borges's idea of translation.[43] Kristal shows compellingly that Borges thought of all writing as translation, not in the strong sense that Octavio Paz employs of writing as a translation of experience, but in the sense of all writing as a stab in the dark at articulating meanings that always remain to some extent elusive.[44] Rather than hoping for a common substratum that would provide the key to universal translation or evoking a "pure language" indistinguishable from the Word of God, Borges delighted in thinking of all writings as drafts in progress, imperfect instantiations never fully one with the significations toward which they gesture. In this view, texts are provocations to go in search of meaning (echoing McGann); when they become instantiated in a given set of words (and we may add, a given medium and performance in that medium), they necessarily miss some possibilities even as they realize others. Hence for Borges it is entirely possible for an original text to be unfaithful to its translation (in the sense of being inferior to its successor), for the translation may realize more fully possibilities that were only nascent in the original. Indeed, this view draws into question the very idea of an "original," for temporal priority does not signify ontological priority when the original is regarded as simply one draft among many. Kristal comments, "Depending on the specific case, [Borges] at times favored a translation over its original, other times an original over its translation, and he was often interested in weighing their relative merits, aesthetic and otherwise."[45]

Borges's idea of "originals" as provocations to go in search of meaning fits well with the idea of Work as Assemblage, for like the restless workings of desire and lines of flight that trace territorializations and deterritorializations of the Body without Organs, texts in an assemblage intermediate one another without necessarily bestowing on any one text the privileged status of the "original." Everything is simultaneously a translation of everything else, each united to the others in a rhizomatic network without a clear beginning or end. That Borges arrived at this view while working exclusively in print should caution us not to overstate the fluidity of electronic texts compared to print. The advantages of programmable media notwithstanding, there is a long history of using the resources of print to achieve fluidity and indeterminacy, as Johanna Drucker, among others, has argued powerfully in her critical writing and demonstrated in her creative work.[46] It remains the case, however, that the resources of print are *different* than the resources of electronic textuality, and that each medium interacts with and influences the others.

How might Borges's perspective apply to media translations? Let us return to consider the works of William Blake in this light. Van Lieshout, a Blake scholar as well as a professional translator, comments that Blake, in running off his books on his own printing press, used the freedom "to recreate every single work over and over again, and he did so consciously and deliberately. . . . Blake would have loved the flexibility and possibility that computers give artists. . . . Basically he was Photoshopping in the early nineteenth century."[47] In this sense, the William Blake Archive, rather than being judged solely on the basis of providing a faithful reenactment of Blake's print works, might be regarded as also providing an opportunity to go freshly in search of meanings highlighted in new ways by electronic media. My UCLA colleague Anne Mellor, a specialist in the Romantic period, observes that the William Blake Archive brings out an aspect of Blake's works that tends to be somewhat obscured by the print medium, namely, its hypertextual links and connections. Like van Lieshout, she suspects that if Blake were alive today, he would find authoring and production systems in programmable media entirely congenial to his vision.[48]

Another example of this kind of intermediation is provided by Raymond Queneau's *Cent mille milliards de poèmes*. One might argue that this work is an attempt to do in a print medium what can be done more easily and "naturally" in programmable media. In the latter, instead of cutting the page into strips and juxtaposing the lines in new combinations that generate a virtually endless variety of sonnets—the operation Queneau suggests in his print version—the entire corpus of possible poems can be generated electronically and presented to the user as a random series of novel productions, as Nicholas Gessler has done in his C++ simulation.[49] A program similar to Gessler's was written by Andrew J. Lurie,[50] who adapted it from the "Chomskybot" program created by John Lawler (and others), which generates new paragraphs using a randomizing program that splices together phrases from Noam Chomsky's writings. This program in turn was adapted from a still earlier program called "foggy," created by one of Lawler's former students and popular around IBM.[51]

Like Borges's idea of translations as drafts circulating along with the original in a stream of provisional attempts, so here programs circulate as patchwork productions building on earlier ones and recycling code. John Lawler's comments are interesting in this regard. He writes, "What I find interesting about [the program] is how it just *hovers* at the edge of understandability, a sort of semantic mumbling, a fog for the mind's eye. . . . Foggy's most interesting effects are in the mind of the beholder."[52] Rather than aiming at a pure language, code here recycles "original" language in random patterns that cross and recross the threshold of intelligibility, inviting the reader's projection into the echoic effects, as if infecting language with the random access memory of computer storage.

Through the feedback loops in which electronic text recycles print and the programs generating electronic text recycle code, we glimpse the complex dynamics by which intermediation connects print and electronic text, language and code, "original" and translation, the specificities of particular instantiations and the endless novelty of recombinations. These dynamics open out onto fundamental questions about the nature of texts, the relation of materiality to content, and the specificities of media. We already know that language matters. Media translation and the conjunctions it performs with print and electronic textualities can give us a deeper appreciation for the corollary propositions that media and materiality also matter.

5 Performative Code and Figurative Language
Neal Stephenson's *Cryptonomicon*

The previous chapter explored the theoretical implications for textuality of translating print literature into digital media. This chapter looks at a work that remains in print but nevertheless bears within its body marks of its electronic composition. With the exception of a handful of fine letterpress books, every book produced in the United States and Europe this year will have been an electronic document in at least one and probably many stages of its existence. Given present modes of book production, it is more accurate to view print as a particular form of output for electronic text than it is to regard print as a realm separate from digital media. Florian Cramer, in thinking about the significance of digital code for literary texts, remarks that "juxtapositions of 'the book' and 'the computer' are quite misleading, because they confuse the storage and analog output media (paper versus a variety of optical, magnetical, and electronical technologies) with the information (alphabetical text versus binary code)."[1] Moreover, Cramer points out that "text and literature are highly privileged symbolic systems in these translation processes because a) they are already coded and b) computers run on code."[2] These comments point to the interpenetration of print with electronic textuality, language with code, even when the focus is on a print book that appears entirely conventional in appearance.

In the contemporary period, print books evolve through the interplay between two different vectors, one rooted in the past and the other arching toward the future, as they negotiate between the centuries-long traditions of bookmaking art and the new possibilities opened by digital media. Tensions between past and future are particularly acute at the present moment when the narrative conventions of the novel, rooted in the seventeenth century, are inscribed with writing technologies profoundly different from the mechanical printing presses with which the history of the novel is deeply entwined. Through what pathways and by what means does the influence of an informatic writing technology, with its complex trading zones in which language and code mutually put pressure on one another, penetrate into a book that on the surface appears as ink marks on paper? Assuming these subterranean perturbations exist, what critical strategies might be used to excavate them?

To explore these questions, I take as my tutor text Neal Stephenson's *Cryptonomicon*. As its name indicates, code is at the center of its thematic concerns, both as cryptological system and computer algorithm. Its material form took shape through the interpenetration of code and language, for Stephenson's compositional habits are typical in combining old with new media. According to his comments in interviews, he writes first drafts with a fountain pen and paper, revising two or three times on paper, and then types the revised version into a computer, revising yet again as he does so.[3]

With an impressive background as a computer programmer, Stephenson does not employ the ubiquitous Windows or even Macintosh but interfaces with the computer through a Unix-based operating system.[4] As his nonfiction work *In the Beginning Was the Command Line* testifies, he shifted from Macintosh to Unix when a crisis erupted in his compositional practices. He regarded this shift as so significant that he wrote a book explaining why Unix is far superior to any other operating system and exhorting his readers to experience similar enlightenment.[5] The crisis that led to his conversion came when he lost a large file that was corrupted so badly it could not be recovered in its entirety. *Cryptonomicon*, published in the same year as *Command Line* and thus in some sense its sibling text, was almost certainly marked by his conversion to Unix, since he switched in 1995 and the book was written from 1995 to 1998. Following this line of thought, we can assume that the clash of operating systems—including all that it implies about the nefarious corporate practices of Microsoft, the capitalistic greed that underlies its ruthless business practices, and the resistance to these practices by open source communities, particularly Unix and the related Linux—penetrated deeply into the electronic structure of this text in physical and material ways. Are there connections between these material manifestations of coding practices and the linguistic surface of the text? Through what means do they mark the work when it is manifested as a print book, that is, when the flickering signifiers of the electronic text have been converted to durable impressions on paper?

To ask these questions is to regard the book not as a fixed and static artifact but as the trace of complex technological, conceptual, linguistic, and cryptological negotiations. In this chapter I argue that in *Cryptonomicon* a series of systematic transformations bears witness to these negotiations. These transformations involve dialectical attempts to mitigate the tensions inherent in the clashes of materiality and abstraction, code and language, hackers and corporate moguls, good profit and evil greed. Cycling through a series of dialectic juxtapositions, the narrative is unable to achieve a final resting point, a resolution stable enough to permit it to effect a rising action that would lead to a satisfying climax and clear denouement. The failure of the text to conform to these expectations signals that despite its traditional physical appearance and conventional narrative techniques, the literary corpus is riven by the writing technologies that produced it. Wrenched from the context of mechanical printing presses and embedded within informational technologies, this novel tries its best to remain a conventional narrative, but the differences between durable marks and flickering signifiers, natural language and computer code, de-form the form and unsettle its dynamics.[6] Finally the text is forced into oxymoronic knots that bring together opposites and entwine them so closely that they cannot be separated. Only through such devices can the text articulate its contradictory enunciations of code/language and the conflicting historical vectors of mechanical past/informatic future.

Math and Lizards: The Dialectic's First Terms

The basic problem for Lawrence was that he was lazy. He had figured out that everything was much simpler if, like Superman with his X-ray vision, you just stared through the cosmetic distractions and saw the underlying mathematical skeleton. Once you found the math in a thing, you knew everything about it, and you could manipulate it to your heart's content with nothing more than a pencil and a napkin. (8)

Sand erupts into the air, like smoke from the burning tires of a racer, and the lizard is rocketing across the beach. It covers the distance to the Imperial Marine in one, two, three seconds, takes him in the backs of the knees, takes him down hard into the surf. Then the lizard is dragging the dead Nip back up onto the land. It stretches him out there among the dead Americans, walks around him a couple of times, flicking its tongue, and finally starts to eat him. (326)

A mathematician coolly controlling the world with a pencil and a napkin, and a primeval lizard so ferocious it erupts into Bobby Shaftoe's nightmares for years to come—these are contraries generating the first dialectical interaction. *Cryptonomicon* testifies eloquently to the importance of code in the contemporary world. Yet when the text pushes to the extreme of seeing the world as *only* code, a counter-resistance begins to build, becoming fiercer as more faith is placed in code. Although this resistance can take multiple forms, its most violent manifestation is animal appetite. As we shall see, the resulting clashes between abstract form and violent appetite remain largely unresolved in the text, leading to further transformations in the dialectic.

An important assumption underlying code's supremacy is the idea that information can be extracted from its material substrate. Once the information is secured, the substrate can be safely discarded. Peering through the window of Bletchley Park's "Ultra"-secret cryptographic decoding facility, Lawrence Pritchard Waterhouse sees a tape running through a machine so fast it smokes and catches fire. Surmising he is witnessing a Turing machine, Lawrence realizes that the "men in the room accept the burning of the tape so calmly" because the tape itself is not important. "That strip of paper, a technology as old as the pyramids, is merely a vessel for a stream of information. When it passes through the machine, the information is abstracted from it, transfigured into a pattern of pure binary data. That the mere vessel burns is of no consequence. Ashes to ashes, dust to dust—the data has passed out of the physical plane and into the mathematical, a higher and purer universe where different laws apply" (195). From here it is a small step to seeing information as immaterial; although information must necessarily be embodied to exist in the world, these embodiments can easily be seen as contingent and dispensable, of no more consequence than the burning tape.

Yet no sooner does someone make this assumption than the text offers a counterexample, an instance where physical instantiation is no mere triviality but essential to the system's operation. One such moment occurs when Lawrence's grandson Randy Waterhouse and his colleagues at their startup Epiphyte Corporation meet with the Sultan of Kinakuta about their scheme to create a data haven in the tiny Sultanate. At first, the Sultan mouths the conventional wisdom that "physical space no longer matters in a digitized, networked world. Cyberspace knows no boundaries" (316). But when he displays a world map with cables depicted between countries and continents, it is "not weblike at all," with only a few intercontinental cables running through "a small number of chokepoints" (317). Geography matters, it seems, even if it is invoked here in the interest of creating "a free, sovereign, location-independent cyberspace" (317). If the dream of a sovereign realm where information can flow freely is to be realized, it cannot be divorced from the real world of geographical specificities, material constraints, and political realities.

As this example illustrates, controlling the flow of information becomes much more problematic when the complexities of coupling it with physical actions are taken into account. The don explains to Lawrence at a high-level strategy meeting after the Allies have broken the Enigma codes that "the Germans have not broken our important cyphers. But they can observe our actions—the routing of our convoys in the North Atlantic, the deployment of our air forces. If the convoys always avoid the U-boats, if the air forces always go straight to the German convoys, then it is clear to the Germans . . . that there is not randomness here. . . . In other words, there is a certain point at which information begins to flow from us back to the Germans" (124). Unlike secret codes, physical actions do not require privileged knowledge to access them, and this tie with the physical world makes every action initiated by the possession of secret information potentially a two-way channel of communication.

Controlling information evolves quickly, then, into a problem of simulating randomness. Indeed, as the don's remarks imply, cryptology can be understood as the art of hiding pattern in randomness, an understanding implicit in the Latin root for "crypt," meaning "hidden, secret." Of course, "crypt" also denotes a burial place, historically often an underground chamber whose location is privileged knowledge. The convergence of the two plots—one focusing on cryptology in World War II, the second a contemporary quest for the recovery of an incredible gold stash buried by the Japanese when they realized the Empire was doomed—is overdetermined not only by the lineages that connect Lawrence Waterhouse, friend and contemporary of Alan Turing, to his nerdy grandson Randy Waterhouse, but also by the secrecy that unites the crypt of gold with the coded information revealing its location, information that is buried in the fiendishly complex Arethusa cryptographic code invented for Göring by Rudolf von Hacklheber, prewar friend and lover of Alan Turing. The mathematical battle of cryptographic codes that stretches across half a century is punctuated by the realities of the physical actions with which codes are correlated. Far from leaving physicality behind, the struggle to control the world through mathematical and cryptological manipulation must contend with the wild, chaotic, and often violent unpredictabilities of a reality too vibrant, alive, and *hungry* to ignore.

When cryptography is used not only for secrecy but also for deception, material specificities become even more important. Echoing an actual British Secret Service maneuver labeled Operation Mincemeat, the text narrates the story of tricking up a body as a secret agent, planting it with false information, and throwing it into the ocean at a point where it is certain to be recovered by the Germans.[7] Participating in the operation is Bobby Shaftoe, the World War II haiku-writing marine whose granddaughter America (Amy) is predestined to hook up with Randy half a century later. Bobby stars in the physically oriented plot that entwines with the cryptological one; he is as adroit at accomplishing the near-impossible in the material world as Lawrence and Alan Turing are in the cryptological realm. In converting the dead butcher's body into a supposed secret agent and therefore into a sign to be read and misunderstood by the Germans, everything depends upon the body's specificities—planted with the magnificent chronometer that must be Swiss rather than English, massaged with the German talcum powder used to ease on the European wet suit, and decorated with the tattoo that happens to read "Griselda" and not, say, "Amy." When he hears the German name, Lieutenant Ethridge tells Bobby, "Battles have hinged on lesser strokes of luck than this one, Sergeant!" Bobby (inappropriately from the lieutenant's point of view but apropos for this argument) uses the comment as an excuse to bring up the rampaging lizard from Guadalcanal that haunts his imagination the way the abject haunts the pure realm of mathematics in the text's Imaginary (152).

The abject is everywhere in this text, smelly, slimy, loathsome, and inescapable.[8] Detachment 2702, dedicated to creating deceptions designed to keep the Germans from realizing that the Allies have broken the Enigma codes, tries to convert the material world into signs, but the abject resists this implicit dematerialization, insisting on its own repugnant physicality. Sent to a bivouac in Italy meant to simulate a secret observation post, Bobby orders his men to dollop barrels of G. I. shit into privy holes, carefully interleaving Italian toilet paper to make it look as though they had occupied the site for months. Shit appears repeatedly in conjunction with secret writing and cryptological codes: in the "old-fashioned two-holer mounted above deep shafts that must descend all the way to hell," where Bobby reads the secret note in which his true love, Glory, arranges their first assignation (46); in the "equatorial miasma" that pervades the tropical climes in which much of the action takes place, so intimately related to diarrhea that as soon as Bobby smells it he "feels his bowels loosening up already" (613); in the vernacular of hacker culture that advocates strong cryptography, where "Randy was forever telling people, without rancor, that they were full of shit" (80); in the exasperation of Doug Shaftoe, Bobby's son, when he exclaims to Randy, "Can't you recognize bullshit? Don't you think it would be a useful item to add to your intellectual toolkits to be capable of saying, when a ton of wet steaming bullshit lands on your head, 'My goodness, this appears to be bullshit'?" (729), a remark that significantly refers to a plot to find the gold's location, which is concealed in the Arethusa code intercepts. Shit even becomes a pseudocode of its own when Detachment 2702 begins to use "shit" instead of "ship" to refer to the "pathetic heap of a freighter" that they use in one of their ruses: "let's get this cabin shit-shape! Where in the hell does the shit's master think he's taking us? And so on" (272). Surely one of the most significant instances occurs when Bobby and his comrades, attempting to rescue crucial Enigma code books from a sinking German submarine, wade through a cabin awash in coded documents and feces, a conjunction that brings the abject into intimate proximity with the secret writing that is supposed to operate in a realm of pure abstraction. Threatening to burst through the sphincters (bodily, social, military, and metaphorical) that seek to contain it, shit refuses to be reduced to only a sign. Expelled in involuntary reaction to intense fear, seeping out in uncontrollable diarrhea, dripping from jungle foliage in brutal marches by the Japanese and Americans in the South Pacific, shit has a material reality that cannot be contained solely within the algorithmic and cryptological.

Next to shit, perhaps the most conspicuous instance of the extent to which the world resists algorithmization is sexuality. Lawrence hypothesizes an inverse relation between his level of sexual frustration and his ability to work, but just when he thinks he can graph the relationship effectively, he discovers that sexual satisfaction is a more complex function than he imagined, depending not only on the time passed since his last ejaculation but also on how the ejaculation was accomplished—by a "manual override," a prostitute, or someone with whom he is emotionally involved. "In other words, the post-ejaculatory horniness level was not always equal to zero, as the naïve theory propounded above assumes, but to some other quantity dependent upon whether the ejaculation was induced by Self or Other" (545) "His life," he concludes, "which used to be a straightforward set of basically linear equations, has become a *differential* equation" (548).

Even the computer, site of digital code abstracted into ones and zeros, has a physical presence so violent it cannot be ignored. When Lawrence demonstrates to his superior officer, Earl Comstock, the computer he has built from mercury vibrating in tubes, it is a violently physical experience: "Hot sonic tongs are rummaging through his viscera, beads of sweat being vibrated loose from his scalp, his nuts are hopping around like Mexican jumping beans" (599). In the fictional world of *Cryptonomicon*, Lawrence gets the idea for this first digital computer from an equally violent encounter with a dusty organ in his beloved Mary's church. The encounter is depicted in a passage reminiscent of his resolve to clear out his own clotted sexual machinery: "Gouts of dust and salvos of mouse droppings explode from the pipes as Waterhouse invokes whole ranks that have not been used in decades" (575). Joining the physical with the abstract, this experience allows Lawrence to see "the entire machine in his mind, as if in an exploded drafts-man's view. Then it transforms itself into a slightly different machine—an organ that runs on electricity, with ranks of vacuum tubes here, and a grid of relays there. He has the answer, now, to Turing's question, the question of how to take a pattern of binary data and bury it in the circuitry of a thinking machine so that it can later be disinterred" (576). The odd terminology used here to describe the operations of electric memory—bury and disinter—further unites the cryptological operations of the computer, as it works to break the Japanese code, with the hidden crypt of gold revealed within the Arethusa code. Neither will be recovered with "nothing more than a pen-cil and a napkin"; both will require engagement with a physical world that cannot be reduced to mathematical abstraction.

The tension between abstraction and violent physicality is, however, it-self a verbal construction and in this sense already takes place in an abstract realm. From this contradiction emerges the next phase of the dialectical transformation, as abstract code and animal appetite merge to create a third term: performative code. Unlike the abstract algorithms Lawrence uses to express mathematical ideas (a practice not uncommon among mathemati-cians in the 1930s, before digital computers were invented), performative code operates as instructions to the machine and therefore initiates action in the world. In this sense, it combines the active vitality connoted by ani-mal appetite with the conceptual power of abstract code. With the collapse of these terms into performative code, signaled in the text by Lawrence's fictional discovery of the digital computer, another term comes into fo-cus as the dialectical complement of performative code, namely, "figurative language."

Stephenson hints at the importance of this conjunction in an interview he gave shortly after *Cryptonomicon* was published. He comments that "it's become evident to me when I looked into the history of computers that they had this intimate relationship with cryptography going back a long way. You could say that writing books about it is a way to explore that relationship." Then he adds, "I could try to get really profound here and say that it has something to do with the process of writing books in general, which is a matter of encoding ideas in words and symbols, but that's sort of a level of navel gazing I will leave to much more sophisticated literary critics."[9] *Command Line*, which as we have seen can be considered the nonfictional companion to *Cryptonomicon*, offers valuable insights into the conjunction between writing novels and writing code—insights that are essential to ex-plicating the next phase of the dialectical transformation.

Commanding Cryptography

Abstract Code + Animal Appetite
$$\downarrow$$
Performative Code + Figurative Language

Stephenson's attitude toward computer code is clear in his quixotic jeremiad, *In the Beginning Was the Command Line*, published first online and later as a short print book. Working through analogy, personal anecdote, and technical exposition, Stephenson tries to persuade the educated public that Unix is a far superior operating system to either Macintosh or Windows. This superiority lies not only in Unix's efficiency and power, nor solely in its economy (it is available for little or nothing over the Web). Equally important is the fact that it allows the user to understand exactly what is happening as typed commands are compiled and executed by the machine. Windows, if not exactly evil, is profoundly misleading because it hides the operations of the machine behind an interface that discourages the user from understanding how the actions of a mouse, for example, get translated into binary code—or even that they do get so translated. To make the point, Stephenson recounts his first experience with computers while in high school, in which he communicated with a mainframe through a teletype machine. Clunky as that interface was, it had the virtue of making clear that the symbol strings he typed in were being converted into binary code through the ASCII conventions of encoding each symbol with eight bits.

Why *should* the user know what is going on in the guts of machine? Or to put it another way, what is wrong with the user staying at the surface, as long as the interface is robust and functional? One problem is that the interface may not really be that robust. To illustrate, Stephenson tells of the day his Macintosh PowerBook "broke my heart," destroying a large document so thoroughly that not even a powerful utilities program could recover it. Since the document was too large to put on a single floppy, Stephenson had stored the only complete copy on the hard drive, so the loss was traumatic.[10] That very day he encountered Unix and became an instant convert. Tested and refined by thousands of hackers, Unix would never make this kind of error, Stephenson maintains, contrasting the open Unix error file with the covert information about errors that corporations like Microsoft bury in their private files. As a result, the information can be obtained only through their professional help line, which Microsoft charges the user to access.

Beyond the issue of robustness lies another reason, more difficult to quantify but perhaps even more important emotionally. The *real* individual, Stephenson implies repeatedly, would not want to put himself at the mercy of large corporations that in effect tell him what to think, deciding what he wants and what is good for him. Such folks are "Eloi," Stephenson suggests, in an allusion to H. G. Wells classic story *The Time Machine*.[11] In Wells's story, the Eloi are small-statured folk apparently living gentle lives in harmony with nature. Yet, as the time traveler Hillyer discovers, their lives are forfeit to the brutal and ugly Morlocks, who live below the surface with their superior technology and apparently regard the Eloi as food animals. Stephenson suggests that nowadays the Morlocks are on the surface running things, while the Eloi stampede stupidly into whatever operating system (or other technology) the Morlocks tell them they should want. At issue is pride, expertise, and, most importantly, control. Those who fail to understand the technology will inevitably be at the mercy of those who do. The implication is that those who choose Unix, even though it is more demanding techni- cally, can escape from the category of the Eloi and transcend to Morlock status where the real power is.

Among the weirder resonances between *Command Line* and *Cryptonomi- con* is the former's allusion to the cannibalistic Morlocks, which echoes the many references to animal appetite in *Cryptonomicon*, including the jun- gle cannibals who devour an unfortunate Filipino as Goto Dengo looks on from his hiding place, so ravenous himself he eats the starch the cannibals leave behind. In a startling reversal, however, *Command Line* reconfigures the Morlocks so that their relevant characteristic is technological prowess. Is their cannibalism merely beside the point in this extended analogy, which has no choice but to drag it along in the same way that analogies always in- clude inappropriate elements if pushed far enough? Or is some covert line of thought connecting the two texts that makes the Morlock/Eloi analogy appropriate in a deeper sense? Is it coincidence that yokes the cannibals' coming-of-age ritual in which an adolescent boy achieves his manhood by killing the intended victim, that is to say, a ritual in which he becomes a real individual, with Stephenson's imagining his Unix conversion as becoming a Morlock?

As the risk of acting out the role of the ironically evoked "much more sophisticated literary critic," I want now to explore the subterranean con- nections between the fictional world of *Cryptonomicon* and the nonfictional conversion narrative in *Command Line*. To write a command line is be in command, that is, to use an operating system that does not disguise the working of the machine, to prefer an interface that makes clear the connec- tion between typing alphabetic symbols and the encoding of these symbols into ones and zeros.[12] Yet in constructing this argument, Stephenson contin- ually uses extended analogies. For example, in addition to the Morlock/Eloi analogy, he imagines a scene of car dealers hawking inferior products that cost a lot (Windows and the Mac OS) while across the street someone is giving away for free beautifully made hefty tanks that get one hundred miles per gallon (Unix). Are these analogies just so much window dressing covering over the guts of the argument, like a Windows interface covering over the real workings of the machine? If the technological elite is distinguished by knowing what is actually going on, why dress the argument up in fancy clothes that pander to the weak-minded who cannot take their facts straight up? Who does the text construct as its audience, Eloi or Morlock, and how can one achieve Morlock status if one is treated by the text as an Eloi who needs analogies to understand what is, after all, a fairly simple and straightforward point?

To entertain these questions is, of course, to suggest that figurative language is to cultural understanding as Windows is to code, a pernicious covering that conceals the truth of things. This is the ancient charge brought by philosophers against rhetoricians, the suspicion of scientists that if humanists really knew what they were talking about they would use equations rather than metaphors, the ideological program of the Royal Society to use plain unadorned language rather than fancy analogies. It is beside my purpose here to rehearse the thousand answers that have been made to these objections to literary language, from Philip Sydney to Gertrude Stein, John Milton to Gillian Beer, Alexander Pope to Arkady Plotnitsky. Rather, I want to highlight the tension between Stephenson's figurative language and performative code. Performative code makes machines do things, and we should be in control of our machines. But figurative language makes people do things, and to be persuasive, to be *effective*, the writer must craft for his readers images that stick in the mind, narratives that compel through memorable scenes and psychological complexities, including paradox, contradiction, irony, and all the rest of the tricks that constitute a writer's trade. Although these tricks can be seen as lies from one perspective, every student of literature understands what it means to say that writers lie to tell the truth.

Stephenson's own explicit justification for figurative language focuses on myths rather than metaphors, or more accurately, myths as analogies. In several of his works, he has characters voice the view that mythic stories conceal profound technological insights, which simply need to be decoded to apply to present-day understandings of natural and artificial cognition. In *Snow Crash*, this device takes the form of an elaborate exposition by the Librarian, an artificial intelligence that summarizes Sumerian myths and explicates their relation to the Snow Crash virus. In *Cryptonomicon*, it occurs when Enoch Root explains to Randy that behind seemingly contradictory myths is a truth on which they converge. Suppose, he says, in an analogy meant to explain analogical thinking, that different people were to present different versions of him. Nevertheless, someone who knew him could see that behind these different representations was a "Root Representation" (800), a play on his name that connects him with the root directory of the computer. Because messing with the root directory can have catastrophic consequences, in large systems it is protected from most users and can be accessed only by the person responsible for the system, the SysOp or Systems Operator. When Enoch Root first sends an e-mail to Randy, Randy pays it special heed because it includes the surname "root," which Randy mistakes as an indication that the sender is a Systems Operator and therefore a knowledgeable and powerful computer expert. In another sense, Root does play this role, although his special expertise stems from his association with the Societas Eruditorium, a shadowy organization that pursues its mysterious ends independent of the national interests at stake in the world war. Although these ends are never made explicit, the implication is that Root, a priest, answers to a higher ethical power than national sovereignty, an ethical imperative that gives special emphasis to Root's explanation about the mythic relation between technology and war. Technology, Root argues, can be used for good or evil ends, and this difference is encoded in the distinction between Athena, goddess of technology and war used for ethical ends, and Ares, the god of violent warfare used simply for destruction and self-gain. As with *Snow Crash*, connecting mythic figures with the contemporary action aims to bring about an ethical understanding of technology, with the result that principled action follows.

These explications of myth do not, however, resolve the deeper contradiction between the up-front nature of code and the devious nature of figurative language. The tension between performative code and figurative language runs through many of Stephenson's books; indeed, it is no exaggeration to say that it is central to his creation of fictive worlds. In *Snow Crash*, he imagines a virus that crashes the operating system of humans, rendering them into automata that can be controlled through a monosyllabic language dubbed "falabala" after the way it sounds. Here language collapses into a kind of code capable of making humans act like computers, forced to run whatever commands the code inputs. At issue are the same concerns evident in *Cryptonomicon* and *Command Line*—control versus being controlled, autonomy versus loss of agency, individualism versus the masses. In *Cryptonomicon*, the same concerns prevail but in a different configuration. Instead of language becoming like code, code becomes like figurative language, creating a deceptive surface that misleads the masses while the cognoscenti penetrate this screen of symbols to extract the meaningful messages hidden within. Cryptanalysis thus becomes like mathematics, revealing the essential information hidden in "cosmetic distractions" such as those Lawrence sees through with his X-ray mathematical vision.

A good illustration of this dynamic occurs in the scene where Randy is thrown into prison on a trumped-up drug charge. To his surprise, his captors return his confiscated laptop, which is protected by the strong cryptography he has installed and hence worthless to his jailers unless they can trick him into voluntarily revealing the encryption key. He suspects, correctly, that his jailers have set up a Van Eck shadowing computer in the adjacent cell so that they will be able to see whatever appears on his screen. A superb hacker, Randy sets a program running in the background that will decode the crucial Arethusa intercepts, but he protects the screen surface by having it run a random display. The results of the background program, rather than appearing on screen, are transmitted by LEDs on the number and cap keys blinking Morse code. This clever ruse recalls the teletype machine through which Stephenson communicated with the mainframe in his high school days and that he likened to a telegraph. Now the computer-as-telegraph connotes not a transparent coupling but precisely the opposite, the triumph of cryptography over political surveillance carried out with malicious intent. These results are consistent with the logic of *Command Line*, for Randy can escape surveillance only because he understands what is really going on inside the machine, whereas his captors are demoted from Morlocks to Eloi because they can see only the deceptive surface he creates.

The configuration in the prison is significant. On one side of the wall are Randy's captors, carrying out covert surveillance under the guise of legitimate political purposes but actually because General Wing wants to find out the gold for personal gain. On the other side is Enoch Root, a cross-cutting character that connects the two generations of conspirators, communicating with Randy using a cryptographic code implemented by manipulating a deck of playing cards. Strong cryptography does more than distinguish the Morlocks from the Eloi; it also allows a freedom-loving band of like-minded hackers to cohere in the midst of the Morlocks who use their power illegitimately. Through this means the hackers are distinguished from the cannibals in a purgative separation that amounts to a distinction between technology used for evil purposes and technology adopted for noble ends.

Just as the active vitality of animal appetite and the conceptual power of abstract code merged in performative code, so the jail scene with Randy signals the merging of performative code and figurative language in the work of the Good Hacker. The Good Hacker reconciles the tensions between a code that honestly testifies to the interior operations of the machine and the deceptive power of metaphoric interfaces (and by implication, figurative language in general). Randy, using his deep understanding of code to create deceptive surfaces, nevertheless uses his expertise for good ends. The conflation prepares for the next dialectical turn, which pits good hackers against evil deceivers.

The Brotherhood of Code

Abstract Code + Animal Appetite
$$\downarrow$$
Performative Code + Figurative Language
$$\downarrow$$
Good Hackers + Evil Deceivers

Being technically proficient with code obviously does not assure that technicians will use their expertise to enhance individual autonomy. Microsoft employs talented programmers who work to create the very interfaces that, in Stephenson's view, seduce and disempower users. Stephenson is well aware of this fact, of course, and frequently constructs plots that pit spirited individualistic hackers against soulless technicians and their evil masters. So strong is Stephenson's sympathy with the hacker versus the large organization that alliances among hackers frequently provide the motive power for his fiction. In *Snow Crash*, for example, the major plot reaches its climax when Hiro Protagonist saves a virtual stadium full of hackers by defeating the software that would crash their neural operating systems, infect them with the Snow Crash virus, and turn them into Bob Rife's minions. In *Cryptonomicon*, much of the action takes place against the canvas of World War II, a military conflict in which national loyalties served to organize immense amounts of manpower and material—a situation ripe for exploitation by the powerful few. Against this volatile backdrop, Stephenson imagines cross-cutting dynamics that organize energies differently, creating small pockets of resistance, subversion, and conspiracy.

We have already considered one of these dynamics, the tension between mathematical abstraction and violent physicality that constituted the first phase of the dialectic. Significantly, the carnivorous lizard with a violent appetite disrupts this stereotypical scene of beachhead warfare when it attacks the Japanese, indicating that the dialectic has the power to intervene and redirect the military conflicts inscribed on the text's surface. Disruption occurs again in the next phase of the dialectic when good hackers are put in conflict with evil deceivers. The good hackers come together to form what might be called the Brotherhood of Code, an alliance that has as its core their expertise in decoding encrypted messages. Although most of the explicit criticism of national agendas is directed against America's enemies (hardly surprising, given the author's nationality), evil deceivers are at work transnationally, including in America. Large organizations are shown to be susceptible to corruption when powerful men subvert their resources to pursue private agendas dictated by greed and arrogance. General Wing pursues the Japanese war gold under the guise of Chinese nationalistic goals; Earl Comstock does the same with the newly formed National Security Agency; his son, Attorney General Paul Comstock, collaborates with the Dentist and his minions in attacking the Epiphyte Corporation's server.

These are the forces against which the Brotherhood of Code struggles, in an unlikely cross-generational conspiracy that includes, during the World War II era: Goto Dengo (a Japanese Imperial soldier), Bobby Shaftoe (an American marine), Oscar Bischoff (a German submarine commander), Rudy von Hacklheber (a high-level German cryptanalyst), Lawrence Pritchard Waterhouse (an American cryptologist working for the British), and Enoch Root (of Societas Eruditorium fame, nominally a Catholic priest and chaplain for the Marine Corps). Almost all of these characters betray organizational loyalties in favor of personal bonds, with cryptography and secret writing at the conspiracy's center.

The Brotherhood of Code injects into the World War II era the same kind of bonding through cryptological expertise that Stephenson in *Command Line* identifies with the open source community. Significantly, the one member of the conspiracy who does not overtly betray his national loyalty is Bobby Shaftoe, killed in a suicide mission on which he is personally dispatched by General MacArthur. And it is Shaftoe, of course, who stars in the physical action in the same way that Rudy and Lawrence dominate in the cryptological arena. Although Bobby participates in the conspiracy, his character is anomalous in that he is not directly involved with decrypting documents, as are the others. Instead, his character illustrates how earlier tensions get integrated into the later dialectical configurations. These tensions are not so much left behind as shifted in their narrative functions when the next phase of the dialectical interaction starts to drive the action.

The conflict between physical action and abstract language, for example, is reiterated in Bobby Shaftoe's meditation on two categories of men, one oriented toward language, the other toward physical action. "Men who believe that they are accomplishing *something* by speaking speak in a different way from men who believe that speaking is a *waste of time*. . . . For them, trying to do anything by talking is like trying to pound in a nail with a screwdriver. Sometimes you can even see the desperation spread over such a man's face as he listens to himself speak." Listening to Enoch Root and Lawrence, Bobby begins "to suspect that there might be a third category of man, a kind so rare that Shaftoe never met any of them until now" (373). Lawrence speaks, Bobby surmises, "not as a way of telling you a bunch of stuff he's already figured out, but as a way of making up a bunch of new shit as he goes along. And he always seems to be hoping that you'll join in. Which no one ever does, except for Enoch Root" (374). Slowly dawning on Bobby is the realization that language might be used not just as a tool for expression but also as a method of exploration. The realization points toward the next phase of the dialectic, which juxtaposes performative code with figurative language. In contrast to the relatively weak rationale that interprets myth as veiled history, Bobby has just discovered a much stronger justification for figurative language. Metaphors and analogies not only express existing ideas; they also lead to new thoughts and possibilities. It is surely no accident that in addition to being a superlative physical specimen, Bobby writes haiku, a poetic form that makes extensive use of metaphor and image.

Like the other configurations before it, the good hackers/evil deceivers configuration becomes unstable, initiating another turn of the dialectical cycle. This time, however, its instability leads to a significantly different outcome. The problem with the configuration becomes apparent in the generation following World War II, when the hackers get together to form the start-up Epiphyte Corporation. As the Internet matured and began to become a commercial enterprise, visionaries saw their utopian dreams being co-opted by mercenary corporate interests. What ensures that Randy, Avi, and their colleagues in Epiphyte will not be similarly co-opted, forced to kowtow to someone like the Dentist, who plots to gain a controlling interest in their fledgling corporation? In its last phase, the dialectic attempts to purge contamination from the Good Hacker and separate it out into a figure of pure evil, whose banishment from the plot can then signal the triumph of the good technology of Athena over the bad technology of Ares. This purgative impulse is, of course, precisely contrary to the dialectic's normal operation of combining contraries. At this point, the dialectic can go no further. The figure of pure evil is indeed produced and expelled, but the dialectic's exhaustion is expressed through oxymoronic knots—life and death, a killing machine and a rescue mechanism, disaster and triumph, greed and altruism—that can be neither untied nor merged into a new synthetic term. Rather than work *through* these dense oxymoronic knots, the text achieves a muted resolution, such as it is, by working *with* them.

Knotty Oxymorons: The Dialectic Exhausted

Abstract Code + Animal Appetite
↓
    Performative Code + Figurative Language
↓
        Good Hackers + Evil Deceivers
↓
           Oxymoronic Knots + (Pure Evil)

The tendency toward oxymoronic entanglement is concentrated around events with life and death consequences, becoming particularly important in the entwining plots of Lawrence's invention of the first digital computer and the burying and disinterring of the Japanese war gold. As we have already seen, both plots involve crypts, the gold because it is buried in an underground installation, the computer because it is linked with cryptology and later with the Epiphyte data haven called "The Crypt." Both plots evolve until they become so knotted into oxymoronic configurations they can go no further.

With the crypt of gold, the oxymorons cluster around the secret intention to make it also a human crypt. In a conversation with Lieutenant Mori (whose name connotes death), Goto understands the truth concealed beneath the lieutenant's riddling discourse (639). The lieutenant promises Goto a reward for work well done, a prize he would presumably want to earn, but Goto realizes this "reward" will in fact be his own death, that which he presumably most fears. The tunnels he has engineered to conceal the Japanese war gold are intended to hold his murdered body once the work is finished. Knowing that Golgotha, "the place of the skull," is associated in the Christian tradition with Christ's betrayal and crucifixion, Goto had privately given this name to the crypt. But when he mutters it and Captain Noda overhears, he dissembles by answering that it is a Tagalog word meaning "hidden glade" (639); sign and signified are further muddled when the captain calls it "Gargotta." As the chain of linguistic signifiers drifts toward nonsense, it resembles a cryptographic code whose hidden meaning can be decoded only by the cognoscenti.

Similar obfuscation takes shape within the physical structure Goto has engineered. He builds into the design certain idiosyncrasies that are highly significant to him but meaningless to his superiors. When the installation is complete and the treasure concealed, the final slaughter is about to begin, but Goto gets "so excited he forgets to die" (734). As he prepares to swim to freedom using the breathing chambers he has designed, the place intended as his burial chamber flips into its opposite: the architecture that will save him. He reflects that "he is an engineer, trapped inside one of his own machines. The machine was designed to keep him alive, and he will never know whether it worked unless it works. After he has achieved that satisfaction, he supposes, he can always kill himself at leisure" (734), a hypothetical outcome that flips again from triumph to presumed despair. The conflation of life and death, presented here as a matter of memory ("he forgets to die"), is deeply bound up with ethical complexities. Earlier, Goto had ordered his soldiers to jump ship rather than go down with the troop carrier, and so had labeled himself unworthy because he chose to live despite the shameful outcome of an American victory (323). Accepting that he is a "bad solider" because he shuns the senseless loss of life, he resolves to save as many men as he can at Golgotha, which finally amounts to a pitiful few. He hopes the gift of life will be enough for them and is shamed when one stops to pick up treasure along the way. "He himself has saved no treasure except these men's lives. But that's not why he feels so bad. He had hoped that being thus saved they would all be noble, and not think of the treasure. But maybe that was too much to hope for" (734).

As future developments make clear, it was indeed too much to hope for. Goto's act of altruism is inextricably entwined with the greed that drives the final portion of the plot. The chief competitor for the gold in the contemporary plot is General Wing, the same Wing who takes off after the escape from Golgotha without bothering to thank Goto for saving his life. Goto continues to believe, as he tells Randy and Avi when they approach him for help in recovering the gold, that gold is the "corpse of value" (858). The real treasure, he explains, is in the head—"the intelligence of the people"—and in the hands—"the work they do" (858). Now a fabulously wealthy and powerful contractor, his success testifies to the wisdom of his view. Only when Avi tells Goto that he wants the gold to attempt to end wars by developing HEAP—the Holocaust Education and Avoidance Pod—does Goto agree to cooperate in the effort.

The scene where Avi and Goto make their pact is awkwardly written in a telling way. When Goto suggests that Avi wants the gold to become rich, Avi's "face turns red, the muscles of his head bulge as he clenches his teeth together, and he breathes heavily through his nose for a while. The Gotos both seem to be rather impressed by this, and so no one says anything for a long time, giving Avi a chance to regain his cool" (858). This heavy-handed indication of moral outrage indicates how desperately Stephenson wants to protect the Good Hacker against the greed that characterizes the evil deceivers, even at the cost of bad writing.[13] Greed sits cheek by jowl with entrepreneurial success, co-optation with individual initiative.[14] Stephenson knows too well the fate of successful dot-coms—sold for fabulous sums to large corporations before the Internet bubble burst—to be sanguine about the prospects for purity in the corporate world or the realm of the Internet, which is increasingly under corporate control. Stephenson's anxiety about protecting the Good Hacker from corruption finds its most extreme expression in the creation of a figure of pure evil, as if by isolating all impurities here he can ensure that they will not contaminate the good characters. This function is fulfilled by the character of Andrew Loeb. Loeb's final attack on Amy has no financial, and indeed no rational, basis at all. "Why does he want to hurt you?" Root asks, to which Randy replies, "Because he's evil." When they finally succeed in killing the madman, "an insect lands on his thumb and starts to eat it" (893) in an ironic assertion of amoral appetite triumphant even over ultimate evil.

In sharp contrast to the unequivocal judgment Randy passes on Loeb are the complexities of the oxymoronic clusters, which bring together opposites so closely entwined that they cannot be separated. Like the gold plot, the cryptology plot enacts these oxymorons by tangling together life and death so that they paradoxically signify each other. The difficult problem that Lawrence must solve before he can invent the first digital computer is how to create machine memory, or in the odd formulation noted earlier, how to "bury and disinter" information. One of the problems he will attack once he has solved this difficulty is decrypting the Arethusa intercepts, which have encoded into them the gold's location. Coincidentally, he also solves the encrypted messages by which the conspirators are communicating with one another. As the conspirators radio messages about meeting at Bobby Shaftoe's memorial service, the crucial word that allows Lawrence to break the code is "funeral." He follows the conspirators to their jungle meeting place, where they have gathered to tap into a small portion of the gold, whose location Goto, now a member of the group, of course knows. When Lawrence reveals himself to Rudy, Rudy "heaves a big sigh. 'So. You win,' he says. 'Where is the cavalry?'" Lawrence jokes, "Cavalry, or calvary?" linking the cliché of cavalry rushing to the rescue with the site of Christ's death. "'I know where Calvary is,' Rudy replies. 'Not far from Golgotha'" (883). As Avi will do half a century later with Goto, Rudy assures Lawrence that "most of [the gold] is going to help victims of war, in one way or another," even though they intend to take enough to make themselves rich. Convinced to help the conspirators, in part because they loyally chose to attend Bobby's funeral despite the risks, Lawrence protects them by destroying the Arethusa intercepts and substituting random numbers. Although he fails to save his friends—Comstock decrypts a message that betrays the location of the conspirators' submarine—Lawrence's substitution of randomness will occupy Comstock for many years as he ruthlessly drives his NSA team to discover a code that is not there.

As these scenes suggest, the oxymoronic clusters are knotted most tightly around gold, not coincidentally the focus for the text's deepest anxieties. The principal gold sites are Golgotha, about which we have already heard; the submarine carrying the conspirators that Comstock sinks and that Douglas Shaftoe, Bobby's son, disinters half a century later; and a mysterious mound of gold bars hidden in the jungle that anticipates and reflects the problems and possibilities of the gold at Golgotha. All three sites provide episodes in which oxymoronic knots express the final perplexities of the dialectic's operation.

In addition to Rudy and Bischoff, the submarine carries some of the gold bars from the Golgotha site and five crates of gold foil plates that Rudy has stashed abroad. The plates Rudy identifies as "cultural treasures," scoffing when Bischoff suggests that they may be encoded with Göring's pornography (851). Careful reading suggests that the plates are in fact the "Leibniz archive" that Rudy had earlier asked Göring to gather for him from Europe's great libraries (503), precious research materials that Rudy has encoded via perforations onto gold foil because he knows the foil will be impervious to salt water. When Bischoff jokes that they should be exporting gold from the Philippines rather than importing it, Rudy explains, "When I export those sheets, I'll do it on wires," suggesting a scene analogous to the burning tape that Lawrence witnesses; the gold foil will be worthless once the information it holds has been extracted. But Bischoff, trying to visualize this scene, imagines it as "wires strung from here to Los Angeles, and sheets of gold foil sliding down them. It doesn't really work" (852).

The fact that the sheets are gold puts them in a different category than the cheap paper tape. When the submarine is discovered decades later by Doug and his crew, they see the gold foil sheets as valuable in themselves, and Randy, although intrigued by the perforations, is apparently never able to decode the information they contain (458–59). Along with the sheets—ambiguously positioned between their material value as gold and their informational value as mathematical archives—are the gold bars from Golgotha, entombed along with those who died in the submarine. The death scene is rich with ironies. Rudy remembers that he has written the Golgotha coordinates on a sheet of paper in his briefcase, and he and Bischoff presciently anticipate that the sunken submarine may eventually be found. Trapped in an oxygen-rich air bubble at the stern of the broken boat, in a scene reminiscent of Goto and his men in the breathing chambers of Golgotha, Rudy and Bischoff realize that if they strike a match to burn the paper, they will be immolated in the resulting flash. Rudy swims to the hatch and opens it, with enough air to make it back to the bubble but not enough to escape. In a knot that ties together life and death, he then tells Bischoff to escape, lighting the match that at once burns the paper, kills him, and provides the illumination Bischoff needs to make it out of the sub.

Decades later, when Doug, Amy, and Randy discover the submerged wreck, they find inside Rudy's briefcase a slip of paper on which is written "WATERHOUSE LAVENDER ROSE" (462), the wedding china pattern that Lawrence had mentioned to Rudy when declining to join the conspirators in favor of becoming a mathematics professor at a small college where he will settle down with his bride, Mary Smith. Randy later confirms that this is indeed his grandmother's pattern, thus enabling him to rediscover the link between the submarine, the conspirators, and his grandfather. When Doug realizes that the hatch is open and presumes that someone was able to escape from the doomed ship, he lights a cigar to mark the occasion, telling Randy, "This is one of the most important moments in your life. Nothing will ever be the same. We might get rich. We might get killed. We might just have an adventure, or learn something. But we have been changed. We are standing close to the Heraclitean fire, feeling its heat on our faces" (442). Far removed from Doug's usual rhetoric, the melodramatic tone underscores the threads knotted together here—the fire that kills Rudy and saves Bischoff reflected in the "flaring safety match" that Doug produces "like a magician," with Randy "staring into the flame"; the solemn toast to "whomever got out," honoring the moment of self-sacrifice that marks a crucial difference between the Brotherhood of Hackers and the greedy bureaucrats who oppose them.

Nevertheless, it remains to be seen whether the gold of Golgotha can be situated so that it can be coded good instead of evil, Athena rather than Ares. Also at issue is the tension between materiality and information, enacted in the submarine scenes in the coexistence of the gold bars and gold foil sheets, but not really resolved. The tension between information and materiality is also performed in a different sense in the ruminations in the text over the nature of money. The opening scene—set in Shanghai, with coolies rushing to redeem notes printed by individual banks as the Marines fight their way to the waterfront and the Japanese attack the city—underscores the fragility of currency. Currency is, Lawrence reflects an ocean away, valuable only as long as people believe it so. Feeling that he knows how the Japanese think, having read their decrypted messages every day, he is sure that "the Nipponese must have given thought to this problem of backing their imperial currency— not just for Australia but New Zealand, New Guinea, the Philippines, Hong Kong, China, Indochina, Korea, Manchuria. . . . How much gold and silver would you need in order to convince that many human beings that your paper currency was actually worth something? Where would you put it?" (812). The answer, of course, is Golgotha. But once the gold is buried and booby-trapped, it will take a major engineering project to unearth it. At one point Randy and Avi wonder whether it needs to be unearthed. Why can't they use the gold to secure the electronic money they are in the process of establishing without needing to dig up the treasure? Isn't it enough that it exists and that they know where it is, even if it is not accessible?

The debate is foreshadowed by the mysterious mound of gold bars they discover in a nearly inaccessible jungle site. A Philippine woman gives the latitude and longitude coordinates to Randy under the guise of a social dance, asking him "What is the value of the following information?" (485). After Doug, Randy, and their crew fight their way to the location, negotiating fierce jungle terrain and rebel roadblocks, they realize that although the unguarded gold appears to be theirs for the taking, there is no way they can actually remove it, given the unstable political and geographical situation. Without possession, access has no meaning.

Does the inverse also hold, that without access, possession has no meaning? When the tremors of underground explosions wake them from their dream of letting the Golgotha gold simply remain underground, they realize that General Wing has marshaled men and material to tunnel diagonally into the stash from the side. The gold cannot be secure, and thus cannot function as a basis for their new virtual currency, unless they physically possess it. Like the Sultan's geography lesson, Wing's run for Golgotha makes clear that even in a world where electronic cash promises to be the currency of the future, the materiality implied by physical possession cannot be ignored. They solve their problem by literally liquefying their assets, setting off enough fuel oil in the Golgotha chambers so that the gold turns to liquid and runs out into the river bed on its own.

The scene provides the narrative's muted climax and abrupt ending, leaving unresolved questions about how the gold will be spent, whether it will go to the HEAP project, the Societas Eruditorium, the Catholic Church, or the Brotherhood of Hackers—all of which are mentioned at one point or another as possible beneficiaries. Like the liquid gold poised between the solid materiality of appetite and the airy vapor of information, the text does not finally answer these questions, perhaps because they cannot be resolved within the parameters of a realistic novel. Apparently the gold has been purified enough to make its moral recovery possible, but not enough to allow a denouement to be written. Even when the plot threads are reassembled into a coherent story, the knots that signify how the action should be valued remain entangled.

The Interpenetration of Technology and Text

Let me now return to consider how the material technology that produced the book enters into its narrative construction. All the terms involved in the dialectical transformations are concerned with situating code in relation to the human world of signs and artifacts, language and objects. More than an abstraction, code has a material efficacy that demands it be recognized as a player in the world. Transparent to the technological elite who understand it, code can also be made deviously obscure; it can be put to socially desirable ends in the hands of idealistic hackers but remains vulnerable to the machinations of evil corporations. Since there is finally no way to ensure that code will not be co-opted, the text signs it with the oxymoronic knots that express the irreducible complexities of its entry into the world. This subterranean narrative, emerging from the operations of the dialectic, is not identical with the surface content and indeed in some ways contradicts it. Rather, this narrative functions as a deep structure within the text, setting up a surface/depth dynamic that mimetically re-creates within the text the surface/depth relation between the screenic text displayed on the computer screen and the coding languages producing the text as a display the reader can access. Thus the narrative implicit in the dialectic reproduces the structural dynamics of the trading zones between code and natural language that digital technologies have made a pervasive feature of contemporary culture.

Further marks of the digital technologies that produced the text can be seen in the way the surface narrative is assembled. As the cryptological and gold plots begin to weave together, it becomes increasingly clear that the novel is functioning as a kind of machine assembling a coherent story out of plot lines that have been fragmented and spliced into one another. Until the final pages, the multiple plots proceed largely independently of one another, with jump cuts across scenes separated by many decades and several continents. One effect of digital text editing has been to change the writing habits of people generally, making cut-and-paste practices much more prevalent than was previously the case with typewriters, when the process was much more laborious. Of course, as a host of literary narratives testify, writers working on typewriters also created cut-and-paste narratives, including such luminaries as Virginia Woolf and John Dos Passos. Nevertheless, in *Cryptonomicon* this technique acquires special significance, for it resonates with the emphasis on burying and disinterring information as the specific technological challenge that led to the invention of the digital computer. In this context, the reader's activity is implicitly imagined as burying the memory of one section in order to cope with new information offered by the next plot thread; later, when the first thread resurfaces again, the reader must disinter that information and link it with the new developments. In effect, then, the reader functions like a digital computer, assembling coherent narratives out of fragmentary strings dispersed throughout the memory space. Like Goto desperately swimming from air pocket to air pocket inside a machine that he himself has built, the reader is trapped inside a machine constructed jointly from the reader's memory and the text's words, at the mercy of a novel that "forgets to die" as it rambles on for hundreds of pages before reaching an inconclusive ending that leaves much undecided.

Further complexities arise when we consider the relation of the Linux operating system to the Macintosh system that Stephenson presumably used when he was drafting the first part of *Cryptonomicon*. As he explains in *Command Line*, Linux operates by giving the user direct access to the commands that control the computer's behavior, whereas the Macintosh operating system offers the user *metaphors* for these commands (e.g., desktop, files, trash bin, etc.) and conceals the actual commands within its hidden coding structures. The fact that the operating system seals off access to the command core has everything to do with the fact it is proprietary software controlled by corporate interests. By contrast, within the Linux system the user can type commands that call up a Windows-like interface, but this metaphoric shell operates as a special functionality within Linux, and it is always possible for the user to regain direct control of the machine by returning to inner core of Linux commands.

In *Cryptonomicon*, this nesting of an inner core within an outer metaphoric shell is reproduced through the fictional compendium of cryptology called the Cryptonomicon, which functions as a *mise en abyme* for Stephenson's novel (to distinguish the two, I will indicate the novel in italics and the compendium without italics). Supposedly, the Cryptonomicon was begun by John Wilkins, not coincidentally the proponent of an analytical language designed to rescue language from a morass of illogical forms and tame its wild metaphoricity by fitting it into a rationally constructed system of roots, prefixes, and suffixes. Since Wilkins, generations of cryptologists have added to the Cryptonomicon, including, in the twentieth century, the cryptological genius William Friedman and the fictional Lawrence Pritchard Waterhouse, second only to Alan Turing in his deep understanding of computers and code. Thus the Cryptonomicon has become a kind of Kabala created by a Brotherhood of Code that stretches across centuries. To know its contents is to qualify as a Morlock among the Eloi, and the elite among the elite are those gifted enough actually to contribute to it.

Containing the Cryptonomicon within itself, Stephenson's novel can be understood as a long footnote to this Kabala, as an explanation in figurative language of the significance of code that the novel posits as the dialectical opposite to the deceptive surfaces and fancy analogies in which it, as a literary work, necessarily indulges. Thus the novel at once contains within its own novelistic body the Cryptonomicon and postulates this fiction as a linguistic Other existing in a space exterior to itself. Elizabeth Weise quotes Stephenson as saying that "language . . . is the reverse of cryptography," because, as she explains, language "is about conveying information, not hiding it."[15] In another sense, however, figurative language hides within linguistic formulations what code reveals. It is significant in this regard that the novel contains an appendix by expert cryptographer Bruce Schneier, explaining the Solitaire encryption algorithm Enoch Root uses to communicate with Randy in jail.[16] This encryption scheme is sufficiently strong that it is possible the National Security Agency would prohibit its exportation in electronic form, the only textual form it monitors. In *Cryptonomicon*, Stephenson included an e-mail from Enoch Root to Randy in which Enoch gives him the Perl script for the Solitaire algorithm (480), leading to the delicious irony that this print book can be exported legally, whereas the code it inscribes with durable marks, if translated into electronic voltages, may not be legally exported.[17] In a literal sense, the text's natural language here operates as a metaphoric shell encapsulating a hidden core of code. Moreover, if Schneier's appendix is sufficiently astute, it could aspire to be included in the Cryptonomicon as a main entry, whereas the best the novel could hope for, as a writing practice linguistic and metaphoric rather than coded and algorithmic, would be to make it into an appendix. In this playfully speculative scenario, *Cryptonomicon* is turned inside out to reveal the Cryptonomicon as the powerful core that can access command lines directly, whereas the novel resembles the Windows or Macintosh operating system that conceals the real command structures from the reader. The oxymoronic knots can now be understood as sites where the reader becomes aware of flips that transform something into its opposite, as here the appendix becomes the core and the novel becomes the appendix. The point of *entangling* the opposites so that they cannot be separated now emerges as a covert justification for figurative language, for effective communication in the digital realm requires an understanding *both* of machine-executable code and human-oriented metaphors.

On multiple levels and in diverse ways, then, *Cryptonomicon* bears witness to the digital technologies that created it. In its structure, dialectical dynamics, and subterranean narrative, it incorporates in linguistic form the crisis in writing practices that materially marked its electronic body, understood simultaneously as a clash of operating systems, a struggle of open source utopianism against capitalistic greed, and an opposition between the command structures of code and the analogical surfaces of figurative language. To probe these complexities, we require critical strategies that are attentive to the technologies producing texts as well as to the texts as linguistic/conceptual structures—that is to say, we require material ways of reading that recognize texts as more than sequences of words and spaces.[18] Rather, they are artifacts whose materialities emerge from negotiations between their signifying structures and the technologies that produce them. Whereas the New Criticism of the mid-twentieth century isolated texts from political contexts and technological productions, the New Materialism I am advocating in this book and practicing in this chapter insists that technologies and texts be understood as mutually interpenetrating and constituting one another.

6 Flickering Connectivities in Shelley Jackson's *Patchwork Girl*

So far in part 2 we have explored intermediation between print and electronic texts in two ways: first, by considering the media translation that occurs when print documents are transformed into an electronic medium like the Web, and second, by exploring a case where a print document in the form of a book nevertheless bears the marks of code within its body. What remains is the instance of a text conceived as a digital artwork from the beginning, a "first generation electronic object," in Matthew Kirschenbaum's apt phrase. Shelley Jackson's brilliantly realized hypertext *Patchwork Girl* is an electronic fiction that manages to be at once highly original and intensely parasitic on its print predecessors. I have chosen *Patchwork Girl* for my tutor text because I think it remains one of the most interesting of electronic fictions and because it is deeply concerned with how digital media enact and express new kinds of subjectivity. To measure the difference between the subjectivity envisioned by *Patchwork Girl* and that associated with the late eighteenth-century and nineteenth-century texts it parasitizes, I will begin by returning to the eighteenth century, when a constellation of economic, class, and literary interests clashed over defining the nature of literary property. Although the decisions that emerged from the ensuing legal battles were no sooner formulated than they were again contested in legal and literary arenas, the debate is nevertheless useful as a foil to Jackson's work, which positions itself against the subjectivity associated with this moment in the print tradition.

Subjectivity and the Legal Fictions of Copyright

In his important book *Authors and Owners*, Mark Rose shows that copyright did more than provide a legal basis for intellectual property. The discussions that swirled around copyright also solidified ideas about what counted as creativity, authorship, and proper literature. One of the important assumptions that emerged out of this debate was the assertion that the literary work does not consist of paper, binding, or ink. Rather, the work was seen as an immaterial mental construct. Here is Justice Blackstone's assessment: "Style and sentiment are the essentials of a literary composition. These alone constitute its identity. The paper and print are merely accidents, which serve as vehicles to convey that style and sentiment to a distance" (quoted in Rose, 89). The abstraction of the literary work from its physical basis, discussed in chapter 4 in terms of editing practices, had the effect of obscuring the work's relation to the economic network of booksellers who purchased shares in the work and used their economic capital to produce books. The more abstract the work became, the further removed it was from the commodification inherent in book sales, and consequently the more exalted the cultural status that could be claimed for it. Cultural capital was maximized by suppressing the relation between cultural and economic capital, although it was primarily the profit motive that stimulated the booksellers' interest in promoting literary works as immaterial works of art. As a result of these representations, literary works operated somewhat like the ideal work discussed in chapter 4, in that they were not to be sullied by the noise of embodiment.

Although Rose does not develop the gender implications of an evaluation that places abstraction above embodiment, his examples reveal that the men producing these discourses had in mind the male writer, whose creative masculine spirit gave rise to works of genius that soared above their material instantiations in books. Thus a hierarchy of values emerged that placed at the ascendant end of the scale the disembodied, the creative, the masculine, and the writer who worked for glory; at the lower end of the scale were the embodied, the repetitive, the feminine, and the writer who worked for money.

Rose traces a series of developments that progressively abstracted the work away from its material instantiation, only to re-embody it in purer, more transcendent form. Although Blackstone located the work both in "style" and "sentiment," subsequent commentators realized that the part of the work that could be secured as private intellectual property, and therefore the part appropriate for copyright protection, was the way ideas were expressed, rather than the ideas themselves. This aspect of the work—"style" or "expression"—was frequently likened to clothes that dressed the thought. Through the clothes of expression, the body of the work entered into social legibility and was recognized as partaking in the social regulations that governed exchanges between free men who could hold private property. As Rose makes clear, it was the author's style—the clothes he selected to dress his thought—that was considered most indicative of his individual personality, so style was also associated with the originality that was rapidly becoming the touchstone of literary value. These interrelations were further extended through metaphors that identified style with the author's face. Note that it was the face and not the body. Not only was the body hidden by clothes; more significantly, the body was not recognized as a proper site in which the author's unique identity could be located. The final move was to reconstitute the author from the "face" exhibited in the style of his works, but by now bodies of all sorts had been left so far behind that critics felt free to attach this ethereal, noncorporeal face to any appropriate subject. (The prime example was the detachment of "Shakespeare" from the historical actor and playwright and the reassignment of his "face" to such august personages as Francis Bacon.) As Rose observes, these developments operated as a chain of deferrals sliding from the embodied to the disembodied, the book to the work, the content to the style, the style to the face, the face to the author's personality, the personality to the author's unique genius. The purpose of these deferrals, he suggests, was to arrive at a transcendental signified that would guarantee the enduring value of the work as a literary property, establishing it as a "vast estate" that could be passed down through generations without diminishing in value.

In the process, certain metaphoric networks were established that continued to guide thinking about literary properties long after the court cases were settled. Perhaps the most important were metaphors equating the work with real estate. The idea that a literary work is analogous to real estate facilitated the fitting together of arguments about copyright with the Lockean liberal philosophy that C. P. Macpherson has labeled possessive individualism.[1] Rose finds it appropriate that James Thomson's long landscape poem *The Seasons* became the occasion for a major copyright case, for it was read as a poet transforming the landscape into his private literary property by mixing with it his imagination, just as the Lockean man who owns his person first and foremost creates private property by mixing it with his labor (113). Whereas the landholder supplies physical labor, the author supplies mental labor, particularly the originality of his unique "style." Rose makes the connection clear: "The Lockean discourse of property, let us note, was founded on a compatible principle—'Every Man has a *Property* in his own *Person*' was Locke's primary axiom—and thus the discourse of originality readily blended with the eighteenth-century discourse of property" (121).

Macpherson pointed out years ago that there is implicit in Locke a chicken-and-egg problem. Whereas Locke presents his narrative as if market relations arose as a consequence of the creation of private property, it is clear that the discourse of possessive individualism is permeated through and through by market relations from the beginning. Only in a society where market relations were predominant would an argument defining the individual in terms of his ability to possess himself be found persuasive. The same kind of chicken-and-egg problem inheres in the notion of literary property. The author creates his literary property through the exercise of his original genius, yet it is clear that writing is always a matter of appropriation and transformation, from syntax to literary allusions and the structure of tropes. A literary tradition must precede an author's inscriptions for literature to be possible as such, yet this same appropriation and reworking of an existing tradition is said to produce "original" work. Arguments about literary property were persuasive in part because they fit together so well with prevailing notions of liberal subjectivity, but that same fit implied common blindnesses.

In particular, anxiety about admitting that writing was a commercial enterprise haunted many of the defenders of literary properties. In a fine image, Rose remarks that "the sense of the commercial is, as it were, the unconscious of the text" for such defenders of literary property as Samuel Johnson and Edward Young (118). There were other suppressions as well. The erasure of the economic networks that produced the books went along with the erasure of the technologies of production, a tradition that continued beyond print technologies to other media, and beyond Britain to other countries. Rose recounts, for example, *Burrow-Giles Lithographic Co. v. Sarony* (1884), the landmark case in the United States in which the court decided that the photograph derived entirely from the photographer's "'original mental conception'" and thus owed nothing to the camera that produced it (cited in Rose, 135). The decision clearly relied on the notion of the author's "originality" as a key component of an artistic work. The commitment to originality led to especially strained interpretations when the work was collaborative, for "originality" implied that the work resulted from the unique vision of one gifted individual, not from the joint efforts of a team of skilled craftsmen. Thus the legal fiction was invented that allowed an organization to become the "author," a fiction routinely evoked to this day for films collaboratively produced by perhaps hundreds of cultural workers. [2]

The patchwork quality of these legal fictions indicates the fragility of the consensus hammered out in the eighteenth century. Over subsequent decades and centuries this consensus was challenged repeatedly in court. It was also challenged through artistic productions that sought to wrench the idea of the writer away from the transcendent ideal of the autonomous creator, from the automatic writing of the Surrealists to the theoretical arguments of Michel Foucault in his famous essay "What Is an Author?" *Patchwork Girl* contributes to these ongoing contestations by exploiting the specificities of the digital medium to envision a very different kind of subjectivity than that which emerged in eighteenth-century legal battles over copyright. Those aspects of textual production that were suppressed in the eighteenth century to make the literary work an immaterial intellectual property—the materiality of the medium, the print technologies and economic networks that produced the work as a commodity, the collaborative nature of many literary works, the literary appropriations and transformations that were ignored or devalued in favor of "originality," the slippage from book to work to style to face—form a citational substrata for Jackson's fiction, which derives much of its energy from pushing against these assumptions. When *Patchwork Girl* foregrounds its appropriation of eighteenth-century texts, the effect is not to reinscribe earlier assumptions but to bring into view what was suppressed to create the literary work as intellectual property. In *Patchwork Girl*, the unconscious of eighteenth-century texts becomes the ground and surface for the specificity of this electronic text, which delights in pointing out that it was created not by a fetishized unique imagination but by many actors working in collaboration, including the "vaporous machinery" of digital text.[3]

Creating a Monster: Subject and Text

Patchwork Girl's emphasis on appropriation and transformation begins with the main character, which is reassembled from the female monster in Mary Shelley's *Frankenstein*. Recall that in *Frankenstein* the male creature, having been abandoned on the night of his creation and having learned through hard experience that humankind finds him repulsive, returns to beg Frankenstein to create a mate for him, threatening dire revenge if he does not. Frankenstein agrees and assembles a female monster, but before animating her, he is struck with horror at the sight of her body and the prospect that she and the male creature will have sex and reproduce. While the howling creature watches at the window, Frankenstein tears the female body to bits. In Shelley Jackson's text the female "monster" (as she refers to herself) reappears, put together again by Mary Shelley. Like the female monster's body, the body of this hypertext is also seamed and ruptured, composed of disparate parts with extensive links between them. The main components of the hypertextual corpus are "body of text," containing the female monster's narration and theoretical speculations on hypertextual and human bodies; "graveyard," where the stories of the creatures whose parts were used to make the female monster are told; "story," in which are inscribed excerpts from the relevant passages in Frankenstein along with the monster's later adventures; "journal," the putative journal of Mary Shelley where she records her interactions with the female monster; and "crazy quilt," a section containing excerpts from Frank Baum's *Patchwork Girl of Oz*, as well as reinscriptions from other parts of the text. [4]

From the hypertext links and metaphoric connections between these parts, a vivid picture emerges that radically alters the eighteenth-century view of the subject as an individual with a unique personality and the Lockean ability to possess his own person. For the female monster, it is mere common sense to say that multiple subjectivities inhabit the same body, for the different creatures from whose parts she is made retain their distinctive personalities, making her an assemblage rather than a unified self. Her intestines, for example, are taken from Mistress Anne, a demure woman who prided herself on her regularity. The monster's large size required additional footage, so Bossy the cow contributed, too. Bossy is as explosive as Mistress Anne is discreet, leading to expulsions that pain Mistress Anne, who feels she must take responsibility for them. The conflict highlights the monster's nature as a collection of disparate parts. Each part has its story, and each story constructs a different subjectivity. In her article "Stitch Bitch," Jackson suggests that what is true for the monster is also true for us: "The body is a patchwork," Jackson remarks, "though the stitches might not show. It's run by committee, a loose aggregate of entities we can't really call human, but which have what look like lives of a sort. . . . These parts are certainly not what we think of as objects, nor are they simple appendages, directly responsible to the brain" (527).

The distributed nature of the monster's subjectivity—and implicitly ours as well—is further performed in the opening graphic. Even before the title screen appears, an image comes up entitled "her," displaying a woman's body against a black ground. Traversing the body are multiple dotted lines, as if the body were a crazy quilt of scars or seams; retrospectively the user can identify this image as representing the female monster's patched body, among other possible referents. Cutting diagonally across the ground of this image is a dotted line, the first performance of a concept central to this hypertext. As the user progresses further into the text, a map view of the different parts opens up, displayed in the Storyspace software (in which the text is written) as colored rectangles that, when clicked, contain smaller rectangles representing paragraph-sized blocks of text or lexias. The lexia "dotted line" explicates the significance of this image: "The dotted line is the best line," this lexia proclaims, because the dotted line allows difference without "cleaving apart for good what it distinguishes" (body of text/dotted line). Hovering between separation and connection, the dotted lines mark the monster's affinities with the human as well as her differences from other people.

The dotted line is also significant because it suggests that the image can move from two to three dimensions, as in a fold-up that lets "pages become tunnels or towers, hats or airplanes" (body of text/dotted line). The movement out of the flat plane evokes the hypertext's stacks, which suggest through their placement a three-dimensional depth to the screen and a corresponding ability to emerge from the depths or recede into them. The text mobilizes the specificity of the technology by incorporating the three-dimensionality of linked windows as a central metaphor for the fiction's own operations. Like the hypertext stacks, the monster will not be content to reside quiescent on the page but moves fluidly between the world represented on the pages of Mary Shelley's text and the three-dimensional world in which Mary Shelley lives as she writes this text. Lying on a plane but also suggesting a fold upward, the dotted line becomes a kind of joint or scar that marks the merging of fiction and metafiction in a narrative strategy that Gérard Genette has called "metalepsis," the merging of diegetic levels that normally would be kept distinct.[5] The line signals the dangerous potential of the monstrous text/body to disrupt traditional boundaries in a border war where the stakes are human identity. In an interview with Rita Raley, Shelley Jackson remarked that "a radical text can't just depict monstrosity, but must be itself monstrous."[6]

In hypertext fashion, let us now click back to "her," the opening graphic, and explore some of the other links radiating out from this lexia. Linked to "her" is "phrenology," a graphic that further performs the metaphoric overlay of body and text. Showing a massive head in profile, "phrenology" displays the brain partitioned by lines into a crazy quilt of women's names and enigmatic phrases. When we click on the names, we are taken to lexias that tell the stories of the women from whose parts the monster was assembled; clicking on the phrases takes us to lexias that meditate on the nature of "her" multiple subjectivities. Thus we enter these textual blocks through a bodily image, implying that the text lies within the represented body. This dynamic inverts the usual perception the reader has with print fiction that the represented bodies lie within the book. In print fiction, the book as physical object often seems to fade away as the reader's imagination re-creates the vaporous world of the text, so that reading becomes, in Friedrich Kittler's phrase (discussed in the prologue and chapter 1), a kind of hallucination.[7] Therefore, the bodies populating the fictional world seem to be figments of the reader's imagination. First comes the immaterial mind, then from it issue impressions of physical beings. Here, however, the body is figured not as the *product* of the immaterial work but a *portal* to it, thus inverting the usual hierarchy that puts mind first. Moreover, the partitioning of the head, significantly seen in profile so that it functions more like a body part than a face delineating a unique identity, emphasizes the multiple, fragmented nature of the monster's subjectivity. The body we think we have—coherent, unified, and solid—is not the body we actually are, Jackson claims in "Stitch Bitch." Like the monster's body, our corporeality, which she calls the "banished body," is "a hybrid of thing and thought. . . . Its public image, its face is a collage of stories, borrowed images, superstitions, fantasies. We have no idea what it 'really' looks like" (523).

Although the monster's embodiment as an assemblage may seem unique, Jackson employs several strategies to demonstrate that it is not nearly as unusual as it may appear. Drawing on the contemporary discourses of technoscience, the lexia "bio" points out that "the body as seen by the new biology is chimerical. The animal cell is seen to be a hybrid of bacterial species. Like that many-headed beast [the chimera], the microbeast of the animal cells combines into one entity, bacteria that were originally freely living, self sufficient and metabolically distinct" (body of text/bio). In this view, the "normal" person is already an assemblage, designed so by evolutionary forces that make Frankenstein appear by comparison as an upstart amateur. Other perspectives yield the same conclusion. Boundaries between self and other are no more secure than those between plant, animal, and human. "Keep in mind," the monster warns us in "hazy whole," that "on the microscopic level, you are all clouds. There is no shrink-wrap preserving you from contamination: your skin is a permeable membrane. . . . If you touch me, your flesh is mixed with mine, and if you pull away, you may take some of me with you, and leave a token behind" (body of text/hazy whole). In "Stitch Bitch," Jackson writes that the mind, "what zen calls monkey-mind and Bataille calls project, has an almost catatonic obsession with stasis, centrality, and unity." The project of writing, and therefore of her writing most of all, is to "dismantle the project" (527).

Following this philosophy, *Patchwork Girl* not only normalizes the subject-as-assemblage but also presents the subject-as-unity as a grotesque impossibility. The narrator satirizes the unified subject by evoking visions of resurrection, when the body will be "restored to wholeness and perfection, even a perfection it never achieved in its original state" (body of text/resurrection). But how can this resurrection be performed? What about amputees who have had their limbs eaten by other creatures? Following the medieval theological notion that the resurrected body will "take its matter, if digested, from the animal's own flesh," the narrator imagines those parts re-forming themselves from the animals' bodies. The "ravens, the lions, the bears, fish and crocodiles . . . gang up along shorelines and other verges to proffer the hands, feet and heads that they are all simultaneously regurgitating whole . . . big toe scraping the roof of the mouth, tapping the teeth from the inside, seeming alive, wanting out" (body of text/resurrection/remade). Bizarre as this scenario is, it is not as strange as the problems entertained by medieval theologians trying to parcel everything out to its proper body. Some theologians theorized that eaten human remains will be reconstituted from the "nonhuman stuff" the creature has eaten, a proposition that quickly becomes problematic, as the narrator points out. "But what (hypothesized Aquinas) about the case of a man who ate only human embryos who generated a child who ate only human embryos? If eaten matter rises in the one who possessed it first, this child will not rise at all. All its matter will rise elsewhere: either in the embryos its father ate . . . or in the embryos it ate" (body of text/resurrection/eaten). This fantastic scenario illustrates that trying to sort things out to achieve a unity (that never was) results in confusions worse than accepting the human condition as multiple, fragmented, chimerical.

Suturing the (Textual) Body: Sewing and Writing in Storyspace

As the unified subject is thus broken apart and reassembled as a multiplicity, *Patchwork Girl* also highlights the technologies that make the textual body itself a multiplicity. To explore this point, consider how information moves across the interface of the CRT screen, compared with books. In print fiction, the reader decodes a durable script to create in her mind a picture of the verbally represented world. With an electronic text, the encoding/decoding operations are distributed between the writer, computer, and user. The writer encodes, but the user does not simply decode what the writer has written. Rather, the computer decodes the encoded information, performs the indicated operations, and then re-encodes the information as flickering images on the screen. As the discussion in chapter 2 makes clear, the transformation of the text from durable inscription into a flickering signifier means that it is mutable in ways that print is not, and this mutability serves as a visible mark of the multiple levels of encoding/decoding intervening between user and text. Through its flickering nature, the text-as-image teaches the user that it is possible to bring about changes in the screenic text that would be impossible with print (changing fonts, colors, type sizes, formatting, etc.). Such changes imply that the body represented within the virtual space is always already mutated, joined through a flexible, multilayered interface with the user's body on the other side of the screen. In "Stitch Bitch," Jackson puts it this way: "Boundaries of texts are like boundaries of bodies, and both stand in for the confusing and invisible boundary of the self" (535).

These implications become explicit in one of the opening graphics of *Patchwork Girl*, "hercut 4." In this image, the monster's body, which was previously displayed with dotted lines traversing it, has now become completely dismembered, with limbs distributed into rectangular blocks defined by dotted lines, thus completing the body/text analogy by making the dispersion of body parts visually similar to the hypertext lexias connected to each other in the Storyspace display by lines representing hypertext links. In addition, the upper right-hand corner of the image looks as though it has been torn off, revealing text underneath. Although fragmentary, enough of the text is visible to allow the user to make out instructions on how to create links to "interconnect documents and make it easier to move from place to [word obscured]." Thus the text underlying the image points to the Storyspace software program used to create the work, so the entire image functions as an evocation of the multilayered coding chains flexibly mutating across interfaces to create flickering signifiers.

In her interview with Rita Raley, Jackson comments that the idea for creating a fiction that would use a patchwork quilt as a central metaphor came to her when she looked at the map view of Storyspace, which appears on the screen as linked and nested rectangular boxes (within boxes within boxes). "When I first started working in electronic media, the applications all seemed fraught with metaphoric implications, which not only bled into the work I was doing but inspired it," Jackson comments. She continues, "I wouldn't have written *Patchwork Girl* at all if I hadn't been puzzling over hypertext in general, and I wouldn't have found the graveyard and quilt metaphors I employed in that piece nearly so ready to hand if I hadn't been using an application, Storyspace, that involved moving little rectangles around inside bigger rectangles!"[8] As these comments suggest, much of the genius of *Patchwork Girl* derives from Jackson's ability to exploit the idiosyncrasies of Storyspace for her own purposes. Created by Mark Bernstein of Eastgate Systems, in collaboration with Jay Bolter and Michel Joyce, Storyspace was one of the first comprehensive hypertext writing systems.[9] When the Web was still in its infancy, Storyspace provided a flexible and relatively easy-to-use tool for creating lexias, linking structures, and "guard fields" (conditional links) that allowed authors to establish pre-scripted sequences. From about 1987 through 1995, first-generation hypertext writers used Storyspace to create some of the first widely discussed literary hypertexts, including Michael Joyce's *afternoon*, Stuart Moulthrop's *Victory Garden*, and, of course, *Patchwork Girl*. These works have often been called (in retrospect) the "Storyspace school" of hypertext writing, and it is worthwhile to consider what such a designation means.

Storyspace is conceived first and foremost as a software for creating and linking blocks of text. The principle unit is what the Storyspace manual calls a "writing space," and although it is possible (with some difficulty, as I found when I tried to use the software) to import images and sound (WAV) files, the basic assumption is that the writing spaces will be filled primarily with text.[10] The software cannot, for example, create animations or accommodate QuickTime movies. It was designed before the Web took off, and its Web capabilities remain limited. To port a Storyspace work to the Web, image files stored in the Storyspace format have to be manually converted into JPEG or GIF files, and the articulation between the text styles used in Storyspace and Web text styles is somewhat unpredictable. Moreover, the different views through which Storyspace displays a work's structure (such as the map view, chart view, and outline view) do not translate to the Web, and so the visual display of structure that is one of Storyspace's strengths is lost in the Web translation. Links from graphics also do not work, and sound files associated with writing spaces will not play. Because of these limitations, someone intending to create a work for the Web would be much better off beginning with a Web authoring tool rather than trying to retrofit a work created in Storyspace for the Web.

In *Patchwork Girl*, Jackson uses only limited graphics and no sound, video, or animation. Moreover, she adapts her text to accommodate the limited ways in which the text's structure can be displayed. A good example is the "crazy quilt" section, in which Storyspace's extremely limited palette of eight colors does not seem overly restrictive, given the fact that crazy quilts were traditionally constructed from fabric scraps and did not necessarily have an artistically compelling or unified color scheme. Her most wide-ranging inspiration, as we have seen, was to use the visual display of nested and linked boxes as metaphors for the fragmented and dispersed body of her protagonist. Working with a software that can seem unbearably restrictive and rigid judged by today's standards of fluid animations, layered images, morphings, and sonic environments, she made a virtue of necessity by appropriating its visual displays and hierarchical structures as primary metaphors for the seamed and ruptured bodies foregrounded in her work.

The specificities of the software sharply distinguish her text from the print works on which she draws. Of course, print texts are also dispersed, in the sense that they cite other texts at the same time they transform those citations by embedding them in new contexts, as Derrida among others has taught us.[11] Nonetheless, the specificity of an electronic hypertext like *Patchwork Girl* comes from the ways in which it mobilizes the resources (and restrictions) of the software and medium to enact subjectivities distributed in flexible and mutating ways across author, text, interface, and user. As we saw in chapters 2 and 4, electronic text is less durable and more mutable than print, and the active interface is not only multilayered but itself capable of cognitively sophisticated acts. By exploiting these characteristics, Jackson constructs distinctions between author and character, user and represented world, as permeable membranes that can be configured in a variety of ways.

In *Patchwork Girl*, one of the important metaphoric connections expressing this flickering connectivity is the play between *sewing* and *writing*. Within the narrative fiction of *Frankenstein*, the monster's body is created when Frankenstein patches the body parts together; at the metafictional level, Mary Shelley creates this patching through her writing. Within *Patchwork Girl*, however, it is Mary Shelley (not Frankenstein) who assembles the monster, and this patching is specifically identified with the characteristically feminine work of sewing or quilting. The fact that this sewing takes place *within* the fiction makes Mary Shelley a character written by Shelley Jackson as well as an author who herself writes. This situation becomes more complex when Mary Shelley is shown both to sew *and* write the monster, further entangling fiction and metafiction. "I had made her, writing deep into the night by candlelight," Mary Shelley narrates, "until the tiny black letters blurred into stitches and I began to feel that I was sewing a great quilt" (journal/written). This lexia is linked with "sewn": "I had sewn her, stitching deep into the night by candlelight, until the tiny black stitches wavered into script and I began to feel that I was writing, that this creature I was assembling was a brash attempt to achieve by artificial means the unity of a life-form" (journal/sewn).

In the Raley interview, Jackson remarks that when she first began writing hypertext she "discovered that the link was not neutral, but was itself a kind of argument, one I should not duplicate in my prose. I had to learn to allow the link to make points that I would formerly have spelled out in words."[12] So here the link between writing and sewing, a stereotypical feminine activity, serves to mark this as a female—and feminist—production. Throughout, the relation between creature and creator in *Patchwork Girl* stands in implicit contrast to the relation between the male monster and Victor Frankenstein. Whereas Victor participates, often unconsciously, in a dynamic of abjection that results in tragedy for both creator and creature, in *Patchwork Girl* Mary feels attraction and sympathy rather than horror and denial. In contrast to Victor's determination to gain preeminence as a great scientist, Mary's acts of creation are hedged with qualifications that signal her awareness that she is not so much conquering the secrets of life and death as participating in forces greater than she. In "sewn," the passage continues with Mary wondering whether the monster's fragmented unity is "perhaps more rightfully given, not made; continuous, not interrupted; and subject to divine truth, not the will to expression of its prideful author. *Authoress*, I amend, smiling" (journal/sewn). The self-conscious placement of herself in an inferior position of "authoress" compared to the male author—surely in relation to her husband most of all—is connected in Jackson's text with subtle suggestions that the monster and Mary share something Mary and her husband do not, an intimacy based on equality and female bonding rather than on subservience and female inferiority. Although Mary confesses to feeling sometimes frightened of the female monster, she also feels compassionate and even erotic attraction toward her creation. Whereas Victor can see his monster only as a competitor whose strength and agility are understood as threats, Mary exults in the female monster's physical strength, connecting it with the creature's freedom from the stifling conventions of proper womanhood. When the female monster leaves her creator to pursue her own life and adventures, Mary, unlike Victor, takes vicarious delight in her creation's ability to run wild and free.

In her comprehensive survey of the status of the body in the Western philosophic tradition, Elizabeth Grosz has shown that there is a persistent tendency to assign to women the burden of corporeality, leaving men free to imagine themselves as disembodied minds—an observation that has been familiar to feminists at least since Simone de Beauvoir.[13] Even philosophers as sympathetic to embodiment as Maurice Merleau-Ponty and Mark Johnson are often blind to issues of gender, implicitly assuming the male body as the norm. The contrast between woman as embodied female and man as transcendent mind is everywhere at work in the comparison between Mary's care for the female monster and Victor's astonishing failure to anticipate any of the male creature's corporeal needs, including the fact that making him seven feet tall might make it difficult for the monster to fit into human society. Whereas the disembodied text of the eighteenth century work went along with a parallel and reinforcing notion of the author as a disembodied face, in Jackson's text the emphasis on body and corporeality goes along with an embodied author and equally material text. "The banished body is not female, necessarily, but it is feminine," Jackson remarks. "That is, it is amorphous, indirect, impure, diffuse, multiple, evasive. So is what we learned to call bad writing. Good writing is direct, effective, clean as a bleached bone.

Bad writing is all flesh, and dirty flesh at that. . . . Hypertext is everything that for centuries has been damned by its association with the feminine" ("Stitch Bitch," 534).

Reinforcing this emphasis on hypertext as "femininely" embodied are links that re-embody passages from Shelley's text in contexts that subtly or extravagantly alter their meaning. A stunning example is the famous passage from the 1831 preface where Mary Shelley bids her "hideous progeny go forth and prosper" (quoted in story/severance/hideous progeny). "I have an affection for it, for it was the offspring of happy days, when death and grief were but words which found no true echo in my heart. Its several pages speak of many a walk, many a drive, and many a conversation, when I was not alone; and my companion was one who, in this world, I shall never see more. But this is for myself; my readers have nothing to do with these associations" (story/severance/hideous progeny). In the context of *Frankenstein*, "hideous progeny" can be understood as referring both to the text and to the male monster. As Anne Mellor points out, taking the text as the referent places Mary Shelley in the tradition of female writers of Gothic novels who were exposing the dark underside of British society.[14] When the monster is taken as the referent, the passage suggests that Mary Shelley's textual creature expresses the fear attending birth in an age of high mortality rates for women and infants—a fear that Mary Shelley was to know intimately from wrenching personal experience. Moreover, in Barbara Johnson's reading of *Frankenstein*, Shelley is also giving birth to herself as a writer in this text, so her authorship also becomes a "hideous progeny."[15] The rich ambiguities that inhere in the phrase make Jackson's transformation of it all the more striking.

In Jackson's work, the passage's meaning is radically changed by the lexia "Thanks," to which it is linked. In this lexia, the female monster says, "Thanks, Mary, for that kindness, however tinged with disgust. Hideous progeny: yes, I was both those things, for you, and more. Lover, friend, collaborator. It is my eyes you describe—with fear, yes, but with fascination: yellow, watery, but speculative eyes" (story/severance/hideous progeny/ thanks). The linked passage changes the referent for "hideous progeny," so that the female monster occupies the place previously held by the male creature, the text of *Frankenstein*, and Mary Shelly as writer. All these, the link implies, are now embedded as subtexts in the female monster, who herself is indistinguishable from the ruptured, seamed textual body that both contains her and is contained by her. "The hypertext is the banished body," Jackson remarks. "Its compositional principle is desire" ("Stitch Bitch," 536). If desire is enacted by activating links, this linked text not only expresses the user's desire but also Mary's desire for her monstrous creation. Its most subversive—and erotic—implication comes in changing the referent for the lost companion "who, in this world, I shall never see more." Now it is not her husband whose loss Mary laments but the female monster—the "lover, friend, collaborator" without whom *Patchwork Girl* could not have been written.[16]

Among *Patchwork Girl*'s many subversions is its attack on the "originality" of the work. "In collage, writing is stripped of the pretense of originality," Jackson writes. "One can be surprised by what one has to say in the forced intercourse between texts or the recombinant potential in one text, by other words that mutter inside the proper names" ("Stitch Bitch," 537). This muttering becomes discernible in Shelley Jackson's playful linking of her name with Mary Shelley's. The title screen of Jackson's work performs this distributed authorship, for it says *Patchwork Girl* is "by Mary/Shelley & herself," a designation that names Mary Shelley, Shelley Jackson, and the monster all as authors.[17]

Jackson's subversions of her publisher's proprietary claims continue in a section entitled "M/S," a naming that invites us to read the slash as both dividing and connecting Mary Shelley and Shelley Jackson.[18] When Jackson reinscribes Shelley's text into hers, the act is never merely a quotation, even when the referents are not violently wrenched away from the originals as in "Thanks"; witness the fact that Jackson divides Shelley's text into lexias and encodes it into the Storyspace software. Rather, the citation of Shelley is a performative gesture indicating that the authorial function is distributed across both names, as the nominative they share between them would suggest (Mary Shelley/Shelley Jackson). In addition, the slash in M/S (ironically interjected into the MS that would signify the "original" material text in normal editorial notation) may also be read as signifying the computer interface connecting/dividing Mary Shelley (a character in *Patchwork Girl*) with Shelley Jackson (the author who sits at the keyboard typing the words that, by conflating Mary's sewing and writing, make "Shelley" into both character and writer).

The computer also actively participates in the construction of these flickering signifiers, in all their distributed, mutable complexity. "There is a kind of thinking without thinkers," the narrator declares, "Matter thinks. Language thinks. When we have business with language, we are possessed by its dreams and demons, we grow intimate with monsters. We become hybrids, chimeras, centaurs ourself: steaming flanks and solid redoubtable hoofs galloping under a vaporous machinery" (body of text/it thinks). The surface of the text-as-image may look solid, this passage suggests, but the "vaporous machinery" generating it marks that solidity with the mutability and distributed cognition characteristic of flickering signifiers. In "Stitch Bitch," Jackson argues that even the subject considered in itself is a site for distributed cognition: "Thinking is conducted by entities we don't know, wouldn't recognize on the street," Jackson writes. "Call them yours if you want, but puff and blow all you want, you cannot make them stop their work one second to salute you" (527).

The trace of flickering signification is as pervasive and inescapable in this text as it is with the constantly refreshed CRT screen. In one of the fiction's climactic scenes, Mary and the monster, having become lovers and grown physically intimate with each other's bodies, decide to swap patches of skin. Each lifts a circle of skin from her leg, and Mary sews her flesh onto the monster, and the monster's flesh onto her own human leg. This suturing of self onto other reveals more than a wish of lovers to join. Because Mary is the monster's creator in a double sense, at once sewing and writing her, the scene functions as a crossroads for the traffic between fiction and metafiction, writer and character, the physical body existing outside the textual frame sutured together with representations of the body in virtual space. Throughout, the narrator has been at pains to point out the parallels between surgery and writing: "Surgery was the art of restoring and binding disjointed parts. . . . Being 'seam'd with scars' was both a fact of eighteenth-century life and a metaphor for dissonant interferences ruining any finely adjusted composition" (body of text/mixed up/seam'd). One of the sutures that reappears in several lexias is the "intertwisted" closing that "left needles sticking in the wounds—in manner of tailors—with thread wrapped around them" (body of text/mixed up/seam'd). Thus a metaphoric relay system is set up between surgery (particularly sutures using needle and thread), sewing, the seamed body, and writing.

Jackson uses this relay system of surgery/sewing/writing to set up an argument about "monstrous" writing that reverberates throughout the text. The narrator points out that "the comparison between a literary composition and the fitting together of the human body from various members stemmed from ancient rhetoric. *Membrum* or 'limb' also signified 'clause'" (body of text/typographical). As the narrator notes, this body/writing analogy allowed rhetoricians to conclude that writing was bad if it resembled a disproportioned or grotesque body. But the analogy was to go only so far; writing was not actually to *become* the body. Decorum dictated that the barrier between the book as physical object and the text as immaterial work be maintained intact. Joseph Addison found any writing distasteful that was configured in the shape of the object it represented, such as George

Herbert's poem "Wings," printed to resemble the shape of wings. The narrator remarks that Addison called this "visual turning of one set of terms into another" the "Anagram of a Man" and labeled it a classic example of "False Wit" (body of text/typographical). This aesthetic judgment is consistent with the assumption that the work is immaterial. Making the physical appearance of the text a signifying component was improper because it suggested that the text could not be extracted from its physical form. According to this aesthetic, bodies can be represented within the text, but the body of the text should not mix with these representations. To do so is to engage in what Russell and Whitehead would later call a "category mistake"—an ontological error that risks, through its enactment of hybridity, spawning monstrous bodies on both sides of the textual divide.

It is precisely such breaches of good taste and decorum that the monster embodies. Her body, "seam'd with scars," becomes a metaphor for the ruptured, discontinuous space of the hypertext, which in its representations also flagrantly violates decorum by transgressively mixing fiction and metafiction in the same chaotic arena. When deciding what skin to swap, the monster, with Mary's consent, significantly decides that "the nearest thing to a bit of my own flesh would be this scar, a place where disparate things are joined in a way that was my own" (story/severance/join). Composed of parts taken from other textual bodies (*Frankenstein* and Frank Baum's *Patchwork Girl of Oz*, among others), this hypertext, like the monster's body, hints that it is most itself in the links and seams that join one part to another. In a passage that conflates body and text, the monster says, "My real skeleton is made of scars, a web that traverses me in three dimensions. What holds me together is what marks my dispersal. I am most myself in the gaps between my parts" (body of text/dispersed). The user inscribes her subjectivity into this text by choosing which links to activate, which scars to trace. Contrary to the dictates of good taste and good writing, the scars/links thus function to join the text with the corporeal body of the user who performs the enacted motions that bring the text into being as a sequential narrative. Because these enactments take place through the agency of the computer, all these bodies—the monster, Mary Shelley, Shelley Jackson, the specificity of the electronic text, the active agency of the digital interface, and we the users—are made to participate in the mutating configurations of flickering signifiers.

As a result of these dotted-line connections/divisions, the text has a livelier sense of embodiment than is normally the case, and the bodies within the text are more densely coded with textuality. "I am a mixed metaphor," the monstrous text / textualized monster declares. "*Metaphor*, meaning something like 'bearing across,' is itself a fine metaphor for my condition. Every part of me is linked with other territories alien to it but equally mine . . . borrowed parts, annexed territories. I cannot be reduced, my metaphors are not tautologies, yet I am equally present in both poles of a pair, each end of the wire is tethered to one of my limbs. The metaphorical principle is my true skeleton" (body of text/metaphor me). The multilayered sense of "metaphor" here—a rhetorical trope of writing that is also a Storyspace link and a scar traversing the monster's body—implies that the movement up and down fictional/metafictional levels is not limited to certain moments in the text but pervades the text as a whole, spreading along with (and becoming indistinguishable from) the "true skeleton" of the text/monster/software. In this fluid movement between bodies inside texts and texts inside bodies, "inside" is constantly becoming "outside" becoming "inside," as if performing at the visible level of the text the linkages between different coding levels within the computer. The dynamic makes real for the user the fact that each visible mark on the screen, in contrast to the flat mark of print, is linked with multiple coding levels whose dimensionalities can expand or contract as the coding commands require. It is not entirely coincidental that the dynamic is also central to Elizabeth Grosz's discussion of "volatile bodies," in which she uses the Moebius strip as a metaphor indicating that bodies are constituted through cultural and linguistic forces that move both from the outside in and from the inside out.[19] Like *Patchwork Girl*, Grosz understands bodies not as static structures but as sites where complex intermediations are enacted.

The dynamic inside/outside/inside is vividly, hauntingly represented in "body jungle," in which the monster dreams herself inside a lush jungle landscape composed of body parts: beating hearts "roost like pheasants on high bone branches"; "intestines hang in swags from ribs and pelvic crests, or pile up like tires at the ankles of legs become trees"; "ovaries hang like kumquats from delicate vines" (story/falling apart/body jungle). The monster imagines passing days and nights in the jungle. "In the morning the convoluted clouds will think about me. They will block my view of the domed sky, which I know will bear faint suture marks, the knit junctures between once-soft sectors of sky." In time she supposes that her legs will be dissolved by the acid dripping from the overhanging stomachs. "My bony stumps will sink deep; I will shuffle forward until I tire, then stand still. I will place the end of a vein in my mouth and suck it. At last I will no longer bother to remove it. . . . I do not know how my skull will open, or if I will still know myself when my brain drifts up to join the huge, intelligent sky." In this vision, she becomes a body part of some larger entity, perhaps the computer that thinks/dreams her, just as her parts were once autonomous entities that have now been incorporated into the larger whole/hole that she is. Jackson remarks in "Stitch Bitch" that in hypertext fiction there are especially powerful opportunities to "sneak up on reality from inside fiction . . . to turn around and look back on reality as a text embedded in a fictional universe" (534).

We can now see that in this text both the construction of multiple subjectivities and the reconfiguration of consciousness in relation to body are deeply bound up with the intermediating dynamics of flickering signification, which is constituted through the fluidly mutating connections between writer, interface, and user. It is not, however, the hypertext structure that makes *Patchwork Girl* distinctively different from print books. As *Dictionary of the Khazars* has taught us (along with similar works), print texts may also have hypertext structures.[20] Rather, *Patchwork Girl* could be *only* an electronic text because the trace of the computer interface, penetrating deeply into its signifying structures, does more than mark the visible surface of the text; it becomes incorporated into the textual body. Flickering signification, which in a literal and material sense can be understood as producing the text, is also produced by it as a textual effect.

Through the complex enactment of linking structures, both within the text and within the distributed cognitive environment in which the text is read, *Patchwork Girl* brings into view what was suppressed in eighteenth-century debates over copyright. Instead of an immaterial work, this text foregrounds the materiality of fictional bodies, authorial bodies, users' bodies, and the writing technologies that produce and connect them. Instead of valorizing originality, it produces itself and its characters through acts of appropriation and transformation that imply that writing and subjectivity are always patchworks of reinscription and innovation. Rejecting the notion of an author's unique genius, this text self-consciously insists on the collaborative nature of its productions, from the monster as assemblage to the distribution of authorship between the monster "herself," Mary Shelley, Shelley Jackson, the user, the computer, as well as other more shadowy actors.

Closure: Link, Lexia, and Memory

To complete the comparison between *Patchwork Girl* and the subjectivity implicit in eighteenth-century debates over copyright, let us now turn to the distinctions between style and idea, form and content, face and body that informed the invention of copyright. Although one could still talk about the "style" of *Patchwork Girl*, the text offers another set of terms in which to understand its complexities: the alternation between lexia and link, the screen of text that we are reading versus the "go to" computer command that constitutes the hypertextual link in electronic media. In *Patchwork Girl* this alternation is performed through a network of interrelated metaphors, including tissue and scar, body and skeleton, presence and gap. Underlying these terms is a more subtle association of link and lexia with simultaneity and sequence. The eighteenth-century trope of the text as real estate has obviously been complicated by the distributed technologies of cyberspace. Moreover, when the print book becomes unbound in electronic media, time is affected as well. The chronotopes of electronic fictions function in profoundly different ways than the chronotopes of literary works conceived as books. Exploring this difference will open a window onto the connections that entwine the link and lexia together with simultaneity and sequence.

With many print books, the order of pages recapitulates the order of time in the lifeworld. Chronology might be complicated through flashbacks or flashforwards, but normally these flashes comprise episodes that stretch for many pages. There are, of course, notable exceptions, for example, Robert Coover's print hypertext "The Babysitter." Choosing not to notice such experimental print fictions, the narrator of *Patchwork Girl* remarks, "When I open a book I know where I am, which is restful. My reading is spatial and even volumetric. I tell myself, I am a third of the way down through a rectangular solid, I am a quarter of the way down the page, I am here on the page, here on this line, here, here, here" (body of text/this writing). In *Patchwork Girl*, as in many hypertexts, chronology is inherently tenuous because linking structures leap across time as well as space. As if recapitulating the processes of fragmentation and recombination made possible by digital technologies, *Patchwork Girl* locates its performance of subjectivity in the individual lexia. Since the past and the future can be played out in any number of ways, the present moment, the lexia we are reading right now, carries an unusually intense sense of presence, all the more so because it is a smaller unit of narration than normally constitutes an episode. "I can't say I enjoy it, exactly," the narrator comments. "The present moment is furiously small, a slot, a notch, a footprint, and on either side it is a seethe of possibility, the dissolve of alphabets and of me" (body of text/a slot, a notch).

Sequence is constructed by accumulating a string of present moments as the user clicks on links, as if selecting beads to string for a necklace. In contrast to this sequence is the simultaneity of the computer program. Within the non-Cartesian space of computer memory, all addresses are equidistant (within near and far memory, respectively), so all lexias are equally quick to respond to the click of the mouse (making allowance for those that load slower because they contain more data, usually images). This situation reverses our usual sense that time is passing as we watch. Instead, time becomes a river that always already exists in its entirety, and we create sequence and chronology by choosing which portions of the river to sample. There thus arises a tension between the sequence of lexias chosen by the user, and the simultaneity of memory space in which all the lexias already exist. The tension marks the difference between the narrator's life as the user experiences it, and that life as it exists in a space of potentiality in which "everything could have been different and already is" (story/rethinking/a life).

When the narrator-as-present-subject seeks for the "rest of my life," therefore, the situation is not as simple as a unified subject seeking to foresee a future stretching in unbroken chronology before her. To find "the rest of my life," the narrator must look not forward into the passing of time but downward into the computer space in which discrete lexias lie jumbled together (in her metaphoric view, which neglects for poetic effect the computer's precise address system). "I sense a reluctance when I tow a frame forward into the view," the narrator says, in an utterance that conflates writer, user, and character, as if reflecting within the jumble of fiction and metafiction the heterogeneous time represented by the lexias. "It is a child pulled out of a fantastic underground hideaway to answer a history quiz. Were you brought out of polymorphous dreams, in which mechanical contraptions, funnels, tubes and magnifying glasses mingled with animal attentions and crowd scenes, into a rigidly actual and bipolar sex scene? Don't worry, little boxy baby, I will lift you by your ankles off the bed. . . . I will show you the seductions of sequence, and then I will let the aperture close, I will let you fall back into the muddled bedsheets, into the merged molecular dance of simultaneity" (story/rest of my life).

The interjection of simultaneity into the sequence of a user's choices makes clear why different ontological levels (character, writer, user) mingle so monstrously in this text. In the heart of the computer, which is to say at the deepest levels of machine code, the distinctions between character, writer, and user are coded into strings of ones and zeros, in a space where the text written by a human writer and a mouse-click made by a human user are coded in the same binary form as machine commands and computer programs. When the text represents this process (somewhat misleadingly) as a "merged molecular dance of simultaneity," it mobilizes the specificity of the medium as an authorization for its own vision of cyborg subjectivity.

Part of the monstrosity, then, is this mingling of the subjectivity we attribute to characters, authors, and ourselves as users with the nonanthropomorphic actions of the computer program. This aspect of the text's monstrous hybridity is most apparent in "crazy quilt," where excerpts from Frank

Baum's *The Patchwork Girl of Oz* increasingly intermingle with other sections of the hypertext and with instructions from the Storyspace manual. Typical is "seam'd," a significantly named lexia that stitches together the Storyspace program and the surgery/sewing/writing metaphoric network established in other lexias: "You may emphasize the presence of text links by using a special style, color or typeface. Or, if you prefer, you can leave needles sticking in the wounds—in the manner of tailors—with thread wrapped around them. Being seam'd with scars was both a fact of eighteenth-century life and a metaphor for dissonant interferences ruining any finely adjusted composition" (crazy quilt/seam'd). The patchwork quality of the passage is emphasized by the fact that another lexia entitled "seam'd" appears elsewhere (body of text/mixed up/seam'd), from which some of the phrases cited above were lifted.

Although memory is equidistant within the computer, such is not the case for human users. In our memories, events take place in time and therefore constitute sequence. The "seam'd" lexia in "crazy quilt" relies for its effect on the probability that the user has already encountered the lexias of which this is a patchwork. Because we have read these lines in other contexts, they strike us now as a crazy quilt, a textual body stitched together from recycled pieces of other lexias and texts. Memory, then, converts simultaneity into sequence, and sequence into the continuity of a coherent past. But human memory, unlike computer memory, does not retain its contents indefinitely or even reliably. If human memory has gaps in it (a phenomenon alarmingly real to me as my salad days recede in the distance), then it becomes like atoms full of empty space, an apparent continuity riddled with holes.

Fascinated with recovering that which has been lost, the narrator recalls a speech made by Susan B. Anthony at a "church quilting bee in Cleveland" in which the monster "was the featured attraction, the demon quilt" (body of text/mixed up/quilting). Anthony (or is it the monster?) remarks that "our sense of who we are is mostly made up of what we remember being. We are who we were; we are made up of memories." But each of us also holds in her mind experiences she has forgotten. Do these memories, the monstrous Anthony speculates, cohere to make another subject, mutually exclusive of the subject constituted through the memories one remembers? If so, then "within each of you there is at least one other entirely different you, made up of all you've forgotten. . . . More accurately, there are many other you's, each a different combination of memories. These people exist. They are complete, if not exactly present, lying in potential in the buried places in the brain" (story/séance/she goes on). Like the eaten body parts incorporated in the animal's flesh that then scrape to get out at the resurrection, like the textual body that exists simultaneously within the equidistant spaces of computer memory, human memory, too, is chimerical, composed of the subject I remember as myself and the multiple other subjects, also in some sense me, whom I have forgotten but who remember themselves and not me.

When the monster offers to buy a past from Elsie, a randomly chosen woman she approaches on the street, this lack of a past is in one sense unique to the monster, a result of her having been assembled and not born, with no chance to grow into the adult she now is. In another sense, this division between the past the monster can remember and the pasts embodied in her several parts is a common human fate. "We are ourselves ghostly," Anthony/herself goes on. "Our whole life is a kind of haunting; the present is thronged by the figures of the past. We haunt the concrete world as registers of past events. . . . And we are haunted, by these ghosts of the living, these invisible strangers who are ourselves" (story/séance/she goes on). Significantly, the hybridity performed here is a mental assemblage that does not depend on or require physical heterogeneity. *Even if* the text were an immaterial mental entity, it still could not be sure of internal cohesion because the human memories that contain it are themselves full of holes and other selves. On many levels and across several interfaces, this monstrous text thus balances itself between cohesion and fragmentation, presence and absence, lexia and link, sequence and simultaneity, coherent selfhood and multiple subjectivities.

How can such a text possibly achieve closure? Jane Yellowlees Douglas, writing on Michael Joyce's hypertext fiction *afternoon*, suggests that closure is achieved not when all the lexias have been read, but when the user learns enough about the central mystery to believe she understands it.[21] Douglas suggests that the privileged lexia in Joyce's text is "white afternoon"— privileged because its transformative power on the user's understanding of the mystery is arguably greater than other lexias. Although *Patchwork Girl* has no comparable central mystery, it does have a central dialectic, the oscillation between fragmentation and recombination. "I believed that if I concentrated on wishing, my body itself would erase its scars and be made new," the narrator confesses. This wishing for wholeness continues in dynamic tension with the simultaneous realization that she is always already fragmented, ruptured, discontinuous (story/falling apart/becoming whole). When this oscillation erupts into a crisis, the text initiates events that make continuation impossible unless some kind of accommodation is reached. The crisis occurs when the narrator awakes one morning to find that she is coming apart. As she tries to cover over the cracking seams with surgical tape, the dispersion rockets toward violence. "My foot strove skyward . . . trailing blood in mannered specks. My guts split open and something frilly spilled out. . . . My right hand shot gesticulating stump-first eastward" (story/falling apart/diaspora). The tide is stemmed when Elsie, the woman whose past the monster bought, comes upon the monster disintegrating in the bathtub and holds onto her. "I was gathered together loosely in her attention in a way that was interesting to me, for I was all in pieces, yet not apart. I felt permitted. I began to invent something new: a way to hang together without pretending I was whole. Something between higgledy-piggledy and the eternal sphere" (story/falling apart/I made myself over). This resolution, in which the monster realizes that if she is to cohere at all it cannot be through unified subjectivity or a single narrative line, leads to "afterwards," in which the monster decides that the only life she can lead is nomadic, a trajectory of "movement and doubt—and doubt and movement will be my life, as long as it lasts" (story/rethinking/afterwards). Thus the narrative pattern of her life finally becomes indistinguishable from the fragmentation and recombination of the digital technology that produces it, a convergence expressed earlier through the metaphor of the dotted line. "I hop from stone to stone and an electronic river washes out my scent in the intervals. I am a discontinuous line, a dotted line" (body of text/hop). Connecting and dividing, the dotted line of the monster's nomadic trajectory through "movement and doubt" resembles the lexia/link, presence/absence pattern of the screenic text. Following this trajectory, she goes on to become a writer herself.

But what does she write—the narrative we are reading? If so, then the authorial function has shifted at some indeterminate point (or many indeterminate points) from Mary Shelley to the monster, recalling the earlier distribution of authorship between M/S. Just as the user can no longer be sure if, within the fictive world, the monster now writes herself or is written by Mary, so the monster is similarly unsure, in part because her body, like her subjectivity, is a distributed function. "I wonder if I am writing from my thigh, from the crimp-edged pancakelet of skin we stitched onto me. . . . Mary writes, I write, we write, but who is really writing?" Faced with this unanswerable question (unanswerable for the user as for the narrator), the monster concludes, "Ghost writers are the only kind there are" (story/rethinking/am I mary).

The larger conclusions suggested by juxtaposing *Patchwork Girl* with eighteenth-century debates crucial to the formation of print literature go beyond showing how this text makes the unconscious of the earlier period into the stage for its performances of hybrid subjectivities. More broadly, *Patchwork Girl* testifies to the importance of materiality in its signifying strategies—in the ways it mobilizes the specificities of the Storyspace software and, beyond this, the specificities of the digital computer. It vividly demonstrates why a linear causal model would be doomed to inadequacy in accounting for its complexities. The text relies as much on print predecessors as on electronic textuality to create meaning; it marshals language and code to produce the text in a literal sense and also to produce discourse *about* the text; and in the central trope of the dotted line, at once continuous and discrete, it enacts the complementary dynamic between the digital and analog. In short, it demonstrates on many levels and in diverse ways—in its aesthetic, its performance of subjectivity, and the multiple causalities that create its flickering connectivities—the importance of intermediation.

3 TRANSMITTING
Analog and Digital

7 (Un)masking the Agent
Stanislaw Lem's "The Mask"

"Transmitting" in this part is considered not in the technical sense of sending encoded packets through fiber-optic cables according to information protocols, an important topic covered in such seminal texts as Alexander R. Galloway's *Protocol* and Geert Lovink's *Dark Fiber*. Rather, here "transmitting" refers primarily to the mechanisms and processes by which informational patterns are transferred between analog consciousness and digital cognition, understanding the latter variously as located in the computer, in human nonconscious processes, and in digital simulations. The focus on staging encounters of consciousness with digital cognition, anticipated in chapter 6, expands the considerations of parts 1 and 2 to subjectivity, narrative, and the relation of the Regime of Computation to human culture and meaning. Chapter 1 raised the critical question of whether the Regime of Computation should be considered as a cultural construction or as an accurate description of reality, and the chapters in this part keep returning to this question from different perspectives. As anticipated in chapter 1, the kind of analysis pursued here will not so much opt for either the constructivist or realist position as explore their co-constitution of each other. The present chapter initiates this broad inquiry by starting locally, that is, by locating the dynamic between digital cognition and analog consciousness *within* the same being.

Although implant devices have become available only recently, speculation on how coding enters into the deep structures of thought predates the technological actuality by several decades. At issue are questions of cooperation and competition between conscious mind and aconscious coding, free will and programmed outcomes, gendered enculturation and the non-gendered operation of algorithms, language and the nonlinguistics operation of code. The assumption that a substrate of code underlies conscious mind profoundly affects concepts of agency and subjectivity. Whereas the Holocaust and other atrocities provide horrifying examples of humans not counting as persons, intelligent software packages offer the spectacle of bots being mistaken for human interlocutors.[1] In light of these complex intermediations, let me advance a proposition: to count as a person, an entity must be able to exercise agency. Agency enables the subject to make choices, express intentions, perform actions. Scratch the surface of a person, and you find an agent; find an agent, and you are well on your way toward constituting a subject, a dynamic explored at length in chapter 8 with regard to Karl Sims's virtual creatures.

As I will demonstrate in this chapter, computer scientists are not the only ones speculating that computational mechanisms underlie and/or interpenetrate human consciousness. Influential cultural theorists, particularly Gilles Deleuze, Félix Guattari, and Jacques Lacan, also speculate on how the digital and analog interact in human cognition. The same kind of ontological perplexity that haunts the Regime of Computation also troubles these theories: is computation here to be considered a metaphor appropriated from information technologies, or an accurate description of psychic processes? If skepticism toward the Regime of Computation is warranted (and I think it is), skepticism toward these cultural theories should not lag behind. The point as I see it, however, is not to determine whether the theories are correct or incorrect but to understand their roles in helping to create a "climate of opinion," as Raymond Williams calls it, in which the complex intermediations between the analog and digital become central to understanding constructions of subjectivity and agency. In the final portion of this chapter, I will turn to a literary text that enacts these issues in particularly powerful ways, Stanislaw Lem's 1976 novella "The Mask." With a narrator hovering between the human and nonhuman, "The Mask" explores with subtle potency the complexities of a conscious mind whose agency is circumscribed by an underlying program that partially dictates the actions mind can perform. As the mind probes the limits of its freedom, it undergoes a transformation into something other than human. Whether the eponymous mask refers to the human skin that encases a metallic robot, or to the mind from which the narrative voice emerges, is one of many ambiguities the story performs as it probes the possibilities for a consciousness that coexists with an underlying program it can sense but never directly know. In imagining this configuration, Lem's fictional anticipation of the unconscious as digital algorithm remains remarkably prescient a quarter of a century later.

The Machine within the Human

In their radical reconceptualization of agency, Deleuze and Guattari reveal that intelligent artifacts played a seminal role in their thinking about agency. Early in *A Thousand Plateaus* they celebrate cellular automata (CA), contrasting them with the centered systems they deplore. As we saw in chapter 1's account of Stephen Wolfram's *A New Kind of Science*, cellular automata are composed of cells, each of which calculates its state depending on the state of its immediate neighbors. Deleuze and Guattari define cellular automata somewhat inaccurately as "finite networks of automata in which communication runs from any neighbor to any other" (17). In fact, as we know, each cell samples only the cells immediately adjacent to it (or in some cases, the next nearest neighbors). By claiming for cellular automata a less rule-bound dynamic than they in fact possess, Deleuze and Guattari imply that any configuration whatever is possible, an idea they push to the extreme in their notions of "deterritorialization" and "reterritorialization." Cellular automata fit Deleuze and Guattari's purpose because they are completely mechanistic, computational, and nonconscious but nevertheless display complex patterns that appear to evolve, grow, invade new territories, or decay and die out. Particularly relevant is the pattern called "Glider," in which a glider-like shape appears at one edge of the screen and moves toward the other edge, as if enacting what Deleuze and Guattari call a "line of flight." Cellular automata appear as well in their description of schizoanalysis, which "treats the unconscious as an acentered system, in other words, as a machinic network of finite automata (a rhizome), and thus arrives at an entirely different state of the unconscious" (18). The implication is that the unconscious, like cellular automata, is mechanistic and rhizomatic.

These ideas have obvious limitations when applied to the human organism. Unlike the free-form patterns of cellular automata, humans have biological requirements that make the skin an organ vital to survival. Yet Deleuze and Guattari leap over this limitation with a powerful performative rhetoric that makes it seem as if the body could deterritorialize and reterritorialize as easily as cellular automata (which themselves, as noted, have limitations Deleuze and Guattari do not accurately represent). As a result of this rhetoric, the body becomes the Body without Organs, an assemblage rather than an organism, which does away with consciousness as the seat of coherent subjectivity (a move alluded to in chapter 4, where it is linked with reconceptualizing the convergent "work" as Work as Assemblage). In the idea of the Body without Organs, humans are conceived as mutating assemblages that can absorb a variety of entities into their environments, including both machines and organic matter. Instead of conscious thought, the Body without Organs is driven by desire. According to Mark Hansen, desire is so central in *A Thousand Plateaus* that it assumes a fetishized quality, flaming with incandescent intensity that alone has the motive force to drive assemblages into new configurations.[2] Indeed, since consciousness is fragmented, the organism dispersed, and signification thrown out, desire is virtually the only agent left on the playing field. "Make consciousness an experimentation in life," Deleuze and Guattari urge, "and passion a field of continuous intensities, an emission of particle-signs. . . . Desubjectify consciousness and passion" (134). The net effect of this rhetorical transmutation is to construct the Body without Organs as an infinite set of cellular automata whose computational rules are re-encoded as desire. This is a much more direct "computationalization" of the human than that imagined by Wolfram, although here computation is understood in psychoanalytic and philosophical terms rather than in engineering and mathematical contexts.

In *A Thousand Plateaus*, at the same time that humans take on attributes of computational media, machines acquire biological traits. Adopting the terminology of biological evolution, Deleuze and Guattari write, "We may speak of a *machinic phylum*, or technological lineage, wherever we find a *constellation of singularities, prolongable by certain operations, which converge, and make the operations converge upon one or several assignable traits of expression*" (406). Endorsing André Leroi-Gourhan's ideas about a "technological vitalism" that takes "biological evolution in general as the model for technical evolution," Deleuze and Guattari assert that "there is indeed a machinic phylum in variation that creates the technical assemblages, whereas the assemblages invent the various phyla. A technological lineage changes significantly according to whether one draws it upon the phylum or inscribes it in the assemblages; but the two are inseparable" (407). By making the phylum depend on the assemblages and the assemblages on the phylum, Deleuze and Guattari suggest that technological evolution produces distinct genetic forms emerging from a daisy chain of interconnections and eluding linear causal explanation.[3] Although Deleuze and Guattari speak of the machinic phylum as "matter in movement, in flux, in variation, matter as a conveyor of singularities and traits of expression" (409), it is not clear what drives these mutations. They attempt to solve the problem by returning to the prime mover in their theory, imagining that machines are also capable of desire.[4]

In "Machinic Heterogenesis," Guattari addresses this point by interpolating the human and mechanical into one another, arguing that the "mechanosphere . . . superimposes itself on the biosphere."[5] Seeking to open Maturana and Varela's self-enclosing concept of autopoiesis to the production of otherness,[6] Guattari argues that even a mechanism as simple as a lock and key has a repertoire of structural forms through which it can move. This deterritorializing or "smoothing" opens the discrete machine to transformation and, by a nonrational leap of inference, to desire;[7] "all machinic orderings contain within them, even if only in an embryonic state, enunciative nuclei [*foyers*] that are so many protomachines of desire" (25). Thus machines are made like humans because they are driven by desire, even as humans are configured like machines because they can be disassembled and reassembled. "It is thus impossible to refuse human thought its part in the essence of machinism," Guattari writes (15). In this view, "human" connotes no essential quality but marks the historical starting point of a certain line of inquiry. If the human has been mechanical all along, anyone who represents it as "contaminated" by the mechanical mistakes his own process of discovery for the hybridization that was always already there.

Clearly the performative force of language plays a crucial role here, as it does in *A Thousand Plateaus*: much is asserted, almost nothing is demonstrated. If language thus possesses a kind of agency, the next step would be to suppose that language itself is a machine and hence subject to the same processes of deterritorialization and reterritorialization that characterize "desiring machines." Guattari edges toward this realization in "Machinic Heterogenesis" when he asks, "But how long can we continue to characterize the thought put to work here as human? Doesn't technico-scientific thought emerge from a certain type of mental and semiotic machinism?" (15). Guattari takes structural semiotics to task because it fails to capture "figures of expression that work as diagrammatic machines in direct contact with technical-experimental configurations" (15). Whereas semiotic systems posit "distinctive oppositions of a phonemic or scriptural order that transcribe enunciations [*énoncés*] into expressive materials that signify," machines operate differently, using a signifying process that "does not derive from repetition or from mimesis of significations" (15). Obscurely expressed, the point here seems to be that semiotics has falsified the workings of language by interpreting it through structuralist oppositions that covertly smuggle in anthropomorphic thinking characteristic of conscious mind. The model for language should instead be machinic operations that do not need structural oppositions; these operations have available to them a materialistic level of signification in which representation is intertwined with material processes. Although the word "code" does not appear in Guattari's essay, it fits well with his vision of a signifying system that is tied directly to the material process of flickering voltages. "Existence is not dialectic," Guattari exclaims. "It is not representable. It is hardly even livable!"

(25). Guattari's lack of reverence for the Lacanian conception of the signifier now becomes explicit. Semiotics is flawed because it "does not get us out of structure, and prohibits us from entering the real world of the machine. The structuralist signifier is always synonymous with linear discursivity," whereas heterogeneous machines refuse to be "orchestrated by a universal temporalization" (23). Nonetheless, Lacan's views have more in common with Guattari's than he acknowledges, for they concur in conceiving of language as a coding machine. Thus the very linguistic processes that reconceptualize human agency by describing it as an intelligent machine are themselves reconceptualized as essentially mechanistic in their operations.

John Johnston, in his important analysis of Lacan's development of a theory of the unconscious, shows that automata theory is crucial to Lacan's thought.[8] The key idea Lacan lifts from automata theory is the notion that inherent in symbol manipulation are certain structural relationships that can be used to program a Turing machine. Recall from chapter 1 that the Turing machine is an abstract computer that can perform any computation that any computer can do, including computing the algorithm that constitutes itself.[9] This very simple machine is composed of three components: a head that reads and writes binary symbols forward and backward on a tape; the tape itself; and the rules for producing a new state from the previous one. Working by analogy (although not always explicitly stating so), Lacan transposes these ideas onto the unconscious, conceiving of it as a machine operating upon language without needing anything like anthropomorphic awareness to perform its operations. Guattari is correct in asserting that linearity is essential to the Lacanian conception of the signifier, but he underestimates the flexibility with which the Turing machine can operate. By folding the abstract operations of calculation into the material operation of the tape, Turing simplified the computational load and achieved an economy of operation that made his Universal machine so powerful an idea that it is routinely regarded as the theoretical basis for modern computers.

Lacan's conception of the unconscious as a kind of Turing machine enables him to accomplish a profound transformation of Freud's view of the unconscious (notwithstanding his claim that he merely makes explicit what is implicit in Freud). When Freud posited the death drive, he thought of it as an unconscious tendency to move toward the inanimate, a return to pre-biological origins. There is a sense in which this view of the unconscious is deeply anthropomorphic, for it identifies the present state of the (conscious) subject with life, from which point the unconscious moves *back* toward the inanimate. By contrast, as John Johnston shows, Lacan envisions language as *beginning* in the mechanistic operations of the unconscious, from which emerge the higher order processes of conscious thought. The direction of the vector changes from back to up, that is, from regression to emergence; equally important, mechanistic operations are conceived as providing the basis for consciousness rather than as representing a return to the preanimate. Thus the important distinction shifts from living/nonliving to mechanistic intelligence/conscious awareness. Given claims by researchers that artificial life is indeed a form of life, the divide between animate and inanimate has become increasingly problematic.[10] Like Lacan, theorists of artificial life focus on the intelligences that can emerge from mechanistic operations in both protein- and silicon-based life forms, an ideal formulated in different terms by Stephen Wolfram in *A New Kind of Science*, as we saw in chapter 1. The difference between Lacan's linear model and Guattari's "heterogeneous machine" pales compared to the looming fact that both envision human cognition as always already interpenetrated by machinic processes, or as John Johnston puts it, as constituted through the "in-mixing" of human psychology with cybernetics.

The net result of these feedback loops between artificial life forms and biological organisms has been to create a crisis of agency, a phenomenon described at length in my book *How We Became Posthuman*.[11] If, on the one hand, humans are like machines, whether figured as cellular automata or Turing machines, then agency cannot be securely located in the conscious mind. If, on the other hand, machines are like biological organisms, then they must possess the effects of agency even though they are not conscious. In these reconfigurations, desire and language, both intimately connected with agency, are understood in new ways. Acting as a free-floating agent, desire is nevertheless anchored in mechanistic operations, a suggestion Guattari makes in "Machinic Heterogenesis." Language, emerging from the operations of the unconscious figured as a Turing machine, creates expressions of desire that in their origin are always already interpenetrated by the mechanistic, no matter how human they seem. Finally, if desire and the agency springing from it are at bottom nothing more than the performance of binary code, then computers can have agency as fully authentic as humans. Through these reconfigurations, Deleuze, Guattari, and Lacan use automata to challenge human agency, and in the process they configure automata as agents.

Machines acting as agents, and humans with their agency rooted in machinic processes—ideas explored in chapter 6 through Shelley Jackson's *Patchwork Girl*—vividly illustrate why notions of personhood have become destabilized. The uncanny similarities between Wolfram's speculations and the theories of Deleuze, Guattari, and Lacan (developed in large part, if not entirely, independently of one another) illustrate how pervasive within the culture these human/machine dynamics have become. To bring into sharper focus the anxieties created by supposing that digital mechanisms underlie analog consciousness, I turn now to Stanislaw Lem's powerful story "The Mask." At the heart of this disturbing tale is a conflict between a conscious mind that can think and an underlying program that determines action. To make the conflict more intense, Lem arranges matters so that conscious mind has no direct access to program, much as we have no direct access to the interior computational modules that, in the view of some evolutionary psychologists, codetermine our behavior.[12] In the disjunction between the representations conscious mind makes to itself and the actions actually taken, the crisis of agency is bodied forth as an inescapable and tragic condition of thinking mind(s).

The Human within the Machine

"The Mask" begins with a threshold. On one side is a consciousness that names "the it that was I" (181). In Polish, the narrator is named throughout with feminine words (for example, "machina," the feminine form of "machine," and the feminine "Maska" of the Polish title). Jerzy Jarzebski and Michael Kandel have observed, however, that at the tale's beginning the narrator is constructed as neuter, a performance Lem enacts by using past-tense verb forms with neuter endings that do not actually exist as such in normal usage (although the neologisms would be recognized immediately by Polish-speaking readers).[13] This linguistic creativity underscores from the outset the importance of gender (albeit here by its linguistic erasure). Using these neologisms, the narrator recounts an experience imaged simultaneously as a birth, a movement down an assembly line, and an erotic encounter. Here the narrator plays a passive role, object of unknown gazing eyes, "snoutlike flattened heads," "pincer hands," and "flat mouths in a rim of sparks" that give a final "quivering kiss" that "tautened the me" and cause the narrator to "crawl into a round opening without light" (181–82). At the moment the narrator crosses the threshold (which is both spatial and linguistic), consciousness undergoes a dramatic change, feeling "the rush of gender so violent, that her head spun and I shut my eyes. And as I stood thus, with eyes closed, words came to me from every side, for along with gender she had received language" (182). At this liminal moment, the narrator moves from an "it" already receding from awareness into a linguistically enculturated "she" whose movement over the palace threshold (for that is where she now perceives herself to be) plunges her into the Symbolic. As her perception snaps into cultural focus, the objects that an instant before it had described as a "colored confusion of vertical trunks," with "globes" containing "tiny buttons bright with water," become the lords and ladies attending a court ball, whose eyes are turning to follow the beautiful woman the narrator has become (182). Thus from the beginning we have reason to doubt that the narrator's consciousness is the seat of identity, for it springs into existence only after another kind of awareness, an awareness that inhabits an "it" and not "she," has moved the narrator through the birth channel and out into the world.

These abrupt transitions between physical spaces are characteristic of the consciousness as long as the narrator remains a woman, suggesting that consciousness here operates as if it were a machine being turned on and off. Precisely because the sphere of consciousness is limited, its operation within that staging area is all the more frenetic as it seeks to establish its conditions of possibility. As the woman progresses into the ball, her consciousness speeds along in a hyperrational mode that Jo Alyson Parker, in her Lacanian analysis of "The Mask," finds impossible to accept as female.[14] Indeed, consciousness suspects its own hyperrationality. As the narrator tries to make sense of her situation, she realizes that "this self-determined thinking of mine seemed in its correctness just a bit too cold, unduly calm, for fear remained beyond it—like a thing transcendent, omnipresent, yet separate—therefore my own thoughts too I held in suspicion" (199). Knowing that she should be afraid but unable to feel the hormonal surges that make fear an experience inhabiting the self, she comes close to being the subject we call Cartesian, doubting everything including her own thoughts.

Why should she feel fear? Although she can think whatever she pleases, she slowly realizes that she is only partially able to control her actions, a prospect that infuses consciousness with dread. She quickly determines that she is intended for Arrhodes, a brilliant thinker who has dared to question the authority of the king. This knowledge comes to consciousness but does not originate there, appearing to the narrator as a predetermined fact. When she drops her fan before Arrhodes in a clichéd gesture of seduction, she feels a blush appear, but like fear, this blush does not inhabit her, appearing to consciousness as if it were a foreign intrusion. "The blush did not belong to me, it spread on my cheeks, claimed my face, pinkened my ear lobes, which I could feel perfectly, yet I was not embarrassed, nor excited. . . . I'll say more: I had nothing whatever to do with that blush, it came from the same source as the knowledge that had entered me at the threshold of the hall" (190). This separation between consciousness and the bodily actions consciousness observes reveals a fatal gap between thought and agency. Although consciousness feels that it comprises an identity in itself—as if it is, as the narrator says, "one"—it must face the fact that another kind of agency also inhabits the body, and moreover an agency to which consciousness has no direct access and that it must strive to apprehend through inferences and observations. "Everyone knows it is impossible to turn the eyeball around," she thinks, "such that the pupil can peer inside the skull" (194).

In her dance of seduction with Arrhodes, the narrator displays a brilliance and satirical edge that both fascinates Arrhodes and makes him afraid, for he senses immediately that this is no ordinary woman, bluntly demanding, "Who are you?" Asking this question of herself, the narrator flashes onto the pasts of three entirely different women: Mignonne from the north, Angelita from the south, and Tlenix, each accompanied by intense though fragmentary sensory memories. [15] She also senses that her choice will determine the "truth," that "each one could take on substance if I acknowledged it," and that "the images unmentioned would be blown away" (192). Consciousness here senses its position as a PROM, a programmable chip that can accept an initial choice of input but that, once the choice has been made, loses this flexibility as input merges with software and software rigidifies into hardware. Significantly, she chooses not to answer Arrhodes, thereby preserving an indeterminacy that she seeks to fill instead with her own option, imagining herself as that quintessentially marginalized female figure, the madwoman tenderly cared for by patronizing relatives.

This identity cannot take, for it has not been included among the possible inputs. Yet the narrator's response is significant, for it shows that consciousness is determined to assert her own agency over and against the other agency inhabiting the body. Conversing with Arrhodes, the narrator tests the limits to which she can go. She tries to say something stupid, knowing that it will be an effective turnoff for Arrhodes, but she finds herself unable to be anything but brilliant. When she tries to warn him outright, telling him in response to his request for an assignation, "Better to say: never and nowhere" (194), she can utter the warning only in the clichéd language of a lover who feigns reluctance to spur on desire. She realizes this too late, desperately adding, "I do not toy with you, my fine philosopher, look within and you will see that I advised you well" (195), another articulation that goes awry because when Arrhodes looks within, he sees only the desire that is real enough to him but that she knows to be a fatal trap set by his deadly adversary, the king. "What I wished to add," consciousness thinks, "I could not utter. I was able to think anything, strange as it may seem, yet in no way find my voice, I could not reach those words. A catch in my throat, a muteness, like a key turned in a lock, as if a bolt had clicked shut between us" (195). As the narrator will come to realize more fully later, the most insidious threat to her agency is not a direct prohibition on her actions. Scary as that is, more frightening is a co-optation that turns whatever she tries to do to the purposes of the other agency inhabiting the body.

The seductive dance continues when the narrator meets Arrhodes the next day in a garden—another abrupt transition preceded by a period of unknowingness; for when she left the ball, she entered into a carriage that was more like a coffin, imprisoning her within a space too small for her to stand fully upright. As she lies in the darkness, she thinks again of her three prearranged pasts and compares them to her dim memories, when she experienced herself as neuter. Becoming increasingly aware not only of the alien agency within her body but also of the exterior agents who arranged for it to be there, she muses on the fact that she can remember the time before. "I think it had to be that way, that it would have been impossible to arrange things otherwise," she speculates (196). Desperately seeking for a way to make her own will count, she tries to put together an identity not predetermined by the other's agency: "Out of discrepant elements I could construct nothing of my own, unless I were to find in the design already existing some lopsidedness, chinks I might penetrate, thereby to rend open the structure and get to the core of it" (202). And so she returns to her memories as a neuter, ironically thinking that "certainly they should at least have wiped out that sequence on my back, the animation of my nakedness, inert and mute, by the sparking kisses, but that too had taken place and now was with me" (202). The memory functions as what evolutionary biologists call a "spandrel," an effect not selected for that emerges because it is genetically entangled with attributes that are selected for. Out of this spandrel, this unplanned excess, she hopes to find the chink that will let her assert agency.

Her desire for an agency she can call her own becomes the driving force of the narrative—or rather, it drives a narrative of self-determination within the larger narrative scripted by the alien agency that also inhabits the body. Thus desire is multiple, living both in consciousness and program. While consciousness knows its desire from the inside, it knows the desire of program from the outside, as if seen from a distance by an observer. "I had love, but elsewhere—I know how that sounds. Oh it was a passionate love, tender and altogether ordinary. I wanted to give myself to him body and soul, though not in reality, only in the manner of the fashion, according to custom, the etiquette of the court. . . . My love was very great, it caused me to tremble, it quickened my pulse, I saw that his glance made me happy. And my love was very small, being limited in me, subject to the style, like a carefully composed sentence expressing the painful joy of tête-à-tête" (208). Her love is great within the scripted confines of the program that has been written to make it so. But for consciousness, love is an alien utterance performed without touching the pulse of thinking mind, which sees but does not experience it. "And so beyond the bounds of those feelings I had no particular interest in saving him from myself or another, for when I reached with my mind outside my love, he was nothing to me" (208–9).

Remembering how she rebelled in the carriage as she realized the limits of her agency, she also recalls the extruded snake head that gave her an injection, turning consciousness off. For consciousness, Arrhodes is important not as a lover but as a potential ally against foreign agents, who themselves have formed an alliance with program across her body's boundaries. "Yet I needed an ally in my struggle against whatever had pricked me that night with venomous metal. . . . Therefore I could not reveal the entire truth to him: that my love and the venomous prick were from one and the same source" (209). Love is a program; passing time is an injection; and both come from agency outside thinking mind.

Because we know the narrator was manufactured and not born, the obvious inference is that her program is composed of algorithms running on some kind of digital mechanism. Lem never reveals the details of her program's operation, however, keeping them deliberately obscure. This makes it possible to think of her program also in cultural terms, an analogy reinforced by the birth imagery at the story's beginning. In this sense, her "program" can also be understood anthropomorphically as equivalent to obsessive/compulsive formations in humans. These subtleties work to encourage our identification with the narrator and to suggest that there may be less difference between her and us than we imagined, a realization in line with the cultural and psychoanalytic theories discussed earlier.

These subtleties come into play partly through the narrator's suggestion that Arrhodes may also be following a cultural program that dictates his actions. Realizing that his banter follows a predictable pattern of sexual foreplay, the narrator intuits that Arrhodes "would surely be conventional in his love" and so "would not accept in me the kind of liberation I desired, the freedom that would cast him off. Therefore I could only act deceitfully, giving freedom the false name of love" (209). For the narrator, one kind of agency comes from program and dictates love; another comes from consciousness, which can exercise agency in this cultural context only by calling it love, although its object is not Arrhodes but the articulation of will independent of program. Arrhodes is not so much a love object to consciousness as a tool she hopes to use to assert her own subjectivity.

The dance of seduction ends with another birth and, with it, a subtle transformation of agency. Ordering Arrhodes to leave her alone in her chateau, the narrator stands before a full-length mirror and, following an inexplicable impulse, cuts herself open from sternum to crotch. When she parts the layers of skin, she sees nestled within her flesh the metallic body of an insectile robot and realizes "it was not it, a foreign thing, different and other, it was again myself" (213). At this moment, Arrhodes comes in and sees her exposed; "it was I, still I, I was repeating to myself when he entered" (213). Gaping at her gaping open, he turns and flees. As the narrator works to free herself from her human mask, "Tlenix, Duenna, Mignonne first sank to her knees, then tumbled face-down to the side and I crawled out of her," whereupon the discarded human skin lies "like a naked thing, her legs thrown apart immodestly" in a seductive pose of which the narrator no longer has need (214–15).

Michael Kandel, in "A Freudian Peek at Lem's *Fiasco*," writes about the pervasiveness of insects in Lem's fiction, noting that "there is something ominous and repugnant about Lem's insects," and observing further that insects, particularly robotic ones, often function as representations of aliens so unlike humans that they remain unfathomable by human characters. "The Mask" uses a highly unusual configuration in combining this alien form with an anthropomorphic consciousness that, moreover, bears the mark of female gender. Throwing aside the shell of a beautiful woman that masked the insectile robot, the narrator now performs a complex balancing act between maintaining the identity of consciousness and dissipating subjectivity throughout the metallic robot body.

In this struggle, gender plays a surprisingly central role. Carol Wald has written brilliantly about "The Mask" as part of a tradition of powerful men using female automata as tools against other men.[16] With the narrator's transformation, the king's plot to assassinate Arrhodes stands fully revealed, but female agency also asserts itself in this design. We learn that the king "had sworn to his dying mother that if harm befell that wise man it would be of his own choosing" (193). Hence the seduction plot. To keep his word to his mother, the king must arrange matters so that Arrhodes *chooses* the narrator and initializes the robot's program, whereupon she metamorphoses into an insectile assassin who will pursue him to the ends of the earth. Male power has the ability to act but only within the constraints imposed by female influence, a formation enacted in a different configuration within the narrator, where male power manifests itself in actions performed by the male-authored program and the consciousness that, as we shall see, continues to be constructed as female.

After the narrator's transformation, consciousness undergoes a subtle but important change. Gone is the hyperrational quality of detached thinking, as if the mind were an engine racing at high rpm while disengaged from the drive train. Consciousness still thinks but now feels more at one with the body, yielding to the "shining metal [that] had written into it movements which I began to execute" (215). Consciousness also finds itself permeated by the exquisite distinctions of smell that the body's superb olfactory equipment makes possible. However, despite this transformation, consciousness continues to desire her own agency, although what that agency might mean becomes more complicated as the sharp division between mind and body eases.

For example, the robot wonders why she pauses for three days after Arrhodes flees before taking up his pursuit. She suspects that this may be her program operating to make sure Arrhodes has time to realize the full terror of his situation. But she also thinks of it as a challenge to her skill as a hunting machine, an opportunity to demonstrate an expertise with which she identifies. Agency here is neither folded back under consciousness nor separated from it; rather, agency of mind and program have blended together to form an uneasy heterogeneous amalgam. Thinking from within this state, consciousness suspects that from the start her agency has been infected with the will of another. Recalling the moment when she split herself open, consciousness realizes "that act of self-evisceration had not been altogether my rebellion. . . . It represented a foreseen part of the plan, designed for just such an eventuality, in order that my rebellion turn out to be, in the end, my total submission" (215). She suspects that the desire authenticating her as an autonomous subjectivity—her intense desire to act as a free agent—has always already been co-opted by program, a thought so scary she can think it only after her metamorphosis, when she accepts program not merely as an exterior function but also an interpenetration of herself. "Thus the hope of freedom could have been just an illusion, nor even my own illusion, but introduced in me in order that I move with more alacrity, urged on precisely by the application of that perfidious spur" (231).

Behind this realization lurks an even more unnerving question. Why does consciousness, obviously necessary for the seduction of the intellectual Arrhodes, need to persist after the narrator's transformation into an insectile robot? The narrative supplies an ad hoc explanation in the monk's suggestion that humans know how to disguise themselves so as to defeat the computations of an algorithmic program; thus the robot's artificial intelligence has been constructed so that it can put "questions to the quarry, questions devised by the foremost experts on the individual characteristics of the human psyche" (229). However, this explanation scarcely suffices to explain the active thoughts of consciousness while on the chase, or her realization that "I was not (after all) a lifeless mechanism equipped with a pair of hunting lungs, I was a being that had a mind and used it" (221). She may have been given a mind for purposes other than her own, but having it, she intends to use it for herself. Still, her mind in its insectile state struggles with other cognitions remote from consciousness. As she continues in the hunt for months, consciousness displays a disconcerting tendency to hibernate. "By now I had forgotten the appearance of this man, and my mind, as if lacking the endurance of the body, particularly during the night runs, drew into itself till I did not know whom I was tracking, nor even if I was tracking anyone; I knew only that my will was to rush on, in order that the spoor of airborne motes singled out for me from the welling diversity of the world persist and intensify" (218). Here agency emerges not from subjectivity but from a cognition that operates independently of conscious mind.

The ambiguity of agency becomes fully apparent when the narrator, having lost the scent, appeals to a wayside monk for help. Woven together in her appeal are falsehood and truth, programmed fate and her own will, prescripted determination to kill Arrhodes and her hope that she can spare him. The monk reveals that Arrhodes had sought sanctuary but was abducted by kidnappers who intended to exploit his fine mind as their tool. The narrator responds by saying that she can kill the abductors, but the monk is also aware of her nature as a programmed assassin. After refusing to give the robot confession because he believes she lacks free will and therefore does not count as a person, the monk asks if she wants the monastery's physician (conveniently a former roboticist) to see if he can defeat the program. Reasoning that he can give her wrong directions to Arrhodes as well as right, she consents to the examination.

The physician finds that her stinger cannot be removed without killing her. But in addition, he also sees "a mechanism which none of your predecessors possessed, a multiple memory of things superfluous to a hunting machine, for these are recorded feminine histories, filled with names and turns of phrase that lure the mind, and a conductor runs from them down into the fatal core. Therefore you are a machine perfected in a way unknown to me, and perhaps even an ultimate machine" (229). Her female gender is thus revealed as somehow essential to her nature even after the seduction plot has ended, linking her femininity to her earlier search for "chinks" in the program that would enable her to "get to the core of it."

Reinforcing this revelation is imagery that figures Arrhodes as her mate as well as her prey. Driven simultaneously by desire and program, her thoughts display a complex ambivalence. When the physician, in one of the anachronistic touches characteristic of Lem's humor, offers to sprinkle iron filings on her core in a move he says will slightly increase her free will, she agrees because she notices that they "both look at me," implying this is a ruse to gain their trust (229). But when she later addresses the reader directly, acknowledging "no doubt you would like to know what my true intentions were in that final run," her thoughts reveal a deep ambivalence about her goal (231).

She says she would like to kill Arrhodes on her own accord, because she knows he cannot possibly love her now that she is no longer a woman, a remark suggesting that she still desires him. She also thinks he owes her his death, for otherwise she would be "big with death, having no one to whom to bear it" (232), a bizarre image that positions him as father to the death her stinger contains and therefore responsible for supporting it. Yet again, she wonders whether, if she kills his abductors and saves him, she might force him "to exchange the disgust and fear he felt towards me for helpless admiration," thus allowing her possibly to "regain—if not him, then at least myself" (232), an idea that links her agency with his admiration.

Why does Lem explicitly include the assertion that gender is connected to her "fatal core," a connection apparently superfluous to the plot now that the robot has shed her human mask? An interview with Lem by Zoran Živković in 1976 throws fascinating light on this question.[17] Connecting his use of a female persona in "The Mask" with the female character of Rheya in *Solaris*, Lem suggests that the two stories represent a significant departure from his usual choice of male protagonists. The passage is so revealing that it deserves to be quoted at length.

Of that which still remains a mystery to me, and there's quite a good deal of it, I would isolate the problem of the being—a being rationally created, evolving from an empirical method, created so to speak just as a house is built. That being, or rather the heroine Hary [Rheya], becomes a person and in that sense acquires a dominant position in relation to her creator. This problem obsessed and occupied me for so long that I returned to it last year, writing a story entitled "The Mask." This piece no longer deals with an artificial human in the third person, and he is not described externally; now it is the heroine herself who speaks in the first person, she is conscious of her origin and status, she gradually finds out the truth about herself. Here too, we have the classical problem of the freedom and non-freedom of the programmed mind.

Why was this problem so interesting that I had to treat it on two occasions? I'm not entirely sure. I'm also not sure why I was interested in precisely a woman, and not in a man or some neutral gender—which is a much more frequent occurrence in my writings. Not only can I not explain this to others but I am unable to explain it to myself. (258)

In *Solaris*, Rheya appears as a creation of the sentient ocean, culled from the deep memories of Kelvin's mind. Visually identical to the wife whom Kelvin lost when she committed suicide, Rheya begins to individuate as a person separate from his perceptions. She has a profoundly different physical structure than humans, and she slowly becomes aware that Kelvin is lying to her about her true nature. Racked by guilt at his wife's suicide, Kelvin tries to get rid of the memories the Rheya simulacrum embodies by ejecting her into outer space, but the simulated Rheya simply reappears, having been reconstituted by the ocean. She finally asserts her autonomy in the only way she believes possible—by committing suicide—and her suicide note is the only communication the reader has from her that is not mediated by Kelvin's perceptions. In "The Mask," the narrator also physically differs from humans, but the split in *Solaris* between a male narrator who speaks and a nonhuman female who acts is now differently arranged, so that the female has the power of articulation and the male-conceived program has the power of action. In both stories, female agency is thrown into question and a female character struggles to assert her independence in her relation with a human male who is at once her lover and antagonist.

Whatever the reasons for this formation, it seems clear that gender is central to the power it exercises over Lem's Imaginary. If it would be presumptuous of me to psychoanalyze Lem, it would be especially so here, in view of his comment that he himself does not know why these female characters fascinate him. I conclude nevertheless that there are deep connections in these narratives between the female's struggle for autonomy within the story and her relation to her creator, understood as a consciousness beyond the reach of the character's introspections, whether a sentient ocean working in collaboration with Kelvin's unconscious, an all-powerful king, or Lem himself. The female's alien nature thus enacts not only her difference from humankind but also her gender-specific difference from her male creator. In these stories, the female is at once the intimate mate and the terrifyingly alien other, bearing within herself the imprint of her creator's will as well as her own ambiguous agency. It is as if the female, to succeed as a character, has to assert an agency independent of the male mind that conjured her into being. The more she tears herself away, the more she achieves reality as an autonomous subjectivity; but the more she achieves autonomy, the more she resists her creator's agency and thereby threatens to defeat her putative purpose for being. Given these complexities, is it any wonder that she is compounded of life and death, love and agony?

These complex interrelations reach explicit articulation within "The

Mask" when the monk demands to know what the narrator will do, now that she has received the treatment to widen slightly her margin of action. When she answers that she does not know—which, given the confused motives described above, is probably accurate—the monk responds, "You are my sister." Stunned, the narrator asks him what he means. "Exactly as I say it," he answers, "and it means I neither raise myself above you nor humble myself before you, for however much we may differ, your ignorance, which you have confessed to me and which I believe, makes us equal in the face of Providence" (226–27).

Harboring an irreducible ambiguity, the monk's response reinscribes within the story Lem's own inability to understand his creative choices. The robot can be understood as like him because she does not know if program will completely determine her actions, which implies that she believes she has free will, however slim the margin. In this sense, she is his sister because she counts as a human person. She may also be like him because he operates according to biocultural programs that dictate his actions, making his consciousness unsure of how he will act, an interpretation consonant with the theories espoused by Deleuze, Guattari, and especially Lacan. In this reading, she is his sister because he counts as a programmed entity. The entangling of meanings here is like the entangling of the female character's agency with her creator's will, so that the story can be understood to be *simultaneously* about human agency and robotic programming, male authorship and female self-birthing, alien creature and ordinary human being.

When she was given birth by the assembly line, the narrator lay passively on her back for most of the journey (202), as she did when the monks operated on her (229). In this position she cannot wield her stinger; for that, she needs to be standing upright so it can emerge from its "ventral shaft" and thrust forward. When she thinks back on the monk's words acknowledging her as his sister, she remarks, "I still could not understand them, but when I bent over them something warm spread through my being and transformed me, it was as if I had lost a heavy fetus, with which I had been pregnant" (230). The image recalls her thinking of the death she carries as Arrhodes's unborn child. Here too the most likely reference for the "heavy fetus" is death, but this time it is her own death as a programmed robot, after which she could possibly be born again as an autonomous person. But the ambiguity lingers, for she also imagines herself *bending over* the monk's utterance, the position from which she can enact the king's command through her phallic stinger. Thus in the same thought she figuratively gives birth to herself as an autonomous agent by losing the king-impregnated fetus of death and adopts the posture that makes her a vehicle for the king's will.

The combination of male and female sexual imagery in this passage appears also in Lem's *Fiasco*, his last published fiction. Michael Kandel, interrogating this story as Lem's farewell text, links the male/female imagery to narrative patterns suggesting that to be born is to be mortal and, in this sense, to receive the sting of death.[18] Kandel quotes what he identifies as a favorite saying of Lem's, "We are born between urine and feces," connecting it with the unremittingly negative associations women have in *Fiasco*. He further suggests that *Fiasco*'s Quintans (versions of the unknowable aliens that populate Lem's fictions) are associated with female sexual imagery. The encounter of humans and aliens that leads to the apocalyptic fiasco of the title thus constitutes an engagement of the explorers with the femininity that marked them from birth as impure incarnations. Kandel reads *Fiasco* as transgressive revenge against humanity for being mired in a messy biology that ensures humans cannot attain the purity of completely rational mind. These narrative patterns form a suggestive context for the female machine in "The Mask."

Her female gender re-marks her phallic stinger with the mortality Lem associates with pregnancy and birth, rendering it at once masculine and feminine (as the image of the stinger as fetus suggests). Moreover, woman as mediating link between an unknowable alien and a male protagonist—the pattern of *Solaris*—is here reimagined as a female consciousness mediating between a male protagonist and an unknowable (to her) program, which operates untouched by the emotional turbulence and irrational desires that Lem hopes humans will overcome. Further complicating these connections is the narrator's metallic body, which is metaphorically comingled with the female pregnancy and birth that Lem associates with "urine and feces," forming an oxymoronic amalgam that at once incarnates and transcends biology. Perhaps these complexities help to explain why "The Mask" (unlike *Fiasco*, with its dark ending) finds in the female mind a measure of compassion that, although it cannot save Arrhodes (described as having a superbly rational mind about to be forced into ignoble slavery), nevertheless restores to him respect and possibly even love.

This ambiguous affirmation occurs when the robot finally tracks Arrhodes to the castle where he has been taken by his abductors, only to discover that a mortal struggle has taken place and that he lies unconscious and bleeding on the stairs. "Had he opened his eyes and been conscious, and—in an inverted view—taken me in entirely, exactly as I stood over him, stood now powerlessly carrying death, in a gesture of supplication, pregnant but not from him, would that have been a wedding—or its unmercifully arranged parody?" (238–39). Both "bride and butcher," the narrator exercises her agency in the only way she can, by delaying her fatal sting while she waits to see if Arrhodes will recover. If he does, she knows that her programming will enact his death, and so enmeshed is her consciousness with program that she does not know "if I truly desired him to wake" (238). Only when he "groaned once more and ceased to breathe" does she alter her posture. Feeling "my mind at rest," she lies down beside him and wraps "him tightly in my arms, and I lay thus in the light and in the darkness through two days of snowstorm, which covered our bed with a sheet that did not melt. And on the third day the sun came up" (239).

Resonating with the Christian story of Jesus's three days in the tomb prior to his resurrection, the three days continue a pattern that has marked her life from the beginning: her courtship lasted three days; she lingered for three days before beginning the hunt; and she experienced three births, first on the assembly line, then in her entry into language and gender, and finally in her metamorphosis into the insectile robot. Does the faint promise of resurrection hint that she can experience a fourth birth, breaking the pattern and becoming at last her own person, now that she has fulfilled her programming? Earlier she had thought about what she would become if she were to abandon her goal and strike out on her own. The king would order robotic dogs to hunt her down as mercilessly as she pursued Arrhodes, and even if she were by some miracle to survive, all human society would find her abhorrent. Significantly, this information comes in the middle of the tale, so that it lingers in the reader's mind as fading memory rather than active narration as the story reaches its end. Granted this slight margin of forgetfulness, we can edge toward asking the question forbidden by the closure of the plot: what kind of life could she be born into? Certainly not into the coherent subjectivity of an independent human who has never had reason to question whether she has free will. But perhaps in these posthuman days, when the crisis of agency is far from resolved, she might count as a person, albeit a nonhuman one. If so, then we can say to her, with all the rich ambiguities that attended the monk's utterance, "You are our sister."

Machine and Human Interpenetrating

In separating consciousness from program, Lem's story anticipates the posthuman subject envisioned by Deleuze, Guattari, and Lacan, a subject in which consciousness, far from being the seat of agency, is left to speculate why she acts as she does. The character in Lem's story is increasingly aware that the origin of agency lies beyond the reach of consciousness, enacted by a computational program ultimately controlled by the external agent that has programmed the code to operate as it does. Even at this deep level, the ambiguity of agency continues, for program is perceived to act both as an agent on its own behalf and as the surrogate for the king's will. The ambiguity is repeated within consciousness, where she perceives herself to be exercising agency in the margins, as it were, the gray areas where the objectives of code might be implemented in ambiguous ways. In these complex reconfigurations of agency, the significance of envisioning the unconscious as a program rather than as a dark mirror of consciousness can scarcely be overstated, for it locates the hidden springs of action in the brute machinic operations of code. In this view, such visions of the unconscious as Freud's repressed Oedipal conflicts or Jung's collective archetypes seem hopelessly anthropomorphic, for they populate the unconscious with ideas comfortingly familiar to consciousness rather than with the much more alien operations of machinic code.

Yet the estrangement from traditional ideas of mind does not stop here, for an even more subversive implication lurks in Lem's story, an implication that the human-sounding voice of the narrator may prevent us from realizing except in retrospect. Given the mechanical origin of the creature, even consciousness must arise from code, for as noted earlier, she has been manufactured rather than born. In this sense, consciousness may also be a mask created to mediate between human readers and an alien core. Even when the machine sheds her human shell, the anthropomorphic thoughts of consciousness function as a mask within the mask, inviting our identification with what must also be a result of machine code.

Whether consciousness can ever emerge from a coded mechanism remains a matter of intense debate. Robotocists such as Hans Moravec and Ray Kurzweil are confident that the equivalent of conscious mind can arise from a coded program, whether evolved through intelligent robots or originating as human consciousness uploaded into a computer.[19] Researchers operating with deeper familiarity with the flesh, such as Antonio Damasio, argue that body and mind are inextricably linked through multiple recursive feedback loops mediated by neurotransmitters, systems that have no physical analogs in computers. Damasio makes the point that these messages also provide *content* for the mind, especially emotions and feelings: "relative to the brain, the body provides more than mere support and modulation: it provides a basic topic for brain representations."[20] It is precisely the disruption of this normal integration between mind and body that makes the intuition of Lem's narrator seem so enigmatic, as when she explains that the love she "feels" for Arrhodes is at once very great and very small.

Nevertheless, with the advent of emotional computing, evolutionary algorithms, and programs capable not only of learning but of reprogramming themselves (as in programmable gate arrays), it no longer seems fantastic that artificial minds may some day achieve self-awareness and even consciousness. Brian Cantwell Smith sees this as opening "a window onto something to which we would not otherwise have any access: the chance to witness, with our own eyes, how intentional capacities can arise in a 'merely' physical mechanism. It is sobering, in retrospect, to realize that the fact computers are computational has placed a major theoretical block in the way of our understanding how important they are. . . . Only when we let go of the conceit that the fact is theoretically important will we finally be able to see, *without distraction*—and thereby, perhaps at least partially to understand— how a structured lump of clay can sit up and think."[21] The central question, in other words, is no longer how we as rational creatures should act in full possession of free will and untrammeled agency. Rather, the issue is how consciousness evolves from and interacts with the underlying programs that operate analogously to the operations of code. Whether conceived as literal mechanism or instructive analogy, coding technology thus becomes central to understanding the human condition.

In this view, agency—long identified with free will and rational mind— becomes partial in its efficacy, distributed in its location, mechanistic in its origin, and bound up at least as much with code as with natural language. We are no longer the featherless biped that can think, but the hybrid creature that enfolds within itself the rationality of the conscious mind and the coding operations of the machine. Who then is the agent that acts? Anticipating these debates, "The Mask" helps us to understand how partial, complex, and intermediated may be the agency we call our own.

8 Simulating Narratives
What Virtual Creatures Can Teach Us

Evolving Virtual Creatures

Yearning for the light, the creatures struggle after it. In water, they grow tails and learn to undulate like snakes. On land, they clump along, relegated by fate and biology to rectangular shapes joined together with moveable hinges. They show extraordinary ingenuity in making the most of these limitations, crawling, hopping, jumping, always toward the light. Then their creator gives them a new goal, a colored cube reminiscent of a squared-off hockey puck. Put into competition with one another, the creatures learn to jostle and shove their opponents, to encircle the cube, to knock it out of the way so their opponents can't reach it. When they meet a new opponent, they develop counterstrategies to meet these challenges. I marvel at their adaptability, cleverness, and determination.

This passage describes my initial interpretations of Karl Sims's evolutionary simulation "Evolved Virtual Creatures."[1] Having watched various audiences view this videotape, I can say that my interpretations are typical. Invariably, viewers attribute to these simulated creatures motives, intentions, goals, and strategies. Even people (like me) who know perfectly well that they are watching visualizations of computer programs still inscribe the creatures into narratives of defeat and victory, cheering the winners, urging on the losers, laughing at the schlemiels. Much more is going on here than simple anthropomorphic projection. "Evolved Virtual Creatures" is a laboratory not only in evolution (its intended purpose), but also in the impact of distributed cognitive systems on traditional modes of description, analysis, and understanding. Here the interactions between analog consciousness and digital program are located at a more conventional site than in chapter 7. Whereas that chapter traced the complex dynamics by which an analog consciousness interacted with an algorithmic program within the same body, here the focus is on embodied humans outside the computer interacting with digital simulations inside the computer. The intermediations that take place across the screenic interface operate in both directions at once: we anthropomorphize the virtual creatures while they computationalize us. In its broader implications, the dynamic suggests further insights into the realist/constructivist divide that we encountered in chapter 1, figured there as a tension between seeing computation as means or metaphor. The emphasis in this chapter will be on interpreting that tension in terms of the transmigrations of inscription versus the embodied instantiations of material entities. But I am getting ahead of my story. Let us first explore the construction and dynamics of the virtual creatures.

Compared to the world in which we live, the environment of "Evolved Virtual Creatures" is extremely simple, so simple that it can be described almost completely.[2] How to define the boundaries of this world is a centrally important issue to which I will return. For now, let us consider the world to be the computer programs, the hardware on which the programs run, and the visualization routines that render these programs as pixilated images of embodied creatures. Even this simple world requires three different modes of interrogation: what it is (the material); what it does (the operational); and what it means (the symbolic). Feedback loops connect the material, operational, and symbolic into an integrated, recursively structured hierarchy reminiscent of the dynamic hierarchies central to the computational worldview discussed in chapters 1 and 2. Emergence is the desired goal of this simulation, as with many others. At the bottom of the hierarchy flicker changing voltages that join the material and operational to create bits, the semiotic markers of one and zero. Logic gates structure signals into bits; bit patterns are fashioned into compiler languages; compiler languages underlie programming languages; and programming languages such as LISP define functions. By the time we arrive at functions, the level at which Karl Sims discusses his design for "Evolved Virtual Creatures," we have reached a point where the patterns created by the programmer become explicit. Instantiated in these patterns are the programmer's purposes in creating this particular hierarchy of materio-semiotic codes.

Sims's design follows John Koza's proposal that evolutionary programs should take advantage of modular structures that can be repeated over and over to create more complex structures.[3] The strategy appears often in nature; a fern, for example, displays a growth algorithm that uses the same basic shape for stems, branches, and leaves.[4] Like the fern, Sims's creatures are built using functions that are repeated with variations to create self-similar morphologies. One function specifies blocks that are multiplied and attached at various positions on a central rectangle to create a "trunk" with several "limbs." Another function specifies the kind of articulation, or joint, between blocks; still another dictates the degrees of freedom through which a joint can move. Recursive loops *within* a function multiply the effects of that function to create more of the same, for example, more limbs of the same shape. Recursive loops *between* functions allow different parts of the creature to evolve together, so that the "brain" or central control circuits coadaptively change with the morphology. The advantages of these modular structures, achieved by using programs called directed graphs, are twofold. In addition to economy of description (because the same module can be used repeatedly with minor variations), the modules also ensure that some structure will persist in the midst of mutation and variation. If all of the programming elements were subject to mutation as independent entities, the resulting complexity would quickly become too chaotic to track effectively. When the elements are grouped and mutated as modules, the spectrum of possible variations is reduced to a manageable level.

The next step moves from the design of individual creatures to a population of creatures. With this step, the symbolic aspects of the program become apparent. The idea is to evolve creatures by introducing diversity into the population and defining fitness criteria that determine which creatures get to reproduce. Diversity is accomplished through sexual reproduction that, following various schemes, combines portions of one creature's genotype with another's. Additional diversity is introduced through mutation. Behaviors take place within an environment governed by an artifactual physics, which includes friction, inertia, momentum, gravity, light, three-dimensional space, and time. Fitness values are determined according to how successful the creatures are in reaching various goals—following a light, moving through fluids and across terrains, cornering the puck while keeping an opponent away from it. To facilitate adaptation to these goals, the creatures are given photosensors that can evolve neurologically to respond to a beacon, the presence of the puck, and positions of competitors, each represented by a differently colored light source.

The designer's intentions, implicit in the fitness criteria he specifies and the values he assigns to these criteria, become explicit when he intervenes to encourage "'interesting'" evolutions and prohibit "inelegant" ones.[5] For example, in some runs of the program creatures evolved who achieved locomotion by exploiting a bug in the way conservation of momentum was defined in the world's artifactual physics: they developed appendages like paddles and moved by hitting themselves with their own paddles. "It is important that the physical simulation be reasonably accurate when optimizing for creatures that can move within it," Sims writes. "Any bugs that allow energy leaks from non-conservation, or even round-off errors, will inevitably be discovered and exploited by the evolving creatures."[6] In the competitions, some creatures evolved to exceptionally tall statures and controlled the cube by simply falling over on it before their opponents could reach it.[7] To compensate, Sims used a formula that took into account the creature's height when determining its starting point in the competition: the taller the creature, the farther back it had to start. The conjunction of processes through which we come to narrativize such images clearly shows that the *meaning* of the simulation emerges from a dynamic interaction between the creator, the virtual world (and the real world on which its physics is modeled), the creatures, the computer running the programs, and (in the case of visualizations) the viewer watching the creatures cavort. In much the same way that the recursive loops between program modules allow a creature's morphology and brain to coevolve, so recursive loops allow the designer's intent, the creatures, the virtual world, and the visualizations to coevolve into a narrative that viewers find humanly meaningful.

An adequate account of the simulation, then, requires expanding the boundaries of the system beyond the programs and the computer to include the virtual world, the creator, and the viewer. The evolutionary dynamics of this larger world function as a distributed cognitive system composed of human and nonhuman actors, each of which acts as an independent cognizer. As Michael Dyer has noted in another context, with distributed cognitive systems there is no free lunch: because all the parts interrelate, if one part of the system can function only as a relatively low-level cognizer, the slack has to be taken up somewhere else by making another part smarter.[8] Compared to artificial intelligence, artificial-life simulations typically front-load less intelligence in the creatures and build more intelligence into the dynamic process of coadapting to well-defined environmental constraints. When the environment fails to provide the appropriate constraints to stimulate development, the creator steps in, using his human intelligence to supply additional adaptive constraints, for instance when Sims put a limit on how tall the creatures can get. But it would be a mistake to see the creator as the court of last resort. The point of such simulations is that the creator does not always need to be as smart as his creatures, for he is counting on their ability to come up with solutions that have not occurred to him. "When a genetic language allows virtual entities to evolve with increasing complexity," Sims observes, "it is common for the resulting system to be difficult to understand in detail. In many cases it would also be difficult to design a similar system using traditional methods. Techniques such as these have the potential of surpassing those limits that are often imposed when human understanding and design is important. The examples presented here suggest that it might be easier to evolve virtual entities exhibiting intelligent behavior than it would be for humans to design and build them."[9]

Since distributed cognitive systems coevolve, the functioning of any one actor can be understood fully only in relation to that actor's interactions with all the other actors. In this context, the narratives humans create for themselves when they watch "Evolved Virtual Creatures" become involved in the coevolutionary processes. Spliced into a distributed cognitive system, we create these narratives not by ourselves, but as part of a dynamic evolutionary process in which we are coadapting to other actors in the system, including pixilated images on a CRT screen and voltages flickering beyond the scale of human perception.

Evolving Narratives

When we attribute motives and intentions to Sims's virtual creatures, we interpolate their behaviors into narratives in which events are causally related to one another and beings respond to their environment in purposeful ways. As Alex Argyros, among others, has suggested, the creation of narrative may itself be an evolutionary adaptation of remarkable importance.[10] With their emphasis on causality, meaningful temporal sequence, and interrelation between behavior and environment, narratives allow us to construct models of how others may be feeling and acting, models that coevolve with our ongoing interior monologues describing and interpreting to ourselves our own feelings and behaviors. When for some reason narratives cannot be constructed, the result is likely to be a world without order, a world of inexplicable occurrences and bewildering turns of events. Simon Baron-Cohen describes such a world in *Mindblindness*, suggesting that it is characteristic of how autistic people perceive their environment. As Baron-Cohen points out, autism is associated with an inability to construct narratives that will make sense of the behaviors of others. Autistic people have no model in their minds for how others act; consequently, they perceive most actions as inexplicable and frightening. Another graphic description of what happens when narratives fail is rendered by Joan Didion in *The White Album*. Recounting a time in her life when she "began to doubt the premises of all the stories I have ever told myself," she lost her sense of living in a coherent world; for as she emphasizes, "we tell ourselves stories in order to live" (11). These accounts demonstrate that narrative has an explanatory force that literally makes the world make sense. It is easy to see why the creation of narratives would confer evolutionary advantages on creatures who construct them. Without the presuppositions embedded in narratives, most of the accomplishments of Homo sapiens could not have happened.

When we construct narratives about virtual creatures, we use an evolved behavior to understand the evolved behaviors acted out in the simulation. It is no accident that in this scenario a feedback loop appears whose recursive structure resembles the recursive structures of the programs generating Sims's virtual creatures. We saw in chapter 1 that across a wide variety of research programs—Stephen Wolfram's cellular automata, Edward Fredkin's digital mechanics, Harold Morowitz's cosmic emergences, and Stuart Kauffman's claims for the evolution of life at the edge of chaos—recursive loops are associated with the emergence of complexity and, consequently, with life, consciousness, and intelligent behavior.[11] Humberto Maturana and Francisco Varela, for example, have suggested that consciousness consists of the ability to make representations of representations (of representations of representations . . .).[12] Luc Steels has named this phenomenon of spiraling recursions "second-order [and higher] emergence" and underscored its importance for artificial-life simulations.[13] First-order emergence, as discussed in chapter 1, is any behavior or property that cannot be found in either a system's individual components or their additive properties, but that arises, often unpredictably, from the *interaction* of a system's components. Second-order emergence arises when a system develops a behavior that enhances its ability to develop adaptive behaviors—that is, when it *evolves the capacity to evolve.*[14] At this point, the simulation really takes off, so it is not surprising that creating such dynamic hierarchies is now the announced goal of artificial-life researchers, as discussed in chapter 1.

In addition to recursive structures, another important element in the creation of narrative is the ability to "see" a scene, either literally or metaphorically in the mind's eye.[15] With training and experience, humans are able to translate a large variety of inputs into these imagined scenarios. No doubt an experienced programmer such as Karl Sims can look at a program's functions and "see" the morphologies and behaviors of his creatures with no more difficulty than an experienced reader of fiction can "see" Isabel Archer in Henry James's aptly entitled novel, *The Portrait of a Lady*. These translation processes draw upon and extend capabilities developed in evolutionary history. Our sophisticated perceptual/cognitive visual processing evolved coadaptively with our movement through three-dimensional spaces; it makes sense, then, that the creation of narrative is tied up deeply with imagining scenes in which actions can take place. When Sims chooses some of his creatures for visual rendering, he taps into this evolutionary history by creating pixilated images that, through culture and training as well as biologically determined capacities, we recognize as representations of three-dimensional creatures. Articulated in this lingua franca of bio-cultural perception, the images allow narrative to kick in with maximum force, for we "see" the action in terms we can easily relate to our ongoing narrativizing of the world.[16]

Let us turn now from the structural preconditions for the creation of narratives to their content. As Jerome Bruner has pointed out, one of the principal purposes narrative serves is to create a sense of *why* things happen.[17] Typically, the narratives we create inscribe actions into a set of more or less canonical stories that invest actions with meaning. When Joan Lucariello studied narratives created by young children, she discovered that unexpected actions (e.g., a description that has Mary crying when she sees her birthday cake and dumping a glass of water all over the candles) stimulated the most vigorous narrative creation.[18] To make sense of these strange actions, the children invented a wide variety of stories that had the effect of suturing the actions back into a predictable and expected range of behaviors. In one small child's account, Mary was upset because her mother would not let her wear the dress she wanted, and that is why she cried and ruined her cake. Presented with noncanonical actions, the children sometimes employed another narrative strategy, namely, marking the behavior as unusual or deviant, which again allowed the social fabric of expectations to be maintained by bracketing this behavior as an exception.[19] It is surely no accident that in his evolutionary simulations Sims designs programs that can be "seen" as creatures striving after a goal and winning against competitors, for these are among the most canonical narratives in traditional accounts of evolutionary history (not to mention in Western capitalist society). The banality of the narrative content suggests that what needs to be sutured here is not so much deviant action as the deviant actor. When we "see" the virtual creatures engaging in these activities, we have models in our minds for what these behaviors mean, and so the creatures, despite their odd shapes and digital insides, seem familiar and understandable.

At this point, some readers may object that however functional narrative may be for everyday social intercourse, it leads to serious mistakes when we use it to understand virtual creatures. Not only do these creatures have nothing in their heads; in a literal sense, they have no heads (because they are virtual, and because their morphology is a series of blocks, the uppermost of which we "see" as the head). Attributing desires to these clumps of blocks is as ridiculous as thinking that electrons have motives. Well, yes and no. Certainly the creatures are merely computer programs that have evolved certain behaviors (and therefore attributes we interpret as embodied action toward a goal) as a result of the fitness criteria used to select which genotypes will be allowed to reproduce—or more accurately, which coding arrangements will be replicated with what variations, since "genotype" and "reproduce" are themselves metaphors designed to reinforce the analogy with biological life forms. On the other hand, these programs are *designed* to simulate biological evolution, and they are visually rendered so that narrative inscription will take place. Thus there is a sense in which we respond correctly, not mistakenly, when we attribute desires to these virtual creatures, for everything about them has been crafted to ensure that such interpretations will occur.

One way to think about this situation is to note that distributed cognition also implies distributed causality. The creatures may not have motives and intentions, but the programmer does (at least in the conventional understanding of human actions). Remember that what we "see" in the visualization is the *global* result of present and past interactions between all the actors in this recursively structured complex adaptive system. When Sims decides which fitness criteria to use, which programs to eliminate, and which to render visually, he injects doses of his human intelligence into the system, along with the attributes we conventionally assign to humans, including desires and intentions. Moreover, his published articles make clear that his intentions affected virtually every aspect of the design, so it is not possible to bracket out his intentions by saying that we should consider only the programs in themselves, not the global system.

Human intentionality, then, infects the creatures, marking them with a trace that cannot be eradicated. Recall that in this recursively structured complex adaptive system, *all* of the actors are involved in, and therefore affected by, the interactions. Is it also the case that the blind operations of the programs infect the humans, marking them with a trace that cannot be eradicated? To entertain this hypothesis is to suppose that the human tendency to anthropomorphize the creatures has as its necessary and unavoidable supplement a countertendency to "see" human behavior as a computer program carrying out instructions, a proposition explored at length in chapter 7 through Stanislaw Lem's story "The Mask." We may think we have desires and intentions (just as we think the creatures do), but our behaviors can be explained materially and operationally in terms similar to Sims's programs, as we saw in the theories of Deleuze, Guattari, and Lacan, discussed in chapter 7. This argument also has been made (admittedly in different terms) by researchers in artificial intelligence and artificial life, including Rodney Brooks and Marvin Minsky.[20] In their view, human behavior is the result of many semiautonomous agents running simple programs. To illustrate, Minsky suggests that "love" is a combination of one agent running an "attraction" program and another agent running a program that shuts off the "critical" agent.[21] Such proposals indicate that anthropomorphizing Sims's creatures is accompanied by what I might call, for lack of a better term, "computationalizing" humans. According to the logic of this relation, blind programs engaging in human-like behaviors make plausible the interpretation of human behaviors as blind programs. We humanize the virtual creatures; they computationalize us; and the recursive loops cycling through the system bind both behaviors together in a network of complex coadaptations—which leaves us with an interesting question: what happens now to narrative and its function of making human sense of the world?

Computing the Human: Analog and Digital Subjects

Following the work of Michel Foucault on the death of the author,[22] Mark Poster, in *What's the Matter with the Internet?* has expanded on Foucault's fourth and final stage of the author's disappearance to suggest that digital technologies and cultures are bringing about a significant reconfiguration of contemporary subjectivity.[23] To illuminate this shift, Poster posits two kinds of subjects: analog and digital. The analog subject is based on relations of resemblance.[24] Although Poster does not use this example, the mind/heart conjunction illustrates the concept. Feelings are imagined as conjoined with the heart, so that what is at the forefront of the mind is mirrored by what is deep inside. Similarly, in the English Renaissance—a period dominated, as Foucault has shown, by cultural relations based on analogy[25]—human sperm was thought to contain a homunculus resembling the man who would grow from the sperm. Walnuts were considered to be "brain food" because walnut meat resembles the human cortex. Analogical relations require that the integrity of the units taken to resemble one another be preserved; otherwise, the correspondence is lost and the relation broken. If one tosses a handful of walnuts into a blender and turns it on, the walnuts are pulverized and no longer resemble a cortex. If walnuts were available only in this form, it seems unlikely that they would have been considered good food for thought. Attributes of the analog subject include, then, a depth model of subjectivity in which the most meaningful part of the self is seen to reside deep inside the body, and the self is further linked with units possessing a natural integrity of form and scale that must be preserved if the subject is to be maintained intact.

Poster focuses his discussion of subjectivity on the "figure of the author" (86), whose construction during the seventeenth and eighteenth centuries required a number of related events, including an increase in literacy, "diminishing personal authority relations" (89), the spread of markets that made books into capitalist commodities, and legal systems of copyright (89). These developments facilitated defining an individual as "interior consciousness, which could then be externalized first in manuscript, then in print" (89). Thus in Poster's view, analog subjectivity is bound up deeply with the dominance of print culture. The origins of print culture are rooted in alphabetic writing, which of course evolved much earlier than the development of capitalism and copyright. Poster notes that alphabetic writing broke the pictorial resemblance that connected an ideogram to the object represented, and in doing so it forged a new connection between a sound and a mark. This connection differed from pictorial writing in that the association of sound with mark was entirely conventional, and the resulting arbitrariness made alphabetic writing much more economical than ideograms (thousands of ideograms versus some thirty letters of the Greek alphabet).[26] The movement from ideogram to alphabet entailed another shift as well, for now the resemblance was not between word and thing but, as Poster puts it, between "a written symbol and its utterance, between two forms of language, writing and speech. The relation between the word and thing becomes conventional, arbitrary, whereas the relation within language between trace and voice is stronger, more direct" (81). Thus to the extent that print can be considered an analog medium, it connects voice to mark and thus author as speaker to the page.

Reinforcing the sense that print texts are "voiced" by an individualistic creator is the uniformity, stability, and durability of print, a point Mark Rose touches upon in *Authors and Owners*, discussed in chapter 6 and developed independently by Poster. "The reader could return time and again to the page and re-examine the words it contained," Poster writers. "A readerly imaginary evolved which paid homage to this wonderful author who was always there in his or her words. . . . The world of analog authors was leisurely, comforting, reassuring to the cognitive function, and expanding through continuous exercise of the visual function" (93). Literary history is largely outside the scope of Poster's analysis, but it has long been recognized in literary studies that the novel reinforced the depth model of interiority and the stability and individuality of the analog subject. As we saw in chapter 6, the legal fight to insure copyright, the cult of the author, print technology, and print culture worked hand in glove to create a depth model of subjectivity in which analog resemblances guaranteed that the surface of the page was matched by an imagined interior within the author, which evoked and also was produced by a similarly imagined interior in the reader.[27]

In contrast to this dynamic are the correspondences that produce the digital subject. Digital technologies employ hierarchical program structures similar to those we see at work in "Evolved Virtual Creatures." The farther down into the coding levels the programmer goes, the less intuitive is the code and the more obscure the meaning; hence the importance of hiding levels of code with which one is not immediately concerned, as discussed in chapter 2. Moreover, with genetic algorithms and programs, the important developments are *emergent* properties that appear at the global level of the system once the programs are set running. The mantra for such programs is "simple rules, complex behaviors," which implies that the farther down into the system one goes, the less interesting it is.[28] Note how this digital model differs from the analog subject, where depth implies a meaningful interiority.

Although the digital subject has depth, the structures governing the relation of surface to interior differ dramatically from the analog subject. The digital subject—say, one of Sims's virtual creatures—instantiates hierarchical coding levels that operate through a dynamic of fragmentation and recombination.[29] Unlike analog subjectivity, where morphological resemblance imposes constraints on how much the relevant units can be broken up, the digital subject allows for and indeed demands more drastic fragmentation. This difference can be seen easily in the greater fragmentation of digital technologies compared to print. In traditional typesetting before the advent of computers, each letter in the alphabet was treated as a distinct unit; in speech, the corresponding phoneme also acts as an intact unit. In contrast are digital sampling techniques, where sound waves may be sampled some forty thousand times a second, digitally manipulated, and then recombined to produce the perception of smooth analog speech.[30] In fact, emergence depends on such fragmentation, for it is only when the programs are broken into small pieces and recombined that unexpected adaptive behaviors can arise. Instead of a depth model of meaningful interiority, the digital subject manifests global behaviors that cannot be predicted by looking at the most basic levels of code with which the program starts. As discussed in chapter 2, complexity becomes visible first at high levels of code, not at the basic levels of machine language. Moreover, the complex emergences bears no analogical resemblance to the mind-numbing simplicity of ones and zeros.

To summarize: the analog subject implies a depth model of interiority, relations of resemblance between the interior and the surface that guarantee the meaning of what is deep inside, and the kind of mind/soul correspondence instantiated by and envisioned within the analog technologies of print culture. The digital subject implies an emergent complexity that is related through hierarchical coding levels to simple underlying rules, a dynamic of fragmentation and recombination that gives rise to emergent properties, and a disjunction between surface and interior that is instantiated by and envisioned within the digital technologies of computational culture.

What happens when we become part of a complex adaptive system by "seeing" the virtual creatures? I suggested earlier that two processes are at work simultaneously: on the one hand, humans anthropomorphize the virtual creatures; and on the other hand, the virtual creatures computationalize the humans. The narratives we construct as we watch the virtual creatures inscribe their behaviors into an analog world, but observant viewers will notice details that cannot be explained by supposing that the complex surfaces are matched analogically with equally complex interiors. One creature, for example, indicates through its movements that it samples the positions of the puck and the opponent once at the beginning of the competition and thereafter ignores all cues about position.[31] Clearly, here is an instance of a relatively simple program creating an impression of surface complexity that contrasts with the simplicity of the underlying rules. As Rodney Brooks frequently points out with the robots he builds, complexity is in the mind of the observer, who attributes to the robot's emergent behaviors more complex thought processes and motivations than in fact are there.[32] Another example is provided by a small mobile robot made by Lego that, on the surface, appears to be capable of following a black line on a white ground.[33] A viewer might suppose that inside the robot is an intelligent program that has an internal representation of a line, and that the robot can so accurately match this representation with what it sees that it can distinguish many different kinds of lines, including ones that are curved and even looped. Underlying the surface complexity, however, are three simple rules: if from white to black, turn right; if from black to white, turn left; if no change, continue straight. Although the robot follows the line overall, this is an emergent behavior. In fact, it simply swerves right when it first comes across a black line on a white background and then, as it begins to veer off the line, immediately turns again, so its "line-following" behavior consists of a series of small swerves that a viewer may interpret as corrections the robot initiates to make sure it follows the line. Simple rules, complex behavior.

On the global level, our narratives about the virtual creatures can be considered devices that suture together the analog subjects we still are, as we move in the three-dimensional spaces in which our biological ancestors evolved, with the digital subjects we are becoming as we interact with virtual environments and digital technologies. In fact, this chapter can be read as one of several narratives in this book designed to accomplish just such a suturing. Hence my insistence on using the plural first person, despite the risk of indulging in oppressive universalisms, for I want to insist that my readers and I participate every day of our lives in the distributed cognitive complex adaptive systems created by digital technologies in conjunction with global capitalism. So pervasive have these technologies become that it would be difficult to find anyone who remains completely outside their reach. Certainly, here in the United States their presence is ubiquitous. In this sense, we do not need to slot Sims's videotape into the VCR to watch virtual creatures. We see them all the time, all around us, including when we look into the mirror.

Scientific Realism and the Transmigration of Form

Let me return to the traditional idea that literary texts are immaterial, critiqued in chapter 4, to explore how the intermediating dynamics of analog and digital extend this critique beyond literary texts to the broader field of inscriptions, including scientific inscriptions. As I hinted at the beginning of this chapter, such considerations are relevant because they shed light on the question posed in chapter 1, namely, whether the Regime of Computation should be understood as a metaphor pervasive in contemporary culture and society, or as an accurate description of reality. It will be useful to place this discussion in the context of scientific realism and how it differs from constructivism.

For the realist, information about physical reality is structured so that it flows from the material (say, a field of morning glories of varied colors) through the operational (experiments in breeding that operate upon the plants and plant genomes to isolate colors from one another) to the symbolic (graphs and charts showing how the colors migrate back to an equilibrium distribution after being separated). The closer the researcher is to the embodied reality of the plants, the fuzzier the picture is likely to be as various sources of "noise" and "contamination" complicate the regularities presumed to be revealed by such inscriptions as graphs and charts. The idea is to remove the noise or, failing that, to compensate for it as much as possible in the experimental design and subsequent analysis, so that the form of the underlying regularities becomes sharp and well-defined.

In the movement from embodied reality to inscription, much is gained and some things are lost. The most important gains, of course, are the regularities revealed through the inscriptions, a point to which I will return. Also important is the implication that once these regularities are durably inscribed, they can circulate through different media without affecting their meaning. If I xerox the chart showing morning glory color distribution and discuss it with my research seminar, everyone assumes we are seeing the *same* graph that appeared in the scientific journal, even though the method of producing the image and the materials composing it (toner ink and copier paper) differ from the original. Similarly, if the researcher illustrates a lecture on her work with slides of the graphs, these count as the same graphs printed on the journal pages. The case would be otherwise if we examined morning glory plants. Say I buy morning glory plants at Home Depot and take them to my seminar. Since they are obviously not the same plants the researcher examined in her test fields some months earlier, questions would inevitably arise about material differences that may exist between our plants and hers. Material embodiments do not circulate effortlessly because they are always instantiated, specific, and located in a certain time and place. By contrast, inscriptions can circulate because cultural conventions privilege the forms expressed by the inscriptions over their instantiations in particular media such as print, Xerox, and photographic negative, which are regarded as passive vehicles for the transmission of the forms.[34]

Normally one says that inscriptions are transportable or transmissible, but perhaps a more appropriate term to describe their circulation is "transmigration." Just as the soul, conceived as a disembodied entity, is thought to move from one corporeal body to another in transmigration, so the abstract form of the inscription is counted as moving from one incorporation to another, despite differences between material instantiations. A partial exception to this convention is the signature, which is presumed to embody the signer's material presence and so not to be transmigratable from one medium to another. A photocopy of a will does not count the same as the original signed document. This presumption of embodiment appears to be giving way with the spread of new communication technologies; faxes, for example, are increasingly accepted as legally binding documents. Even here, however, there continues to be some whiff of embodiment, for a fax occupies a different legal position than e-mail, which has no signatures that can be linked with embodiment.

Inscription, then, is crucially important to the transformation of embodied reality into abstract forms. Bruno Latour and Steve Woolgar, imagining themselves to be naive anthropologists visiting a biological laboratory, emphasize that what would first strike such observers is the "strange mania for inscription" that obsesses the scientific workers, from laboratory technicians scribbling in laboratory notebooks to senior scientists writing journal articles.[35] Defining an inscription device as "any item of apparatus or particular configuration of such items which can transform a material substance into a figure or diagram," Latour and Woolgar note that "inscriptions are regarded as having a direct relationship to the original substance" (51). For our purposes, it is worth noting that many, perhaps most, scientific instruments produce inscriptions through morphological proportionality to physical properties. Sound waves hit a membrane, and the vibrations capture an analog resemblance, which is conveyed through a linking mechanism to a pen tracing a line on graph paper, and the line in turn bears an analog resemblance to the vibrations. Even though scientific instrumentation increasingly uses digital technologies for analysis and imaging, some portions of the chain that employ analog representation usually remain, typically at the beginning and end of the process. Further developing the discussions in chapters 1 and 2 about the synergistic interactions between the digital and analog, I will here call this digital/analog structure the "Oreo," for like the two black biscuits sandwiching a white filling between them, the initial and final analog representations connected with embodied materialities sandwich between them a digital middle where fragmentations and recombinations take place.

An example of an Oreo structure is positron emission tomography, or PET images. The process begins with the ingestion of radioactive substances by the patient. Using analog proportionality, an instrument senses the decay of these substances, and the results are inscribed as an array of numerical data. These data are then digitally analyzed and manipulated to create lifelike analogical resemblances that humans interpret as metabolic processes occurring within the cortex. These images are often interpreted as "thinking in action," but they may be understood more accurately as the Oreo effect in action. Analog resemblance appears at the bottom of the Oreo because the embodied materiality of radioactive decay connects to the apparatus of inscription through relations of resemblance. Only after this resemblance has been captured as a number indicating the level of radioactivity at a certain position in the brain can it be digitized and manipulated as part of a data array. Similarly, at the top of the Oreo analog resemblance is the mode best suited to the sophisticated visual/cognitive perceptual skills we have developed through eons of moving through immensely complex three-dimensional environments. Compare the accessibility of a PET image with that of a data array displaying numbers that stand for radioactivity levels. It would take hours or days to extract from this display the intuitive understanding we gain from a glance at the image. Where linkages between embodied materialities are key, analog resemblances are also likely to be crucial.

By contrast, the digital middle of the Oreo also offers distinctive advantages. Moving from analog resemblance to coding arrangements opens possibilities for leveraging that is unthinkable with analog resemblance, which by virtue of *being* a resemblance must preserve proportional similarity. The difference can be illustrated with a typewriter and a computer word processing program. To make a letter darker on a typewriter, proportionately more ink and/or pressure must be applied for each letter. To make a screen of letters bold, a single keystroke will suffice. Coding arrangements have powerful transformative properties precisely because they have been freed from the morphological resemblances of analog technologies. The power of codes should not, however, obscure the fact that the bold letters on screen also have a material basis; at the point where the embodied materiality of changing voltages is transformed into binary code, analog resemblance necessarily reenters the picture.

To clarify this point, let us consider in more detail how electronic voltages are fashioned into a bit stream. As we saw in chapter 2, the voltages are rarely, if ever, captured in their initial phase as the discrete step function we are accustomed to call one and zero. Rather, the voltages as initially inscribed have a "fall-off" error, a trailing off that represents the noise of embodiment as it is registered by the electronic inscription apparatus. Sophisticated electronics are necessary to rectify this "error" and make it into the binary signals of one and zero. Although we may think of the computer as the digital middle of the PET scan, it too has an analog bottom and, insofar as humans need to interact with its processes, an analog top as well. Wherever different embodied materialities are linked, analog resemblance is likely to enter the picture, for it is the dynamic that mediates between the noise of embodiment and the clarity of form.

Let me return now to inquire about the status of the forms transmigrating through inscriptions, an issue that goes to the heart of the differences between realist and constructivist viewpoints. From a realist point of view, the forms are always already instantiated in the embodied reality, and the inscriptions merely reveal their true nature. From a constructivist point of view such as that articulated by Bruno Latour in *Science in Action*, the forms do not precede the inscriptions but are produced by them. In making this argument, constructivists point toward the contingencies and local conditions that always accompany embodied reality: the air pump cannot produce the same results in Holland as in England;[36] two equivalent scientific instruments cannot be calibrated to produce the same results unless someone who knows how to calibrate the first instrument physically travels to the second one.[37] Few doubt that regularities exist in nature, but the problem comes when these regularities are seen as "laws" that can be abstracted from embodied contexts and expressed as the transmigrating forms of scientific inscriptions. As Evelyn Fox Keller wittily puts it, every scientist knows what hard work it is to get nature to obey the laws of nature. Does nature count as the abstracted form or the embodied materiality, which is always more complex than the form allows?

Whereas the realist assumes that information is structured so that it flows from the material through the operational to the symbolic, the constructivist often assumes that it flows from the symbolic (Enlightenment ideas about clarity of vision as an enactment of rationality) through the operational (Bentham's plans for a model prison) to the material (the construction of the Panopticon). Notice that the two positions are symmetrical, each tracing the flow in the opposite direction from the other. To break open the hegemony of scientific realism, no doubt it was helpful to take the strong counterposition that "truth effects" are produced by social processes rather than by experimental apparatus. But such strategies are limited in their options by the very assumptions they resist. Defining himself by what he revolts against, the revolutionary ends up looking like his opponent reflected in a mirror.

Work in the cultural and social studies of science has been marked by various strategies to escape the limitations imposed by these symmetry relationships. For example, the Latour of *We Have Never Been Modern* (1993) differs significantly, it seems to me, from the Latour of *Science in Action* (1987), for in the later work Latour, acknowledging the limitations of earlier constructivist arguments, insists that the objects of scientific research are at once discursively constructed, socially produced, *and* materially real, a position he articulates even more forcefully in voicing concern about how radical constructivist positions can be appropriated for such reactionary purposes as denying the Holocaust.[38] I want to put Sims's virtual creatures into conversation with these ongoing debates, for I think these creatures have something important to contribute. They suggest other ways to skew the symmetry relations of the materialist/discursive divide and to rethink the transmigrations of forms through inscriptions that have the effect of leaving embodied reality behind.

Digital Creatures and Hybrid Subjectivity: From Form to Process

Unlike the forms that experiments in the natural world abstract from embodied materiality, often with great effort and ingenuity, the forms underlying the virtual creatures are easily accessible and open to view. At the bottom of the hierarchy are the ones and zeros of binary code. Some see the emergence of complexity out of these simple elements as confirming the computational nature of reality, as we saw in chapter 1. Whereas scientific analysis leaves behind the complexity of the real world—which is to say, the messiness of embodied materiality—in the (necessary and useful) analytical division of an environment into discrete components and in the abstraction of form out of these components, complexity is precisely what is produced by the recursively structured adaptive systems of artificial life.[39] Although this complexity is generated from simple elements, it is not reducible to their combined properties, nor it is predictable from them, for it emerges dynamically from their interactions—which implies that if you have only the inscription of abstractions understood as forms that transmigrate *through* media but that are not affected *by* media, then the most interesting part of reality may have slipped through your fingers. Focusing on the complexity of intermediating processes helps to remind us what is left out of account when embodied materiality is reduced to inscription.

In the case of virtual creatures, it is difficult or impossible to think of forms transmigrating from embodied materiality to the electronic inscriptions we see on the CRT screen, for the complex structure of the Oreo necessarily complicates that picture. The complexity the creatures display is not inherent in the binary code; rather, it is *produced* as the program runs. "But you have forgotten," the realist objects, "that the creatures are simulations. As such, they occupy a different ontological niche than an inscription emerging from an embodied materiality that is the object of an experiment. It is no wonder that forms do not transmigrate, for the images do not represent preexisting reality." To this objection, I would respond that the simulations, although they do not represent a preexisting reality, nevertheless are themselves real, in the sense that they exist as objects in the world. Moreover, the evolutionary processes by which they are generated are no less real than the evolutionary processes that produced us as viewers, as Harold Morowitz's cosmic view of emergence demonstrates.[40] In Latour's terminology, they are quasi objects, hybrid entities produced through nature/culture.[41] They differ from the inscriptions of a biological laboratory not in being purely "artificial" in contrast to the "natural" organisms of the laboratory, but in the processes that produce them. When we see them, they are images on a CRT screen. Beneath that, they are functions in a LISP program, on down through the coding levels to the bottom layer where the voltages are being fashioned into bit streams. Their "bodies" have a material instantiation, but this instantiation differs radically from the inferences we make when we "see" them as creatures moving in three-dimensional space. To bridge the gap between our narrative inscription of the creatures and the materio-semiotic apparatus producing them, I find it useful to think of them as processes rather than as bodies. As emphasized in chapter 2 in the discussion of code running in the machine, the creatures' bodies are literally processes—electron beams scanning across the screen, code being compiled or interpreted in the computer—and their morphological and neurological properties are the result of generations of processes congealed and expressed in what we "see" as their bodies.

And how do we "see" the creatures, or anything else for that matter? Also through processes that bring the world into existence for us. As Brian Massumi argues elegantly in "The Brightness Confound," there is a sense in which the world is not a collection of preexisting objects but a continuing stream of processes. Although we customarily assume that the world preexists the processes, from a perceptual point of view the processes come first, and the objects we take as the world emerge from them. It is precisely this flux, this ongoingness of process from which the world emerges, that the realist in effect erases by privileging the underlying forms as the essential reality. Hence the significance of the virtual creatures, for they make this move impossible. There are no forms underlying them that are adequate to account for their emergence, no mechanisms that can be seen as allowing preexisting forms to transmigrate out of embodied materiality to become the complex inscriptions we see. When I suggest that we are virtual creatures, I mean to foreground the importance of processes for us as well. Processes connect the embodied materiality of the creatures with the bodies we see; processes connect our visual/cognitive perceptions of them with the narratives we construct; and processes are reinscribed and reinterpreted as narrative representations when we make the creatures characters in stories of defeat and victory, evolution and development. In distributed cognitive environments like those created when humans and nonhuman actors collaborate to create and understand the virtual creatures, embodied materialities interacting through complex processes disrupt the story of transmigrating forms and instead stimulate narrative inventions that foreground emergence and flux, perception and process.

The shift, then, is not merely from analog to digital subjectivity, both of which could be described as realist entities. Rather, the more profound change is from form to process, from preexisting bodies to embodied materialities that are linked to one another by complex combinations of processes based both in analog resemblances and coding relationships. When we inscribe ourselves as actors in these distributed cognitive environments, we become neither the interiorized analog subject of print culture nor the binary code of the digital subject; rather, we become a hybrid entity whose distinctive properties emerge through our interactions with other cognizers within the environment. These cognizers include the congealed processes embodied in such mundane objects as the chair I am sitting on, the keyboards I tap, and the yellow legal pad on which I scribble notes as I peer at the screen. Print culture and print subjectivity do not disappear but mutate, as distributed cognitive environments stimulate new kinds of narratives, including this one on the page you are reading.

The hybrid subjectivity emerging from distributed cognitive environments is playfully enacted in Jim Campbell's art installation "I Have Never Read the Bible." To make the installation, Campbell recorded his voice articulating the twenty-six letters of the alphabet while Mozart's *Requiem* played in the background. He then scanned an English translation of the Bible and converted it to binary code. A computer program was used to associate the sound of his voice articulating a letter with the corresponding mark, now residing in the computer as a coding string. After these coding arrangements were complete, another program was used, in conjunction with a synthesizer, to reproduce the articulated letters in the order in which they appear in the Bible. The result is a "reading" of the Bible letter by letter, from beginning to end, a process that the installation takes thirty-seven days to complete, running twenty-four hours a day. Meanwhile, the background music that in the original recording was a coherent performance of the *Requiem* has also been scrambled, with a bit of music playing only as long as it takes to articulate each letter. This musical soup serves as an audible reminder that we should not mistake the analog reproduction of sound for the coherent original, for the frothy digital middle of the Oreo has intervened and left tangible evidence of its process of fragmentation and recombination.

In the installation, the voice and scrambled music issue from a nineteenth-century edition of *Webster's Dictionary*. Heavy with materiality, the dictionary testifies to the anarchic status of the book as it hangs on the wall, whispering to the viewer "I-N-T-H-E-B-E-G-I-N-N-I-N-G-W-A-S-T-H-E-W-O-R-D. . . ." Performing the "voiced" text of analog subjectivity, the installation simultaneously hybridizes this subjectivity by embedding it in a new context. Visibly testifying to this new context is the cable running out of the dictionary to an electronic (and presumably digital) device below. The choice of the dictionary as the "voiced" text foregrounds the issue of meaning, for the dictionary's function is to define words, to match one signifier with other signifiers in correspondences that clarify meaning. In Campbell's installation, however, the signifier is not the flat mark of print culture. As if testifying to this change, the *Webster's Dictionary* that hangs on the wall cannot be opened, for it has been hollowed out to conceal the electronic gear within. Rather, the signifier has become a complex chain of digital codes and analog resemblances with rich internal structures articulated together through a series of dynamic processes in a configuration that I have called the flickering signifier.[42]

Meaning emerges not through correspondences between the flat marks but through the interactions of human and nonhuman cognizers distributed throughout the environment. The hybridity of the situation is highlighted in the installation's title. The point, after all, is that "*I* Have Never Read the Bible," that is, the artist as a singular subject has not read it. Rather, "reading" here is a distributed activity taking place partly in the articulations of the artist, partly in the "voiced" text, partly in the Oreo structures of the scanner, computer, and synthesizer, and partly in the perceptions of the viewer who not only makes words out of the voiced letters but also makes meaning out of her interpolation into this distributed cognitive environment.

What kind of subject am I as I stand musing before this installation? I certainly am not the autonomous liberal self that located identity in consciousness and rooted it in my ability, first and foremost, to possess my own body. Rather, as I think about my connection to virtual creatures, I am tempted to fashion myself in their image, seeing myself as a distributed cognitive system composed of multiple agents that are running the programs from which consciousness emerges, even though consciousness remains blissfully unaware of them. I am one kind of material embodiment; the virtual creatures are another; and we are connected through intermediations that weave us together in a web of jointly articulated cognitive activities. I think, therefore I connect with all the other cognizers in my environment, human and non-human, including both the dynamic processes that are running right now as you decode these letters and all the dynamic processes that have run in the past and congealed to create this paper, this ink, this old language made of nouns and verbs that I am trying to fashion to new purposes that will allow you to see my body, your body, the bodies of the virtual creatures, not as nouns that enact verbs, but as dynamic intermediations that weave together the embodied materialities of diverse life forms to create richly complex distributed cognitions. That is what virtual creatures can teach us.

9   Subjective Cosmology and the Regime of Computation
Intermediation in Greg Egan's Fiction

I would like not to like Greg Egan's fiction. He espouses many of the ideas I argued against in *How We Became Posthuman*, including the near-future prospect of uploading human consciousness into a computer and, in the longer term, a postbiological future for (post)humanity in which embodiment will have gone beyond even computers to become entirely optional, with people choosing whether to have bodies, grow new ones, or remain incorporeal. Moreover, he is still developing as a writer, and many of his works lack rich character development, sacrificing it for the sake of the highly speculative ideas he explores. Despite my disagreement with his conclusions about the future and notwithstanding the literary deficiencies, I find myself drawn to his fictions and admiring them almost in spite of myself. This chapter explores that reluctant fascination. The trajectory of the previous chapters has arced toward the conclusion that human bodies, cultures, and artifacts are becoming increasingly entwined with intelligent machines. Also at issue is the impact of the imagined future on the present, which as we saw in chapter 1 is an important dynamic braiding together the Universal Computer as metaphor with it as means. Egan's fiction, pushing the possibilities for the Computational Universe to extremes, invites us to think about how far the entanglement of humans and computers can or should go.

The Legacy of Alan Turing

To set the scene for Egan's speculative fiction, let us flash back to that seminal moment in 1950 when Alan Turing proposed the Turing test as an operational procedure whereby the question "Can machines think?" could be answered.[1] Two related trains of development spun off from that influential paper. First, many researchers considered Turing's proposal an invitation to develop intelligent machines, and within a decade artificial intelligence had become a flourishing research field. When skeptics objected that these early computers were not able to exercise judgment (as Joseph Weizenbaum asserted in 1976) or to think creatively and intuitively, arguing that these modes of thought remain the exclusive province of humans, researchers turned their attention to creating programs that could achieve these qualities.[2] For example, John Koza and his collaborators have worked to use genetic programs to design band-pass filters.[3] They have demonstrated that these programs can successfully design circuits previously thought to require the creativity and intuition that only highly skilled and experienced electrical engineers possess. Although one could argue that Turing's provocation has not been definitively answered in a philosophical sense, in my view it has met the fate of many such questions: it has not so much been answered as rendered increasingly uninteresting or even irrelevant. As the cognitions that intelligent machines can perform have deepened and broadened, we can exclude what they do from our definition of "thinking" only if we narrow the range of what counts as thinking so significantly that it becomes questionable whether many humans can think.

Similarly, the proposition that intelligent machines can have minds seems highly controversial, if not downright false, to many people today. Yet already researchers are engaged in developing intelligent machines that can perform mind-like activities. Consider Rodney Brooks's "Cog" project, the information-filtering ecology developed by Alexander Moukas and Pattie Maes, neural nets of many different kinds, Gerald Edelman's neurologically accurate NOMAD robot (Neurally Organized Mobile Adaptive Device), and many others.[4] In my view it is only a question of time before the activities performed by these and other machines become so mind-like that this too will become an uninteresting or irrelevant question. One development following from Turing's paper, then, has been the increasing sophistication of intelligent machines, as researchers have overcome barrier after barrier that has been postulated definitively to separate machines from the kinds of thinking that humans do.

A second development from Turing's paper was to set off debates concerning what we mean when we use words like "thinking," "mind," and "alive." These are notoriously controversial terms, and there exists neither a universal consensus about what they mean nor definitive demonstrations of what they are. Instead, when someone maintains that machines can think, that computers have minds, or that digital simulations are alive (assertions with complex histories of debate, research, and controversy), the terms themselves undergo transformation and modification as new players vault onto the field. A good example is the term "artificial life." Christopher Langton argues that the study of artificial life should be seen as part of theoretical biology, which, in turn, should endeavor to define life based on two distinct lineages: life forms based on carbon and those based on silicon.[5] Obviously, were one to reason on this basis the meaning of "life" would shift significantly. Similar dynamics are at work with the proposition that computers have minds, and the results can be seen, for example, in Daniel C. Dennett's *Kinds of Minds*, where he argues that it makes sense to talk about the mind of a cell or even of DNA.

These two dynamics—the continuing development of intelligent machines and the shifting meanings of key terms—work together to create a complex field of interactions in which humans and intelligent machines mutually constitute each other. Neither kind of entity is static and fixed; both change through time, evolution, technology, and culture. In other words, to use an aphorism that cultural materialists have long realized as a truth of human culture: what we make and what (we think) we are coevolve. The parenthesis in the aphorism marks a crucial ambiguity, a doubleness indicating that changes in cultural attitudes, in the physical and technological makeup of humans and machines, and in the material conditions of existence develop in tandem. For example, upright posture and the use of tools are considered by anthropologists to have coevolved dynamically in synergistic interactions. Walking upright made tool use easier, and tool use considerably increased the fitness advantages of bipedalism. Moreover, tool use is associated with the beginnings of human culture. Along with language, the development of artifacts and technologies are routinely considered as distinguishing characteristics setting human societies apart from other primate groups.

When I wrote in chapter 1 that I wanted to consider the Regime of Computation as both means and metaphor, the complex interaction of "what we make" and "what (we think) we are" is what I had in mind. Almost certainly, some of the insights of the Regime of Computation will bring about change in theories of how complexity arises, for example, Wolfram's key point that simple cellular automata can create complex patterns, and his and his employee Matthew Cook's demonstration that the simple CA described by Rule 110 is interconvertible with a Universal Turing machine. Wolfram's other, more far-reaching claims put pressure on competing ideas and theories, forcing them to modify some of their conclusions and speculations even as they, in turn, force the modification or rejection of some of Wolfram's claims.[6] The bold vision that Wolfram, Fredkin, Morowitz, and others espouse of a Universal Computer generating physical reality is meanwhile circulating in cultural arenas, as Greg Egan's novels, along with much else, testify.

The Universal Computer is already providing new ways to make old arguments about the contested term "human." For example, it transforms the scale at which claims about uploading consciousness might take place. In Hans Moravec's famous uploading scenario, published in 1990, consciousness is transferred directly into a computer, based on Moravec's reasoning that if consciousness is essentially an information pattern, then reproducing that pattern in artificial media will re-create consciousness in the same form it is experienced in a human.[7] As I observed in *How We Became Posthuman*, such a view ignores the vast differences separating human embodiment from computer architecture, not to mention the complex feedback loops that connect human cognition with embodied processes, as Antonio Damasio has shown compellingly.[8] But in the Regime of Computation, one does not need to make such simplistic assumptions in order to see cognition as a computational process. If computation generates physical reality at the subatomic level, then one can claim that in this sense cognition is computational, even while conceding differences in embodiment and the integral relation between embodiment and human cognition. The complexity of these dynamics simultaneously interacting with one another is intermediation in the broadest sense—claims about physical reality, cultural attitudes, and technological developments coevolving in relationships of synergy, contestation, competition, and cooperation.

Obviously, this is a huge topic and the subject of hundreds of books, from such majestic works as Manuel Castells's Information Age trilogy and Alan Liu's *The Laws of Cool* to more specialized studies such as Mark Poster's *What's the Matter with the Internet?*[9] The area of my own interest—indicated by the subtitle of this book, *Digital Subjects and Literary Texts*—focuses on making, storing, and transmitting as crosscutting topics that imply technological functions but that also engage cultural and artistic concerns. These concerns include the way code modifies our understandings of speech and writing systems, the interaction of print and electronic textuality, and the transformation of subjectivities as human and computer cognitions dynamically alter the meaning of thinking and mind. The crucial point to which I keep returning is the necessity to think these dynamics together, which requires recognizing that multiple causalities simultaneously interact with one another as both means and metaphors.

This is a more difficult, and perhaps more subtle, approach than I employed in *How We Became Posthuman*. I continue to think that my analysis there of how information lost its body accurately depicts much of the cybernetic thinking of the last half of the twentieth century, but that approach must be modified to account for the complexities of the Regime of Computation, which is a larger and more ambitious project than even the far-reaching dreams of the mid-twentieth century cyberneticians. Indeed, since in many ways twentieth-century cybernetics prepared the way for the Regime of Computation, it would not be entirely inaccurate to name the contemporary emphasis on emergence "third-order cybernetics" because it subsumes and transforms the reflexivity characteristic of second-order cybernetics. There are also, however, significant differences. The Regime of Computation is not a dematerialized theory, as was the Shannon/Weaver version of information theory central to the formation of cybernetics.[10] The Regime of Computation presumes and requires materiality at the same time that it transforms our understanding of the nature of materiality. This difference, among others, is why I have preferred to speak of the Regime of Computation, so as not to obscure the ways in which this twenty-first-century vision differs from the cybernetic paradigm.

Having presented a number of case studies showing that the complex dynamics of making, storing, and transmitting are changing contemporary ideas about language, textuality, and cognition, I turn in this final chapter to test the limits of the Regime of Computation. Egan's novels are particularly rich resources in this regard because he envisions the human/computer connection not as a question of technology (shades of Heidegger) but as an ontological inquiry into the relation of humans to the universe. In his "subjective cosmology" trilogy—*Quarantine*, *Permutation City*, and *Distress*—each of the novels speculates that there are deep connections between human consciousness and the computational processes that generate the universe, although each novel's vision of what this means remains distinct. Moreover, each novel carries within its fictional world seeds of resistance to the work's governing assumptions, thus performing many of the same ambivalences that I feel toward the Computational Universe. Indeed, in some ways my relation to these texts mirrors and inverts the dynamics of the texts themselves. Whereas they enact ideological programs through which run threads of resistance and subversion, I encounter them with major resistance through which run threads of admiration and fascination.

From Egan's fiction and interviews, it is clear that he places a high value on intellectual honesty. "What's important to me in every book is to push the ideas as far as I can, and to be as honest about the subject as I can," he remarks.[11] For him, intellectual honesty includes the willingness both to follow an idea through to its logical conclusion and to look hard at the differences between what we wish were true and what is actually the case.

A pithy bit of dialogue from *Distress* illustrates his commitment. Andrew Worth, in a moment of cynicism, remarks to Kuwale that "the truth is whatever you can get away with." Kuwale responds, "No, that's journalism. The truth is whatever you can't escape" (307). For Egan, humans *can* escape biology. What we cannot escape, in Egan's view, is the materiality of a physical universe that constitutes us as physical beings even as our participatory understanding co-constitutes it. In Egan's fiction, I encounter the farthest reaches of the Computational Universe. Whether I—indeed, all of us—can escape its implications is the scary and fascinating issue his novels invite us to engage. I begin the engagement by positioning the Computational Universe not only as a metaphor but as a *pathological* metaphor, that is to say, as a symptom.

Computation as Symptom

As outlined in chapter 1, if we read Stephen Wolfram's claims for the Computational Universe as cultural metaphor, we can trace a feedback loop between Wolfram's cultural situation—his location at a moment in human history when computer technology is widely available and exponentially increasing in memory capacity and processor speed—and his belief that physical reality is computational in nature. Such feedback loops (more clearly seen in retrospect than at the time) often develop, as in the example of eighteenth-century views of the universe as a clockwork mechanism, which I noted in the introduction. The appropriation of computation as a cultural metaphor is an instance of a more general dynamic in which cultural, historical, and linguistic presuppositions, invisible to someone because he simply assumes them to be true, constitute the framework in which problems are constructed and judgments made. This dynamic has much in common with the symptom. Useful for explicating its psychological aspects is Slavoj Žižek's *Enjoy Your Symptom!*

Taking his cue from Lacan's notorious dictum that "the letter always arrives at its destination," Žižek identifies the characteristic structure of the symptom as "*the mechanism of teleological illusion*" (9). He explains it with a joke: "Daddy was born in Manchester, Mummy in Bristol and I in London: Strange that the three of us should have met!" (9).[12] The mechanism, then, involves reasoning backward from one's present position and seeing prior contingent events as constituting a necessary and inevitable teleological progression to that point. The letter always arrives at its destination because, as Žižek points out, following Barbara Johnson, its destination is wherever it arrives. The metaphor of the letter is appropriate because a letter presumably contains a message addressed to someone other than the sender. Yet like a psychoanalytic symptom that indicates not a supposed physical ailment but repressed psychological trauma, the letter reaches its destination as soon as it is sent because the message points back to the sender rather than to a supposed other.

What letter does Wolfram send, and how does it function as a symptom? His vision of a Computational Universe is clearly indebted to the computer technology that makes his research possible. Creating complex patterns through CA simulations, he reasons backward to posit cellular automata as the mechanism that creates all complex systems, including the hardware and software running the simulations as well as his own perceptual/cognitive system enabling him to arrive at this conclusion. In a symptomatic view, the letter Wolfram sends in *A New Kind of Science* has as its addressee Wolfram's beliefs themselves, or more accurately the cultural formations that make computation seem so fundamental that it *must* turn out to be at the bottom of things (and us). Like the fantastic premise of the film *Paycheck*, he shoots a laser beam out into the universe to have it return and illuminate the back of his head. The letter arrives at its destination when we understand the teleological illusions that complete the (short) circuit between Wolfram's interpretation of complex systems and the cultural context of computation in which he is embedded.

As Žižek notes, similar backward reasoning is also characteristic of the so-called "anthropic principle." The strong version of this principle puts together a series of contingent physical qualities—the expansion rate of the universe, the freezing point of water, and so on—to show that if everything had not been just this way, the evolution of intelligent life would have been impossible, with the implication that the universe has been constructed precisely to enable intelligent life to emerge.[13] The weak version of the principle insists that any explanation about the origin of the cosmos must be consistent with the emergence of intelligent life, since it did after all evolve. Both versions reason backward to convert contingency into necessity and in this sense participate in symptomatic psychology. One might imagine a computational version of the anthropic principle using reasoning similar to Richard Dawkins's argument in *The Selfish Gene*, where he argues that humans are ways for genes to make more genes. In this scenario, the Universal Computer kept computing, computing, and computing through evolutionary eons until it was finally able to create consciousness capable of recognizing the Universal Computer's own natural mechanisms and then to re-create them in artificial media. Humans, in this view, are the computer's way to make more computers.[14] Take away the implication of the

Universal Computer's intentionality, and the scenario is close to Morowitz's postulation of the fourth stage of emergence as a reflexive turning back of computational mind to Computational Universe. However problematic this backward reasoning may be, the scenario makes clear why reflexivity is an important characteristic of the computational vision.

Žižek further associates the symptom with the observation that "there is no metalanguage" (12). He draws a connection between teleological reasoning and an insight central to quantum mechanics and contemporary science studies: we always participate in what we observe. He writes, "What we can see, as well as what we cannot see, is always given to us through a historically mediated frame of possibilities" (14–15). "At this level," he continues, "the impossibility of metalanguage equals the impossibility of a neutral point of view enabling us to see this 'objectively,' 'impartially': there is no view that is not framed by a historically determined horizon of 'preunderstanding'" (15). For Žižek, the reflexive entangling of subject and object takes the form of a certain excess or surplus, manifesting itself when the sender of a letter "always says more than he 'intended to say'" (14). In psychoanalytic terms, this becomes the repressed, with symptoms functioning to announce "returns of the repressed" (14).

In terms less oriented to psychology, the surplus reveals that the sender is implicated in the message, in the sense that the message is never objectively external to his perspective but is formed within and through that perspective, a dynamic central to Donna Haraway's concept of situated knowledge. [15] This notion of surplus suggests that Wolfram's interpretations of his simulations have a "repressed" aspect. Many commentators have remarked on his reluctance to credit the research of others and on his repeated insistence that he alone deserves the credit for inventing the "new kind of science." His promotion of his own work implies that he puts his mark on the universe and sees that handprint as synonymous with the way the universe actually is. Moreover, he interprets objections to his conclusions as evidence that he is correct, asserting that "traditional science" always resists the arrival of new paradigms. In Wolfram's self-insulating reasoning, the more other scientists object to his problematic extrapolations, the more certain he is that he is right. [16] We may conclude that Wolfram, more than most scientists, is blind to his own blind spots.

In its broadest conceptual form, the "blind spot" results not from a specific failure of vision but from the inevitable partiality of the viewer's perspective. "In what I see, in what is open to my view," Žižek writes, "there is always a point where 'I see nothing,' a point which 'makes no sense.' . . .

This is the point from which the very picture returns the gaze, looks back at me" (15). For Niklas Luhmann, this blindness is implicit in the cut that distinguishes a system from its environment. "Observing means making a distinction and indicating one side (and not the other side) of the distinction," he writes in a typical formulation.[17] While the cut enables the system to come into view as such, it also necessarily introduces an area beyond the realm of analysis that the cut makes possible. "Reality is what one does not perceive when one perceives it," as Luhmann puts it.[18] Whereas Luhmann emphasizes the blindness that unavoidably accompanies analytical insight, Žižek interprets the blind point as a gesture toward the frame that paradoxically encloses it. "The 'horizon of meaning' is always linked, as if by a kind of umbilical cord, to a point within the field discovered by it; the frame of our view is always already framed (re-marked) by a part of its content" (15). Paradoxes of representations that contain within themselves the frames enclosing them have been explored extensively by Douglas R. Hofstader in *Gödel, Escher, Bach.* Their pertinence here is their association with the symptom and the mechanism of teleological illusion.

As we shall see, the overlaps between Žižek's analysis of the symptom and Egan's subjective cosmology are extensive. There is, however, a significant difference that I want to note here. Egan's orientation is toward computation and quantum physics rather than psychoanalysis, and this difference in theoretical orientation leads him to conclusions very different from those Žižek espouses. A striking incongruity between Žižek and Egan lies in their attitudes toward death. For Žižek, death is the ultimate destination of the letter. "The only letter that nobody can evade, that sooner or later reaches us, i.e., the letter which has each of us as its infallible addressee, is death. We can say that we live only in so far as a certain letter (the letter containing our death warrant) still wanders around, looking for us" (20). By contrast, Egan views death as a consequence of our biological embodiment and speculates that it may become optional when technological advances allow human consciousness to be simulated within computational media. In this aspect of his writing, Egan would seem to have a technophilic orientation that is dramatically opposed to Žižek's psychoanalytic approach. I will argue, however, that his novels are ambiguously coded, and thus can be read both as technophilic extrapolations of the Regime of Computation and, more subtly, as critiques that interpret the Computational Regime as a symptom of our present cultural condition. This ambiguity makes Egan's novels ideally positioned to interrogate the deeper implications of the Regime of Computation as means and metaphor, symptom and reality.

Permutation City: The Letter Arrives as Death and Simulation

If the ultimate message the letter carries when it arrives at its destination is our own death, then in *Permutation City* the letter, like a charmed ritual in a fairy tale, announces itself three times. The first announcement comes when Paul Durham, the novel's protagonist, has himself scanned and the information uploaded into a computer.[19] Awakening to consciousness as a Copy, the simulated consciousness (whom I will call Paul, to distinguish him from Durham, the "real" person) finds the simulated life not worth living, feeling deeply troubled by the knowledge that he, like his environment, is an artifact produced by a machine. If in creating a Copy, Durham sends a letter, then Paul is the faux Durham who reads in it the necessity of his death. He consequently tries to "bale out" [*sic*]—the euphemism for Copies committing suicide. But this time the letter appears not to arrive, for he discovers that his original has illegally sabotaged the software and condemned him to continue living. Fifth in a line of Copies, all of whom "baled out" within fifteen minutes of (re)gaining consciousness, Paul has no choice but to perform the experiments that his original has preestablished.

The experiments are designed to test the nature of consciousness and, specifically, its relation to identity. They suggest that our sense of continuous selfhood is an illusion—that we are never who we think we are. At first these conclusions seem to apply only to simulated consciousness, but through a bizarre twist of plot Egan generalizes them to "real" identities. The experiments consist of Durham altering the processor speeds so that Paul's consciousness is generated not continuously but once every thousandth of a second, then hundredth, tenth, and finally only every ten seconds. Despite the intervening times, Paul perceives his consciousness as a continuous flow. This result is consistent with what we already know about computation. Data can be stored randomly throughout computer memory and still assembled in the correct order by the program, so dispersion in computational space has no relation to the simulation's continuity. Moreover, the simulation's outcome does not depend on processor speed. Whether a program runs fast or slow, the same result obtains, as we know from the ordinary practice of running simultaneous applications on our desktop. Hans Moravec, director of the mobile robotics laboratory at Carnegie-Mellon University and patron saint to uploaders, refers to these properties in *Robot: From Mere Machine to Transcendent Mind*: "A simulation's internal relationships would be the same if the program were running correctly on any of an endless variety of possible computers, slowly, quickly, intermittently, or even backwards and forwards in time, with data stored as charges on chips, marks on a tape, or pulses in a delay line, with the simulation's numbers represented in binary, decimal, or roman numerals, compactly or spread widely across the machine. There is no limit, in principle, on how indirect the relationship between simulation and simulated can be" (192). Although Moravec's publication came too late for Egan to have consulted it, similar ideas were afloat at the time he wrote *Permutation City*; and indeed he notes explicitly in an interview that such ideas were paramount in his mind when he wrote the novel.[20]

There is, however, an apparent fallacy here that obtains if a simulation is computing emergent phenomena (and presumably there would be no point in doing the simulation if emergence were not the concern). The time can be delayed in any variety of ways, as Moravec and Egan suggest, but one cannot in the general case run a simulation backward or in random order and be assured of producing the same outcome, for each successive clock-tick within the computer presupposes the previous one and uses its results as a basis for its own computation. (Exceptions that prove the rule are the special cases of reversible cellular automata, which can be run backward.)[21] Because there may be many paths to any given point in a simulation, running it backward could easily result in creating a different "past" than existed when the simulation ran forward.[22] Paul perceives that his consciousness continues uninterrupted, but this does not assure either him or us that the consciousness so produced is the *same* consciousness he would otherwise have had if the simulation had run forward. In the novel, Paul recognizes this fact and develops the "dust" hypothesis, generalizing from his experience as a simulation that all consciousness is actually discrete and discontinuous. In this view, everyone assembles his or her consciousness (and therefore identity) from the random noise of the universe (the "dust") to produce the illusion of continuous mind.

In effect, then, Paul recognizes the symptomatic mechanism of putting together contingent events so that they seem to reach a teleological end point. However, Paul's interpretation of this mechanism profoundly subverts the symptom's meaning in psychoanalytic theory. Paul's recognition of the radical contingency of human identity does not signal that he has finally uncovered the short circuit the symptom creates and, by implication, the trauma it covers over. On the contrary, the teleological illusion is transformed so that it now represents the ordinary "sane" belief that human consciousness is continuous. Paul is judged insane because he believes that the symptomatic mechanism, far from being psychopathological, is the usual way that discontinuous consciousness interacts with the universe to convince itself that it is continuous and ontologically stable. On a metaphysical level, this formation implies that computation has been transformed from a metaphor into the means by which reality is generated, a means that includes the illusions of those who think the Universal Computer is (only) a metaphor.

Paul's realization of this "truth" is accomplished through a plot development so implausible that its only justification is the necessity to redirect the letter so that it is forwarded through Paul back to Durham. Paul discovers that he is not the Copy but instead has been tricked into believing so by a plot Durham and his girlfriend hatched before erasing the knowledge of it from Paul's memory. Through this fantastic turn of events, Paul and Durham are reunited as Paul Durham. Awakened in the real world, Paul remains passionately convinced that all experience is digital and discontinuous. Moreover, he thinks that Paul and Durham really did have two distinct pasts, although the commonsense (i.e., "sane") view would be that he had simply been mistaken, the victim of an elaborate hoax. Because he believes that "Paul Durham" has at least two forking lifelines, and potentially many more possible permutations, he is declared insane and subjected to brain surgery. Although the operation supposedly cures him, he continues to believe in the dust hypothesis. "Paul Durham" now represents not so much a coherent identity as an infusion of Paul the Copy into Durham the person, and Paul Durham sees everyone's consciousness, including his own, as an operating system running on the Universal Computer, plucking data from here and there to assemble a contingent reality that always could have been different—and in fact always *is* different, playing out diverse trajectories in multiple parallel universes.

Computation in the conventional sense mimics this diversity on a small scale by multiplying the original into a Copy, which as soon as it is created begins diverging from the original. The Universal Computer operates on a vastly larger scale, creating infinite multiplicities whereby Paul Durham (and everyone else) is continually diverging from himself. He has the *illusion* of possessing a continuous identity, but the dust hypothesis dictates that we understand this identity as the result of tracing one contingent path through infinitely many branching points. Each branching produces an incrementally different identity than the others, resulting in infinitely many selves, each of which presumes that it is the unique result of an illusory teleology.

A similar idea is explored in *Quarantine*, Egan's novel preceding *Permutation City*. Here the mechanism is not a Computational Universe but the "many worlds" hypothesis of quantum theory. In the novel, scientist Chung Po-Kwai explains in a lengthy infodump (as it is known in SF circles) that quantum wave equations predict the probabilities for such actions as ion deflection and radioactive decay, but they do not specify how a *given* ion will deflect or how a *particular* particle will decay, which must be determined by measurement (127–35). Before the measurement, the particle's state is indeterminate, but after the measurement, future measurements always give the same result. This fact has led some quantum theorists to suggest that measurement (or more generally, observation) *determines* the result, in effect collapsing the wave function so that it leads to a unitary reality that did not exist as such before the measurement.[23] Egan takes this hypothesis and runs with it, postulating that the "observer function" is located in the human brain. Moreover, he also sets up the plot so that characters can learn to turn the observer function on and off. He further imagines that the ability to do so can be duplicated in software and computer viruses, making it potentially available to everyone.

In the novel, when the wave functions are not collapsed, every particle in the brain exists in more than one state, leading to billions of possible selves, each generated from a state incrementally different than every other. In the same way that quantum computing uses quantum indeterminacies to create multiple computing states, each of which is capable of carrying out an independent computation, so all the possible selves of the protagonist Nick Stavrianos in his uncollapsed or "smeared" state can carry out different permutations of the same task to discover the one possibility out of billions that will successfully complete the task.[24] Thus in his smeared state Nick is able to open secure locks, break complex cryptological codes, and stroll past guards without being seen. When the wave function is collapsed, all but the successful self disappears. Since which self is successful varies from task to task, Nick's impression of having a continuous consciousness is revealed as an illusion produced by jumping from self to self to self, each of which exists for a brief time as an autonomous entity until the wave function collapses and all memories of alternate states are erased, leading to the impression that only one self has existed.

As readers, we become aware of this process through discrepancies that reveal that the self narrating a given section is not the same as the self narrating the next one. For example, an accomplice sets Nick the task of finding the ten-digit code that will open a lock. This self tries the combination 1450045409 (195). But then the narrator of the next section, the self who survived because his was by chance the winning combination, reveals that the correct code (which he used) was 9999999999 (196). The experience of a continuous self is thus the teleological obsession naturalized so that it becomes the normal way humans experience the world. Before human observers force the world to become a unitary chain of events by collapsing the wave functions of everything within their sphere of observations, the universe in its uncollapsed state proceeds as an unimaginably vast series of computations continuously diverging from one another. This "smeared" state, although inimical to normal human consciousness, is by implication how the (inhuman) cosmos works. The anomalous position of humans within the universe becomes clear when unknown agents (presumably a vastly superior alien race) "quarantine" our solar system by encapsulating it within a huge impenetrable barrier to protect themselves against the human activity of collapsing everything they observe into a single lifeline. By the standards of the smeared universe, human consciousness is pathological by its very nature, as the title *Quarantine* suggests.

Egan's story suggests that recognizing the difference between the human teleological illusion and cosmic indeterminacy does indeed induce trauma, but with two crucial differences from Žižek's version. First, this is not the psychopathology of a single individual but the trauma of an entire world; and second, the pathological state for humans is revealed to be the uncollapsed, smeared state that is normal for the rest of the universe. Indeed, it is this "normal" state that leads to the disaster alluded to in *Quarantine*'s subtitle, *A Novel of Quantum Catastrophe*. When the inhabitants of New Hong Kong are infected with an engineered virus that causes them all to become smeared simultaneously, the bizarre and fatal results spawn all manner of monstrosities, from buildings growing flesh to people sprouting roots that sink into the ground. Astronomically improbable, these anomalies show that for humans, the teleological illusion is an essential defense necessary for human existence. Indeed, the teleological illusion as Egan envisions it is precisely that which is necessary to *prevent* human psychopathology, whereas for the rest of the universe the reverse its true: the smeared state is healthy and the normal human state is pathological. The criteria defining psychopathology are thus rendered contingent, depending on whether the reference is to humans or the postulated alien races that have cordoned off human observers to protect their worlds from becoming collapsed.

Like *Quarantine*, *Permutation City* supposes that a coherent identity is made to appear only by ignoring all the branching points and following a single trajectory through multiple proliferating selves. Here, however, the mechanism is significantly different from the quantum mechanics of *Quarantine*; rather, it reenvisioned as an inference emerging from the Computational Regime. Pushed to its logical conclusion, the dust hypothesis implies that not only multiple identities but multiple worlds can be assembled, all running on the underlying Universal Computer. The twenty-line poem that serves as an epigraph hints at this ontology. Each line is an anagram of "Permutation City" (as are the chapter titles of part 1).[25] A note explains that the poem was "found in the memory of a discarded notebook" in a psychiatric hospital, implying that it was written by Paul Durham while he was institutionalized. In addition, as Ross Farnell notes in one of the few critical articles on *Permutation City*, the short story "Dust," of which the novel is an expansion, is scattered throughout the novel's three-hundred-plus pages.[26] This dispersion further suggests that the novel itself could exist in countless permutations, of which we know only one. Egan thus carries over into this work *Quarantine*'s subtle implication that the coherence of the narrator's voice amounts to a teleological illusion created by the reader. The logic of Egan's fictional world implies that there may be as many narrators (and different permutations of the novel we read) as there are billions of alternative selves created by the endlessly proliferating branchings.

In *Permutation City*, the reflexive entwining of frame and picture that Žižek associates with the teleological illusion breaks into visibility through Egan's equivocation on a central point, namely, the position of consciousness within the simulation. Recall that Morowitz had no qualms about situating an observer function inside the computation that would mimic the role of an observer outside the simulation, watching it evolve. Egan joins these two functions into a paradoxical reflexive loop when he supposes that consciousness can at once assemble the dust that *produces* the simulation and simultaneously be *produced by* the simulation, thus entangling the picture and the frame that encloses it. As if picking up Žižek's image of an umbilical cord that connects the frame to a mark within the picture, Egan repeatedly creates scenes in which an umbilical cord metaphorically appears at precisely the moment that the reflexive entwining of frame and picture creates a crisis, a point to which we will return.

Yet despite this similarity between Egan's fiction and Žižek's analysis, there remain significant differences as well, particularly with regard to the teleological illusion. To develop these differences further, let us pick up the narrative at the point where Paul, in the grip of his obsession with the dust hypothesis, risks everything to buy up for a brief few minutes most of the planet's computing power to launch his "Garden of Eden" configuration, on the chance that once a seed for a simulated world is created and given an initial push, it can take off on its own and begin to run directly on the Universal Computer, envisioned as a TVC (Turing von Neumann Chiang) cellular automaton (183).[27] Because the platform would be the structure of the universe itself, Paul thinks it can grow and expand constantly as it assembles the dust, bringing space and time into existence through its computations.

At this point, the fiction has only a tenuous connection to reality, for no simulation has ever succeeded in escaping the bounds of the program that creates it, not to mention catapulting out of the computer to run on the same platform that produces our reality. In this respect, *Permutation City* resembles David Cronenberg's surrealistic film *Videodrome* more than it does scientific research on artificial life. In supposing that a simulation can begin to run on the Universal Computer from the force of its internal coherence, Egan goes beyond Wolfram in making reality and simulation permeable to one another.[28] In another sense, however, Egan's novel fully supports Wolfram's implication that the same computational mechanisms that create his simulations underlie physical reality; for once the Garden of Eden seed begins to run on the Universal Computer, there *is* no a priori ontological distinction between reality and simulation. Such a stance is inimical to the distinction between fantasy and reality on which the concept of the psychoanalytic symptom depends.

Notwithstanding Egan's technophilic extrapolations, significant threads of resistance run through *Permutation City*. Having the simulation leap out of the computer to run on the Universal Computer opens Durham's project to a critique of the kind Robert Markley undertakes when he contrasts the "freedom" of cyberspace with its cost in economic and social resources.[29] The novel makes clear that Durham's ambitions are severely constrained as long as he is confined to computing with finite resources. Only if the configuration runs on the Universal Computer will memory storage be able to increase without limit and without the vulnerabilities to which physical hardware is subject. This premise enables Paul to persuade his wealthy clients to underwrite his project, for he offers them the ultimate insurance from all contingencies: immortality. In psychoanalytic terms, the promise of immortality is an attempt to delay the letter indefinitely so that it never arrives. The phantasmatic aspect of Durham's obsession is emphasized by Maria De Luca's skepticism toward his project. Although she agrees to help him, she voices continuing resistance to his ideas, making clear to him (and to us) that she regards his obsession as a pathological attempt to continue by other means the delusions he suffered while institutionalized for mental illness.

Another aspect of the novel's resistance appears when the letter proves stronger than the fantasy of its infinite deferral. If the letter announces itself the first time to Paul, the Copy who finds simulated life not worth living, then it proclaims its arrival a second time to the Paul Durham who remains behind in the "real" world after his Copy, along with some fourteen other Copies (plus stowaways), are launched on the Universal Computer. So convinced is Durham that this launch can become reality that after completing the send-off and spending a night of disastrous sex with Maria, he commits suicide in a disembowelment that metaphorically resembles birth. This ghastly birth simulation, centered on his abdomen, conflates death and birth, the umbilical cord of a newborn with the intestines that spill from Durham's abdomen. This event transforms the meaning of the umbilical cord's appearance in psychoanalytic theory. Instead of functioning as a recognition of reflexivity, Durham's suicide makes the situation *less* reflexive, for it invests all that might remain of his identity in the Copy residing in Permutation City, capitol of the simulated world Elysium. That Durham now finds "real" life not worth living ironically mirrors and inverts his Copy's earlier attempt at suicide. Thus the letter has circulated through the faux Durham to arrive at the original Paul Durham.

In another permutation of this logic, the third letter arrives at its destination when a Copy chooses to accept himself as the addressee, even though it was sent by his original. The arrival of this letter enacts yet another variation on the theme of identity constantly diverging from itself. In Permutation City, how closely a Copy mirrors its original is negotiable, for a simulated consciousness can *choose* how much of the original personality and memories to retain, and how much to modify or edit. If one finds oneself unhappy in Permutation City, for example, it would be possible to edit one's program so that unhappiness is impossible. Of course, precisely to the extent that such changes are made, the Copy diverges from its original identity, the preservation of which was the presumed reason to create the Copy. This is the dilemma facing Thomas Riemann, a multibillionaire who had a Copy loaded into the Garden of Eden configuration as insurance against the possibility that his existing Copy, running on his own secure hardware after his death, might encounter political and economic backlashes that would endanger its existence. A Copy of a Copy, the Riemann consciousness in Permutation City has chosen to retain a small scar on his forearm and the memory to which it is metonymically associated. The scar recalls for Thomas a moment of cowardice when as a young man he became involved with a woman of questionable reputation and during an argument pushed her against a brick wall, seriously injuring her. Rather than call an ambulance and face the resulting disgrace and probable disinheritance, Thomas brutally continued to beat her until she died.

This shameful memory has become so integral to his identity that he believes if he were to abandon it, his entire life would no longer make sense to him. He cannot resist playing the memory of that disastrous night over and over again, which he experiences each time as if it were happening anew. Since it is a simulation, at any point he can edit the memory or even change the outcome, but each time, for thousands of repetitions, he makes the same fatal choice at the decisive moment. After hundreds of thousands of repetitions resulting in a mounting score that he incises into his abdomen with a knife, he finally breaks clear and makes the ethical choice to call an ambulance. In doing so, he accepts the consequences of his actions, which is to say, he accepts the letter that has been following him around. He subsequently falls into a coma, an appropriate plot development that metes out a simulated death to a simulated consciousness.

Riemann's acceptance of the letter coincides with the climactic final crisis, marked by the arrival not so much of a different letter as the same letter in different form. This crisis represents the novel's strongest resistance to its own premises. Significantly, it serves to disentangle metaphor and means. When Paul Durham designed Permutation City, he wanted to include the seed of another simulated world, differing from Permutation City because it is intended to evolve life from mutating bacteria, thus building a reality from the ground up. To facilitate the evolution of this simulation within the simulation, called the Autoverse, Paul arranged matters so that the processing time for the Autoverse runs much faster than for Permutation City. Whereas only seven thousand years have passed for the Copies, three billion years have elapsed for the Autoverse. During this time, highly intelligent life forms—human-sized insects called the Lambertians—have evolved. In contrast to the evolutionary processes that create the Lambertians, the Copies have been constructed using ad hoc algorithms that simulate respiration, circulation, and so on. The Lambertians are thus more coherent than the Copies, making sense as emergent processes all the way down to the atomic level. Their scientists have lately begun to question how their world came into existence. When Paul communicates the answer that he assumes is correct—the Autoverse was created by (the originals of) the Copies—the Lambertians reject the idea as an untenable ad hoc hypothesis. With that, they begin deconstructing the world of Permutation City.

This contestation can be understood in terms of metaphors versus means. In a certain sense, everything in the simulated world of Permutation City functions as a metaphor. One of the ways Thomas Riemann propped himself up, for example, was to take a swig from his C&O bottle. Although the name sounds like a whiskey, C&O stands for Confidence and Optimism, and the "bottle" is a metaphor for changing the code that computes his simulated consciousness so that he feels more confident and optimistic. Like the trash icon on a computer desktop, the "bottle" has no intrinsic relation to the underlying code, connecting Riemann to a lost world of real objects rather than to the simulated world of Permutation City in which he actually lives. The

Lambertians, by contrast, have no need of ad hoc metaphors unrelated to the materiality of their environment. Whatever metaphors they presumably use have coevolved in synchrony with their world, making their world epistemologically as well as ontologically superior to Permutation City. Their triumph over Permutation City functions to distinguish metaphors that obscure the material basis for existence from those that illuminate it (a distinction, as we have seen, crucial to Neal Stephenson's *Cryptonomicon*). Through the Lambertians, then, the novel enacts a cautionary tale about confusing metaphor and means, thus performing another resistance to its premises.

When the Lambertians refuse to accept their subaltern status, the supposedly infinite deferral implied by Paul's assertion that the denizens of Permutation City would be immortal abruptly collapses and the fatal letter arrives after all. Although Paul and Maria, as well as the other Copies, plan to re-create themselves (or more precisely, generate Copies of their Copies) by launching a new Garden of Eden configuration, they are unable to drag Riemman's unconscious body with them, so he becomes a remainder, symbolically accepting the letter announcing their mortality. When the Lambertians refuse to accept Durham's explanation, he is confronted with the realization that evolution is not teleological and that emergence will not necessarily lead to the result its creator envisioned. If in one sense *Permutation City* supports Wolfram's thesis by deconstructing the distinction between simulation and reality, in another sense it reveals the power of simulation to determine its own future, independent of what its creator intends or desires. Juxtaposed with Wolfram's claims that he alone deserves credit for the "new kind of science," *Permutation City* implicitly critiques the creator's ability to lay claim to his creations. Precisely because Egan takes the Computational Regime seriously as the means by which reality is produced, he refuses to confine it within the preconceptions of its creator, whatever those might be.

Distress and the Participatory Universe

As we have seen, *Quarantine* entangles human consciousness with the production of a single lifeline for the solar system, whereas *Permutation City* suggests that human consciousness itself is produced by assembling the universe's "dust." In *Distress*, the last novel in Egan's subjective cosmology trilogy, human consciousness is envisioned as essential to producing the universe's cosmology. Here Egan's fiction engages the most grandiose of the teleological illusions that Žižek discusses: the anthropic principle linking the evolution of the cosmos to the evolution of intelligent life. *Distress* also provides the trilogy's richest character development, as if Egan recognizes that a more vibrant sense of the narrator's humanity is necessary to complement the inhuman dimensions of the universe's birth and evolution. Indeed, bringing the scale of individual humans into connection with the scale of the universe is the novel's central project.

Distress foregrounds the paradox hovering in the margins of the earlier texts, namely, a consciousness that simultaneously assembles the dust (or quantum states) and is assembled by it. Andrew Worth, a science journalist working on contract for the television channel SeeNet, grabs the assignment to cover a high-level scientific conference on competing versions of a Theory of Everything, or TOE. He stumbles across the Anthrocosmologists (ACs), a cult that believes that the articulation of a successful TOE will not so much describe a preexisting world as actually bring the postulated universe into being. Amanda Conroy, drawing on physicist John Wheeler's controversial interpretation of quantum indeterminacy (with a wink by the author to those who have read *Quarantine*), explains that "it's easy enough to see that a coin is neither 'heads' nor 'tails' while it's still up in the air, spinning—but what if it's not even *any particular coin*? What if there really are no preexisting laws governing the system you're about to measure" (208).[30] In this conjecture, observation (more precisely, articulation) determines not only quantum states but the very law-like structures that define and generate the states. In the view of the ACs, the more questions that scientists ask, "the more precisely the universe takes shape" (208). "If an event doesn't take place unless it's observed," Conroy argues, "then a law doesn't exist unless it's understood" (209). As she points out, however, "understanding" here implies not simply a claim to understand, in which case the universe would be fractured into as many worlds as there are competing interpretations. Rather, an understanding powerful enough to affect the world would have to be coherent, consistent, and rich enough to account for the universe's diverse manifestations.

The reasoning extends to the breaking point those arguments advanced by constructivist critics within science studies that laws of nature do not exist until they are discovered. Most critics acknowledge that *something* exists, but they argue that the ways in which that something is articulated and understood deeply affect how it will be integrated into existing frameworks of knowledge, transforming them in the process.[31] There is reason to think that Egan has little patience with social constructivism, which is lampooned in *Distress* through a caricature "Ignorance cult" called "Culture First." Characteristically, however, Egan confronts this presumed enemy not by debunking but by appropriating and expanding its claims. The strategy recalls the motto that truth is "what you can't escape." If he cannot escape the kernel of truth in the view that the laws of nature are invented rather than discovered, he will make the truth his own by pushing it to the limit.

The strategy is enacted when the dialogue suddenly veers toward fringe cosmology. "Imagine this cosmology," Conroy tells Worth. "Forget about starting the universe with just the right finely-tuned Big Bang needed to create stars, planets, intelligent life . . . and a culture capable of making sense of it. Instead, take as your 'starting point' the fact that there's a living human being who can explain an entire universe, in terms of a single theory. Turn everything around, and take it as the only thing given that this person exists" (212). This is the anthropic principle gone wild. As we have seen, even the strong version of the anthropic principle traces a historical trajectory, albeit one that has as its necessary teleological endpoint the emergence of intelligent life. This version goes further: erase history, start with a single person (called the Keystone by those who take the theory seriously), and add the requirement that the Keystone bring history into being (instead of the idea that history brings intelligent life into being).

If this theory were articulated by someone who believed himself to be the Keystone, we might justifiably consider him a megalomaniac. When pronounced by someone who identifies another person as the Keystone (as do fringe ACs), it becomes enormously important who that person is. If the "wrong" person becomes the Keystone, that person could create an apocalypse by theorizing a universe inimical to intelligent life and perhaps to life of any kind. Translated into psychoanalytic terms, the belief in the Keystone combines scapegoating with a strong teleological illusion, identifying as the letter's addressee a consciousness uniquely invested with cosmic powers of creation and uncreation. Conroy's comments set the stage for Andrew's discovery of several groups of fringe Anthrocosmologists, from those who believe that their life depends on having the "right" Keystone, to even more extreme groups who prefer that the universe retain its infinite capacity for change, which they think they can accomplish by assassinating everyone capable of articulating a TOE at all.

At the center of the maelstrom is Violet Mosala, the brilliant South African twenty-nine-year-old Nobel Prize physicist who is one of the top three TOE contenders. Significantly, her theory has something in common with the teleological illusion as analyzed by Žižek. It is abstract and formal, having little content, which she supplies by putting in constants already known, such as the speed of light. She reasons that since we already know these things to be true, they must be consistent with a correct TOE; her critics (including Andrew Worth) suspect that this makes her theory tautological.

In much the way that the teleological illusion reads backward through contingent events to arrive at a present thus made necessary and inevitable, so Mosala's theory synthesizes her logical framework with what already exists to create a TOE that appears fated to be the correct interpretation.

The addition of known data to Mosala's theory recalls the ad hoc nature of the Copies, whose reality was vulnerable to deconstruction precisely because it had not emerged from the ground up. *Distress* explores the inverse proposition; instead of a more robust reality deconstructing Permutation City, Mosala's theory, because it lacks robust content, threatens to deconstruct the universe. Captured by an extremist AC group, Andrew tries desperately to dissuade them from their deadly designs on Mosala. They explain their violent intentions by running a simulation for him that first shows an incredibly complex web of interconnected threads representing the universe's knowledge content. When they put in Mosala's theory, these threads begin to unravel until finally there is nothing. One of their scientists explains, "Her TOE can't survive its own expression. It can make her the Keystone. It can grant her a seamless past. It can manufacture twenty billion years of cosmology. But once it's been stated explicitly, it will resolve itself into pure mathematics, pure logic" (321). The letter's arrival, as they see it, will be the uncreation of the universe, as Mosala's TOE "goes through all the labor of creating a past—only to reach the conclusion that it has no future" (321).

As we have seen, Žižek uses the letter's arrival to signify an unraveling of the teleological illusion, so that the sender is finally forced to recognize the psychological mechanisms embedded within the illusion. In Žižek's construction, the problem is precisely that the symptomatic patient mistakes his subjective contingencies for an objectively existing reality. Egan, by contrast, entwines the teleological illusion with an abstract and formal TOE, thereby situating the compound in a borderland indeterminably located between the subjective and objective. It is subjective insofar as it embodies Mosala's vision; if another scientist becomes the Keystone (as the fringe ACs hope will happen when they take Mosala out of the picture by infecting her with a deadly virus), the consequence would presumably be a different kind of universe. On the other hand, the compound is objective in the sense that her TOE expresses formal relationships that must logically cohere for her TOE (or any other) to have efficacy. Only if it coheres would it have the power to become objective in the strong sense of actually determining the universe's structure.

This entanglement of the subjective and objective, the human with the cosmological, is bound up with another drama played out between human identity and embodied instantiation, a drama performed most powerfully through Andrew's role in the unfolding events. He has had implanted in his abdomen a sophisticated hardware and software system that can record events electronically; the implant is appropriately dubbed "Witness." The implant promises objectivity, for it will simply record whatever is to be seen. Yet Andrew must evoke the software through a conscious act of will, and he also directs what it records by his glance, so the result is a synthesis of his subjective intention with the intelligent machine's operation. His psychology therefore inevitably affects the electronic record, and there are early hints that his psychology is unusual. We learn that he has never had a relationship last longer than eighteen months and that he lacks an intuitive feeling for intimacy, attempting to make up for it by a list of rules that he recites to himself, the first rule being to pretend to his partner that there are no rules. When he interviews a leader of Voluntary Autistics, subsequent events intimate that Andrew himself is probably a high-functioning autistic, an inference that later becomes important in linking Andrew's subjective worldview with the nature of the world itself.

Significantly, Andrew's realization of his own physicality is bound up with his intestinal tract and specifically with the small aperture through which the equipment was inserted into his abdomen. Infected with an engineered strain of cholera by the fringe ACs, he realizes that "this diseased body was my whole self. It was not a temporary shelter for some tiny, indestructible man-god living in the safe warm dark behind my eyes. From skull to putrid arsehole, this was the instrument of everything I'd ever do, ever feel, ever be" (272). Yet there are layers to this realization; he knows, but he does not know fully. Sliced across the abdomen by a military robot, he later feels an inexplicable impulse to probe the wound with his fingers, pushing until he feels his small intestine. Thinking "this was the part of me that had almost killed me" (when he had uncontrollable diarrhea), he realizes that "*the body is not a traitor; it only obeys the laws it must obey in order to exist at all*" (422).

His confrontation with his own physicality is thus staged as a realization that he is bound by the laws that the TOE articulates. In a certain sense, his identity is nothing other than this articulation. The connection is further strengthened when he is kidnapped and forced to pull the embedded coils of software out of his abdomen. As he extracts the umbilical-like artifact, he engages in a performance that demonstrates the inevitable entwining of the subjective and objective. The action eerily echoes and inverts the scene in *Permutation City* where Paul Durham stabs himself in the abdomen. Whereas Paul's suicide is a renunciation of embodiment, Andrew's extraction of his software is connected with his realization that he *is* his body. As he pulls the coils of optic fiber from his belly, the scene functions as if bringing literally into bloody view the symbolic umbilical cord that Žižek identifies with the place where the frame enters the picture. When he later probes his intestine through the reopened wound, he thinks, "I wanted to stare into a mirror and proclaim: *This is it. I know who I am, now. And I accept, absolutely, my life as a machine driven by blood, as a creature of cells and molecules, as a prisoner of the TOE*" (422). If the Lacanian mirror stage enables the subject to (mis)recognize himself as a coherent body, here the (missing) mirror reflects back to Andrew an image of himself as a manifestation of the universe's realization through the Theory of Everything, which as its name redundantly implies must include Andrew's subjective being within its scope.

The point is made explicit when Andrew attempts to goad a fringe AC scientist by suggesting that he is content to be a bit player in a drama directed by the successful TOE theorist. The scientist responds, "The universe is not a *dream*. The Keystone is not . . . the avatar of some slumbering god-computer in a higher reality, threatening to wake and forget us. The Keystone anchors the universe *from within*. There's nowhere else to do it" (319). Although events prove the scientist wrong in thinking that a single person would be the Keystone, the narrative sustains and expands the central insight that we are always in the position of changing the world while simultaneously being changed by it, for the only possible positions we can occupy are inside that same world.[32]

Distress creates several metaphors for this reflexive entwining. Shortly after Andrew arrives at Stateless, the island anarchy where most of the novel is set, a woman tells Andrew her story of treading water with her sister for hours after a shipwreck, each holding up the other in a fashion that recalls Escher's drawing of a right hand drawing a left hand drawing a right hand. Stateless itself embodies the same reflexive metaphor, for it literally floats on top of the ocean through nano-engineered organisms that generate the gases holding up the island, even while the island holds them up. Although the island would seem to be hopelessly vulnerable to any attack, when EnGenuity (the corporation claiming proprietary rights to the nanotechnology that created the island) uses ruthless mercenaries and military robots to intimidate and slaughter the inhabitants, the anarchists triumph by simply allowing the portion of the island holding the invaders to sink.

The scene of Andrew accepting his body as truly himself and not merely as a container sets the stage for the climax, in which the union of the subjective and objective rockets to cosmological proportions. Knowing she has been targeted, Mosala activates a Kaspar clonelet, an artificial intelligence software that instantiates certain aspects of her mind. Yet as the clonelet completes and extends Mosala's synthesis, Distress (an informational disorder in which the victims feel unbearable anguish from informational overload) begins exponentially claiming victims. The problem, Andrew intuits, is that the TOE is being put together by a nonhuman intelligence. To integrate humans into the picture, the TOE must be interpreted by a human being, who turns out, as readers might have guessed, to be Andrew himself—and yet not him; for once he has given human form to the understanding, many others follow, so the TOE ends up being created not by a single Keystone but by millions of people working cooperatively together.

In conveying the resulting transformation, Egan strives to represent a world that is at once infused with human meaning and objectively true; he calls this world the "participatory universe." Significantly, the last remaining obstacle to Andrew's attempt to articulate the TOE is empathy, which he now understands in the terms set out earlier by the Voluntary Autistics: empathy is a trick evolution played on the human species to insure that pair bonding, and thus sexual reproduction, would take place. The illusion that we can understand another person's feelings is replaced by the TOE, a greater understanding that does not require the exclusivity of pair bonding. The lasting relationship for which Andrew yearned is finally accomplished with Akili Kuwale, an "asex" who has had "vis" body surgically altered to remove sexual allure and the possibility for sexual union. "The deepest truth about the body," Kuwale tells Andrew, "is all that restrains it, in the end, is physics. We can shape it into anything the TOE allows" (404).[33] In this curious configuration, the body is accepted as a "prisoner to the TOE" at the same time that it is liberated from its evolutionary bondage to reproductive urges, as if to accomplish the former the latter must also take place.

As this formation suggests, physics consistently trumps biology in Egan's work. In the later novel Schild's Ladder, set in the far future (i.e., from six hundred to one thousand years hence), humanity has become so thoroughly postbiological that most people no longer feel anxiety about losing their birth bodies. This is not the case in Quarantine, Permutation City, and Distress, all near future works (i.e., a few decades away). In this subjective cosmology trilogy, the protagonists struggle with their physicality and its limitations: witness Nick's anxiety when he realizes the discontinuities of consciousness, Paul's intense horror at finding that his body is a simulacrum, and Andrew's painful coming to terms with his embodiment. These texts suggest that this is the price that must be paid to achieve a subjective cosmology: humans must first recognize themselves as creatures of the cosmos before they are allowed to understand that they are creators of it as well.

The friction between struggling with embodiment and Egan's belief in a postbiological future can be seen as an admirable commitment on his part to look hard at his own premises. In Egan's fiction, there is the lingering suspicion that humans represent one small part of an immense universe, and this suspicion often translates into a healthy skepticism that Egan seems to harbor with regard to his own assumptions. Like Žižek, Egan would agree that we always say more than we know, in the sense that the range of our knowledge has limits we do not see. For Egan, however, the letter's arrival is not associated particularly with repression (although he is not unaware of this possibility, as his characterization of Andrew Worth indicates). Rather, the letter points toward our local and limited understanding of the nature of the physical universe. Egan would almost certainly find Žižek's psychoanalytical approach distressingly parochial. He has made his views clear in an interview: "When it comes to deep self-modification of the personality . . . either while remaining in our bodies, as in *Quarantine*, or once we're uploaded as software, as in *Permutation City*—that's a very complex issue, which . . . the majority of my work is trying to address in various ways. It might take 50 years, or it might take 500, but eventually we're going to have unlimited control over whatever physical substrate is 'executing' our minds, and I'm trying to map out some of the benefits and some of the dangers of that."[34] To invest everything in a theory of the unconscious based on our physical and mental structures, as Žižek does, would in Egan's view be presumptuous because it holds the entire span of the far future hostage to our present local conditions.

At almost every point where I find myself resisting Egan's vision— notably his vision of a postbiological future and the expansion of human powers necessary to create the participatory universe—I find this resistance inscribed and recognized within the text. Egan has Andrew Worth acknowledge, for example, that the participatory universe is not entirely benign. Nine million people, we are told, committed suicide (!) rather than join in this vision. Since they presumably would have resisted the instantiation of this vision if such resistance were possible, this revelation, arriving a page from the end, suggests that the participatory universe can also be seen as the compulsory universe.

Finally what attracts me—*compels* me—to engage with Egan's fiction is his refusal to make things easy for himself, a refusal that might well be called by such names as "honesty" and "integrity." If I attempt to be equally honest myself, I am forced to agree that it is difficult to imagine where humans will be in another thousand years; they might indeed invent a postbiological future for themselves. It seems certain that the next century will see increasing convergences between humans and intelligent machines through such developments as implants, pervasive computing, robots with ever more sophisticated sensors and actuators, quantum computing, and the increasing convergence of biology and computation through nanotechnology and other means.

As the scope of our technological prowess increases, so do threats to our biological existence—through acid rain, greenhouse effects, and other environmental degradations, not to mention genocidal campaigns of ethnic cleansing and military adventures intent on making other cultures conform to what we think they should be. Amid these disasters, we could do worse than attend to the implication in Egan's subjective cosmology trilogy that "what we make" and "what (we think) we are" are deeply intertwined. Whatever the future, the teleological illusion operates strongly in his fiction to remind us that we are both in the world and of it—a truth that becomes only more inescapable as we create machines in our image and reenvision ourselves as computational mechanisms like them.

Epilogue
Recursion and Emergence

Long before Stephen Wolfram's book, Francis Bacon also called for a new kind of science that was even more ambitious and far-reaching than Wolfram's vision. *Novum Organon*, routinely regarded as providing the foundations of modern science, envisioned a masculine science based on empirical practices that, in Bacon's high expectations, would repair the damage done with the Fall from Eden and restore to "man" dominion over the earth. Bacon understood full well the dangers of believing in cultural metaphors and constructed a typology of blind spots to warn practitioners against them. However necessary his strategic separation of the subjective and objective may have been at a time when alchemy flourished and astrology was a state science, it left a damaging legacy by associating science with mastery, control, and domination, underwritten by the premise that one can act without simultaneously being acted upon. Over the intervening centuries, the tragic implications of that assumption would be played out again and again in fiction and reality, from Mary Shelley's *Frankenstein* to the looming problems in the new millennium of global warming.

An important contribution of mid-twentieth-century cybernetics was the construction of theories and workable technologies that instantiated feedback loops connecting human and machine, dominator and dominated, subject and object. Yet even the most insightful and reflective of the cyberneticians stopped short of seeing that reflexivity could do more than turn back on itself to create autopoietic systems that continually produce and reproduce their organization. Heinz von Foerster's classic work *Observing Systems* shows him coming to the threshold of a crucial insight and yet not quite grasping it: the realization that reflexivity could become a spiral rather than a circle, resulting in dynamic hierarchies of emergent behaviors. By the time scientists began to use this idea as the basis for new kinds of technologies, cybernetics had already lost its utopian gloss, and the new fields would go by the names of artificial life, complexity theory, and cellular automata.

The crucial question with which this book has been concerned is how the "new kind of science" that underwrites the Regime of Computation can serve to deepen our understanding of what it means to be in the world rather than apart from it, comaker rather than dominator, participants in the complex dynamics that connect "what we make" and "what (we think) we are." Amid the uncertainties, potentialities, and dangers created by the Regime of Computation, simulations—computational and narrative—can serve as potent resources with which to explore and understand the entanglement of language with code, the traditional medium of print with electronic textuality, and subjectivity with computation.

A major implication of entanglement is that boundaries of all kinds have become permeable to the supposed other. Code permeates language and is permeated by it; electronic text permeates print; computational processes permeate biological organisms; intelligent machines permeate flesh. Rather than attempt to police these boundaries, we should strive to understand the materially specific ways in which flows across borders create complex dynamics of intermediation. At the same time, boundaries have not been rendered unimportant or nonexistent by the traffic across them. Biological organisms are not only computational processes; natural language is not code; and fleshly creatures are composed of embodiments that differ qualitatively from artificial life forms. Boundaries are *both* permeable and meaningful; humans are distinct from intelligent machines even while the two are become increasingly entwined.

Informing these interactions is a vision of computational media as instantiations of the world's active agency. Disrupting the standard story of scientific realism, the computational processes that create and implement this agency have the potential to inspire another kind of narrative in which humans are not seen as subjects manipulating objects in the world. It is possible, of course, to inscribe computational media into scenarios of mastery, familiar at least since Bacon, in which the subject/object dichotomy provides the basic assumption for action. Popular culture offers us myriad stories of this kind, from the *Terminator* films to *A. I.* and *The Matrix* to Philip K. Dick's *Do Androids Dream of Electric Sheep?* A central dynamic in these works is the artificial life form that refuses to accept its status as a passive object and asserts its right to become a subject capable of autonomous action, which when pitted against human agency generates the conflict on which the story turns. However this power struggle is played out and whatever its outcome, the subject/object dichotomy remains intact, as does the implication that subjects have the right to dominate objects. If we interpret the relations of humans and intelligent machines only within this paradigm, the underlying structures of domination and control continue to dictate the terms of engagement.

This book has focused on narratives of a different kind that offer ways out of the subject/object divide. In these stories, human action and agency are understood as embodied processes sharing important characteristics with the processes taking place within computational media, including possibilities for evolution and emergence. In my view, an essential component of coming to terms with the ethical implications of intelligent machines is recognizing the mutuality of our interactions with them, the complex dynamics through which they create us even as we create them. The preceding chapters have staged that central realization at many points and in different ways: Wolfram looking at his cellular automata; the monster in *Patchwork Girl* looking for her consciousness in the guts of the machine; humans gazing at Karl Sims's virtual creatures; Andrew Worth probing inside his wound to extract Witness.

Encountering intelligent machines from this perspective enables me to see that they are neither objects to dominate nor subjects threatening to dominate me. Rather, they are embodied entities instantiating processes that interact with the processes that I instantiate as an embodied human subject. The experience of interacting with them changes me incrementally, so the person who emerges from the encounter is not exactly the same person who began it. What I think of as my human legacy—the language I speak, the books I read, the digital art and information I peruse, the biology I inherit from eons of evolutionary dynamics, the consciousness that generates my sense of identity—is already affected by the intermediating dynamics of my interactions with intelligent machines, and will surely be transformed even more deeply in the decades to come. The challenge, as I see it, is to refuse to inscribe these interactions in structures of domination and instead to seek out understandings that recognize and enact the complex mutuality of the interactions. "What we make" and "what (we think) we are" coevolve together; emergence can operate as an ethical dynamic as well as a technological one. Realization arrives not in an instant but in successive cycles of awareness, each building on what came before. So it has been for me in writing this book, and perhaps for you in reading it. As is always the case where dynamical emergences are involved, at the end we begin again.

Notes

Prologue

1. Anne Balsamo, *Technologies of the Gendered Body*, 133.

2. I have borrowed the term "Robo sapiens" from Peter Menzel and Faith D'Alusio, *Robo sapiens*, a photographic excursion into some of the newest accomplishments in robot engineering.

3. Hans Moravec, *Mind Children*, passim. For example, in the prologue Moravec predicts that "a postbiological world dominated by self-improving thinking machines would be as different from our world of living things as this world is different from the lifeless chemistry that preceded it" (5). He continues his exploration of robot intelligence and a postbiological world in *Robot*.

4. Bruno Latour, "A. N. Whitehead and Richard Powers."

5. Stephen Wolfram, *A New Kind of Science*.

6. The similarity between the clockwork metaphor in the eighteenth century and the pervasiveness of computer metaphors in the twentieth century has been widely noticed in the scientific community, by skeptics as well as advocates of the Computational Universe. See, for example, Seth Lloyd, "How Fast, How Small, and How Powerful? Moore's Law and the Ultimate Laptop."

7. Marjorie Hope Nicolson, *Newton Demands the Muse*.

8. Friedrich A. Kittler, *Essays*, 40.

9. Friedrich A. Kittler, "The Mother's Mouth," in *Discourse Networks*, 25–70.

10. Nicholas Gessler, personal communication.

11. Marie-Laure Ryan, *Possible Worlds, Artificial Intelligence, and Narrative Theory*.

Chapter One

1. Hereafter when "code" and "language" appear together, "language" refers to natural language and "code" to digital computer code, unless otherwise specified.

2. The concept of the feedback loop was developed in first-order cybernetics during the 1930s and 1940s. Although the idea of circulating the output of a system back into the system as input is ancient, dating back to self-governing devices developed by the Greeks in the classical period, it was not until the twentieth century that the feedback loop was explicitly

linked with informational circuits, where it began to have much broader applicability. I use "feedback loop" to apply both to physical devices and to recursive conceptual structures.

3. Ferdinand de Saussure, *Course in General Linguistics*.

4. Stephen Wolfram, *A New Kind of Science*; Edward Fredkin, *Introduction to Digital Philosophy*; Harold Morowitz, *The Emergence of Everything*; Ellen Ullman, *Close to the Machine*; Matthew Fuller, *Behind the Blip*; Matthew G. Kirschenbaum, "Editing the Interface"; Bruce Eckel, *Thinking in C++*.

5. See, for example, Jacques Derrida, *Positions*, 22.

6. Quoted in Alan Bass, "Translator's Introduction," in Jacques Derrida, *Writing and Difference*, xiii. In *The Parasite*, Michel Serres explored extensively the notion of the parasite in relation to noise in communication systems. Derrida's grammatology can be understood as an intense dose of noise injected in Saussurean linguistics.

7. Leonard M. Adelman, "Molecular Computation of Solutions to Combinatorial Problems"; Daniel Hillis, *The Pattern on the Stone*; John von Neumann, *Theory of Self-Reproducing Automata*.

8. Alan Turing, "On Computable Numbers, with an Application to the Entscheidungs-problem." For an analysis of the evolution of the logic underlying Turing's construction of the Universal Computer, see Martin Davis, *The Universal Computer*.

9. Von Neumann, *Theory of Self-Reproducing Automata*, 91–156. Steven Levy, in *Artificial Life*, gives an account of von Neumann's self-reproducing machine. His account is based on the rather sketchy information given by Arthur W. Burks (who edited and compiled von Neumann's incomplete manuscript after the latter's death) of what Burks calls the kine-matic model of self-reproduction. Burks's version can be found in von Neumann, *Theory of Self-Reproducing Automata*, 74–90.

10. Konrad Zuse, *Rechnender Raum*.

11. See, for example, Christopher G. Langton, "Computation at the Edge of Chaos."

12. For a downloadable version of the game in Java, see John Conway, *Game of Life*.

13. The following scheme represents a typical configuration; many other arrangements are possible. The cells can be configured so that they can occupy more than two states; they can be arranged in one, two, or n-dimensions; and they can reference not only their nearest and next nearest neighbors but also states of their neighbors one or more steps back. Of course, the rules can also change, as can the colors used to represent the states.

14. Rule 110 is illustrated in Wolfram, *A New Kind of Science*, 53. The patterns are much easier to comprehend in the simple illustrations Wolfram gives, but if one must rely on words, the patterns can be described as follows. If a given cell and both its neighbors are the same color, in the next generation the cell will be white. If it and the left neighbor are the same color, in the next generation the cell will be black. If it and the right neighbor are the same color, in the next generation the cell will be that color. If both the cell's neighbors are a different color than it is, in the next generation it will be black.

15. Arthur K. Cebrowski and John J. Garstka, "Network-Centric Warfare." For a sobering analysis of the problems involved in this revolution in military affairs, see Stephen J. Blank, "Preparing for the Next War."

16. It is possible, of course, to freight one and zero with considerable metaphysical bag-gage, if one is inclined to do so. In "Language as Information," Johanna Drucker instances

the case of the Renaissance type designer Geofroy Tory, who argued that the "full set of symbols of human language, and thus of cosmic as well as human thought, are comprised at base of two elements: the I and O. For Tory these are essential elements: the masculine principle of the vertical thrust and the feminine principle of procreative fullness" (214–15). In *Snow Crash*, Neal Stephenson also includes a long disquisition by the Librarian (an artificial intelligence manifested as a hologram) on similar ideas in Sumerian culture regarding the one and zero.

17. Edward Fredkin, "History," in *Introduction to Digital Philosophy*, chap. 9, para. 7.

18. In *Order out of Chaos*, Ilya Prigogine and Isabelle Stengers argue that dissipative processes create new information, as, for example, in a multiparticle collision in which the collision serves as a coordination point correlating the particles' momenta and positions. Such creation explains, they argue, why time can go only forward, for as billions or trillions of such events occur, an infinite "information barrier" is created that separates the past from the future.

19. Edward Fredkin, "Conservation of Information," in *Introduction to Digital Philosophy*, chap. 11, para. 3.

20. Edward Fredkin, "Thinking about Digital Philosophy," in *Introduction to Digital Philosophy*, chap. 34, para. 1.

21. Edward Fredkin, "DP and Biology," in *Introduction to Digital Philosophy*, chap. 4, para. 7.

22. Ray Kurzweil, "Reflections on Stephen Wolfram's *A New Kind of Science*." For another review, see Lawrence Gray, "A Mathematician Looks at Wolfram's New Kind of Science."

23. In February 2003, Stephen Wolfram gave a lecture at the California Institute of Technology in Pasadena. After the lecture, Wolfram's work was discussed by a panel of Caltech scientists. In that discussion, artificial-life researcher Christopher Adami made the point that Wolfram had seriously underestimated the importance of evolution.

24. See, for example, the UNITN call for papers for the conference "Dynamic Ontology: An Inquiry into Systems, Emergence, Levels of Reality, and Forms of Causality" (January 24, 2003).

25. Pierre Teilhard de Chardin, *The Phenomenon of Man*.

26. Stuart A. Kauffman, *The Origins of Order*; see also the more general version, *At Home in the Universe*.

27. The role of the observer in evolutionary processes is central to second-order cybernetics. The observer also plays a crucial role in the interpretation of artificial-life simulations. When Conway's *Game of Life* is perceived as a living entity, for example, this perception may be related analogically not so much to the evolution of life itself as to the evolution of the perceptual mechanisms within humans that trigger the thought "This entity is living." An especially interesting treatment of processes within an observer that stand in a metaphorical or analogical relation to processes in the external world is presented in Mary Catherine Bateson, *Our Own Metaphor*.

28. Thanks to Nicholas Gessler for drawing my attention to these agendas. See, for example, AAAI, *Computational Synthesis*.

29. Nicholas Gessler, personal communication.

30. Each year John Brockman poses a question on his Web site and invites well-known scientists to post their answers. In 2004 the question was "What is your law?" to which Seth Lloyd responded with "Lloyd's It from Qubit Law." A "qubit" is a quantum bit, that is, a bit generated by a quantum computer. His law implies that all of "it"—the universe—comes from quantum bits generated by the universe understood as a quantum logic circuit, in effect, a quantum computer.

31. John Brockman, "What's Your Question?" More discussions on Seth Lloyd's vision of a Computational Universe can be found in Seth Lloyd, "How Fast, How Small, and How Powerful? Moore's Law and the Ultimate Laptop," where he calculates the absolute limits of computations that could be performed by an "ultimate laptop" one liter in volume and one kilogram in weight; see also Seth Lloyd, "Ultimate Physical Limits to Computation." Lloyd later realized that he was not sufficiently ambitious (as he says) and that the real issue was the computational limits of the universe understood as a quantum computer, a question he addressed in "Computational Capacity of the Universe." Thoughtful responses to Lloyd's vision of a Computational Universe can be found at John Brockman, "Joseph Traub, Jaron Lanier, John McCarthy, Lee Smolin, Philip W. Anderson, Anthony Valentini, Stuart Hameroff, and Paola Zizzi Respond to Seth Lloyd."

32. Nicholas Gessler, "Evolving Artificial Cultural Things-That-Think and Work by Dynamical Hierarchical Synthesis." Intermediation has a rich history that adds to its connotations. "Intermedia" is the term for the hypertext authoring system developed at Brown University by the Institute for Research in Information and Scholarship (IRIS). It also appears in numerous corporation names and art groups, for example, the Palindrome Inter.media Performance Group, a German-American dance group based in New York and Nümberg, Germany.

33. Lev Manovich, *The Language of New Media*; Friedrich A. Kittler, *Gramophone, Film, Typewriter*.

34. Kittler, *Gramophone, Film, Typewriter*, 25–114, esp. 48–49.

35. Friedrich A. Kittler, *Discourse Networks*.

36. In my view, this helps to explain the notable resurgence of interest in the book in the twentieth century, both for artists' books and for book technology in general.

37. Richard Grusin and Jay David Bolter, *Remediation*.

38. Ibid., 273.

39. Referencing the full range of the extensive literature on the Prisoner's Dilemma is beyond the scope of my purposes here. For a good introduction to game theory in the context of John von Neumann's seminal work in the field, see William Poundstone, *Prisoner's Dilemma*. For an explanation of how the Prisoner's Dilemma can be adapted for computer programs, and how it gives rise to emergent cooperation when it is iterated, see Robert Alexrod, *The Evolution of Cooperation*.

40. Kittler, *Gramophone, Film, Typewriter*, 46.

41. See, for example, ibid., 76.

42. See Donald MacKay, *Information, Mechanism, Meaning*.

43. To be fair, Hansen's work comes a decade after *Discourse Networks*, Kittler's major book. Kittler's prior entrenchment helps to explain why Hansen has to push hard on the position Kittler articulates to make room for his own ideas.

44. Hans P. Moravec, *Mind Children* and *Robot*; Ray Kurzweil, *The Age of Spiritual Machines*.

45. Sha Xin Wei, "A Tgarden as a Phenomenological Experiment."

46. In "It's Not the Technology, Stupid!" a presentation at the annual convention of the Modern Language Association in 2003, Jerome McGann articulated this belief with great conviction and force.

47. Jerome J. McGann, D. G. Rossetti Hypermedia Archive.

Chapter Two

1. Brian Cantwell Smith, *On the Origin of Objects*, 76.

2. Ferdinand de Saussure, *Course in General Linguistics*, 67.

3. Jacques Derrida, *Positions*, 17.

4. Jacques Derrida, *Of Grammatology*, 52.

5. Jonathan Culler, *Ferdinand de Saussure*, 33.

6. Working against these interpretations of Saussure are a number of critics who have argued that his theories were misinterpreted in poststructuralism. Among them are Raymond Tallis, *Not Saussure*, a work that argues in favor of restoring the notion of reference, and Paul J. Thibault, *Re-reading Saussure*, a study that emphasizes Saussure's theory as a model of social/semiological interactions. In *The Visible Word*, a careful analysis of Saussure's theory in historical context, Johanna Drucker seeks to recuperate from Saussure a revitalized role for the materiality of the sign.

7. In *The Visible Word*, Johanna Drucker concludes that "there would seem to be no possibility of generating a concept of materiality out of Saussure's theory of the sign." She notes, however, that "there is one loophole in his argument, namely his view of inflection as altering the value of the sign" (23).

8. Peter Gendolla, Jörgen Schäfer, and Maik Pluschke, e-mail message, February 3, 2004. See also, Peter Gendolla, Jörgen Schäfer, and Maik Pluschke, "Literatur in Netzen/Netzliteratur."

9. Friedrich Kittler, "There Is No Software," in *Essays*, 147–55.

10. Languages that are compiled perform the translation into binary code as a batch run, whereas interpreted languages perform translation into binary code command by command. The advantage of interpreted languages, although they eat up more run time, is increased flexibility and error control.

11. Jacques Derrida, "Différence," in *Margins of Philosophy*, 1–28, esp. 6.

12. A trail-off error denotes a voltage packet that instead of looking like a step function ⌐⌐ trails off at the end of the packet ⌐⌐.

13. Jacques Lacan, *Le Séminaire XX: Encore*, 22, 35. "Function as intended" should be interpreted in context of the program's structure and design. A virus, worm, or Trojan horse, for example, may be intended to crash the system.

14. Jacques Derrida, "Signature Event Context," in *Limited Inc*, 1–24, esp. 9.

15. It is true that bits can be put in any context whatever, but their order signifies a specific meaning that is in general nontransferable. To take Derrida's observation to this level (or for language, to the level of the individual letter) would reduce iterability to a trivial proposition, so I assume this is not what he means.

16. Ellen Ullman, *Close to the Machine.*

17. Ellen Ullman, "Elegance and Entropy."

18. For a brief introduction to the lambda calculus, see Don Blaheta, "The Lambda Calculus."

19. Alexander R. Galloway, *Protocol*, 165.

20. J. L. Austin, *How to Do Things with Words.* Jacques Derrida, "Limited Inc a b c . . . ," in *Limited Inc*, 29–110. This famous response to John R. Searle's "Reiterating the Differences: A Reply to Derrida" demonstrated with acerbic wit why writing cannot, in Derrida's view, be assimilated into speech. Indeed, Derrida's response to Searle's "Reply" launched a brilliant counterattack by assimilating speech into writing.

21. William R. Paulson, *Literary Culture in a World Transformed.* Paulson decries the esoteric nature of much of literary theory, especially deconstruction, and calls for a return to language that ordinary people can understand.

22. See the Open Source Initiative for a statement of principles: "The *basic idea behind open source* is very simple: When programmers can read, redistribute, and modify the source code for a piece of software, the software evolves. People improve it, people adapt it, people fix bugs. And this can happen at a speed that, if one is used to the slow pace of conventional software development, seems astonishing. We in the open source community have learned that this rapid evolutionary process produces better software than the traditional closed model, in which only a very few programmers can see the source and everybody else must blindly use an opaque block of bits. Open Source Initiative exists to make this case to the commercial world." The success of this and related initiatives can be seen in the movement of Macintosh to a Unix platform.

23. Jonathan Culler briefly reviews this history in *Ferdinand de Saussure*, 45–56. Johanna Drucker in *The Visible Word* also reviews the historical context to evaluate the role of materiality in pre-Saussurean linguistics as well as in Saussure's own theory (9–47).

24. There seems to be slippage here between the elementary unit of a language, such as a letter, and larger units such as words, phrases, sentences, and so on. As indicated in note 15 above, it is trivial to observe that letters are iterable, for this is the nature of alphabetic language. For Derrida's observation to have force, it must apply to larger units, and the larger the unit, the less the observation applies to content-bound code at the binary level.

25. Rita Raley, "Machine Translation and Global English."

26. The importance of this aesthetic to electronic literature is discussed in Rita Raley, "Reveal Codes."

27. Harold J. Morowitz, *The Emergence of Everything.*

28. Andrew Koenig and Barbara E. Moo, "Preface."

29. Bruce Eckel discusses the distinction between early and late binding in *Thinking in C++*, 40.

30. For a discussion of this interpenetration, see Raley, "Machine Translation and Global English."

31. Ibid.

32. For discussions of these practices, see Rita Raley, "Reveal Codes" and "Interferences." A discussion can also be found in N. Katherine Hayles, "From Object to Process." For a carefully nuanced analysis of works using "broken code" versus code that will actually run, see John Cayley, "The Code Is Not the Text (Unless It Is the Text)."

33. Wendy Hui Kyong Chun, "On the Persistence of Visual Knowledge."

34. A playful example of such subversion was the hack into the Google home page that, for a brief time, answered the Google search "Evil as the devil himself" by directing the user to the Microsoft home page. Alexander R. Galloway has an illuminating discussion of hacking as a social good in *Protocol*, 146–207.

35. Matthew Fuller, *Behind the Blip*; Matthew G. Kirschenbaum, "Virtuality and VRML."

Chapter Three

1. G. M. Foster, "Peasant Society and the Image of Limited Good."

2. Mark Poster, *What's the Matter with the Internet?*

3. Charles Ostman, "Synthetic Sentience."

4. For a discussion of the ambiguities in Stephenson's fiction, see N. Katherine Hayles, "From Utopia to Mutopia."

5. C. B. Macpherson, *The Political Theory of Possessive Individualism*.

6. The idea that virtual technologies subvert the traditional assumption that one body houses one subject is explored in Allucquère Rosanne Stone, *The War of Technology and Desire at the Close of the Mechanical Age*.

7. Robert Markley, "Boundaries: Mathematics, Alienation, and the Metaphysics of Cyberspace."

8. In *Networking*, Laura Otis traces the extensive analogies in nineteenth-century British science and literature between telegraph lines (and communication lines generally) and the nerves of the human body.

9. Stuart Hutchinson's stout defense of Mr. Mudge in "James's 'In the Cage': A New Interpretation" is no doubt correct, in that Mr. Mudge is shown to have virtues that the girl underplays in her desire to be superior to him. Nevertheless, Mr. Mudge has his feet planted firmly in the regime of scarcity; indeed, that is one of his principal strengths.

10. For a discussion of information as pattern and randomness, see N. Katherine Hayles, *How We Became Posthuman*, chap. 2.

11. Ralf Norrman, *Techniques of Ambiguity in the Fiction of Henry James*, 139–40.

12. The girl's correction causes Lady Bradeen to blush and exit the office, never to return, for it indicates how much the girl knows about her putative affair with the captain. Andrew Moody, in "'The Harmless Pleasure of Knowing,'" provides useful historical context for concerns about privacy in a telegraph service that was constituted through human interactions rather than anonymous, impersonal service.

13. Ralf Norrman, in "The Intercepted Telegram Plot in Henry James's 'In the Cage,'" carefully traces out the possibility that the girl's "correction" distracted Lady Bradeen from making the correction she likely intended, not to the place-name but the number code. I would add only that it is entirely possible that both the place name and the number code are in error.

14. Jennifer Wicke, "Henry James's Second Wave."

15. In "Philip K. Dick and Criticism," Carl Freedman discusses the cultural context for the novels of the 1960s, pointing out that commodification and conspiracy assumed unusually large importance in those years in the United States. Scott Durham, in "P. K. Dick: From the Death of the Subject to a Theology of Late Capitalism," has a fascinating analysis of the movement from the subversion of the subject to the subversion of the narrative viewpoint,

which is stabilized again in Dick's late works, particularly the VALIS trilogy, by the turn to theology. As the succeeding paragraphs will make clear, this argument is relevant to *The Three Stigmata of Palmer Eldritch*, which Durham briefly discusses.

16. In the course of the narrative we learn that there are six off-world colonies, all of them dismal.

17. In Dick's books, the instability in the subject is often preceded by a rift in the family corporation, as in *We Can Build You* and, in a different way, *The Simulacra*.

18. Kim Stanley Robinson, *The Novels of Philip K. Dick*, 61.

19. In *Networking*, Laura Otis describes Samuel Morse's belief that telegraphy involved no temporal gap; before empirical evidence showed otherwise, Morse asserted that telegraph signals traveled at two hundred thousand times the speed of light. By the time of Tiptree's story, no such illusions about simultaneity were possible.

20. As Andrew Moody ("'The Harmless Pleasure of Knowing'") and Ric Savoy ("'In the Cage' and the Queer Effects of Gay History") both note, it was a concern of the upper-class patrons of telegraphy that the telegraphists might learn information from the telegrams they sent, which they could then use to blackmail their wealthy clients. As Tiptree's story suggests, by the late twentieth century the object of this concern had shifted from the individual agent to the corporation, for in her story it is the corporation who will intervene in the messages for its own profit.

21. I am indebted to Carol Wald for her astute reading of this story in "The Female Machine," where she closely analyzes the significance of the waldo as a potentially independent agent.

22. In *The Fiction of James Tiptree Jr.*, Gardner Dozois comments on the importance this casting of the story as a "tale of the future" has in the construction of the narrative voice.

23. Wicke, "Henry James's Second Wave," 148.

24. Savoy, "'In the Cage' and the Queer Effects of Gay History."

25. For a discussion of gender politics in Dick's novels and its enactment in his character systems, see Hayles, *How We Became Posthuman*, chap 7.

26. Timothy Lenoir, personal communication.

Chapter Four

1. Jorge Luis Borges, "The Don Quixote of Pierre Menard."

2. Dene Grigar, "Mutability and Medium."

3. Library of Congress, William Blake Archive.

4. Jerome McGann, *The Textual Condition*.

5. Matthew G. Kirschenbaum, "Materiality and Matter and Stuff."

6. Matthew G. Kirschenbaum, "Editing the Interface," esp. 46.

7. McGann, *The Textual Condition*.

8. Peter L. Shillingsburg, "Text as Matter, Concept, and Action."

9. Hans Zeller, "A New Approach to the Critical Constitution of Literary Texts," esp. 258.

10. Allen Renear, "Out of Praxis."

11. Mats Dahlström, "When Is a Webtext?"

12. Suggesting that the OHCO scheme "made a virtue of necessity," John Unsworth comments, "I think it is important to recognize that the necessity of ordered hierarchies . . .

is really a function of the exigencies of programming software to process SGML" (e-mail message, August 29, 2002).

13. Renear, "Out of Praxis," sec. 5.3.15. See also Allen Renear, "Philosophy and Electronic Publishing."

14. Dino Buzzetti, "Digital Representation and the Text Model."

15. Dahlström, "When Is a Webtext?"

16. McGann uses the term "text" in a rather different way than it is used in deconstructive criticism, which he dismisses too lightly in a few condescending sentences.

17. In a practical sense, of course, the D. G. Rossetti Hypermedia Archive also aims for accurate simulation of Rossetti's materials.

18. Janet Murray, *Hamlet on the Holodeck*; Espen Aarseth, *Cybertext*.

19. Relevant here may be the context in which Web material is often read, a mode of superficial perusing that Alan Liu, in "The Humanities: A Technical Profession," calls "low cognitive reading." Given the low intellectual value of much material on the Internet (banner advertisements, spam e-mails, Web sites that contain misleading or incorrect information, etc.), the expectation may naturally arise that first-generation digital content (as distinct from print materials translated onto the Web) will not be intellectually or aesthetically challenging. Adding to this impression is the fact that people often read Web material while undertaking other activities such as talking on the telephone, reading material in other windows, instant messaging, and so on, all contributing to what Walter Benjamin called a "state of distraction" ("The Work of Art in the Age of Mechanical Reproduction," 240). Of course, one could counter with the large amount of print materials that are also suitable for "low cognitive reading," including junk mail, advertisements, glossy magazines devoted to Hollywood celebrities, and so on.

20. Matthew Kirschenbaum has a version of this argument in "Editing the Interface," calling the contrast between stable print and fluid electronic text "patently false" (24). To my mind, this claim simply means that the argument has to be made more carefully; it *cannot* be taken to mean that important distinctions between electronic text and print do not exist.

21. Mats Dahlström, "Drowning by Versions."

22. In this essay, which appears in *Essays* (147–55), Kittler argues that because everything ultimately reduces to voltages, "there is no software." One could equally well argue that with firmware, PROMs, programmable gate arrays, and other forms of evolvable hardware, everything is becoming software. Perhaps the more accurate point is that the multiple layers of coding and bit stream information are connected in complex ways that make hard-and-fast divisions difficult to maintain. In *Dig[iT]al Poet(I)(c)s*, Loss Pequeño Glazier quotes David Siegel to the effect that "documents are becoming applications" (28), a cogent observation that sums up this situation.

23. Rita Raley, "Reveal Codes," 10.

24. For a fuller version of this argument, see N. Katherine Hayles, *Writing Machines*.

25. Similar problems of identity/difference emerge in many different fields concerned with data that cluster rather than converge into a point; a notorious example is predicting future outcomes when many variables are involved. Steven Bankes has developed sophisticated software to analyze such data clusters and to draw conclusions from them that give

workable prognostications, even when uncertainty is high. See, for example, Steven Bankes, "Computational Experiments and Exploratory Modeling."

26. David Silver has argued that such clusters should form part of the interpretive context for any text in the cluster; I am indebted to him for drawing this kind of phenomenon to my attention. In "Looking Backwards, Looking Forward," he anticipates a third phase of cyberculture studies: "critical cyberculture studies," which would include analyses of the discursive interactions between different Web sites and between virtual and real communities.

27. In "Requiem for a Reader?" Jack Post writes about this Web site at length, clearly showing its complexities and identifying it as a new electronic genre. The Web site is at http://www.requiemforadream.com.

28. McGann, *The Textual Condition*.

29. Gilles Deleuze and Félix Guattari, *A Thousand Plateaus*.

30. Roland Barthes, *S/Z*.

31. Glazier, *Dig[iT]al Poet(I)(c)s*, 96–125; John Cayley, "Of Programmatology."

32. Johanna Drucker, "Theory as Praxis."

33. John Cayley, "The Code Is Not the Text (Unless It Is the Text)"; Rita Raley, "Interferences."

34. Warren Weaver, "Translation." I am grateful to Rita Raley for drawing this essay to my attention.

35. Warren Weaver, "The New Tower," esp. vii.

36. Weaver, "Translation," 22.

37. Rita Raley, "Machine Translation and Global English."

38. W. J. Hutchins, "Warren Weaver Memorandum July 1949."

39. In *Chinese Dreams*, Eric Hayot, exploring Ezra Pound's (and others') complex engagements with China, comments on Pound's modernist poetry as "English-as-Chinese," that is, English written as if it had been translated through Chinese (49ff.). These sinographic influences serve as a serendipitous counterpart to Warren Weaver's imaginary Chinese-as-English.

40. Weaver, "Translation," 23.

41. Marc Damashek, working under the auspices of the National Security Agency, has created a program that comes close to realizing Weaver's dream, for it can prepare a précis of any article in any language; see Damashek, "Gauging Similarity with N-Grams: Language-Independent Categorization of Text."

42. I am grateful to Jules Van Lieshout for providing me with a written copy of this presentation and for meeting with me in person to discuss further his ideas and experiences.

43. Efrain Kristal, *Invisible Work*. I am grateful to Efrain Kristal for conversations regarding his conclusions in this book, including the contrast between the views of Borges and Octavio Paz.

44. Octavio Paz, "Translation."

45. Kristal, *Invisible Work*, xv. In "The Homeric Versions," Borges offers a succinct expression of the view that a translation can be superior to the original: "To assume that every recombination of elements is necessarily inferior to its original form is to assume that draft nine is necessarily inferior to draft H—for there can be only drafts. The concept of a 'definitive text' corresponds only to religion or exhaustion" (69).

46. For books in which Johanna Drucker makes the argument that print is remarkably fluid and complex, see *The Century of Artists' Books* and *The Visible Word*. For a creative text that demonstrates and illustrates these possibilities, see her *Otherspace*. Matthew Kirschenbaum makes a similar point in "Editing the Interface."

47. Jules van Lieshout, e-mail message, December 2003.

48. Anne Mellor, personal communication.

49. Nicholas Gessler, "Sonnet."

50. Andrew J. Lurie, "Now May I Offer You a Poem."

51. The history of "Chomskybot," as well as the program itself, can be found at John Lawler's Web site, see especially the links "Chomskybot" and "What's it all about?"

52. Ibid., answer to the question "What the hell *is* this, anyway?" under the link "What's it all about?"

Chapter Five

1. Florian Cramer, "Digital Code and Literary Text," 1.

2. Ibid., 2.

3. See John Markoff, "Behind Happy Interface, More Complex Reality." See also Harper-Collins, "A Talk with Neal Stephenson," where the interviewer remarks of *Quicksilver*, a prequel to (though written after) *Cryptonomicon*, "This is the book you are writing with a fountain pen," and Stephenson replies, "I've written every word of it so far with a fountain pen on paper." Markoff also reports in June 1999 that Stephenson "now writes with fountain pens on a thin masonite 'laptop' board that he travels with. He has taken to traveling without a portable computer, saying that he had decided to give up 'on the hassle.'"

4. Now, of course, Macintosh itself has gone to a Unix-based operating system, as Stephenson recognizes in this comment on his Web site: "*In the Beginning Was the Command Line* is now badly obsolete and probably needs a thorough revision. For the last couple of years, I have been a Mac OS X user almost exclusively" (under "Author" and "Juvenilia").

5. This book was originally commissioned by *Wired*, which declined to publish it. It was then published online at the Avon Web site, but the demand was so severe, with one hundred thousand people logging on, that it crashed the servers. On this basis, Avon decided it had sufficient audience for a print book.

6. By "conventional narrative" I refer to the predictability of popular literature in providing readers with a beginning, middle, and end, enacted through a series of rising actions resulting in a climax and denouement. Of course, these expectations have been disrupted by all manner of modernist and postmodernist experimental fiction, from Virginia Woolf's *The Waves* to David Foster Wallace's *Infinite Jest*. In *Cryptonomicon*, however, the inability of the text to create a conventional narrative is, I argue, specifically linked to the intermediating dynamics of code and language, print and digital technologies.

7. Jim McCellan reports in "After *Snow Crash*'s Cyberpunk, It's Cyberpunk" that when Stephenson read about this incident, he found it so intriguing it became the kernel for *Cryptonomicon*.

8. For an insightful discussion of the abject in relation to cyberspace, transnational politics, and global capital, see Terry Harpold and Kavita Philip, "Of Bugs and Rats: Cyber-Cleanliness, Cyber-Squalor, and the Fantasy-Spaces of Informational Globalization."

9. Markoff, "Behind Happy Interface, More Complex Reality."

10. John Markoff (ibid.) reports that Stephenson "acknowledges that when he returned home he was able to salvage an earlier version from a backup disk. But the event was clearly traumatizing and it undermined his trust in the Macintosh operating system forever." I thought it was possible that the "large file" may have been *Cryptonomicon*, published in the same year as *Command Line*. Although Stephenson makes a point on his Web page of declaring that he does not answer e-mail, as it detracts from the concentration he needs to do his writing, he does give the e-mail address of his literary agent, listed as Kristin Lang at Darnansoff, Verrill, Feldman Literary Agents in New York City. I sent Lang an e-mail with my question—was the large file Stephenson lost related to *Cryptonomicon*?—and she gave me the answer in return e-mail after checking with Stephenson: no.

11. H. G. Wells, *The Time Machine*.

12. As Alan Liu, a reader for the University of Chicago Press, pointed out, Unix also uses metaphors in the sense that it employs shell accounts controlled by the command core. To this extent, then, Stephenson's characterization of Unix tends to romanticize it.

13. I am not alone in thinking that this part of the book is weak. Paul Quinn, in "The How of the Crypt," writes of this part of the book, "The weakly worked idea that Randy's business partner, Avi, seeks wealth in order to educate the world in the prevention of another Holocaust seems in this context ultimately muddled, if noble."

14. The scene with the Sultan in which Randy and Avi survey their potential partners (316–17) makes clear how real the risk of co-optation is, as it includes, in addition to the Sultan, former bagmen for President Marcos, drug dealers, and international gangsters.

15. Elizabeth Weise, "Cracking *Cryptonomicon*: Stephenson Weaves 50-Year Tale of Intrigue."

16. Bruce Schneier, "The Solitaire Encryption Algorithm."

17. The irony remains intact even though in the first edition the copy editors unfortunately made an error that prevents the code from running, an error Stephenson corrects on the Web. See his "*Cryptonomicon* cypher-FAQ."

18. The phrase "sequences of words and spaces" alludes, of course, to the arguments made in chapter 4.

Chapter Six

1. C. B. Macpherson, *The Political Theory of Possessive Individualism*.

2. The fiction of individual authorship for collaborative work is visibly reinforced for me when I sit through film credits—a pervasive practice here in Los Angeles where the credits are often scrutinized more avidly than the film itself—and see roll up on the screen this disclaimer: "For purposes of copyright, [the film studio's name] is the sole author of this film."

3. The phrase "vaporous machinery" comes from *Patchwork Girl* (body of text/it thinks). A note on citations from *Patchwork Girl*: I identify them using slashes to indicate a jump in directory level, moving from higher to lower as is customary in computer notation. The uppermost level is always a name the user would see on the screen when opening the highest level of the map view in Storyspace, and the lowest level is the lexia in which the quotation appears. Thus the citation "body of text/it thinks" indicates that within the major textual component entitled "body of text" is a subsection entitled "it thinks," which when opened also contains the quoted passage.

4. This list omits the graphics, of which there are several as the hypertext opens.

5. Gérard Genette, *Narrative Discourse*.

6. Shelley Jackson, "'Of Dolls and Monsters.'"

7. Friedrich A. Kittler, "Gramophone, Film, Typewriter," in *Essays*, 238–49, esp. 240.

8. Jackson, "'Of Dolls and Monsters,'" 1–2.

9. Storyspace version 2.0.3 also lists John B. Smith as a coauthor.

10. I used the 2001 copyright version, Storyspace 2.0.3, for PC. The PC version seems to be much buggier than the Macintosh version, perhaps because Storyspace was designed originally for Macintosh and the PC version was derived from that.

11. Jacques Derrida, "Signature Event Context."

12. Jackson, "'Of Dolls and Monsters,'" 2.

13. Elizabeth Grosz, *Volatile Bodies*.

14. Anne K. Mellor, *Mary Shelley*, 52–69.

15. Barbara Johnson, "My Monster/My Self."

16. The lexia's explosive potential may explain why it is partially hidden. It can be seen in the Storyspace chart view but is not visible in the more frequently used map view.

17. In a perhaps intentional irony, the Eastgate title screen inscribes Jackson's name as the "authorized" signature, along with the usual warnings about copyright infringement, even though the entire thrust of Jackson's text pushes against this view of a sole author who produces an original work.

18. M/S can also be read as an allusion to masochism and sadism, an erotics that weaves throughout the text, notably in the female monster's appropriation of a thief's leg and in other scenes of bodily fragmentation and recombination.

19. Grosz, *Volatile Bodies*.

20. Milorad Pavić, *Dictionary of the Khazars*. This marvelous work weaves a metanarrative out of discrete entries within a "dictionary" composed of three parts. The various entries are elaborately cross-linked, both thematically and through the author's eccentric link/symbol system. For a fuller explication, see N. Katherine Hayles, "Corporeal Anxiety in *Dictionary of the Khazars*."

21. Jane Yellowlees Douglas, "'How Do I Stop This Thing?'"

Chapter Seven

1. The literature on this phenomenon is extensive. For a technical survey, see Derek Munneke, Kirsten Wahlstrom, and Linda Zaccara, "Intelligent Software Agents on the Internet"; for a discussion of the psychological aspect of bots, see Leena Saarinen, "Chatterbots," which also discusses Joseph Weizenbaum's famous "Eliza" program.

2. Mark Hansen, *Embodying Technesis*. Although he makes important points, Hansen's interpretation is flawed insofar as he fails to recognize the importance of agency in Deleuze and Guattari's rhizomatic philosophy. For them, agency continues to play a central role, but its locus is displaced from consciousness into aconscious processes.

3. In another context, Francisco Varela calls such dynamics "co-dependent arising," to emphasize the mutual interdependence of each component on the others; see Francisco J. Varela, Even Thompson, and Eleanor Rosch, *The Embodied Mind*.

4. For a critique of the idea that computers and intelligent machines can be considered alive (and by implication, have such experiences as desire), see Peter Swirski, "A Case of Wishful Thinking."

5. See especially page 17.

6. See Humberto R. Maturana and Francisco J. Varela, *Autopoiesis and Cognition*.

7. In *A Thousand Plateaus*, Deleuze and Guattari contrast smooth and striated space. Whereas smooth space is continually transformative and fluid, striated space (by analogy, I suppose, with muscle tissue) is hierarchical, locked in, structurally rigid.

8. John Johnston, "The In-Mixing of Machines: Psychoanalysis and Cybernetics." I am grateful to John Johnston for sharing this essay with me prior to publication.

9. Alan M. Turing, "On Computable Numbers, with an Application to the Entscheidungsproblem."

10. Christopher Langton, "Artificial Life."

11. See especially chapters 4, 5, and 9. The crisis of agency is also implicit in such works as Marvin Minsky, *The Society of Mind*, which conceptualizes human intention and agency as subroutines run by semiautonomous agents. Also revealing is the furor over the research of Benjamin Libet, Anthony Freeman, and Keith Sutherland, *The Volitional Brain*; and Benjamin Libet, C. A. Gleason, E. W. Wright, and D. K. Pearl, "Time of Conscious Intention to Act in Relation to Onset of Cerebral Activities (Readiness Potential)." Libet and his collaborators demonstrated that research subjects started the muscular actions to raise their arms before they were consciously aware that they were going to do so, thus bringing into question whether the conscious mind is the source of agency. Libet's experiments have been extensively critiqued in Daniel Dennett, *Freedom Evolves*, 228–42.

12. Jerome Barkow, Leda Cosmides, and John Tooby, *The Adapted Mind*.

13. I am grateful to Jerzy Jarzebski and Michael Kandel for this information. Kandel illustrates using the verb *czuc* (to feel). "A man would say 'czulem' ('I felt'); a woman would say 'czulam' ('I felt'). A nongendered robot would say 'czulom' ('I felt'). Using the vowel 'o' is Lem's neologism. The verb form is quite strange, but a Polish reader would understand immediately" (e-mail message, January 6, 2004).

14. Jo Alyson Parker, "Gendering the Robot."

15. There is a minor inconsistency in the story with regard to these three names, which I take to be an error on Lem's part.

16. Carol Wald, "The Female Machine." I am grateful to Wald for making her essay available to me before publication, and also for calling my attention to "The Mask."

17. Zoran Živković, "The Future without a Future."

18. Michael Kandel, "A Freudian Peek at Lem's *Fiasco*."

19. Hans Moravec, *Mind Children* and *Robot*; Ray Kurzweil, *The Age of Spiritual Machines*.

20. Antonio R. Damasio, *Descartes' Error*, xvii.

21. Brian Cantwell Smith, *On the Origin of Objects*, 75–76.

Chapter Eight

1. My thanks to Karl Sims for making the videotape available to Nicholas Gessler, and to Nicholas Gessler for allowing me to view it. I am also indebted to Nicholas Gessler for many of the ideas in this chapter. He conveyed them to me over several years of ongoing discussions, and by now they are so woven into my own thoughts that I am no longer sure which started as his suggestions. Let me simply say, then, that this chapter could not have been written without his help.

2. The world of "Evolved Virtual Creatures" is described in Karl Sims, "Evolving Virtual Creatures"; his "Evolving 3-D Morphology and Behavior by Competition" is also relevant. A movie of "Evolved Virtual Creatures," as well as an interview with Sims discussing his work, can be found at http://www.biota.org/ksims/index.html.

3. John R. Koza, *Genetic Programming* and *Genetic Programming II*, where Koza shows how genetic programming can itself dynamically evolve the functions it needs to evolve further. Koza calls these Automatically Defined Functions (AFTs) and remarks, "Hierarchical organization and reuse [of AFTs] seem to be required if automatic programming is ever to be scaled up from small problems to large problems" (4).

4. Benoit Mandelbrot, in *The Fractal Beauty of Nature*, discusses how relatively simple computer algorithms can generate complex plant shapes.

5. Sims, "Evolving 3-D Morphology," 31, 29.

6. Sims, "Evolving Virtual Creatures," 18.

7. Sims, "Evolving 3-D Morphology," 29.

8. Michael G. Dyer, "Toward Synthesizing Artificial Neural Networks That Exhibit Cooperative Intelligent Behavior." I am indebted to Michael Dyer for conversations clarifying these issues for me.

9. Sims, "Evolving 3-D Morphology," 38.

10. Alex Argyros, *A Blessed Rage for Order*.

11. Stephen Wolfram, *A New Kind of Science*; Edward Fredkin, *Introduction to Digital Philosophy*; Harold Morowitz, *The Emergence of Everything*; Stuart A. Kauffman, *The Origins of Order*.

12. Humberto R. Maturana and Francisco J. Varela, *Autopoiesis and Cognition*.

13. Luc Steels, "The Artificial Life Roots of Artificial Intelligence."

14. A point made by Richard Dawkins in *The Blind Watchmaker*.

15. I use "see" in quotations marks to imply not only the physical act of visual perception but also the culturally conditioned cognitive processes by which we invest what we see with meaning.

16. I recently came across an advertisement for an academic job encouraging "visible minorities" to apply, a phrase I had not heard before and that immediately evoked thoughts of Ralph Ellison's *Invisible Man*. Leaving aside the complex cultural history embedded in this phrase, it serves the purpose here of highlighting the importance of making bodies *visible* if they are to enter into the canonical narratives of a culture, a requirement that seems both strange and familiar when applied to visualizations of virtual creatures.

17. Jerome Bruner, *Acts of Meaning*.

18. Joan Lucariello is cited in Bruner, *Acts of Meaning*, 81–82, 157 n. 26, where the source is identified as "private communication."

19. Ibid.

20. Marvin Minsky, *The Society of Mind*; Rodney A. Brooks, "Intelligence without Representation." See also Luc Steels and Rodney A. Brooks, *The Artificial Life Route to Artificial Intelligence*.

21. Marvin Minsky, "Why Computer Science Is the Most Important Thing That Has Happened to the Humanities in 5,000 Years." I am grateful to Nicholas Gessler for providing me with a transcript of this lecture.

22. Michel Foucault, "What Is an Author?" 119.

23. See especially the chapter "Authors Analogue and Digital," 78–100. I am grateful to Mark Poster for making this chapter available to me before its publication and for his correspondence on the ideas it expresses.

24. Poster's discussion can be clarified by noting that analog technologies do not necessarily rely on resemblance, only on morphological proportionality. A phonograph record, for example, does not look like the sound waves it captures and reproduces, but there is a morphological proportionality between the sound waves and the spacing of the record grooves. Analog relations that depend on resemblance are more properly called analogies (or analogizing relations). Analogies are a subset of analog relations, which also contain the relations, typical of analog technologies, that depend on morphological proportionality.

25. Michel Foucault, *The Order of Things*.

26. For a discussion of the digital nature of alphabetic language versus ideogrammatic writing, see John Cayley, "Digital Wen." Robert K. Logan, in *The Alphabet Effect*, also argues that the switch from pictorial representations to alphabetic representation, in its much greater economy, is a move toward the digitalization of language. In this view, alphabetic writing is not primarily analog but digital. See also Logan's interesting arguments about computational language as an advance on natural languages, in *The Fifth Language*.

27. See Mark Rose, *Authors and Owners*.

28. For a discussion of this mantra in the context of artificial life, see N. Katherine Hayles, *How We Became Posthuman*, 222–46.

29. In *City of Bits*, William J. Mitchell highlights the importance of fragmentation and recombination across a variety of architectural sites and social practices in the digital age.

30. This example comes from Poster, "Authors Analogue and Digital," 79.

31. This behavior was pointed out to me by Nicholas Gessler.

32. Rodney A. Brooks, *Cambrian Intelligence*.

33. The robot was displayed in an art show entitled "The Art and Aesthetics of Artificial Life," which featured images, simulations, and installations created by artificial-life techniques; the show, curated by Nicholas Gessler, was exhibited at the UCLA Center for Digital Arts from June 22–July 23, 1998.

34. In *How We Became Posthuman*, I discuss the dialectic between incorporation and inscription as two alternating ways of understanding written documents. In *Writing Machines*, I explore the implications of seeing all texts, especially literary ones, as material instantiations.

35. Bruno Latour and Steve Woolgar, *Laboratory Life*, 50. See also Timothy Lenoir, "Inscription Practices and the Materialities of Communication," his excellent introduction to *Inscribing Science*.

36. Steven Shapin and Simon Schaffer, *Leviathan and the Air Pump*, 235–44.

37. H. M. Collins, *Changing Order*.

38. Bruno Latour, *We Have Never Been Modern*; Bruno Latour, "Why Has Critique Run Out of Steam?"

39. In *How the Laws of Physics Lie*, Nancy Cartwright clearly analyzes the kinds of complexities that are left behind when a holistic interactive environment is divided into separate components.

40. Morowitz, *The Emergence of Everything*.

41. Latour, *We Have Never Been Modern*, 50.

42. See my discussion in *How We Became Posthuman*, chap. 2.

Chapter Nine

1. Alan M. Turing, "Computing Machinery and Intelligence."

2. Joseph Weizenbaum, *Computer Power and Human Reason.*

3. John R. Koza et al., *Genetic Programming III.*

4. For a description of the "Cog" project, see Rodney Brooks, *Flesh and Machines*; for the information-gathering ecology of Alexandros Moukas and Pattie Maes, see their "Amalthea"; for a description of the NOMAD project, see Neurosciences Research Foundation, "NOMAD."

5. Christopher Langton, "Artificial Life," 1.

6. For an example of this kind of negotiation already underway, see Scott Aaronson, "On *A New Kind of Science* by Stephen Wolfram." Aaronson argues that Wolfram's prediction, reasoning from his cellular automata model, of "long-range threads" between quantum particles is not consistent with Bell inequality violations, which have been verified as quantum effects. In the same review, however, he shows that some of Wolfram's claims can be upheld, although he argues that they are not as new or revolutionary as Wolfram asserts.

7. Hans Moravec, *Mind Children*, 109–10.

8. Antonio R. Damasio, *Descartes' Error* and *The Feeling of What Happens.*

9. Manuel Castells, *The Rise of the Network Society*; *The Power of Identity*; and *End of the Millennium.*

10. Claude Shannon and Warren Weaver, *The Mathematical Theory of Communication.*

11. Greg Egan, "Interview with Greg Egan," by Russell B. Farr.

12. The joke recalls Stanislaw Lem's spoof review of a nonexistent text on "my impossible life," in which the narrator recalls the details of how his mother and father met, calculates the probability of each event, and concludes that, statistically speaking, the odds of him existing are so infinitesimal that his life must be considered an impossibility; see Stanislaw Lem, "*De Impossibilitate Vitae* and *De Impossibilitate Prognoscendi* by Cezar Kouska."

13. The central text is John D. Barrow and Frank J. Tipler, *The Anthropic Cosmological Principle*. For an overview of similar effects both within the fields of cosmology and quantum mechanics, and more generally, see Nick Bostrom, *Anthropic Bias.*

14. I first heard this idea in a conversation with John Cayley, but since he expressed horror at the thought, I am not sure he would want it attributed to him. Consider it an emergent phenomenon from our conversation in March 2004.

15. Donna Haraway, "Situated Knowledge."

16. In February 2003, Stephen Wolfram gave a lecture at the California Institute of Technology in Pasadena. After the lecture, a panel of Caltech scientists discussed Wolfram's work. When the moderator, Steven Koonin (a physicist), asked the panel if Wolfram's "new kind of science" would be viewed as a paradigm shift in twenty years, the answer was a unanimous "no." Wolfram riposted that this reaction is exactly what one would expect in response to a revolutionary paradigm shift. Koonin replied that this is also what one would expect if the "new kind of science" was not a paradigm shift, implicitly acknowledging Wolfram's self-insulating reasoning.

17. Niklas Luhmann, "The Paradox of Observing Systems," esp. 43.

18. Niklas Luhmann, "The Cognitive Program of Constructivism and a Reality That Remains Unknown"; quoted in N. Katherine Hayles, "Theory of a Different Order," esp. 14.

19. For a fascinating account of actual communities of uploaders, see Richard Doyle, "Uploading Anticipation, Becoming Silicon," in *Wetwares: Experiments in Postvital Living*, 121–41.

20. Greg Egan, "An Interview with Greg Egan: Counting Backwards from Infinity." Egan states, "I believe that all of Durham's computer experiments would work exactly as described—the Copy would be oblivious to whether it was being run on one computer in one place, or scattered all over the planet. You could certainly argue that, with the time-reversed experiments, the experience of the Copy would first arise whenever the 'subjectively final' state of mind was pre-loaded with memories—by whatever means—as well as when that state of mind was played backwards, later. But I don't think that changes anything."

21. Stephen Wolfram discusses reversible cellular automata in *A New Kind of Science*, 435–57, 1017–21. See also Kwangh Yung Paek, "Reversible Cellular Automata."

22. Nicholas Gessler drew my attention to this apparent fallacy in *Permutation City*, although on consideration I believe that it is not actually a mistake Egan makes but an intentional provocation to further thought, a provocation evident in Paul's "dust" hypothesis, which I discuss in the following paragraphs.

23. For a discussion of quantum indeterminacy, see Arkady Plotnitsky, *Complementarity*. In "Agential Realism," Karen Barad also has an interesting discussion of Bohr's interpretation of quantum mechanics and its implications for feminist theory. The fact that the wave function equations have more than one solution implies the possibility of branching worldlines, an interpretation developed in the so-called "many worlds" hypothesis.

24. For an explanation of quantum computing, see Michael A. Nielsen and Isaac L. Chuang *Quantum Computation and Quantum Information*, which includes discussions of quantum cryptography (relevant to Nick's opening a lock), quantum temporality, and quantum algorithms. For a somewhat more technical treatment, see Mika Hirvensalo, *Quantum Computing*.

25. All but two of the chapters in part 1 (before Paul commits suicide) are entitled "(Rip, tie, cut toy man)," if focalized on Paul, or "(Remit not paucity)," if focalized on other characters; both titles are anagrams of "Permutation City." The two anagrammatic variations of the repeating titles are "(Toy man, picture it)" for chapter 16, where Paul's realization that he never was the Copy deepens his obsession, and chapter 20, "(Can't you time trip?)," which recounts the realization of Peer, another simulated Copy, that he can never know how many identical cycles he may have acted out if his memory has been programmed to erase them, further reinforcing the idea that continuity of consciousness is an illusion.

26. Ross Farnell, "Attempting Immortality"; Greg Egan, "Dust."

27. While Turing and von Neumann are, of course, well-known names, to my knowledge "Chiang" has yet to make a contribution worthy of adding his name to this illustrious list.

28. *Permutation City* was published seven years before Wolfram's master work, so this work is not a direct influence on Egan's novel. However, Egan has remarked in interviews that he has a background in computer programming, and he clearly knew about CAs prior

to the publication of Wolfram's book. When *A New Kind of Science* appeared, Egan wrote a favorable review of it and published it on his Web site; see Greg Egan, "Stephen Wolfram's Science."

29. Robert Markley, "Boundaries."

30. Hugh Everett, a Ph.D. student working with John Wheeler as his advisor, advanced the "many worlds" hypothesis in 1957. Everett suggested that when a quantum system encounters a measuring device, it splits into many waveforms, each representing a different value of the quantum states. To account for the fact that these multiple states are not recorded by the measuring device, Everett suggested that the measurement device itself must split into as many versions of itself as there are quantum states. Following this logic to its conclusion then leads to the idea that for every such splitting, multiple worlds are constantly proliferating.

31. The arguments are too extensive to rehearse here. Crucial texts, however, are Bruno Latour and Steve Woolgar, *Laboratory Life*; Steven Shapin and Simon Schaffer, *Leviathan and the Air Pump*; and Donna Haraway, *Simians, Cyborgs, and Women*. For my own modest contribution, see N. Katherine Hayles, "Constrained Constructivism."

32. The situation is beautifully captured in the fictional Nobel Laureate address that Stanislaw Lem imagines in "The New Cosmogony." The narrator has received the Nobel Prize for inferring the existence of beings so advanced that they have learned how to transform the laws of physics. When they do so, however, they also necessarily alter the conditions of their existence, for they are part of the universe they are transforming. Like Egan, Lem imagines a species that can transcend the biology that evolution has given them; what they cannot transcend is the reflexivity inherent in their position within the universe upon which they are experimenting.

33. Far from seeing the sexual drive as an essential and major component of human psychology, Egan's fiction consistently represents sex as painful, unsatisfying, and ridiculous. In *Permutation City*, when Paul Durham attempts to have sex with Maria (the only time we see him engage in sexual activity), he is wrenched by testicular cramps so excruciating that he cannot continue. In *Distress*, sexual relationships are associated either with pain, as when Andrew lacerates his chest with knife wounds when Gina tells him she is leaving him, or with a pleasurable intimacy that exists only when penetrative sex is constituted as impossible or forbidden, as in the scene where Andrew encounters Kuwale's surgically altered body. When in *Schild's Ladder* Tchicaya proposes a sexual interlude with Yann, an "incorporeal" who has never known a permanent bodily form, Yann finds the activities Tchicaya proposes so ludicrous that he breaks out laughing. In the subjective cosmology trilogy Egan insists that his protagonists struggle with their embodiments, but the disappearance of sex is nevertheless more often greeted with relief than nostalgia.

34. Greg Egan, "Interview with Greg Egan," in *Ibn Qirtaiba*.

Works Cited

AAAI. *Computational Synthesis: From Basic Building Blocks to High Level Functionality, Papers from the 2003 AAAI Spring Symposium.* Technical Report SS-03020. Menlo Park, CA: AAAI Press, 2003.

Aaronson, Scott. "On *A New Kind of Science* by Stephen Wolfram." *Quantum Information and Computation* 2, no. 5 (September 2002): 410–23.

Aarseth, Espen J. *Cybertext: Perspectives on Ergodic Literature.* Baltimore: Johns Hopkins University Press, 1997.

Adelman, Leonard M. "Molecular Computation of Solutions to Combinatorial Problems." *Science* 266 (November 1994): 1021–24.

Alexrod, Robert. *The Evolution of Cooperation.* New York: Basic Books, 1985.

Argyros, Alex. *A Blessed Rage for Order: Deconstruction, Evolution, and Chaos.* Ann Arbor: University of Michigan Press, 1991.

Austin, J. L. *How to Do Things with Words.* 2nd ed. Edited by Marina Sbisa and J. O. Urmsson. Cambridge, MA: Harvard University Press, 1975.

Bacon, Francis. *The New Organon.* Edited by Lisa Jardine, Michael Silverthorne, Karl Ameriks, and Desmond Clarke. Cambridge: Cambridge University Press, 2000.

Balsamo, Anne. *Technologies of the Gendered Body: Reading Cyborg Women.* Durham, NC: Duke University Press, 1996.

Bankes, Steven. "Computational Experiments and Exploratory Modeling." http://www.evolvinglogic.com/Learn/absandpapers/validation.html.

Barad, Karen. "Agential Realism: Feminist Interventions in Understanding Scientific Practice." In *Science Studies Reader,* edited by Mario Biagioli, 1–11. New York: Routledge, 1999.

Barkow, Jerome, Leda Cosmides, and John Tooby. *The Adapted Mind: Evolutionary Psychology and the Generation of Culture.* Oxford: Oxford University Press, 1992.

Baron-Cohen, Simon. *Mindblindness: An Essay on Autism and Theory of Mind.* Cambridge, MA: MIT Press, 1995.

Barrow, John D., and Frank J. Tipler. *The Anthropic Cosmological Principle.* New York: Oxford University Press, 1986.

Barthes, Roland. *S/Z*. Translated by Richard Miller. New York: Hill and Wang, 1974.

Bateson, Mary Catherine. *Our Own Metaphor: A Personal Account of a Conference on the Effects of Conscious Purpose on Human Adaptation*. Washington, DC: Smithsonian Institution Press, 1972.

Benjamin, Walter. "The Task of the Translator." In *Illuminations: Essays and Reflections*, edited by Hannah Arendt, translated by Harry Zohn, 69–82. New York: Schocken Books, 1969.

———. "The Work of Art in the Age of Mechanical Reproduction." In *Illuminations: Essays and Reflections*, edited by Hannah Arendt, translated by Harry Zohn, 217–52. New York: Schocken Books, 1969.

Birkerts, Sven. *The Gutenberg Elegies: The Fate of Reading in an Electronic Age*. New York: Ballantine Books, 1995.

Blaheta, Don. "The Lambda Calculus." http://www.cs.brown.edu/courses/cs173/2003/Text book/lc.pdf.

Blank, Stephen J. "Preparing for the Next War: Reflections on the Revolution in Military Affairs." In *In Athena's Camp: Preparing for Conflict in the Information Age*, edited by John Arquilla and David Ronfeldt, 61–77. Washington, DC: Office of the Secretary of Defense by National Defense Research Institute, RAND, 1997.

Bolter, Jay David, and Richard Grusin. *Remediation: Understanding New Media*. Cambridge, MA: MIT Press, 2002.

Borges, Jorge Luis. "The Don Quixote of Pierre Menard." In *Ficciones*, translated by Anthony Kerrigan, 79–88. New York: Grove Press, 1989.

———. "The Homeric Versions." In *Selected Non-Fictions*, edited by Eliot Weinberger, translated by Esther Allen, Suzanne Jill Levine, and Eliot Weinberger, 69–75. New York: Penguin, 1999.

Bostrom, Nick. *Anthropic Bias: Observation Selection Effects in Science and Philosophy*. Studies in Philosophy. New York: Routledge, 2002.

Brockman, John. "Joseph Traub, Jaron Lanier, John McCarthy, Lee Smolin, Philip W. Anderson, Anthony Valentini, Stuart Hameroff, and Paola Zizzi Respond to Seth Lloyd." Edge. http://www.edge.org/discourse/information.html.

———. "What's Your Question?" Under "World Question Center." Edge. www.edge.org.

Brooks, Rodney A. *Cambrian Intelligence: The Early History of the New AI*. Cambridge, MA: MIT Press, 1999.

———. *Flesh and Machines: How Robots Will Change Us*. New York: Pantheon, 2002.

———. "Intelligence without Representation." *Artificial Intelligence* 47 (1991): 139–59.

Bruner, Jerome. *Acts of Meaning*. Cambridge, MA: Harvard University Press, 1990.

Buzzetti, Dino. "Digital Representation and the Text Model." *New Literary History* 33 (2002): 61–88.

Cartwright, Nancy. *How the Laws of Physics Lie*. Oxford: Oxford University Press, 1993.

Castells, Manuel. *End of the Millennium*. London: Blackwell, 2000.

———. *The Power of Identity*. London: Blackwell, 2003.

———. *The Rise of the Network Society*. London: Blackwell, 2000.

Cayley, John. "The Code Is Not the Text (Unless It Is the Text)." *Electronic Book Review* (September 2002). http://www.electronicbookreview.com/v3/servlet/ebr?command= view_essay&essay_id=cayleyele.

————. "Digital Wen: On the Digitization of Letter- and Character-Based Systems of Inscription." In *Reading East Asian Writing: The Limits of Literary Theory*, edited by Michael Hockx and Ivo Smits, 227–94. London: Routledge Curzon, 2003.

————. "Of Programmatology." *Mute* (Fall 1998): 72–75.

Cebrowski, Arthur K., and John J. Garstka. "Network-Centric Warfare: Its Origin and Future." *Naval Institute Proceedings Magazine* (January 1998). http://www.usni.org/Proceedings/Articles98/PROcebrowski.htm.

Chun, Wendy Hui Kyong. "On the Persistence of Visual Knowledge." Paper presented at the annual convention of the Modern Language Association, San Diego, CA, December 28, 2003.

Collins, H. M. *Changing Order: Replication and Induction in Scientific Practice*. London: Sage Publications, 1985.

Conway, John. *Game of Life*. http://www.bitstorm.org/gameoflife/.

Coover, Robert. "The Babysitter." In *Pricksongs and Descants: Fictions*, 206–39. 1969. Reprint, New York: Grove Press, 2000.

Coverley, M. D. *The Book of Going Forth by Day*. http://califia.hispeed.com/Egypt/.

Cramer, Florian. "Digital Code and Literary Text." *Beehive* 4, no. 3 (November 2001). http://beehive.temporalimage.com/archive/43arc.html.

Culler, Jonathan. *Ferdinand de Saussure*. Rev. ed. Ithaca, NY: Cornell University Press, 1986.

Dahlström, Mats. "Drowning by Versions." *Human IT* 4, no. 1 (2000): 7–38.

————. "When Is a Webtext?" *TEXT Technology: The Journal of Computer Text Processing* 11, no. 1 (2002): 139–61.

Damashek, Marc. "Gauging Similarity with N-Grams: Language-Independent Categorization of Text." *Science* 267 (February 10, 1995): 843–48.

Damasio, Antonio R. *Descartes' Error: Emotion, Reason, and the Human Brain*. New York: Putnam, 1994.

————. *The Feeling of What Happens: Body and Emotion in the Making of Consciousness*. New York: Harvest, 2000.

Danielewski, Mark Z. *House of Leaves*. New York: Pantheon, 2000. House of Leaves. http://www.houseofleaves.com.

Davis, Martin. *The Universal Computer: From Leibniz to Turing*. New York: W. W. Norton, 2000.

Dawkins, Richard. *The Blind Watchmaker*. New York: Norton, 1986.

————. *The Selfish Gene*. New York: Oxford University Press, 1989.

Deleuze, Gilles, and Félix Guattari. *A Thousand Plateaus: Capitalism and Schizophrenia*. Translated by Brian Massumi. Minneapolis: University of Minnesota Press, 1987.

Dennett, Daniel C. *Freedom Evolves*. New York: Vintage, 2003.

————. *Kinds of Minds: Toward an Understanding of Consciousness*. New York: Basic Books, 1996.

Derrida, Jacques. *Limited Inc*. Translated by Samuel Weber. Evanston, IL: Northwestern University Press, 1998.

————. *Margins of Philosophy*. Translated by Alan Bass. Chicago: University of Chicago Press, 1984.

————. *Of Grammatology*. Translated by Gayatri C. Spivak. Baltimore: Johns Hopkins University Press, 1977.

————. *Positions.* Translated by Alan Bass. Chicago: University of Chicago Press, 1982.

————. *Writing and Difference.* Translated by Alan Bass. Chicago: University of Chicago Press, 1980.

Dick, Philip K. *The Simulacra.* London: Metheun Paperbacks, 1964.

————. *The Three Stigmata of Palmer Eldritch.* 1964. Reprint, New York: Doubleday, 1965.

————. *We Can Build You.* London: Grafton Books, 1969. First published as *A. Lincoln, Simulacrum.*

Didion, Joan. *The White Album.* New York: Simon and Schuster, 1979.

Douglas, Jane Yellowlees. "'How Do I Stop This Thing?' Closure and Indeterminacy in Interactive Narratives." In *Hyper/Text/Theory*, edited by George P. Landow, 159–88. Baltimore: Johns Hopkins University Press, 1994.

Doyle, Richard. *Wetwares: Experiments in Postvital Living.* Minneapolis: University of Minnesota Press, 2003.

Dozois, Gardner. *The Fiction of James Tiptree Jr.* San Bernadino, CA: Borgo Press, 1984.

Drucker, Johanna. *The Century of Artists' Books.* New York: Granary Books, 1996.

————. "Language as Information: Intimations of Immateriality." In *Figuring the Word: Essays on Books, Writing, and Visual Poetics*, 213–20. New York: Granary Books, 1998.

————. *Otherspace: A Martian Typography.* Atlanta: Nexus, 1992.

————. "Theory as Praxis: The Poetics of Electronic Textuality." *Modernism/Modernity* 9, no. 4 (2002): 683–91.

————. *The Visible Word: Experimental Typography and Modern Art, 1909–1923.* Chicago: University of Chicago Press, 1994.

Durham, Scott. "P. K. Dick: From the Death of the Subject to a Theology of Late Capitalism." *Science-Fiction Studies* 15 (1988): 173–86.

Dyer, Michael G. "Toward Synthesizing Artificial Neural Networks That Exhibit Cooperative Intelligent Behavior: Some Open Issues in Artificial Life." *Artificial Life* 1, nos. 1/2 (Fall 1993/Winter 1994): 111–35.

Eckel, Bruce. *Thinking in C++.* Englewood Cliffs, NJ: Prentice Hall, 1995.

Egan, Greg. *Distress.* London: Orion/Millennium, 1995.

————. "Dust." In *The Year's Best Science Fiction: Tenth Annual Collection*, edited by Gardner Dozois, 87–112. New York: St. Martin's Press, 1993.

————. "An Interview with Greg Egan: Counting Backwards from Infinity." *Eidolon.net: Australian SF Online.* http://eidolon.net/index.html (accessed August 8, 2004). Site now discontinued.

————. "Interview with Greg Egan." *Ibn Qirtaiba* 18 (September 1996): n.p.

————. "Interview with Greg Egan." By Russell B. Farr. *Piffle and Other Trivia* 26 (September 1997). http://gregegan.customer.netspace.net.au/INTERVIEWS/Interviews.html#Piffle.

————. *Permutation City.* London: Orion/Millennium, 1994.

————. *Quarantine.* London: Century/Legend, 1992.

————. *Schild's Ladder: A Novel.* New York: EOS, 2003.

————. "Stephen Wolfram's Science." Under "Bibliography" and "Non Fiction." Greg Egan's Home Page. http://gregegan.customer.netspace.net.au/index.html.

Farnell, Ross. "Attempting Immortality: AI, A-Life, and the Posthuman in Greg Egan's *Permutation City.*" *Science-Fiction Studies* 27 (2000): 69–91.

Foerster, Heinz von. *Observing Systems.* 2nd ed. New York: Intersystems Publications, 1982.

Foster, G. M. "Peasant Society and the Image of Limited Good." *American Anthropologist* 67, no. 2 (1965): 293–315.

Foucault, Michel. *The Order of Things: An Archeology of the Human Sciences.* New York: Vintage Books, 1970.

———. "What Is an Author?" *Language, Counter-Memory, Practice: Selected Essays and Interviews by Michel Foucault,* edited by Donald F. Bouchard, translated by Donald F. Bouchard and Sherry Simon, 113–138. Ithaca, NY: Cornell University Press, 1977.

Fredkin, Edward. *Introduction to Digital Philosophy.* http://www.digitalphilosophy.org.

Freedman, Carl. "Philip K. Dick and Criticism." Editorial introduction to *Science-Fiction Studies* 15 (1988): 121–30.

Fuller, Matthew. *Behind the Blip: Essays on the Culture of Software.* New York: Autonomedia, 2003.

Galloway, Alexander R. *Protocol: How Control Exists after Decentralization.* Cambridge, MA: MIT Press, 2004.

Gendolla, Peter, Jörgen Schäfer, and Maik Pluschke. "Literatur in Netzen/Netzliteratur." http://www.litnet.uni-siegen.de/Literatur%20in%20Netzten%20-%20Netzliteratur.pdf.

Genette, Gérard. *Narrative Discourse: An Essay on Method,* translated by Jane E. Lewin. Ithaca, NY: Cornell University Press, 1983.

Gessler, Nicholas. "Evolving Artificial Cultural Things-That-Think and Work by Dynamical Hierarchical Synthesis." http://www.sscnet.ucla.edu/geog/gessler/cv-pubs/03naacsos.pdf.

———. "Sonnet." http://www.sscnet.ucla.edu/geog/gessler/borland/samples.htm.

Glazier, Loss Pequeño. *Dig[iT]al Poet(I)(c)s: The Making of E-Poetries.* Tuscaloosa: University of Alabama Press, 2002.

Gray, Lawrence. "A Mathematician Looks at Wolfram's *New Kind of Science.*" *Notices of the American Mathematical Society* 50, no. 2 (February 2003): 200–11. http://www.ams.org/notices/200302/fea-gray.pdf.

Grigar, Dene. "Mutability and Medium." Paper presented at a conference on Computers and Writing, Normal, IL, May 2002.

Grosz, Elizabeth. *Volatile Bodies: Toward a Corporeal Feminism.* Bloomington: Indiana University Press, 1994.

Grusin, Richard, and Jay David Bolter. *Remediation: Understanding New Media.* Cambridge, MA: MIT Press, 2000.

Guattari, Felix. "Machinic Heterogenesis." In *Rethinking Technologies,* edited by Verna A. Conley, 13–27. Minneapolis: University of Minnesota Press, 1993.

Gunder, Anna. "Forming the Text, Performing the Work—Aspects of Media, Navigation, and Linking." *Human IT* 5, nos. 2–3 (2001): 81–206.

Hansen, Mark B. N. *Embodying Technesis: Technology Beyond Writing.* Ann Arbor: University of Michigan Press, 2000.

————. *New Philosophy for New Media.* Cambridge, MA: MIT Press, 2003.

Haraway, Donna. *Simians, Cyborgs, and Women: The Reinvention of Nature.* New York: Routledge, 1991.

————. "Situated Knowledge: The Science Question in Feminism as a Site of Discourse on the Privilege of Partial Perspective." *Feminist Studies* 14, no. 3 (1988): 575–99.

HarperCollins. "A Talk with Neal Stephenson." Cryptonomicon. http://www.cryptonom icon.com. Under the link "Chat with Neal (4/19)."

Harpold, Terry, and Kavita Philip. "Of Bugs and Rats: Cyber-Cleanliness, Cyber-Squalor, and the Fantasy-Spaces of Informational Globalization." *Postmodern Culture* 11, no. 1 (2000). http://muse.jhu.edu/journals/postmodern_culture/toc/pmc11.1.html.

Hayles, N. Katherine. "Constrained Constructivism: Locating Scientific Inquiry in the Theater of Representation." In *Realism and Representation: Essays on the Problem of Realism in Relation to Science, Literature, and Culture,* edited by George Levine, 27–43. Madison: University of Wisconsin Press, 1993.

————. "Corporeal Anxiety in *Dictionary of the Khazars*: What Books Talk about When They Talk about Losing Their Bodies." *Modern Fiction Studies* 43 (Fall 1992): 800–820.

————. "From Object to Process: Cinematic Implications of New Media Poetry." *Future Cinema: The Cinematic Imaginary after Film,* edited by Peter Weibel and Jeffrey Shaw, 316–23. Cambridge, MA: MIT Press, 2003.

————. "From Utopia to Mutopia: Recursive Complexity and Nanospatiality in *The Diamond Age.*" In *World Weavers: Globalization, Science Fiction, and the Cybernetic Revolution,* edited by Wong Kin Yuen, Gary Westfahl, and Amy Chan Kit Sze. Hong Kong: Hong Kong University Press, forthcoming.

————. *How We Became Posthuman: Virtual Bodies in Cybernetics, Literature, and Informatics.* Chicago: University of Chicago Press, 1999.

————. "Theory of a Different Order: A Conversation with Katherine Hayles and Niklas Luhmann." *Cultural Critique* 31 (Fall 1995): 7–36.

————. *Writing Machines.* Cambridge, MA: MIT Press, 2001.

Hayot, Eric. *Chinese Dreams: Pound, Brecht, Tel Quel.* Ann Arbor: University of Michigan Press, 2004.

Hillis, Daniel. *The Pattern on the Stone: The Simple Ideas That Make Computers Work.* New York: Perseus Books Group, 1999.

Hirvensalo, Mika. *Quantum Computing.* Berlin: Springer Verlag, 2001.

Hofstader, Douglas R. *Gödel, Escher, Bach: An Eternal Golden Braid.* New York: Basic Books, 1979.

Hutchins, W. J. "Warren Weaver Memorandum July 1949." http://ourworld.compuserve. com/homepages/WJHutchins/Weaver49.htm.

Hutchinson, Stuart. "James's 'In the Cage': A New Interpretation." *Studies in Short Fiction* 19 (1982): 19–26.

Jackson, Shelley. "'Of Dolls and Monsters': An Interview with Shelley Jackson." By Rita Raley. *The Iowa Review on the Web* (March 1, 2002): 1–4. http://www.uiowa.edu/%7Eiare view/tirweb/feature/jackson/jackson.htm.

————. *Patchwork Girl by Mary/Shelley and Herself.* Watertown, MA: Eastgate Systems, 1995. http://www.eastgate.com/catalog/PatchworkGirl.html.

————. "Stitch Bitch: The Patchwork Girl." *Paradoxa* 4 (1998): 526–38.

James, Henry. "In the Cage." In *The Complete Tales of Henry James.* Vol. 10, edited by Leon Edel, 139–242. London: Rupert Hart-Davis, 1964.

Johnson, Barbara. "My Monster/My Self." *Diacritics* 12 (1982): 2–10.

Johnston, John. "The In-Mixing of Machines: Psychoanalysis and Cybernetics." Unpublished manuscript.

Kandel, Michael. "A Freudian Peek at Lem's *Fiasco*." Paper presented at a conference on The World according to Lem: Science Fiction and Futurology, University of Alberta, Edmonton, AB, September 29, 2003.

Kauffman, Stuart A. *At Home in the Universe: The Search for Laws of Self-Organization and Complexity.* New York: Oxford Press, 1996.

————. *The Origins of Order: Self-Organization and Selection in Evolution.* New York: Oxford University Press, 1993.

Kirschenbaum, Matthew G. "Editing the Interface: Textual Studies and First Generation Electronic Objects." In *TEXT: An Interdisciplinary Annual of Textual Studies.* Vol. 14, edited by W. Speech Hill and Edward M. Burns, 15–51. Ann Arbor: University of Michigan Press, 2002.

————. "Materiality and Matter and Stuff: What Electronic Texts Are Made Of." *Electronic Book Review* 12 (2002). http://www.altx.com/ebr/riposte/rip12/rip12kir.htm.

————. "Virtuality and VRML: Software Studies after Manovich." In *The Politics of Information: The Electronic Mediation of Social Change*, edited by Mark Bousquet and Katherine Wills. Alt-X Press eBook, 2004. http://www.altx.com/ebooks/infopol.html.

Kittler, Friedrich A. *Discourse Networks, 1800/1900.* Translated by Michael Metteer. Stanford, CA: Stanford University Press, 1992.

————. *Essays: Literature, Media, Information Systems.* Edited by John Johnston. Amsterdam: G+B Arts, 1997.

————. *Gramophone, Film, Typewriter.* Translated by Geoffrey Winthrop-Young and Michael Wutz. Writing Science Series. Stanford, CA: Stanford University Press, 1999.

Koenig, Andrew, and Barbara E. Moo. "Preface." In *Accelerated C++.* Redwood City, CA: Addison-Wesley, 2000. http://www.acceleratedcpp.com/details/preface.html.

Koza, John R. *Genetic Programming: On the Programming of Computers by Means of Natural Selection.* Cambridge, MA: MIT Press, 1992.

————. *Genetic Programming II: Automatic Discovery of Reusable Programs.* Cambridge, MA: MIT Press, 1994.

Koza, John R., Forrest H. Bennett III, David Andre, and Martin A. Keane. *Genetic Programming III: Darwinian Invention and Problem Solving.* San Francisco: Morgan Kaufmann Publishers, 1999.

Kristal, Efrain. *Invisible Work: Borges and Translation.* Nashville, TN: Vanderbilt University Press, 2002.

Kurzweil, Ray. *The Age of Spiritual Machines: When Computers Exceed Human Intelligence.* Oxford: Oxford University Press, 2000.

————. "Reflections on Stephen Wolfram's *A New Kind of Science*." KurzweilAI.net. http://www.kurzweilai.net/articles/art0464.html.

Lacan, Jacques. *Le Séminaire XX: Encore.* Paris: Seuil, 1975.

Langton, Christopher G. "Artificial Life." In *Artificial Life*, edited by Christopher Langton, 1–17. Redwood City, CA: Addison-Wesley, 1989.

———. "Computation at the Edge of Chaos: Phase Transition and Emergent Computation." *Physica D* 42 (1990): 12–37.

Latour, Bruno. "A. N. Whitehead and Richard Powers." Paper presented at a conference of the Society for Literature and Science, Paris, France, June 24, 2004.

———. *Science in Action: How to Follow Scientists and Engineers through Society*. Cambridge, MA: Harvard University Press, 1987.

———. *We Have Never Been Modern*. Translated by Catherine Porter. Cambridge, MA: Harvard University Press, 1993.

———. "Why Has Critique Run Out of Steam? From Matters of Fact to Matters of Concern." *Critical Inquiry* 30, no. 2 (Winter 2004): 225–48.

Latour, Bruno, and Steve Woolgar. *Laboratory Life: The Social Construction of Scientific Facts*. London: Sage, 1979.

Lawler, John. John Lawler. http://www-personal.umich.edu/~jlawler.

Lem, Stanislaw. "*De Impossibilitate Vitae* and *De Impossibilitate Prognoscendi* by Cezar Kouska." In *A Perfect Vacuum*, translated by Michael Kandel, 141–66. New York: Harvest, 1983.

———. "The Mask." In *Mortal Engines*, translated by Michael Kandel, 81–239. San Diego: Harcourt, 1992. First published in English 1977 by Seabury Press. First Polish edition 1976.

———. "The New Cosmogony." In *A Perfect Vacuum*, translated by Michael Kandel, 197–238. New York: Harvest, 1983.

———. *Solaris*. Translated by Joanna Kilmartin and Steve Cox. New York: Berkley, 1971.

Lenoir, Timothy. "Inscription Practices and the Materialities of Communication." Introduction to *Inscribing Science: Scientific Texts and the Materiality of Communication*, edited by Timothy Lenoir, 1–19. Stanford, CA: Stanford University Press, 1998.

Levy, Stephen. *Artificial Life: The Quest for a New Creation*. New York: Pantheon Books, 1992.

Libet, Benjamin, Anthony Freeman, and Keith Sutherland. *The Volitional Brain: Neuroscience of Free Will*. Thorverton, UK: Imprint Academic, 1999.

Libet, Benjamin, C. A. Gleason, E. W. Wright, and D. K. Pearl. "Time of Conscious Intention to Act in Relation to Onset of Cerebral Activities (Readiness Potential): The Unconscious Initiation of a Freely Voluntary Act." *Brain* 106 (1983): 623–42.

Library of Congress. William Blake Archive. Edited by Morris Eaves, Robert Essick, and Joseph Viscomi. http://www.blakearchive.org.

Liu, Alan. "The Humanities: A Technical Profession." Paper presented at the annual convention of the Modern Language Association, San Diego, CA, December 28, 2003.

———. *The Laws of Cool: Knowledge Work and the Culture of Information*. Chicago: University of Chicago Press, 2004.

Lloyd, Seth. "Computational Capacity of the Universe." *Physical Review Letters* 88, no. 23 (June 10, 2002): 237901.

———. "How Fast, How Small, and How Powerful? Moore's Law and the Ultimate Laptop." July 23, 2001. http://www.edge.org/3rd_culture/lloyd/lloyd_print.html.

————. "Lloyd's It from Qubit Law." http://www.edge.org/q2004/page5.html#lloyd.

————. "Ultimate Physical Limits to Computation." *Nature* 406 (2000): 1047–54.

Logan, Robert. *The Alphabet Effect: The Impact of the Phonetic Alphabet on the Development of Western Civilization.* New York: St. Martin's Press, 1987.

————. *The Fifth Language: Learning a Living in the Computer Age.* North York, ON: Stoddart, 1997.

Lovink, Geert. *Dark Fiber: Tracking Critical Internet Culture.* Cambridge, MA: MIT Press, 2002.

Luhmann, Niklas. "The Cognitive Program of Constructivism and a Reality That Remains Unknown." In *Selforganization: Portrait of a Scientific Revolution,* edited by Wolfgang Krohn, Gunter Kuppers, and Helga Nowotny, 64–85. Dordrecht: Kluwer Academic, 1990.

————. "The Paradox of Observing Systems." *Cultural Critique* 31 (Fall 1995): 37–56.

Lurie, Andrew J. "Now, May I Offer You a Poem." http://develop.www.umich.edu/lurieabin/queneau.

MacKay, Donald. *Information, Mechanism, Meaning.* Cambridge, MA: MIT Press, 1969.

Macpherson, C. B. *The Political Theory of Possessive Individualism: Hobbes to Locke.* New York: Oxford University Press, 1988.

Mandelbrot, Benoit. *The Fractal Beauty of Nature.* San Francisco: W. H. Freeman, 1982.

Manovich, Lev. *The Language of New Media.* Cambridge, MA: MIT Press, 2002.

Markley, Robert. "Boundaries: Mathematics, Alienation, and the Metaphysics of Cyberspace." In *Virtual Reality and Their Discontents,* edited by Robert Markley, 55–77. Baltimore: Johns Hopkins University Press, 1996.

Markoff, John. "Behind Happy Interface, More Complex Reality." *New York Times,* June 3, 1999, sec. G7, col. 1.

Massumi, Brian. "The Brightness Confound." In *The Body Mechanique,* 81–94. Wexner Center Exhibit Catalogue. Columbus: Ohio State University, 1998.

Maturana, Humberto R., and Francisco J. Varela. *Autopoiesis and Cognition: The Realization of the Living.* Dordrecht: D. Reidel, 1980.

McCellan, Jim. "After *Snow Crash's* Cyberpunk, It's Cyberpunk." *Guardian* (London), October 14, 1999, 2.

McGann, Jerome J. The D. G. Rossetti Hypermedia Archive. http://www.iath.virginia.edu/rossetti/fullarch.html.

————. "It's Not the Technology, Stupid!" Paper presented at the annual convention of the Modern Language Association. San Diego, CA: December 28, 2003.

————. *Radiant Textuality: Literature after the World Wide Web.* London: Palgrave Macmillan, 2001.

————. *The Textual Condition.* Princeton, NJ: Princeton University Press, 1991.

McKenzie, D. F. *Bibliography and the Sociology of Texts.* Cambridge: Cambridge University Press, 1986.

Mellor, Anne K. *Mary Shelley: Her Life, Her Fiction, Her Monsters.* New York: Routledge, 1988.

Memmott, Talan. *Lexia to Perplexia.* http://www.uiowa.edu/~iareview/tirweb/hypermedia/talan_memmott/.

Menzel, Peter, and Faith D'Alusio. *Robo sapiens: Evolution of a New Species.* Cambridge, MA: MIT Press, 2000.

Minsky, Marvin. *The Society of Mind.* New York: Simon and Schuster, 1988.

————. "Why Computer Science Is the Most Important Thing That Has Happened to the Humanities in 5,000 Years." Keynote address at a conference on artificial life. Nara, Japan, May 15, 1996.

Mitchell, William J. *City of Bits: Space, Place, and the Infoban.* Cambridge, MA: MIT Press, 1996.

Moody, Andrew. "'The Harmless Pleasure of Knowing': Privacy in the Telegraph Office and Henry James's 'In the Cage.'" *The Henry James Review* 16 (1995): 53–65.

Moravec, Hans. *Mind Children: The Future of Robot and Human Intelligence.* Cambridge, MA: Harvard University Press, 1990.

————. *Robot: Mere Machine to Transcendent Mind.* New York: Oxford University Press, 2000.

Morowitz, Harold. *The Emergence of Everything: How the World Became Complex.* New York: Oxford University Press, 2002.

Moukas, Alexandros, and Pattie Maes. "Amalthea." MIT Media Lab. Research Group Projects and Descriptions. http://www.media.mit.edu/research/ResearchPubWeb.pl?ID=284.

Munneke, Derek, Kirsten Wahlstrom, and Linda Zaccara. "Intelligent Software Agents on the Internet." http://www.cis.unisa.edu.au/~cisdm/papers/iagents/IntelligentAgentsInternet.html.

Murray, Janet. *Hamlet on the Holodeck: The Future of Narrative in Cyberspace.* Cambridge, MA: MIT Press, 1998.

Neurosciences Research Foundation. "NOMAD." Neurosciences Institute. http://www.nsi.edu.

Nicolson, Marjorie Hope. *Newton Demands the Muse: Newton's "Opticks" and Eighteenth-Century Poets.* Princeton, NJ: Princeton University Press, 1946.

Nielsen, Michael A., and Isaac L. Chuang. *Quantum Computation and Quantum Information.* Cambridge: Cambridge University Press, 2000.

Norrman, Ralf. "The Intercepted Telegram Plot in Henry James's 'In the Cage.'" *Notes & Queries* 24 (1977): 425–27.

————. *Techniques of Ambiguity in the Fiction of Henry James, with Special Reference to "In the Cage" and "The Turn of the Screw."* Acta Academiae Aboensis, ser. A, Humaniora, 54, no. 2. Abo: Abo Akademi, 1977.

Open Source Initiative. Open Source. http://www.opensource.org/.

Ostman, Charles. "Synthetic Sentience." Interview with Galen Brandt. *Mondo 2000* 16 (1998): 35.

Otis, Laura. *Networking: Communicating with Bodies and Machines in the Nineteenth Century.* Ann Arbor: University of Michigan Press, 2001.

Paek, Kwangh Yung. "Reversible Cellular Automata." http://sjsu.rudyrucker.com/~kwanghyung.paek/paper/.

Parker, Jo Alyson. "Gendering the Robot: Stanislaw Lem's 'The Mask.'" *Science-Fiction Studies* 19 (1992): 178–91.

Paulson, William R. *Literary Culture in a World Transformed*. Ithaca, NY: Cornell University Press, 2001.

Pavić, Milorad. *Dictionary of the Khazars: A Lexicon Novel*. Translated by Christina Pribicevic-Zoric. New York: Vintage, 1989.

Paz, Octavio. "Translation: Literature and Letters." In *Theories of Translation*, edited by Ranier Schulte and John Biguenet, 152–62. Chicago: University of Chicago Press, 1992.

Plotnitsky, Arkady. *Complementarity: Anti-Epistemology after Bohr and Derrida*. Durham, NC: Duke University Press, 1995.

Post, Jack. "Requiem for a Reader? A Semiotic Approach of Reader in Text in Electronic Literature." Unpublished manuscript.

Poster, Mark. *What's the Matter with the Internet?* Minneapolis: University of Minnesota Press, 2001.

Poundstone, William. *Prisoner's Dilemma*. New York: Anchor, 1993.

Prigogine, Ilya, and Isabelle Stengers. *Order out of Chaos: Man's New Dialogue with Nature*. New York: Bantam Books, 1986.

Queneau, Raymond. *Cent mille milliards de poèmes*. Paris: Gallimard, 1961.

Quinn, Paul. "The How of the Crypt." *Times Literary Supplement*, November 5, 1999, 24.

Raley, Rita. "Interferences: [Net.Writing] and the Practice of Codework." *Electronic Book Review* (September 2002). http://www.electronicbookreview.com/v3/servlet/ebr?command=view_essay&essay_id=rayleyele.

———. "Machine Translation and Global English." *Yale Journal of Criticism* 16, no. 2 (Fall 2003): 291–313.

———. "Reveal Codes: Hypertext and Performance." *Postmodern Culture* 12, no. 1 (September 2001). http://muse.jhu.edu/journals/postmodern_culture/toc/pmc12.1.html.

Renear, Allen. "Out of Praxis: Three (Meta)theories of Textuality." In *Electronic Text: Investigations in Method and Theory*, edited by Kathryn Sutherland, 107–26. Oxford: Clarendon Press, 1997.

———. "Philosophy and Electronic Publishing: Theory and Metatheory in the Development of Text Encoding." *The Monist* 80, no. 3 (1997): 348–67.

Requiem for a Dream. http://www.requiemforadream.com.

Robinson, Kim Stanley. *The Novels of Philip K. Dick*. Ann Arbor, MI: UMI Research Press, 1984.

Rose, Mark. *Authors and Owners: The Invention of Copyright*. Cambridge, MA: Harvard University Press, 1993.

Ryan, Marie-Laure. *Possible Worlds, Artificial Intelligence, and Narrative Theory*. Bloomington: University of Indiana Press, 1992.

Saarinen, Leena. "Chatterbots: Crash Test Dummies of Communication." Master's thesis, Media Lab, University of Art and Design, Helsinki, Finland. http://www.mlab.uiah.fi/www/projects_and_publications/final_thesis/saarinen_leena.

Saussure, Ferdinand de. *Course in General Linguistics*. Translated by Roy Harris. Peru, IL: Open Course Publishing Co., 1988.

Savoy, Ric. "'In the Cage' and the Queer Effects of Gay History." *Novel* 28 (1995): 284–307.

Schlossberg, Edwin. *Wordswordswords*. West Islip, NY: Universal Limited Arts Editions, 1968.

Schneier, Bruce. "The Solitaire Encryption Algorithm." In *Cryptonomicon*, by Neal Stephenson, 911–18. New York: Avon, 2002.

Searle, John R. "Reiterating the Differences: A Reply to Derrida." *Glyph* 1 (1977): 198–208.

Serres, Michel. *The Parasite*. Translated by Lawrence R. Shehr. Baltimore: Johns Hopkins University Press, 1982.

Shannon, Claude, and Warren Weaver. *The Mathematical Theory of Communication*. Urbana: University of Illinois Press, 1949.

Shapin, Steven, and Simon Schaffer. *Leviathan and the Air Pump: Hobbes, Boyle, and the Experimental Life*. Princeton, NJ: Princeton University Press, 1986.

Sha Xin Wei. "A Tgarden as a Phenomenological Experiment." http://www.gvu.gatech.edu/people/sha.xinwei/topologicalmedia/tgarden/index.html.

Shelley, Mary Wollstonecraft. *Frankenstein: The 1818 Text, Contexts, Nineteenth-Century Responses, Modern Criticism*. Edited by Paul J. Hunter. New York: W. W. Norton, 1996.

Shillingsburg, Peter L. *Scholarly Editing in the Computer Age: Theory and Practice*. 3rd ed. Ann Arbor: University of Michigan Press, 1966.

———. "Text as Matter, Concept, and Action." *Studies in Bibliography* 44 (1991): 43–83.

Silver, David. "Looking Backwards, Looking Forward: Cyberculture Studies 1990–2000." In *Web Studies: Rewiring Media Studies for the Digital Age*, edited by David Gauntlett, 19–30. Oxford: Oxford University Press, 2000.

Sims, Karl. "Evolved Virtual Creatures." http://www.biota.org/ksims/index.html.

———. "Evolving 3-D Morphology and Behavior by Competition." Unpublished manuscript.

———. "Evolving Virtual Creatures." Paper presented at the SIGGRAPH annual conference, Orlando, FL, July 24–29, 1994. Published in Annual Conference Series, *Computer Graphics* 28 (July 1994): 15–22.

Smith, Brian Cantwell. *On the Origin of Objects*. Cambridge, MA: Bradford Books, 1996.

Steels, Luc. "The Artificial Life Roots of Artificial Intelligence." *Artificial Life* 1, nos. 1/2 (Fall 1993/Winter 1994): 75–110.

Steels, Luc, and Rodney A. Brooks, editors. *The Artificial Life Route to Artificial Intelligence: Building Embodied Situated Agents*. Hillsdale: Erlbaum Associates, 1995.

Stephenson, Neal. *Cryptonomicon*. New York: Avon, 2002.

———. "*Cryptonomicon* cypher-FAQ." Under question 13, "Hey, the perl script doesn't work! What's the deal?" http://www.well.com/user/neal/cypherFAQ.html.

———. *The Diamond Age; or, A Young Lady's Illustrated Primer*. New York: Bantam, 2000.

———. *In the Beginning Was the Command Line*. New York: Avon, 1999.

———. Neal Stephenson. http://www.nealstephenson.com.

———. *Snow Crash*. New York: Bantam, 2000.

Stewart, Garrett. *Reading Voices: Literature and the Phonotext*. Berkeley: University of California Press, 1990.

Stone, Allucquère Rosanne. *The War of Technology and Desire at the Close of the Mechanical Age*. Cambridge, MA: MIT Press, 1996.

Swirski, Peter. "A Case of Wishful Thinking." In *Between Literature and Science: Poe, Lem, and Explorations in Aesthetics, Cognitive Science, and Literary Knowledge*, 127–32. Montreal, QC: McGill-Queen's University Press, 2001. http://www.scienceboard.net/community/perspectives.64.html.

Tallis, Raymond. *Not Saussure: A Critique of Post-Saussurean Literary Theory.* London: Macmillan Press, 1988.

Teilhard de Chardin, Pierre. *The Phenomenon of Man.* New York: Perennial, 1976.

Thibault, Paul J. *Re-Reading Saussure: The Dynamics of Signs in Social Life.* London: Routledge, 1997.

Tiptree, James Jr. "The Girl Who Was Plugged In." In *Her Smoke Rose Up Forever: The Great Years of James Tiptree Jr.,* 44–79. New York: Arkham House Publishers, 1990.

Turing, Alan M. "Computing Machinery and Intelligence." *Mind* 59 (1950): 433–60.

———. "On Computable Numbers, with an Application to the Entscheidungsproblem." *Proceedings of the London Mathematical Society,* ser. 2, 42 (1936): 230–65.

Turkle, Sherry. *Life on the Screen: Identity in the Age of the Internet.* New York: Simon and Schuster, 1997.

———. *The Second Self: Computers and the Human Spirit.* New York: Simon and Schuster, 1984.

Ullman, Ellen. *Close to the Machine: Technophilia and Its Discontents.* San Francisco: City Lights Books, 1997.

———. "Elegance and Entropy." Interview with Scott Rosenberg. *Salon 21st* (October 9, 1997). http://archive.salon.com/21st/feature/1997/10/09interview.html.

UNITN. "Dynamic Ontology: An Inquiry into Systems, Emergence, Levels of Reality, and Forms of Causality, Trento University, Trento, Italy." September 8–11, 2004. http://www.unitn.it/events/do/.

Unsworth, John. "The Importance of Failure." *Journal of Electronic Publishing* 3, no. 2 (December 1997). http://www.press.umich.edu/jep/03-02/unsworth.html.

Van Lieshout, Jules. "The New Alchemists." Paper presented at the annual convention of the Midwest Modern Language Association, Chicago, IL, November 9, 2003.

Varela, Francisco J., Even Thompson, and Eleanor Rosch. *The Embodied Mind: Cognitive Science and Human Experience.* Cambridge, MA: MIT Press, 1991.

Von Neumann, John. *Theory of Self-Reproducing Automata.* Edited by Arthur. W. Burks. Urbana: University of Illinois Press, 1966.

Wald, Carol. "The Female Machine: From von Neumann to Richard Powers." Unpublished manuscript.

Weaver, Warren. "The New Tower." Foreword to *Machine Translation of Languages,* edited by William N. Locke and A. Donald Booth, v–vii. Cambridge, MA: MIT Press; New York: John Wiley & Sons, 1950.

———. "Translation." In *Machine Translation of Languages,* edited by William N. Locke and A. Donald Booth, 15–23. Cambridge, MA: MIT Press; New York: John Wiley & Sons, 1950.

Weise, Elizabeth. "Cracking *Cryptonomicon*: Stephenson Weaves 50-Year Tale of Intrigue." *USA Today,* April 28, 1999, D1.

Weizenbaum, Joseph. *Computer Power and Human Reason: From Judgment to Calculation.* New York: W. H. Freeman, 1976.

Wells, H. G. *The Time Machine: An Invention.* New York: Modern Library, 2002.

Wicke, Jennifer. "Henry James's Second Wave." *The Henry James Review* 10 (1989): 146–51.

Winson, L. J. Dark Lethe. http://www.darklethe.net.

Wolfram, Stephen. *A New Kind of Science.* New York: Wolfram Media, 2002.

Zeller, Hans. "A New Approach to the Critical Constitution of Literary Texts." *Studies in Bibliography* 28 (1975): 231–65.

Živković, Zonran. "The Future without a Future: An Interview with Stanislaw Lem." *Pacific Quarterly (Moana): An International Review of Arts and Ideas* 4, no. 3 (1979): 255–59.

Žižek, Slavoj. *Enjoy Your Symptom! Jacques Lacan in Hollywood and Out.* New York: Routledge, 2001.

Zuse, Konrad. *Rechnender Raum.* Schriften zur Datenverarbeitung, Band 1. Braunschweig: Friedrich Vieweg & Sohn, 1969.

Index

signifier, and, 68; unconscious and, 191; worldview of, 8, 16, 30–31, 38

code book, 75

codework, as a creole, 60

coevolution: in Prisoner's Dilemma, 32–33; processes, 197

cognition, 200, 212–13; distributed, 197, 200, 212–13; human, 217

command: executable, 53; lines, 141; "reveal code," 54–55

commodification, and literary work, 144, 147

compiling, 59

complexity: in cellular automata, 216; emergence and, 26, 198; as emergent property of computation, 41; emerging from simple program, 20; of evolutionary simulations, 210; of flickering signifiers, 157; levels of, 29; location of, 41, 85–86; surface, 204; theory, 3, 242

computation, 2; and computational irreducibility, 18; and computational perspective, 21; and computational practice, 4; as cultural metaphor, 219; definition of, 17–18; as fundamental process, 30; as generator of reality, 55, 217; as ontology, 3; in *Permutation City*, 225–32; requirements for, 22; simulations and, 6; worldview of, 17, 30, 39, 47. *See also* Regime of Computation

computational universe, 22; ambiguity in, 20; as cultural icon, 4; in Egan's fiction, 214–43; as means, 4, 20, 22; as metaphor, 4, 20, 22, 219–22

computer: in *Permutation City*, 225–32; quantum, 30, 222. *See also* Universal Computer

computer games, 5, 36

consciousness, 10, 11; analog, 193; simulated, in *Permutation City*, 223–32; uploading, 217

constraints, 42–43; adaptive, 196; in C++,

58; in *Cryptonomicon*, 120; in dream of information, 62–86; environmental, 196; imposed by morphological resemblance, 203

constructivism, 50; in *Distress*, 233; social, 205–9

Conway, John, *Game of Life*, 18

Cook, Matthew, and cellular automata, 216

Coover, Robert, "The Babysitter," 162

Copy, in *Permutation City*, 11, 223–32, 235

copyright, 10, 106, 202; in *Authors and Owners*, 144–47

cosmology, subjective. *See* subjective cosmology

Coverley, M. D., *The Book of Going Forth by Day*, 54

Cramer, Florian, 117

creatures, virtual, 193–213

criticism, textual, 104–8

crypt, in *Cryptonomicon*, 121, 124, 133

cryptanalysis, in *Cryptonomicon*, 129

cryptography: in *Cryptonomicon*, 121, 129, 131; and relation to writing books, 124

cryptology, in *Cryptonomicon*, 121, 135

Cryptonomicon (Stephenson), 1, 10, 31, 117–41, 232; Bobby Shaftoe, 119, 121–22, 131; Earl Comstock, 1, 123, 131, 136; Enoch Root, 128–29, 131; the Good Hacker, 129–32, 134; Randy Waterhouse, 121, 127–30

Culler, Jonathan, 43–44

cybernetic difference, 90

cybernetics: contribution of, 241–42; in-mixed with human psychology, 177; paradigm, 218

cyberspace, 162; in *Cryptonomicon*, 120; in *Permutation City*, 229–32

cybersystem, in "The Girl Who Was Plugged In," 80–83, 85

Cybertext (Aarseth), 36–38, 99

Dahlström, Mats, 95, 97–98, 101–2

Damasio, Antonio, 191, 217

Danielewski, Mark, *House of Leaves*, 105–6

encapsulation, in C++, 58
encoding, of print texts, 95–96
Enigma codes, in *Cryptonomicon*, 122
ergodic literature, 36–38, 44
errors: coding, 68; control, 43; file, in Unix, 125; trail-off, 46
evolution: biological as model for technological, 174; cosmological, 233–40; in humans and intelligent machines, 216; of the posthuman, 26; of virtual creatures, 193–97, 211
explanations, discursive, 5, 6

feedback: intermediating, 62, 64; in simulations, 25
feedback cycles, 22
feedback loops, 15, 20, 31–33, 37–39, 116, 177, 194, 198
figurative language, in *Cryptonomicon*, 10
Finlay, Ian Hamilton, 108
fitness criteria, 195, 199
fitness values, 195
Foggy, computer simulation, 116
FORTRAN, 57
Foster, G. M., 62
Foucault, Michel, 34, 147, 201
Fredkin, Edward, 15–16, 54, 216; digital mechanics, 198; *Digital Philosophy*, 22–23
free will, in "The Mask," 190, 192
Fuller, Matthew, 16, 61
function, wave, in *Quarantine*, 226

Galloway, Alexander R., 50; *Protocol*, 171
Game of Life (Conway), 18
garble, in "The Girl Who Was Plugged In," 80, 82
gender: implications of, in information technologies, 1; implications of, with copyright, 144; in "The Mask," 178, 183–92; in *Patchwork Girl*, 155
gendered enculturation, 171
gender hierarchies, 85–86
Genette, Gérard, 149

genotypes, of virtual creatures, 199–200
Gerstack, John J., 20
Gessler, Nicholas, 5, 28, 31, 116
"Girl Who Was Plugged In, The" (Tiptree), 79–86; Delphi, 79–83, 85; GTX, 79–83, 85; P. Burke, 79–83, 85; Paul Isham, 79–83, 85
Glazier, Loss Pequeño, *Dig(iT)al Poet(I)(C)s*, 54, 108–9
grammatology, 40–61
Grigar, Dene, 89
Grosz, Elizabeth, 155, 160
Grusin, Richard, *Remediation*, 32–33
Guattari, Félix, 172; Body without Organs, 106–7, 115, 173–74; "Machinic Heterogenesis," 174–75, 177; and "The Mask," 190–91; schizanalysis in, 173; and Sims's "Evolved Virtual Creatures," 200; *A Thousand Plateaus*, 173–76
Gunder, Anna, 91–94

Hackers, Brotherhood of, 137–38
Hansen, Mark B. N., 33–36; embodiment and, 35; *New Philosophy for New Media*, 34
Hayles, N. Katherine: *How We Became Posthuman*, 2, 63, 177, 214, 217; *My Mother Was a Computer*, 7; *Writing Machines*, 2
Herbert, George, 158–59
hierarchies, dynamical, 25, 28, 30, 194, 198, 241; emergences, 28
Hillis, Daniel, 17
Hofstader, Douglas, 222
Homo sapiens, 1
How We Became Posthuman. See under Hayles, N. Katherine
humanist tradition, 2
human lifeworld, 6, 7, 62
Hutchins, W. J., 110
hybridity: in "I Have Never Read the Bible," 212; in *Patchwork Girl*, 165
hybridization, 125

messages: decrypted, 138; encrypted, 131, 135; in "The Girl Who Was Plugged In," 81

metalepsis, 149

metamorphosis, in "The Mask," 184

metaphor, 4

metaphysics: classical, 17, 22, 51–52; of presence, 40, 42, 46–47

MEZ (Mary-Anne Breeze), 60

Microsoft, 60, 118, 125; Windows, 118, 127, 140; Windows 95, 51; Windows XP, 51; Word, 46

Miller, J. Hillis, 40

Milton, John, 127

Minsky, Marvin, 200

monster, female: in *Patchwork Girl*, 147–63; subjectivity of, 148

Moo, Barbara E., 58

Moravec, Hans, 1, 35, 191; *Robot*, 223–24; uploading scenario of, 217

Morowitz, Harold, 5, 15–16, 54, 198, 216; emergence, 210; *The Emergence of Everything*, 25–27; and observer function, 228

morphology: self-similar, 194–95; of virtual creatures, 196, 198–99

mother, as computer, 1

Mother Nature, 4

mother's voice, in print texts, 4

Moukas, Alexander, 215

Moulthrop, Stuart, 99; *Victory Garden*, 153

Murray, Janet, 99

mutation, in virtual creatures, 194

My Mother Was a Computer (Hayles), 7

Myst (game), 105

nanotechnology, 63

narrative, 6, 55; in *Cryptonomicon*, 10, 139; importance of, 199; in the Regime of Computation, 27; and simulations, 242

narrative ambiguities, 53

narrative pathways, 50

narrative viewpoint of virtual creatures, 197–205

nature: code the lingua franca of, 8, 55; Mother Nature, 4

navigation, in William Blake Archive, 90

network: autocatalytic, 27; economic, 146–47

network-centric warfare, 21–22

Newton, Sir Isaac, laws of motion, 3

Nicolson, Marjorie Hope, 3

noise: and alteration of identity, 75; and artistic effects, 94; of code, 68; of embodiment, 35, 145, 205, 208; in "The Girl Who Was Plugged In," 85; in telegram, 69; in *The Three Stigmata of Palmer Eldritch*, 75

nonlinear behavior, 5

noosphere, 26

Norrman, Rolf, 67

Of Grammatology (Derrida), 40–61

OHCO (Ordered Hierarchy of Content Objects), 95

Ong, Walter, 39–40

ontology, 4; dynamic, in simulations, 25; in *The Three Stigmata of Palmer Eldritch*, 76

Operation Mincemeat, 121–22

Oreo, structure of, 207–8, 212

originality, Shelley Jackson's comments on, 157; of literary work, 146; in *Patchwork Girl*, 161

Ostman, Charles, 63

oxymoronic knots, in *Cryptonomicon*, 119, 132–39, 141–42

Parker, Jo Alyson, 179

Patchwork Girl (Jackson), 10, 107, 143–67, 177, 243; dotted line in, 148–49, 152, 159, 166–67; encoding and decoding in, 151; sewing in, 152–55; writing in, 152–55

pattern, 66, 70, 81

Paulson, William R., 57

Pavić, Milorad, *Dictionary of the Khazars*, 91, 161

Paycheck (film), 220

performance, in electronic texts, 103

Permutation City (Egan), 22, 223–32; Autoverse in, 231–32; dust hypothesis in, 225–27; "Garden of Eden" simulation in, 228–29; Lambertians, 231–32; Maria De Luca, 229, 232; Paul Durham, 223–32; Thomas Riemann, 230–31

person, autonomous, in "The Mask," 188

phonemes, 56

photograph, 46

phylum, machinic, 174

physicality, of texts, 97–104; difference from materiality, 103–4

physics: artifactual, 195; quantum, 222

Plotnitsky, Arkady, 127

polymorphism, in C++, 48

Pope, Alexander, 127

Portrait of a Lady, The (James), 198

possessive individualism, 63, 76, 82, 83–86, 145–46

possibilities, emergent, 7

possibility space, 26

"possible worlds," 6

Post, Jack, 106

postbiology: in Egan's fiction, 214–40; future in relation to, 2, 11, 239–40

Poster, Mark, 63; *What's the Matter with the Internet?* 201–3, 217

posthuman, 2; age of, 35; in Egan's fiction, 214–40; evolution of, 26

posthuman collectives, 68

posthuman future, 11

poststructuralism, 43

pregnancy, in "The Mask," 189

presence and absence, dialectic of, 66, 70

Prigogine, Ilya, 23

Principle of Computational Equivalence, 18

print: age of, 97; compared to electronic textuality, 89–116; interpenetration of, 117

print books, 117–18

print-centric notion of electronic media, 93

print environment, 94

print subjectivity, 211

print tradition, 143–47

Prisoner's Dilemma, 32–33

process, 209–13; computational, 242; embodied, 217, 243; intermediating, 210

program: digital, and analog consciousness, 193; evolutionary, for virtual creatures, 193–213; ideological, 218; object-oriented, 58, 60; in "The Mask," 182–92

projection, anthropomorphic, 5, 193

property: intellectual, 143–47; literary, 143–47; morphological and neurological, in virtual creatures, 210

prosthesis, in *The Three Stigmata of Palmer Eldritch,* 73, 76

prostitution, 67, 83–86; male homosexual, 83–84

Protocol (Galloway), 171

quantum mechanics, 3; *Digital Philosophy* and, 24

quantum physics, 222

Quarantine (Egan), 22, 225–27

Queneau, Raymond, *Cent mille milliards de pòemes,* 115–16

Radiant Textuality (McGann), 97–104, 107–8

Raley, Rita, 54, 103; *Global English* and, 60; interview with Shelley Jackson, 149, 152, 154

randomness, 66, 121

Reading Voices (Steward), 53

realism, scientific, 205–9, 242

reflexivity, 26; in von Foerster, 241

Regime of Computation, 8, 18, 21–30, 38, 40–42, 54, 55, 76, 86, 171–72, 205, 216–18, 242. *See also* computation

remediation, 32–33

Renear, Allen, 95–96; analysis of OHCO, 95; antirealism in text encoding, 96–97; and Platonism in text encoding, 96; and pluralism in text encoding, 95

representation: analog, 6, 207; digital, 6

Requiem for a Dream (film), 106

Storyspace software, 148, 151–54, 160, 167
subject: analog, 201–5; as assemblage, 150; autonomous, 82; Cartesian, in "The Mask," 179; digital, 5, 10, 201–3; embodied, 33–38; fragmented, 10; liberal, 10, 63, 76, 79–80, 84
subjective cosmology: in *Distress*, 232–40; in Egan's fiction, 214–40; fringe, 234–40
subjectivity, 3, 10, 11, 172, 242; analog, 202–3, 212; connected with writing, 4; constituted through bits, 16; and copyright, 143–47; depth model of, 201; in "The Girl Who Was Plugged In," 81; hybrid, 5, 166, 212; liberal, 72, 146; in *Patchwork Girl*, 147–67; postbiological, 6; print, 211; transformation of, 217; unified, 166; and Work as Assemblage, 106
supplementarity, 68
surgery, in *Patchwork Girl*, 158
Surrealists, 146
Suvin, Darko, 72
swarms, 20
Sydney, Philip, 127
Symbolic, in "The Mask," 178
symptom: in *Permutation City*, 223–32; in Slavoj Žižek, 219–22
system: complex, 5; complex adaptive, 200, 204; cryptological, 118; distributed cognitive, 193, 196–97, 204, 213; legacy of speech and writing, 39–61; machinic, 61; multiagent social, 18; multilayered hierarchical, 32, 175; multileveled complex, 24; operating, in computer, 126, 140–42; semiotic, 175; signifying, in Guattari, 175

Teilhard de Chardin, Pierre, 26
TEI (Text Encoding Initiative), 95
telegraph, 8, 65; in *In the Beginning Was the Command Line*, 129; in "In the Cage," 62–71, 83–85; and telegraphist, 64, 66; and telegraphy, 64
telegraph boys, 83

telegraph cage, 64, 65
teleological illusion, 219–22; in *Distress*, 234–40; in *Permutation City*, 234–40
text: algorithmic, 99; definition of, 91–97; electronic, 10, 38, 98, 154, 159; monstrous, in *Patchwork Girl*, 160
textons, 36
textuality, 3, 11; electronic, 16, 37, 44, 90–116, 167; embodied, 97–104; instantiated, 103. *See also* literature
thermodynamics: first law, 62; second law, 20, 62
Thousand Plateaus, A (Deleuze), 173–76
Three Stigmata of Palmer Eldritch, The (Dick), 9, 64–65, 71–86; Anne Hawthorne, 77; Barney Mayerson, 73–79; Can-D, 71–74, 85; Chew-Z, 72–79, 85; code book in, 75; Leo Bolero, 73–79; Palmer Eldritch, 72–80; Perky Pat, 71–74, 79, 84; Roni Fugate, 84–85; stigmata in, 74; Walt, 71–72
TIB (The Information Block), 112
time-travel, 83
Tiptree, James, Jr., 9, 64. *See also* "The Girl Who Was Plugged In"
Tower of Babel, 110
tower of languages, 54–55
trace, the, 41, 46
transcendental signified. *See* signified
transformation, dialectical, in *Cryptonomicon*, 139
Transistor to Transistor Logic (TTL), 43
translation: in "The Don Quixote of Pierre Menard," 109; of language, 110–16; of media, 89–116, 143
translation machine, 111–12
transmigration, 194, 209
transmitting, 171, 217–18; as a dynamic, 6–7
trauma: in *Quarantine*, 227; and the symptom, 220
Turing, Alan: in *Cryptonomicon*, 121–22, 124, 140; and Universal Computer, 228
Turing machine, 18, 176–77
Turing test, 214–15